1986

LANGUAGE, SEXUALITY AND II
POUND'S CANT(

LANGUAGE, SEXUALITY AND IDEOLOGY IN EZRA POUND'S *CANTOS*

Jean-Michel Rabaté

State University of New York Press
Albany

First published in USA by
STATE UNIVERSITY OF NEW YORK PRESS

For information write to:
State University of New York Press
State University Plaza
Albany, NY 12246

Library of Congress Cataloging in Publication Data
Rabaté, Jean-Michel, 1949–
Language, sexuality and ideology in Ezra Pound's
Cantos
Bibliography: p.
Includes index.
1. Pound, Ezra, 1885–1972.   Cantos.   2. Pound,
Ezra, 1885–1972 – Philosophy.   3. Sex in literature.
4. Philosophy in literature.   5. Psychoanalysis and
literature.   I. Title.
PS3531.082C2875 1986   811'.52   84–23926
ISBN 0–88706–036–6
ISBN 0–88706–037–4 (pbk.)

Contents

v

Preface

My first thanks go to Colin MacCabe, without whose confidence and friendship this project would never have been undertaken. Six or seven years ago, even before I had completed the thesis of which this is part translation, part re-elaboration, he and Stephen Heath had asked me to write a book on Pound, which has then for a long time been announced under a different title.

As it is, I wish to dedicate it to Eva Hesse, who has set up in Germany and elsewhere standards of intellectual rigour and curiosity in the understanding of modern poetry – of Pound in particular – which this work could only hope to emulate.

I also benefited from long, funny and stimulating discussions of Pound and China with Joel Shapiro, with whom I had started working on a parallel undertaking which unhappily never materialised. I am also extremely grateful to Chris Sutcliffe and Tina Kendall who read the early stages of the manuscript and improved the language.

Finally, I owe to both Christine Brooke-Rose and to Mary de Rachewiltz the pleasure and the honour to have been acquainted with the truly living Poundian spirit at Brunnenburg, Tirol, and at the Beinecke Library of Yale, a spirit which helped me to adopt a less dogmatic approach to Pound's poetic achievement in several instances, and guided me through the complex periplus of which this book is but a testimony.

J.-M.R.

Acknowledgements

The author and publishers are grateful to all the copyright-holders who have given permission to reproduce material in copyright.

Extracts from the following works by Ezra Pound are reprinted here by permission of Faber & Faber Ltd, London, and New Directions Publishing Corporation, New York, on behalf of the Ezra Pound Literary Property Trust (all rights reserved):

The Cantos, copyright 1934, 1937, 1940, 1948, © 1956, 1959, 1962, 1963, 1968, 1972, 1975 by Ezra Pound;

Collected Shorter Poems (US title *Personae*), copyright 1926 by Ezra Pound;

ABC of Reading, copyright 1934 by Ezra Pound;

The Literary Essays of Ezra Pound (edited by T. S. Eliot), copyright 1918, 1920, 1935 by Ezra Pound;

Selected Letters of Ezra Pound 1907–1941 (edited by D. D. Paige), copyright 1950 by Ezra Pound;

Selected Prose 1909–1965 (edited by W. Cookson), copyright © 1973 by The Trustees of the Ezra Pound Literary Property Trust;

Gaudier-Brzeska, copyright © 1970 by Ezra Pound, all rights reserved;

Women of Trachis, © 1956, 1957 by Ezra Pound;

Jefferson and/or Mussolini, copyright 1935, 1936 by Ezra Pound;

Natural Philosophy of Love, copyright 1922, 1926 by Ezra Pound;

Ezra Pound Speaking (edited by Leonard W. Doob), © 1978 by The Trustees of the Ezra Pound Literary Property Trust (Greenwood Press).

Extracts from *The Classic Anthology Defined by Confucius*, copyright 1954, 1955 by Ezra Pound are reprinted here by permission of Faber & Faber Ltd, London, and Harvard University Press, Cambridge, Mass.

Abbreviations Used for the Works of Pound

ABCR   *ABC of Reading* (1934: repr. London: Faber, 1961)
CEP   *Collected Early Poems of Ezra Pound*, ed. Michael John King (New York: New Directions, 1976)
Con   *Confucius: The Great Digest, The Unwobbling Pivot, The Analects* (New York: New Directions, 1969)
CSP   *Collected Shorter Poems* (London: Faber, 1952)
GB   *Gaudier-Brzeska: A Memoir* (1916; repr. New York: New Directions, 1970)
GK   *Guide to Kulchur* (1938; repr. New York: New Directions, 1970)
J/M   *Jefferson and/or Mussolini* (1935; repr. New York: Liveright, 1970)
L   *The Selected Letters of Ezra Pound, 1907–1941*, ed. D. D. Paige (1950; repr. New York: New Directions, 1971)
LE   *Literary Essays*, ed. T. S. Eliot (London: Faber, 1954)
PD   *Pavannes and Divagations* (1958; repr. London: Peter Owen, 1960)
P/J   *Pound/Joyce, The Letters of Ezra Pound to James Joyce, with Pound's Essays on Joyce*, ed. Forrest Read (London: Faber, 1968)
SP   *Selected Prose 1909–1965*, ed. William Cookson (London: Faber, 1973)
SR   *The Spirit of Romance* (1910; repr. with additions New York: New Directions, 1968)
T   *Translations* (1953: enlarged edn London: Faber, 1970)
WT   *Sophocles: Women of Trachis* (1956; repr. London: Faber, 1969)

The most easily accessible edition of the *Cantos* is the new complete edition published by Faber in 1975, which includes the drafts and fragments, and for the sake of convenience I refer only to this edition; for an idea of the complexities of the several 'collected' editions see Barbara Eastman's *Ezra Pound's Cantos: The Story of the Text 1948–1975* (Orono: University of Maine Press, 1979).

Introduction

We are at the crisis point of the world.   (*Con.*, p. 89)

    1. He said: Not to know the decree (the sealed mouth [*L* adds 'of heaven', not to recognise destiny]) is to be without the means of being a proper man (the ancestral voice incomplete).
    2. Not to know the rites is to be without means to construct.
    3. Not to know words (the meaning of words) is to be without the fluid needful to understand them. (*Con.*, p. 288)

The scope of Pound's achievements, the breadth of his axes of reference, the passions he continues to raise among his audience – all this challenges current critical assumptions about the act of reading and indeed forces one to meet the challenge with renewed and clearly defined critical ambitions and mounting philosophical claims. Are the *Cantos* a very subjective testimony, the log-book of an exploration, the record of a 'single man's effort', or the unavoidable introduction to our position as readers in an age which calls itself 'post-modern'? The very difficulty of deciphering them reveals the paradoxical confrontation of an urge towards synthesis, even when it exhibits its totalitarian nature, and the opening of a new space of writing where anarchy and difference come into play.

Political, economical, ideological readings of Pound cannot be dissociated from attention to the language as it is presented through its articulation, its enunciation, and understood in its relation to a more comprehensive European crisis, into which Heidegger can also provide useful insights.

Pound and Heidegger: sites and monuments

Placing the names of Pound and Heidegger side by side generally calls

1

up a monstrous image of two difficult writers, who have little in common apart from a highly specific and idiomatic command of language. One could even be tempted to draw a superficial and antagonistic contrast between the shrill exuberance of a wild American swooping down on literary circles in London and Paris before leaving for Fascist Italy in an effort to master the new creative movements, and the deep calm of Heidegger's silent meditations in woods, echoing through a few privileged texts and providing them with a metaphysical locus. Besides, if a certain number of critics have perceived the need to allude to Heidegger when discussing the *Cantos*,[1] it remains to be demonstrated that they have more than a small number of parallel themes in common, and that they share an identical problematics of language. My belief is that only a detour through Heidegger can permit one to understand the 'foundational' position of Pound as a poet, and to understand its imbrication in a general historical perspective. If Heidegger is nowadays gradually being acknowledged as a major influence in continental thinking, to such an extent that a discussion of his concepts remains a prerequisite of any introduction to either Lacan's version of psychoanalytical theory or Derrida's deconstructive strategies, here I shall have recourse to his approach to language both for methodological and historical reasons. Pound and Heidegger have both attempted a general survey of the question of language in its relation to 'metaphysics' at large, without eschewing the problems of politics, art and even changes in the modern way of life.

Anyone vaguely familiar with Heidegger will immediately wonder how his 'essentialist' philosophy of Time and Being can be reconciled with Pound's deep commitment to polytheism, with his polyphonic mode of writing poetry, and his dismissal of abstruse and abstract modes of reflection, while it seems dubious that Pound could have fitted in Heidegger's canon, alongside with Hölderlin, Trakl and Rilke for instance. Nevertheless Heidegger's meditation is indispensable to anyone who attempts to look back on the whole expanse of Western philosophy and values, and to question concepts generally taken for granted, such as 'time', 'essence', 'gods', 'thing', 'difference'. On the other hand, since he also is part of the closure of the metaphysical history of Being he announces, he cannot avoid being committed to the inescapable drift of history: I shall give one precise example of such symptomatic coincidence between Pound and Heidegger in the thirties.

But, first, in order to reach the broadest possible basis for a communal set of questions linking Heidegger and Pound, I would select three points of contact and interaction: the idea of the radical finitude of man, a sense of the multiplicity of Being, and a deep comprehension of the 'turns' of epochal history. For Pound as for Heidegger, man is to be understood as limited by death, searching for expression and survival in the immortality afforded by works of art, but not in a transcendent other world.

> and Kung gave the words 'order'
> and 'brotherly deference'
> And he said nothing of the 'life after death'.
>
> (Canto XIII, p. 59)

Heidegger's first philosophy was indeed to stress the fact that human existence is bounded by death and finds authenticity only in so far as it poses the question of its mortality, and any escape route towards the heavens rules out the possibility for an intuition of ontological difference between an existing being and that which makes it be a being, or Being. Besides, such a finitude finds an expression in the language of multiplicity, for Heidegger repeatedly acknowledges his debt to Brentano's dissertation *On the Manifold Sense of Being in Aristotle*, which was prefaced by the sentence from the Greek philosopher: *to on legetai pollakhos* ('being is said in many ways', or, as Heidegger subsequently rephrases it, 'A being becomes manifest (*sc.* with regard to its Being) in many ways'[2]). A similar Greek, hence 'foreign' but perhaps 'original' paradigm recurs throughout Pound's writings when he alludes decisively to his favourite Homeric hero and persona Odysseus, who is praised for having gained a wide knowledge of 'men and cities': *pollon d'anthropon iden* ('he saw many men') echoes through the *Cantos* and the prose essays as giving the key to an understanding of human existence and anthropological values.

There is finally a deep historical convergence between what the historians of philosophy have called the 'reversal' or 'turn' in Heidegger's thought, which leads Richardson, for instance, to distinguish between Heidegger I and Heidegger II,[3] and the shift in Pound's writing after the crucial experience of near-execution and savage confinement in Pisa. The comparison would remain formal if one could not prove that Pound's reversal of attitude had been in fact prepared by the internal logics of his thought and writings, exactly as Heidegger's 'reversal' owes something to his brief political engagement. The thinker of *Time and Being*,[4] who understands language as the Temple of Being, and the 'second Pound', irretrievably deprived of his Fascist utopia, but also brought to a foundational questioning of 'belief' – both write from a vertiginously close experience of the limits of language.

I should furthermore like to suggest such a parallel between Pound and Heidegger so as to open to examination a set of critical, historical and theoretical questions. For they are contemporaries in more than one sense, both having attempted to cover the whole field of Western metaphysics by orienting it in a new context: this meant for Pound a decentring, by means of other models of civilisation and perception, of time units, idioms, rhythmic patterns of language, whilst for Heidegger it entailed a return to a pre-Socratic insight into Being which could be used to subvert the concepts of classical philosophy. Pound wished to start his *Cantos* by a translation of the passage in which Odysseus visits the Underworld in the Odyssey, not only because this afforded him a perspectivistic play with a series of 'Englishes' but also because it was a return to a kind of pre-origin: 'The Nekuia (Descent to the Dead) shouts aloud that it is *older* than the rest, all that island, Cretan, etc., hinter-time' (*L*, p. 274). The paradox is that both attempted to sum up culture and elaborate an all-inclusive conceptual framework, thereby succumbing to the dangerous lure of totalities, finally to disrupt the foundations of the idea of totality, Heidegger by a novel practice of poetic language wedged into philosophical discussion, Pound by the introduction of foreign material, of documents, archives, economic theory, into a poetic voice belonging to more classical models of polyphony.

The historical turning-point which affected both of them can be dated to the years 1933–6, when Heidegger was momentarily drawn into the educational policy of Nazism, becoming Rector of Freiburg University, before skilfully managing a retreat into private meditation of poetic texts, and from the moment when Pound declared himself an unconditional supporter of Mussolini – that is, after he actually met him.[5] The crystallisation of commitments around 1933 is striking; both responded to the tide of history as it swept over Europe, while maintaining the claims of a foundational approach to language.

The point of the comparison is to show that one cannot dissociate the 'aberrations' from the 'sacramental' or 'transcendental' moments which would redeem them: at this level, the criticism of thinkers such as Adorno, who is indeed all too prone to reject the whole of Heidegger's philosophy as 'jargon of authenticity',[6] is a welcome antidote, just as the rejection of what appeared inacceptable in

Pound's ideology by his friends and emulators such as Williams, Olson or Duncan provokes a fresh readjustment. An attempt to rethink the whole work of Pound and Heidegger is thus necessary, for in their momentary or lasting delusions – which no one ought to forget, or forgive – there can be seen the epochal fate of this century's thought. As Heidegger puts it in a phrase which retains its relevance for Pound's individual destiny: 'He who thinks greatly must err greatly.'[7] Such erring is integral to the process of thinking, a process never dissociable from the writing of poetry. No one who attempts to redefine the fundamentals of man's relationship to language can do it without risking obscurity, madness, or political delusion – a risk for which Pound fully paid.

If the turning-point is thus to be situated in the middle thirties, Italy provides an ideal meeting-place for Pound and Heidegger, and indeed on 2 April 1936 Heidegger gave a lecture, 'Hölderlin and the Essence of Poetry', in Rome while Pound was trying from Rapallo to have his *ars poetica* reprinted: the *Chinese Character* was published in March 1936 by Stanley Nott.[8] And, if Heidegger had chosen to stop in Rapallo on his way back to Germany, he might have been delighted to hear that an American poet in exile was proposing that the municipality of Rapallo should erect a building for the Fascists of the city, which could also serve as a library accessible to tourists.[9] But in 1936 Heidegger was eluding the issues of politics and economics, backing away from Nazism and finding in poetry a field of investigation which could keep up a façade of conformity and yet articulate elements of criticism. This is why what he had to say about Hölderlin at that time can serve as a relevant introduction to the question of poetic enunciation in Pound's *Cantos*.

The Rome conference condenses a series of lectures held at the University of Freiburg during the winter of 1934–5, and the notes (only published in 1980) throw a keener light on Heidegger's position than the published essay:[10] they are more openly 'political', and they clearly situate the poet's voice in the gap between enunciation and enounced statement. Heidegger believes apparently in the necessary alliance of three mythical figures, the poet, the thinker and the statesman (called *Staatschöpfer* or even *Führer*), and the lectures end with a quotation from Hölderlin which takes on an ominous quality: 'We learn nothing more difficult than the use of the national.' But other elements in these lectures, precisely when they leave the level of myth and lead to a theory of reading, move towards anti-Nazi theses: Heidegger refuses to have anything to do with the interpretation of poetry in the name of the 'soul of a culture' (Spengler) or of the 'soul of a race' (Rosenberg).[11] He is against any *Blut und Boden* interpretation of Hölderlin[12] and refuses the concepts of traditional criticism, such as 'metaphor'.

What matters most is the organisation of the poem in its enunciatory movement. The poem, which begins as a first-person speech, lets other speakers intervene in their turn: the enunciating voice allows one to perceive the resonance of other voices, among which are those of the poet and his audience. 'We are swept along in a dialogue which brings language to the condition of language' (*Gesamtausgabe*, vol. 39, p. 45). This movement is described as a 'whirlpool' or a 'vortex' (*Wirbel*) of voices: we must enter the vortex in order to understand what language has to say, and this movement organises the series of positions tenable at different points of time. Every stanza turns around, revolves in the vortex and posits a different subject, 'if', Heidegger writes, 'one can still speak of "places" in a vortex' (p. 47). The vortex or *Wirbel* defines the locus of the intersubjectivity created by the poem as a 'We' (*wir* in German). The poem has stated that 'We – mankind – are a dialogue [*Gespräch*]',[13] and in the poetic dialogue, when the enounced appears as shifting play of enunciation, language comes into its own as language. Poetry implies an experience of language as a circle of hearing and uttering, for no one can speak from outside the *Wirbel* since it predetermines the dialogic nature of the subject. From the vortex of voices emerges a moving pattern of enunciating energies, close to the self-enunciation of language, mediated by a basic *mood* (*Stimmung*).

The concept of *Grundstimmung* is very important for an understanding of Pound's poetry, for here, as with Pound's intuition of the 'gods', it would be easy to mistake the concept for a purely subjective moment. We shall have to understand how this 'basic mood' does not belong to the poet any more than it belongs to language itself, for it belongs to the world, to time or history, seen in its epochal destination. In the case of 'Germanien', the 'basic mood' is determined by four elements: (1) the poet's confrontation with the gods but also with their disappearance; (2) his insertion into the earth; (3) his opening to the world; (4) the definition of his being-there, or *Da-sein*, as mortal (*Gesamtausgabe*, vol. 39, pp. 139–41).

The eternity of the gods is not granted once and for all, and the paradox which Heidegger identifies in Hölderlin's later poetry is that the gods belong to time, can even be constituted by time (Hölderlin writes in his annotations to *Oedipus Rex*, 'God, who is nothing but time'[14]). Thus their eternal 'mood' can vanish as soon as it appears, leaving the poet with the dire task of having to sing of this disappearance to his people. In the same way, Pound could say that the gods were but the names found for some 'delightful psychic experience', while asserting that they exist outside our consciousness.[15] This accounts for his curious oscillation between an enlightened rationalism with strong moralistic and political leanings, and a more mystical sense of contemplation: the return of the gods is precisely situated in this interval.

However, for Heidegger the withdrawal or the return of the gods to Germany can be expressed in a communal language, which is the speech of the people. But language for Heidegger cannot be adequate to the naming of the gods: there is a lack which comes from the decentred position of the subject. The speaking subject labours under the delusion that he possesses language, owns it, is master over it, when in fact language merely speaks through us: 'Die Sprache spricht' ('language speaks'). 'We do not have a language, language has us, in a good and a bad sense' (*Gesamtausgabe*, vol. 39, p. 23). Therefore language appears in its whole ambivalence: it is the most dangerous possession of man, for its owns him and makes him a 'keeper of Being' – later Heidegger will speak of man as the 'shepherd of Being'. The danger lies in the fact that this exposure to the gods brings one too close to madness, while a language which protects too much from the gods falls back into the necessary trivialities of everyday speech. Pound feels too this discontinuous and intermittent paradise, and expresses the dual powers of language in germane terms: 'As language becomes the most powerful instrument of perfidy, so language alone can riddle and cut through the meshes' (*LE*, p. 77). And in the *Guide to Kulchur* Pound states the thesis 'that our time has overshadowed the mysteries by an overemphasis on the individual' (p. 299), and goes on with a sentence which could be taken from Heidegger's lecture – 'Only in the high air and the great clarity can there be a just estimation of values' – to conclude, 'I assert that the Gods exist' (ibid.).

A detailed comparison between the positions of Hölderlin and Pound would lead us too far.[16] I wished above all to use these remarks of Heidegger to point towards a common definition of the poetic utterance. For the main question posed by Heidegger is, 'What does *dichten* really mean?' Pound's famous false etymology is well known ('Dichten = Condensare' – *ABCR*, p. 36), and Heidegger, who is more informed of German roots than Pound, recalls the derivation from the Old German *tithôn*, with its parallels in Latin, *dictare, dicere* in the frequentative, meaning to declame and write poetry. In a more original – and daring – sense, *tithôn* can be derived from *deiknumi* in Greek, which means 'to show'. The 'saying' is always a 'showing', a truth-telling which discloses the truth (or *aletheia*): *deixis* lies behind poetry, which leads one to the second paradox that language in poetry speaks of itself in order to show, to point at, to designate. Of course, in 1934 Heidegger could not proceed in this contradictory fashion; it is only later, in *On the Way to Language*, that he is able to connect the 'saying' (*die Sage*) with the 'showing' (*die Zeige*) – precisely at the time when Pound attempts to define tradition as 'Sagetrieb', but I shall develop this in Chapter 6.

The theoretical connection between *deixis* and enunciation will be made in an attempt to relate Pound's belief in 'reference' to particular objects and his constant reminder that what matters is the position of the speaking subject, since his referents can only be determined with respect to the interlocutors. Thus, what Heidegger enables us to grasp, the gap between the absence of the gods and their return hollowing language out for a particular discourse to emerge therefrom, can apply for Pound, who appears caught up in a contradiction between reference to historical facts and reverence of gods, values, heroes, and so on. Between tragedy and paradise, there opens the space of an idiom, since, as Heidegger writes, 'What is spoken is never, and in no language, what is said.'[17]

The poet shall have to learn that he becomes the 'Other' when he attempts to speak of the gods; he is a 'demi-god' himself, because he is 'excluded': such a notion is precisely one that Adorno selects to make fun of, and, indeed, Heidegger's concepts should not all be accepted uncritically; but, as they closely comment on actual texts, their logic and progression cannot stand apart from what they determine as the 'fate' of poetry since the Romantic period. Heidegger's idea of truth as 'disclosure' and revelation cannot be separated from the 'foundational' situation of language: 'One essential way in which truth establishes itself in the beings it has opened up is truth settling itself into work. Another way in which truth occurs is the act that founds a political state.'[18] The link between the creation of a language and the foundation of a city or state is one of Pound's major motifs in the *Cantos*.

A few arguments of Heidegger's discussion will be brought out in stronger relief if they are submitted to Adorno's criticism, especially as this criticism is voiced in a paper on Hölderlin, 'Parataxis', which defines one of the major modes of poetic composition for Pound. In this paper Adorno launches a severe attack on Heidegger's mystique of language. His strictures can be summed up by a passage which voices the main charge against an 'essentialist' reading of Hölderlin:

By discarding at once the aesthetics of content, the necessary aesthetic element is misread as being real, without any consideration of the dialectical rupture between form and truth-content. It is thus that Hölderlin's authentic rapport with reality, a critical and utopian relationship, is fashioned. What he is supposed to have celebrated as Being found in his work no other place than the determined negation of beings. By a premature affirmation of the reality of the poetic element, one disguises the tension toward reality of Hölderlin's poems, one neutralises his work, which then merely becomes equated with fate.[19]

Adorno's dialectical optimism, which relies on the glib distinction between form and content, knowing quite well that the eventual sleight of hand of synthesis brings about their adequation, might appear as dated as Heidegger's stilted language; he nevertheless helps one to read Heidegger against himself, so to speak, while the stress he lays on parataxis as the primordial mode of construction echoes Pound's own poetic practice; Adorno provides a theoretical foundation that can bridge the gap between the current empiricism regarding Pound's poetry (Hugh Kenner is probably the most brilliant representative of this school, and I can only refer to his pioneering analyses of the ellipsis of verbs and of the 'parataxis of sound' employed by Pound[20]) and a more 'metaphysical' approach.

Adorno brands Heidegger as undialectical and reactionary because he accepts the form and content of the poem at face value instead of following the complex gestures of language which cannot be reduced to the motto of 'language speaks'. Hölderlin's oracular utterances adding names of gods, and Pound's ideogrammic procedure of 'heaping up' the components of thought have in common the profound passivity of the subject as he writes, which allows him to be the recipient of quotations and other discourses. 'By severing all ties which connect it to the subject, language speaks in the place of the subject who cannot speak from himself – Hölderlin was probably the first artist to sense this.'[21] Parataxis logically transforms itself into a series of incantations, a mere string of proper names: 'The dissociation into names is the innermost tendency of Hölderlin's parataxis' (*Noten zur Literatur III*, p. 197). Adorno suggests here a first way of approaching the paradox raised by Heidegger, who left pure *deixis* and pure self-referentiality in an unstable coexistence; in the *Cantos*, a similar passivity is 'at work' behind Pound's often vehement praise of 'factive', i.e. creative, personalities and his bold layering of languages and idioms.

Such passivity might be the object of psychological or even psychoanalytical investigation, and if Adorno's 'negative dialectics' can offer a usable model for an understanding of Pound's 'weakness of ego'[22] it will by now have become clear that a 'foundational' approach to language can only rule out such attempts because they remain within the field of anthropology. The question nevertheless remains open, for Pound himself has been responsible for many confusions, since he avowedly transformed the *Cantos* into his own 'record of struggle' by taking his life, his subjectivity as basic paradigm for all humanity. And, the more he feels himself entangled in the writing of his huge 'palimpsest', the more he quotes from purely private readings and references, the more hieratic, impersonal, anonymous he sounds – until, in the last drafts and fragments, Pound's voice is heard as indissociable from that of Herakles, the demigod reconciled with the idea of death through an oracle, or Dante, the arch-poet guided to the vision of the mystic rose. Pound's gradual acceptance of this passivity, from an 'omniformis' spirit which still engages with the synthetic process of history to the 'mind unstill as Ixion', ever turning in gyres of remorse at times yielding to intense moments of self-vindication, brings about a slower and slower swirl of insights into the nature of beauty and light.

Language as such can take on its full function when it is seen as the locus from which the poet can speak as the Other of the System; he can utter this otherness between transgression and provocation – in Adorno's terms – or as the sacrifice of his self – in Heidegger's terms – to create the 'pure idiom', analogous to the 'prose of sacred texts' (*Noten zur Literatur III*, p. 184), a synthesis of love and desire. The methodological tension only briefly adumbrated here can find a tentative resolution in Lacan's conception of the speaking subject split by desire. A title such as 'Subversion of the subject and dialectic of desire' could bridge the conceptual gap I have just opened: the essential and the dialogical readings, the anthropological and the theological, are both implied and fused by Lacan's positioning of the Other in language.

Lacan translated Heidegger's paper in *Logos*,[23] an article in which Heidegger starts from the semantic ambiguity of *logos*, which cannot be reduced to *ratio* or *verbum* but signifies to say, to utter, to enunciate (*legein*) and the utterance, what has been said (*legomenon*). *Logos* soon is identified with its etymological sense of 'gathering' as reading and writing, and the importance of this short text is decisive for Lacan's subsequent conceptual elaboration. Besides, it is used as a guide to literature for an analyst unwilling to submit the literary text to 'wild' interpretations. Heidegger's respect for the signifier and the exact phrasing of Greek philosophers or German poets can be taken as a warning not to 'psychoanalyse' the author. Such a warning has been repeatedly issued by Lacan (who expresses the same respect for artists and creators as Freud when faced with Goethe, Nietzsche or Shakespeare) whenever he has directly commented on writers. This, for instance, is what he has to say about Marguerite Duras:

A subject is a scientific term, and as such calculable, and a reminder of its status should put an end to what must now really be called by its name: the boorishness, or the pendantry of a certain type of psychoanalysis. If this aspect of their frolics can become manifest to those who engage with them, it could signal to them that they are slipping into some kind of silliness: that for instance of attributing an author's avowed technique to some neurosis: loutishness; and of demonstrating how it stems from the explicit carrying out of the mechanisms which constitute its unconscious edifice: stupidity.[24]

When referring to Lacan, I shall thus be wary of such direct exploitation of his concepts, and refuse to study Pound's unconscious, his obsessions and manias, his phobias or neuroses, in order to hear the voice at work in the writing and the writing which embodies the voice: in so doing, I shall yet need to know a little more about the logic – the calculability – of this voice, of the structure of its division, and of the relationship between the dialogic subject (*wir*) and the vortex (*Wirbel*) of Pound's poems. The subject at stake will therefore be the poetic subject in general, as underwritten or signed by a name: Ezra Pound.

The subject of the enunciation

By the end of the seventies a theoretical battle seemed to have been won by those who wished to replace the static linguistic analysis of utterances by the apprehension of the dynamic process underlying them. Roland Barthes was superbly heralding the triumph of the linguists who had been elaborating the concept of enunciation for more than a decade:

> The statement [*énoncé*] which is the ordinary object of linguistics is generally seen as produced by the absence of the enunciator. Enunciation itself, which exposes the place and the energy of the subject, even his lack (not to be confused with his absence), aims at the real nature of language. . . . Words are no longer mistaken for instruments, they shoot forth like projections, explosions, vibrations, machineries, flavours; writing turns knowledge into a festivity.[25]

But just a little earlier, Barthes had shown how the voices in a text are always inhabited by ghosts and codes: 'Alongside each utterance, one might say that off-stage voices can be heard: they are the codes; in their interweaving, these voices (whose origin is lost in the vast perspective of the already-written) de-originate the utterance.'[26]

Both notions – enunciation as the subjective process of the production of speech, and the lack of a real origin in the text – must together be brought to bear on Pound's own practice of posturing as the dominant authorial voice in his text. Pound plays the role of the chronicler who arranges the quotations and decides to intervene or not; when he does, the 'voice' we hear has quite an ambiguous status. In Canto xxiv, for instance, Pound quotes from an account of Niccolo d'Este's travels to Jerusalem, and he translates the Italian text written by an obscure scribe:

> 'Here Christ put his thumb on a rock
> 'Saying: hic est medium mundi.'
> (That, I assure you, happened.
> Ego, scriptor cantilenae.)
> For worse? for better? but happened.
> After which, the greek girls at Corfu . . . .   (p. 112)

Does Pound limit his intervention to the wry remark 'For worse: For better?' or is the whole parenthesis to be ascribed to his voice? Indeed the quotation marks have closed, and the anaphora linking the two occurrences of 'happened' tends to confirm the validity of what is said. But in fact the chronicle only records mythical events at this point, which Pound cannot pretend to have verified: he then opts for a playful attitude to his source and to historical verisimilitude (not to mention truth) while baffling the reader with 'scriptor cantilenae' in place of the original *scriptor historiae*. This endless process of division among voices sketches the problem of enunciation in the *Cantos*.

The field of enunciation was covered by rhetorical modes of analysis from Aristotle to Boethius,[27] but the purpose of their classification was to give a set of rules for the constitution of an art of persuasion (including all sorts of strategies which would be relevant to Pound's poetic discourse) rather than a real grasp of the mechanism of enunciation. To link a working concept of enunciation with an understanding of the encroachments of the Unconscious on subjectivity has been Lacan's main effort. His emphasis on the place of the subject, which reveals a lack, a modality of his fading away in language – and not the pure absence of formalist or structuralist linguistics – lends its specific overtones to the first quotation from Barthes.

Since Lacan started utilising linguistic concepts with a Freudian slant, more than one linguist has been disturbed by his off-hand annexations, such as his treatment of Saussure's distinction between 'signified' and 'signifier', with his notoriously allegorical reading of the line dividing them as the 'bar' of repression.[28] But it was with the displacement of the linguistics of the signifier by the linguistics of enunciation, affording him the tools with which to break away from the implicit functionalism of Saussurean theory, that Lacan was able to find the specific locus of this theory. As Jean-Luc Nancy points out, 'The theme of the subject of the enunciation finally enabled and urged psychoanalysis to criticise the science from which it believed it could borrow this subject: linguistics.'[29] The suspicion nevertheless remains that, far from having achieved the 'subversion' of the subject promised by Lacan, psychoanalytical discourse might indeed have reinvested the subject with another discourse, that of the theory of the lack which constitutes it. By positing a gap between the subject and the 'real', Lacan's theory presents itself as the only bridge between the two sides of the chasm dividing the subject. Anyhow, the only way to situate the subject in this controversy is to go back to the original discussion.

The first textual mention of the opposition between the subject of the enunciation and the subject of the utterance, or statement, or enounced,[30] was made by Benveniste[31] just at the time when Lacan was groping, with the help of Heidegger, toward the same intuition, corroborated by Freud's last paper on the *Spaltung* or 'splitting' of the ego. Lacan used the term in 'Subversion of the Subject and Dialectics of Desire' before fully elaborating it in the 1964 *Séminaire*.[32]

Benveniste's paper is crucial for an understanding of Lacan's theory because he radically refuses the notion of language considered as an instrument. For him, subjectivity is nothing but a speaker's ability to posit himself as subject in language: 'He is "ego" who utters "ego" ' (p. 260). Subjectivity implies a dialogic and reciprocal constitution of subjects: 'I only use *I* when I address myself to someone who will be a you in my allocution. The condition of dialogue constitutes the *person* for it implies the reciprocity through which I become *you* in the allocution of he who in his turn designates himself by I' (ibid.). 'I' therefore only refers to the 'individual act of discourse' which utters it, the reality of language deriving from this self-reference in the present of an action.

The scheme can of course be reversed and apply to another subject, who then becomes co-enunciator and not merely 'addressee' of a message. This is verified by the analysis of performative verbs, when the action is the utterance of the verb, but which is warranted by the hearer only if he acknowledges the other's position of discourse. The speaker and the enunciator have to coincide so that, for instance, a promise may be valid. Now all the terms needed for Lacan's theory of a subject split between enunciation and enounced have been introduced.

Lacan's pronouncements lose a little of their cryptic character if one keeps in mind the basic situation of discourse constituted by analysis: an analysand is asked to say whatever comes to his mind and speaks not *to* the analyst, but to the wall, while the analyst, unseen, keeps silent for the greater part of the session. From this pattern, one can learn that 'I' am only subject in so far as I am a *'speaking* subject'; the 'subject' has to be generated from the general structures of language, desire and the family, which operate the mediation from the status of being just an 'infant' to that of being a 'person'. Language conditions the category of the person, which cannot be restricted to the 'ego' of Freud's topography. A first disjuncture between the 'ego' and the 'I' is necessary to understand what Lacan means by 'subject', a subject who is mainly the subject of psychoanalysis. 'It is therefore always in the relation between the subject's ego [*moi*] and the "I" [*je*] of his discourse that you must understand the meaning of the discourse if you are to achieve the delienation of the subject.'[33]

At this point, it is convenient to define the psychoanalytic process as a technique aiming at turning the analysand into a subject. But this subject is neither a 'full subject' nor a 'person', and there is the greatest danger in attempts to replace this subject by an imaginary version, thereby reducing the gap opened in its autonomy by Freud's 'Copernician revolution'. Lacan insists that analysis has been perverted by a movement which has centred everything around the ego, misreading the Freudian motto 'Wo Es war, soll Ich werden' and distorting it into an 'adequation' of the patient's ego with that of the analyst. The processes of 'transference' and 'resistance' which make up most of the dialogue between analyst and analysand can be defined by a theory which finds a renewed rigour in linguistic models:

> The kernel of our being does not coincide with our self [*moi*]. This is the meaning of analytic experience. . . . But do you think it suffices to say: the 'I' of the subject is not his ego [*moi*]? It is not enough, for nothing implies a reciprocity for you who think spontaneously, as it were. And you currently begin thinking that this 'I' is the real ego. You imagine that the ego is only an incomplete, erroneous form of the 'I'. Thus, no sooner has this decentring been achieved, a decentring so essential to Freud's discovery, than it has been reduced.[34]

For Lacan, indeed, the ego is not a pure 'mistake', a mere bubble to be pricked, since it fulfils a function – that of an imaginary reconstruction of an asymbolisable real into a reality defined by the web of fantasies which render the real less painful, less foreign, less disturbing. But, as soon as a subject speaks, he enters the realm of language, through which the promise of truth can be made. Although this truth cannot be uttered entirely, it speaks at times through the habitual disguises used by the self in its 'misconstruction' (*méconnaissance*): such is the case of parapraxes, lapsus, jokes, dreams and so on, the usual direct formations of the Unconscious. To say, along with Freud, that the Unconscious tells me the truth of what I really wish does not immediately imply that I, as a subject, can become aware of this truth, or that I am sure of uttering it. Even if I guess that this truth is located in the 'Other' place of the Unconscious, no warrant exists for it (or, as Lacan says, there is no Other of the Other). Thus an absence of reciprocity, a disalignment, a fundamental disparity, all brand the speaking subject with the seal of desire.

The speaking subject affords the only possible mode of access to truth, a truth of which he is unaware most of the time. Speech provides a key to the truth of psychoanalysis, because the Unconscious possesses the structure of language. But, before embarking on a description of the workings of such a language, a distinction should be made between three terms:

(1) *language* as a general structure introduces us to the laws of combination and selection (the reference to Jakobson is explicit here), since the principles of metaphor and metonymy can be superimposed on Freud's 'condensation' and 'displacement' in the process of the dreamwork;

(2) *discourse* is a social formation of language which situates the subject within his family, in which a place is prepared for him even before his birth by a name, a set of expectations, a series of values and standards of behaviour by which he is to fail or to succeed, thus paying off his symbolic debt;

(3) *speech* is produced by the subject in a dialogic situation; 'empty speech' may be opposed to 'full speech' (*Ecrits/S*, p. 40). It remains the privileged medium of analysis: 'psychoanalysis has only a single medium: the patient's speech. That this is self-evident is no excuse for our neglecting it. And also speech calls for a reply. I shall show that there is no speech without a reply, even if it is met only with silence, provided it has an auditor' (ibid.).

Therefore, no one can pretend to be the subject of 'language': his speech is always a combination of discourses, and this is why the analyst keeps silent. He stands in a sort of 'neutrality', being neither the one nor the other, but the void which lets the Other speak. What the analysand receives is nothing but his own discourse, but inverted by the decentring produced by the Other. 'The Unconscious is the discourse of the Other by which the subject receives his own forgotten message under the inverted form which corresponds to promise.'[35]

Speech becomes the paradoxical locus of a dialogue with silence and otherness. If I seek the response of the Other when speaking, it is my question, my demand which constitutes me as a subject. Even when I am by myself, the fact that I can speak implies at least two subjects; if they are then confronted, the nature of their relationship is closer to that of a pact than to mirror images. For instance, if I say, 'You are my master', I really mean, 'I am your slave, disciple, etc.', which goes beyond any reciprocal scheme. Another instance, the instance of the Law which will guarantee 'mastery' is needed. As we shall see, this Law and the discourse of the Other are identical.

Before elaborating the distinction between the subject of the enunciation and the subject of the enounced, Lacan had only worked with the
simpler distinction between the subject of the signifier and the subject
of the signified. In this pattern, the signified was defined as 'representing a subject for another signified', which reversed the traditional
distinction between signified and signifier. For, if, along with Peirce's
theory of the 'interpretants' of signs,[36] Lacan states that a subject is
only a link in a chain of language, instead of an idealised absolute
origin of signification, the real subject is to be found in the subject of
the signifier: he will adhere to the chain of words, names, puns and
metaphors or metonymies, and not be limited to the false consciousness of being signified by those same terms. 'Is the place that I occupy
as the subject of a signifier concentric or excentric, in relation to the
place I occupy as subject of the signified? – That is the question. It is
not a question of knowing whether I speak of myself in a way that
conforms to what I am, but rather of knowing whether I am the same as
that of which I speak' (*Ecrits/S*, p. 165).

Thus, once the question of the subject appears as distinct from that
of the ego, the play on the signifier (*S*) and the signified (*s*) as in
Saussure's model of the sign *S* and on the crossing of the line separating
signifier from signified can point toward a third 'S', namely that of the
subject:

> This crossing expresses the condition of passage of the signifier into
> the signified that I pointed out above, although provisionally
> confusing it with the place of the subject. It is the function of the
> subject, thus introduced, that we must now turn to since it lies at the
> crucial point of our problem. 'I think, therefore I am' (*cogito ergo
> sum*) is not merely the formula in which is constituted, with the
> historical high point of reflection on the conditions of science, the
> link between the transparency of the transcendental subject and his
> existential affirmation.
>
> (*Ecrits/S*, p. 164)

The reference to the Cartesian *cogito* is central, and it can stand for the
paradigm of all subjective delusions centred around vain autonomy
and self-love, whilst constituting science through the mathematisation
of the given. Lacan's own algebrical formulas build up a series of
'graphs'; they all articulate the subject's desire onto metaphor and
metonymy; desire will be caused by the lack of an imaginary object
receding along the chain of signifiers, and a symptom will be expressed

by a rupture of the bar of repression, writing on the body the unutterable 'message' of the Unconscious. All this sets up a kind of game in which the subject has to learn that his fate is determined from where he is not, since he would really be at a loss to situate himself in the Unconscious. Lacan can therefore state the formula, 'I think where I am not, therefore I am where I do not think.' Or again: 'I think of what I am where I do not think to think' (*Ecrits/S*, p. 166). But the mere inversion of the Cartesian model seems just a little too glib, and offers only a brittle countermodel. The model will only gain its scientific rigour when Lacan is in a position to understand the verb *cogito* as the place of the enunciation. The sentence then becomes quite simply, 'Cogito: "ergo sum".' An *ergo* has replaced the ego, for the ego is not the 'I' of discourse, but only the 'metonymy of its signification' (p. 307). The opacity of the signifier once more determines the false transparency of self-consciousness, and opens a play of utterances founded on a striking parataxis.

To postulate a Freudian Unconscious determined in itself like a language by the interplay of metaphor and metonymy working through signifiers (and not defined by the 'communication of ideas' or signs, if by a sign one means something for someone) implies that it needs an enunciative subject. Such a subject, when he speaks, says more than he knows, and not less. The unconscious is what the subject of the enunciation utters unwittingly: it is utterable, but without the conscious knowledge of the subject, and his utterance does not leave him the wiser for it. Enunciation is neither masterable nor measurable. The Unconscious can be defined as an utterance produced by an enunciation which escapes any subjective control. The aim of the 'talking cure' can be made explicit: it situates the subject in this gap which threatens the consistency of any discourse, but allows for real speech. Truth is always approached *in statu nascendi*, for it can never be identified with a word or a signifier (this is why 'desire' is not the truth of analysis if it is reduced to a keyword such as 'libido').

An enunciator is not an 'ego', a 'person'; there is no knowledge available about him. Although he is constantly positing himself by reference to a present time and to a specific organisation of space, there is no logical or 'ergological' bridging of the gap from his existence to his imaginary pole as Freudian 'Ego'. 'For this ego, which is notable in the first instance for the imaginary inertias that it concentrates against the message of the unconscious, operates solely with a view to covering the displacement constituted by the subject with a resistance that is essential to the discourse as such' (*Ecrits/S*, p. 169). It would be too simplistic to reduce the two clinical terms of 'resistance' and 'transference' to a greater emphasis on the pole of the ego for the former, on the pole of the enunciation for the latter, but this nevertheless indicates a certain direction in the process of Lacan's thinking. For no enunciator can stand on his own; he is always a co-enunciator. What remains to be demonstrated is the fact that this function opens up the space of radical otherness by presenting the dialogue as founded by the third person.

The theme of the subject of the enunciation enables Lacan to go beyond the dialectics of 'representation' so powerfully expressed by 'a signifier represents a subject for another signifier'. On the contrary, the subject of the enunciation is not represented by his utterance:

> We can try, with methodological rigour, to set out from the strictly linguistic definition of the I as signifier, in which there is nothing but the 'shifter' or indicative, which, in the subject of the statement, designates the subject in the sense that he is now speaking.
>
> That is to say, it designates the subject of the enunciation, but it does not signify it. (*Ecrits/S*, p. 298)

Lacan adds as a proof of this that the subject as such may be entirely missing from the utterance – that is, not represented by a signifier. It can be reduced to pure *deixis* or 'monstration', to the French *ne* used as expletive, to the ambiguity of adverbs, and so on . . . . The list would be endless, since ellipsis itself can reveal this ghost of a function, which may be hidden in the trace of an intonation. To distinguish the adverb as used by the subject of the enunciation and as proposed to the addressee, one has merely to compare 'Quite frankly, this play is no good!' with 'Quite frankly, did you enjoy it?' In the second example, 'frankly' predetermines the future enunciation of the hearer. 'Quite frankly, you enjoyed it' would be entirely ambiguous, and the epitome of expressions which lend themselves to analytic interpretation.

Pound had grasped this particular mobility of certain adverbs, and used the same example to make his point clear; he quotes approvingly de Gourmont's sentence 'Franchement d'écrire ce qu'on pense, seul plaisir d'un écrivain', and comments,

> 'To put down one's thought frankly, a writer's sole pleasure.' That phrase was the centre of Gourmont's position. . . . 'Franchement', 'Frankly' is 'Frenchly', if one may drag in philology. If, in ten lines or

in a hundred pages, I can get the reader to comprehend what one adjective *means* in literature. (*SP*, pp. 386–7)

This leads him to comment on de Gourmont's poems, 'The first difficulty in a modern poem is to give a feeling of the reality of the speaker, the second, given the reality of the speaker, to gain any degree of poignancy in one's utterance' (p. 388). In fact, the ultimate degree of poignancy is only attained when the risk of total loss threatens the subject – this will be the lesson learnt in Pisa. Anyhow, the vanishing subject cannot be adequately represented by a signifier: style and affects have to meet him at the empty place he leaves.

If the subject of the enunciation is not represented but only indicated if it can be missing as a signifier, it then means that the logic of the signifier is not wholly adequate to the task of defining its role. The subject is a 'discontinuity in the real', a 'fading' presence which finds its theoretical status in a re-elaboration of Freud's formula, 'Wo Es war, soll Ich werden' suggested by Lacan in these words: 'An enunciation that denounces itself, a statement that renounces itself, ignorance that dissipates itself, an opportunity that loses itself, what remains here if not the trace of what *must* be in order to fall from being?' (*Ecrits/S*, p. 300). The expression is set in parallel with one of Freud's famous ones: 'He did not know that he was dead.' This refers to the ghost of a father, but can also be read as the hint that the father is a key to the symbolical 'Name-of-the-Father', or the agency of the dead father in any subject's unconscious. Lacan comments thus: 'If the figure of the dead father survives only by virtue of the fact that one does not tell him the truth of which he is unaware, what, then, is to be said of the *I*, on which this survival depends?' (ibid.). The 'I' is then a 'being of non-being', a single 'cut in discourse' whose elusive being is pinpointed by the analyst when he achieves the same 'cut in a false discourse'. The sentence can illustrate the relation of the subject to discourse and to the signifier, 'a relation that is embodied in an enunciation whose being trembles with the vacillation that comes back to it from its own statement' (ibid.). This confirms both the split nature of the subject and its determination by the discourse, which rebounds, so to speak, from the locus of the Other. The levels of the enunciation and of the statement are always sliding off one another.

Lacan says that the 'I' of 'I think' is marked by a 'sort of abortion'.[37] For the subject is not only secondary to the signifier, not only taken apart between his imaginary lures and the persistent dimension of truth which is opened in spite of himself by his speech; he is spoken through or by desire: 'Whatever animates, that which any enunciation speaks of, belongs to desire' (ibid.). Such a desire, which may be just the desire to deceive, accounts for the discrepancies which reign within the subject; objective truth is no proof against it, as the Jewish joke recorded by Freud ('Why are you telling me you are going to Lemberg, so that I believe you are going to Cracow, while in fact you are going to Lemberg?') so masterfully shows.

The term 'Desire' – used by Alan Sheridan to translate Lacan's *désir* instead of the standard translation of *Wunsch* into 'wish' – is necessary to hint at the way the dialogic situation is structured by its appeal to the Other. Benveniste had already noted that the third person, the divine 'He', is the Absent par excellence. But he did not see it as a condition for dialogue. This step is taken by Lacan, who seems to follow closely Freud's analysis of the *Witz* ('jokes' is a weak approximation). Freud insisted that there must always be three persons, or at least three imaginary roles for a good joke to be effective. 'Generally speaking, a tendentious joke calls for three people: in addition to the one who makes the joke, there must be a second who is taken as the object of the hostile or sexual aggressiveness, and a third in whom the joke's aim of producing pleasure is fulfilled.' [38] This finally provides a set of formal criteria enabling us to distinguish between *der Witz* or *le mot d'esprit*, in which the unconscious achieves direct expression, and the comic or humour, which is the product of conscious or preconscious elaboration: 'The psychical process in jokes is accomplished between the first person (the self) and the third (the outside person) and not, as in the case of the comic, between the self and the person who is the object.' [39]

The pleasure gained in a joke establishes a sort of short-circuit within the circuit of desire, which is basically triangular. The economy of wit, a typical language production, adumbrates the general economy of exchange, the exchange of persons, things and words. The Oedipal stages and the child's acquisition of language are contemporaneous, and both demonstrate that Law and Desire are not opposed, as would commonly be believed, but reconciled. They appear linked as two sides of a coin because language is a condition of the unconscious, and not the reverse, as Lacan repeats.

Thus the Oedipal pattern is also a linguistic process of learning, dealing mainly with personal pronouns. If the father remains a second person for the child, superposable onto the mother, he will never be capable of 'laying down' the law, or of acting as its representative; the child then runs the risk of remaining a prisoner of an imaginary identification with either his mother or his father, which can lead to psychosis or neurosis.[40] In the ideal pattern of normality, the subject has been confronted by a father and a mother who exchanged words and desire, so that the mother could be able to acknowledge the father as a subject for her. This dialogue and the situation of desire is the condition of possibility for the child to assume the role of a subject. For the 'I' and 'you' can only be permutated when set off against the invocation of a third person, a 'he' who is present by his very absence. It would be wrong to identify this 'he' with the father, since the role can be played by the mother, who at one point plays the function of the big Other. Father and mother alternatively exchange the position of 'I' and 'you' against which the child can start being both an 'I' and a 'he'.

As a language, the Unconscious defines a structure, a pattern of tropological realisations (metaphor/metonymy), not a content; the only statement enounced as such is embodied in the name: the name chosen for the child, weighted with all the imaginary overtones latent in the 'I' and 'you's psyches, and streamlined by the symbolic debt owed to the 'Name-of-the-Father'. This name designates the subject as shifter; it does not 'represent' him. It is imposed on him first from the outside, and this exteriority is necessary since exclusion from the dialogue between mother and father turns the infant into the empty centre which will then be filled by a voice. It is imposed secondly by a relation of desire, against which he will have to define a position in terms of the Law. After the 'he' of the infant has undergone castration, utter absence and lack, he can be generated as a 'one' among others. This symbolic death by displacement is the only mode of access to discourse.

The genesis of the 'he' or 'she' allows for the disjuncture of the 'I' itself between the subject of the enunciation and the subject of the statement. Their coincidence is by definition impossible, for the subject of the enunciation never realises a self in a statement, never 'expresses' himself, nor abolishes himself in discourse. On the contrary, it is generally the lack of this lack which precipitates the subject towards neurosis or psychosis: it suffices for him to become identified with a statement and somehow stuck to it or by it (for example, the injunction to be a substitute for some dead relative, the command to be 'good' and without life and desire, etc.), and he may never be free to organise a real speech. He will be cut off from the symbolic realm opened by the Other, and will probably have to relive another kind of symbolic death in the process of analysis to be the 'subject of his discourse' again. In the normal condition of mildly neurotic subjects (equivalent to the average notion of 'normality') the split nature of subjectivity implies that any statement is an enigma when referred back to the speaking subject, a puzzle or rebus pointing towards the shifting dispersal area that he is. 'He does not know' defines the subject at the level of his enunciation. Of course, he wishes to know, especially as soon as he is engaged in a talking cure; he wishes to penetrate back to his origins. But the analytic process will slowly demonstrate to him that the radical incompatibility between the wish to know and his desire or the truth of desire is that which founds his split nature. His 'ineffable, stupid existence' as S, barred subject, is determined by the discourse of the Other. The very simple schema L maps it clearly:

S stands for the subject, O for the locus of the Other or the unconscious 'from which the question of his existence may be presented to him', o, the objects of the subject, around which his desire is hinged, and o' his ego, or mirror-image of the objects (*Ecrits/S*, pp. 193–4). 'The Other therefore, is the locus in which the I who speaks to him who hears is constituted, that which is said by the one being already the reply, the other deciding, upon hearing him, whether the one has or has not spoken' (p. 141, modified).

The ancient dichotomy opposing universal and particular can no more be thought out in terms of the difference between the subject of the signifier and the subject of the signified, but only between the subject of the enunciation and the subject of the enounced. The literary text constitutes the space of its language by the same division. Dante offers the initial paradigm of this process when he decides to open his *Commedia* by the disjunction between a collective subject and the subject who says 'I' but who stands for all of us:

> Nel mezzo del cammin di *nostra* vita
> *Mi* ritrovai per una selva oscura...

Eliot has learnt from this archetypal disjuncture the way to dramatise the aporetic nature of enunciation, while enabling the reader to achieve a certain amount of transference with the text. Prufrock can only utter the celebrated 'Let us go then, you and I' because Guido da Montelferro thought he could reveal his secret to Dante and remain assured of his silence, not believing that live men can go down to Hell. The epigraph to 'The Love Song of J. Alfred Prufrock' encapsulates the sly machinery of all the dramatic ironies attendant on the modernist desire to 'tell it all' while staying aware of the subject's division:

> S'io credessi che mia risposta fosse
> a persona che mai tornasse al mondo,
> questa fiamma staria senza più scosse.
> Ma per ciò che giammai di questo fondo
> non tornò vivo alcun, s'i'odo il vero,
> senza tema d'infamia ti rispondo.[41]

Only one year after *Prufrock* had been published in *Poetry*, Pound showed he had understood the consequences of such dialogic paradoxes for his conception of the 'masks':

> In the 'search for oneself', in the search for 'sincere self-expression', one gropes, one finds some seeming verity. One says 'I am' this, that, or the other, and with the words scarcely uttered one ceases to be that thing.
>
> I began this search for the real in a book called *Personae*, casting off, as it were, complete masks of the self in each poem. I continued in long series of translations, which were but more elaborate masks.
>
> Secondly, I made poems like 'The Return', which is an objective reality, and has a complicated sort of significance. . . . Thirdly, I have written 'Heather', which represents a state of consciousness, or 'implies', or 'implicates' it.
>
> A Russian correspondent, after having called it a symbolist poem, and having been convinced that it was not symbolism, said slowly: 'I see, you wish to give people new eyes, not to make them see some new particular thing.' (*GB*, p. 85)

I wanted to give the quotation as completely as possible, for, if it is often reproduced, the whole context is generally lost; what matters is to see the connection between a theory of the discrete and discontinuous nature of the speaking subject, an affirmation of the 'objective' nature of the return of the gods ('The Return'), and finally the appeal to the auditor or an audience who is to be modified by the reading-experience as much as the poet has been; to give people new eyes or new ears is the fundamental aim of Pound's writing, and it is

founded on a sense of division *and* of the possibility of finding a
language, or a series of languages to communicate this division.

'The Tragic Double of our Day'

> We are too late for the gods and too early for Being. Being's
> poem, just began, is man.
> (Heidegger, *Poetry, Language, Thought*, p. 14)

In his Preface to the English version of the *Four Fundamental Concepts
of Psycho-analysis* Lacan writes decisively, 'A certificate tells me that I
was born. I repudiate this certificate: I am not a poet, but a poem. A
poem that is being written, even if it looks like a subject.'[42] The Other
is there, busily laying down the law of what shall turn out to be my fate,
the poem inscribed in my flesh and in my life; by another torsion, or by
a speeding up of the whirls of signifiers and voices, the poet can
approach this disturbing knowledge, the knowledge of his own
undoing, and write from this point where his *aphanisis*, his disappearance, will turn into its contrary, the *apophansis*, or judgement, or
manifestation to the light, of truth.

A reading of Pound's early poems would have to attach itself to the
discovery of these moments or 'moods' through which the speaker
suddenly understands this division – whether he sees it as a division
between 'souls', 'feeling myself divided between myself corporal and a
self aetherial' (*CEP*, p. 8) or a division between self and others, 'I? I?
I? / And ye?' (p. 35), or between self and images of the self, 'And then
for utter loneliness, made I / New thoughts as crescent images of *me*'
(p. 36) – and systematises it in a whirlpool of metamorphoses, through
which souls keep exchanging identities. This is the subject of 'Histo-
rion':

> No man hath dared to write this thing as yet,
> And yet I know, how that the souls of all men great
> At times pass through us,
> And we are melted into them, and are not
> Save reflexions of their souls.   (p. 71)

Such a lability of the poetic subject only reveals with greater emphasis
the process which constitutes human speech. But in the *Cantos* the
vortex of voices and souls has become a vortex of texts, in a whirling

vortextuality, as it were, for the voices come back as ghosts who ask for blood, wish to be placated or pushed away. The Nekuia offers the paradigm of a pre-text, *vor-* or *Ur-*text, behind which one may always further recede, until a new form has been found and frozen on the page.

Pound after Yeats plays on the etymology of 'per-sona', a mask through which a voice can be mimicked; but masks possess still another aperture, the two holes for the eyes; and it might not be so self-evident that the attempt to give 'new eyes' to the audience should be equated with the revitalisation of speeches. The division of the subject as he speaks and misses the object of his desire, the several time-lags brought about by discrepancies in historical rhythms, the gap between will and action Dante underlines among his characters – all this leads to another type of dissociation, and Canto vii relates it to a division in being.

Canto vii begins by recalling the themes of Canto ii, with Eleanor spliced in with Homer's blindness, and the empty voices of the old men on the wall at Troy, refusing beauty and its evil consequences; she embodies the destructiveness of her sex, and yet appears as more 'alive' than these doomed phantoms of the past:

> ῎Ελανδρος and ῾Ελέπτολις, and
> poor old Homer blind,
> blind as a bat,
> Ear, ear for the sea-surge;
> rattle of old men's voices.   (p. 24)

And the other elements which compose this complicated ideogram (the visit to Henry James, to Vanderpyl, the memory of a friend who committed suicide[43]) all suggest the essential emptiness and tawdriness of modern times; the basic situation of Prufrock has been reversed, for instead of hearing the women in the room who 'come and go, talking of Michelangelo', the poet only hears 'old dry dead talk, gassed out' in the 'petrefaction of air', while the lure of the mermaids in their cave keeps all its positive value:

> And all that day
> Nicea moved before me
> And the cold grey air troubled her not
> For all her naked beauty, bit not the tropic skin,
> And the long slender feet lit on the curb's marge
> And her moving height went before me,
> We alone having being.   (p. 26)

The image of perpetual desire is contrasted with the empty talk, and the theme of love – presented in all its sensuousness – embodies the only stable basis for the will: 'The live man, out of lands and prisons,/ shakes the dry pods,/ Probes for old wills and friendships' (p. 27). By a kind of grammatical hesitation, 'we alone having being' sounding so close to 'we alone having been', the inner life resists the erasure of time ('Time blacked out with the rubber' – p. 25) since it keeps the present value of the gerund/noun. Being is the consequence of the fusion of feminine beauty and masculine will; Eros is thus another of its names, as the reference to Dido shows: 'Dido choked up with sobs, for her Sicheus/Lies heavy in my arms, dead weight/ Drowning, with tears, new Eros' (pp. 26–7).

It is only after the Pisan experience that Pound can reconcile Time and Being, or even identify them in the writing of the traces left in his memory; the carving of the living ridge among past and present images brings back the dead to life in a different way. The eyes themselves will be shown to keep and produce the vision, and they will even later give forth the power of Love: 'UBI AMOR IBI OCULUS EST'.[44] But, at that moment, life has encompassed death in a general sense of flowing which coincides with the movement by which the world is a world: 'Trees die & the dream remains' (Canto xc, p. 609). The 'seeing eye' (*chien*, made up an eye and two legs, meaning to see) sees that the paradise is outside the vision:

> to 'see again',
> the verb is 'see', not 'walk on'
> i.e. it coheres all right
>   even if my notes do not cohere.
> Many errors,
>   a little rightness,
> to excuse his hell
>   and my paradiso.   (cxvi, pp. 796–7)

Who is 'he'; who is 'it'? One would be too easily contented by answering that the 'he' is Dante; as for this 'it', it would be as well to leave open the whole range of its indeterminacies; Pound explains that his 'notes' do not 'cohere' because he is not a 'demi-god', which leaves 'it' – the world? the dream? the thing? logos? language? the revelation of truth? love? – in its coherence: 'it' speaks all right. But, even if 'it' speaks, 'I' cannot utter it; its coherence is outside, in the realm of the Other, forsaken, foreclosed.

If Pound is really, as Olson intelligently put it, the 'Tragic Double of our day' and 'the demonstration of our duality',[45] it is not primarily because he enacts the division between 'reactionary politics', 'as retrogressive as the Czar', and a revolutionary language. The division is constitutive of his language and his politics, and it appears idle now to minimise the potential rifts and inconsistencies in both; in this creative fissiparity, his writings tend to disrupt the monologist features of our dominant metaphysical discourse while attempting to regain the lost paradise of an utterance that would be able to tell the full truth. In this movement, Pound presents a mirror to our division, a duplication of our duplication, a division of our division, symptomatically living through the tragedy of writing as duplication and division and founding his poetics on it.

This is why his language is both private paratactical idiom and the speech of a whole people, intent on the celebration of its vanishing gods; this is why it has recurrently to dramatise its own utterance and the splitting of the utterance, as it hesitates between logorrhea and silence, between shrill self-assertion and a surrender to intertextual dispersion. The impossible task Pound sets out for his poem is the writing of the suture at the juncture of the imaginary and symbolic realms. It leaves him only one object which eludes him, whether he calls it money or the gods: that trace of an inexpressible radiance coming at the place of the real.

Money will enable him to link the verbal seal with the symbolic seal, since it opens the problematics of the name and the bearer of the name, of the signature and its underwriting, and of the circulation of signs in what can also be understood as hermeneutical circle. All these points will be treated by the following chapters, as they will try to map out the periplus of a broken voice among the signs of its desire. When money, for instance, comes to the fore as the main object of investigation, it appears as both real and symbolic, which leaves Pound incapable of thinking the process of capitalistic production. Yet this inability affords him a much greater leverage to bypass most 'metaphysical' traps of our present-day ideologies, and to deconstruct, by a radical 'step back out' of the system of the production of signs, values and merchandise, the ontological site of the logics of production.

Being unable to confront the problem of production forces him to deal with empirical reality as if itself was already an ideogram, and finally in a nominalist fashion (although his explicit ideology runs counter to the nominalist 'philology' he hates), using a kind of Occam's razor to effect a linguistic castration of the system of signs. Hence the fundamental gesture of dissociating, splitting up words so as to find roots (thus the subtraction of *usus* from *usura*) which are splintered in their turn. In such a disintegrating palimpsest, the incestuous game that quotations, codes and records play with the poet strand him or 'shore' him between saturation (when awestruck he beholds the sacred text) and suturation: being ordered to speak with the 'sealed mouth' of heaven so that the 'ancestral voice' might be complete.

1 Symptoms and Voices: the Articulations of the Subject

> To write, in the sense of Flaubert and de Goncourt, is to exist, to differentiate oneself. To have a style means that one speaks a particular dialect in the midst of a common language, but unique and inimitable, so that it will however remain the language of everybody and the language of one at the same time.   (Rémy de Gourmont, *La Culture des Idées*[1])

The *Cantos* and *Finnegans Wake*, those two gigantic 'universal histories', have often been compared on grounds of a common illegibility and opacity of verbal texture, but the experience induced by the two texts is fundamentally different; one starts reading *Finnegans Wake* in much the same way as one learns a foreign language[2] – that is by mastering the various linguistic rules, the polysemic procedures, the system of punning *double-entendre* which fuses different personalities, until the axes of a microcosm start giving a shape to what slowly dawns on the reader as an equivalent of the world, when he grasps that the irreducible indeterminacies are meant to mirror a cosmological concept. The *Cantos* requires another approach, closer to the experience of slowly mastering a chronicle of an unknown country, such as China, a country which remains different from our own since its language is quoted but not translated, because it is not the language that is meant to be taught, but the entire system of values which underlie it. The ideal reader would then not have to turn insomniac to recapture all the distorted dreams of humanity, but he would have to wake up a Chinese himself, metamorphosed from the inside by the process of accretion and dislocation, of inculcation and illumination. Thus the *Cantos* offers not so much a 'conjuration' – for the powerful idea of the 'conjuration' is already part and parcel of the thematic network of the poem – nor the equivalent of the process of acquisition of a new language, but simply opens the way to an entire 'education', in the etymological sense of 'leading someone' to a personal development through knowledge and interest, and modification of character. The values Pound writes about exist for him independently of his text, although they cannot survive outside the dialogic situation opposing guide and reader–pupil. If the text is not a mirror to the whole cosmos, it is a mirror of the general interpretative process on which his 'education' is founded. And the term, or *telos*, of the long journey on which we embark with Odysseus on Canto I is not fixed by the terms of the reading itself, for Pound knows that the main revelation of the ultimate object, whether he calls it 'the gods' or 'the mysteries', has to escape, to elude him: 'The mysteries are *not* revealed, and no guide book to them has been or will be written' (*L*, p. 327).

Thus the 'education' towards beauty or light or order will have to follow Pound's own personal progress through cultures, will imitate his readings, his commitments, his agonies and despair – an *imitatio Poundi* which fortunately can be relieved by sudden outbursts of critical negation or by a wry but pervasive sense of humour. 'There is no substitute for a lifetime' must be the conclusion of any serious reading of the *Cantos*,[3] so intensely can one feel the poem's intricate connection with its author's life, and so strongly does it appeal to the most basic beliefs and responses of any reader, who has to measure a feeling of personal time and history with that of the *ego scriptor*.

Although I shall attempt here to give a rapid sketch of the logics of discourse contained in the structure of the *Cantos*, they are too closely inscribed in history to possess any preconceived scheme which could subsume the discontinuous 'decades' by a neat pattern. Even the most comprehensive of such plans, the Dantean division between Hell, Purgatory and Paradise, which Pound clearly had in mind for his poem, was savagely rebutted by a history whose evolution was dramatically ironic: for Pound was ready by 1940 to write his Paradise, having composed his Hell and Purgatory. He wrote in 1939, 'My economic work is done (in the main). I shall have to go on condensing and restating, but am now definitely onto question of BELIEF' (*L*, p. 328). In 1944, the Salò Republic brought renewed hopes for a final implementation of the economic theories he had fought for, and he could write confidently, but for the last time,

> For forty years I have schooled myself, not to write an economic history of the US or any other country, but to write an epic poem which begins 'In the Dark Forest', crosses the Purgatory of human

error, and ends in the light, and 'fra i maestri di color che sanno'. For this reason I have had to understand the NATURE of error. (*SP*, p. 137)

'To school', 'error' and 'light' are three terms I wish to underline because they delimit stages in an initiation which underwent the most blatant denial history could afford, while keeping both their order and value. The usually bleak dramatic irony of history took the shape of a complete reversal or *peripeteia* and plunged Pound in the midst of apocalypse instead of letting light pour, and yet this turned out to be his major chance: the twist of fate which took the opposite direction of his utopia was allowing him the opportunity of writing for all men; one shudders to envisage what Pound might have become had the Axis forces mastered all Europe and America remained neutral.

I shall then show how the 'schooling' cannot be separated from the 'nature of the error' in an analysis of the properties of Pound's voices (the plural is necessary). From the idea of generalisable mistakes and blunders as key to the interpretative process of reading, I shall study the rates of individual delivery as determined by speed and rhythms at the level of the individual, by symptoms at the level of whole cultures; but the insight into the radiant light of the 'gods' will remain central, as a keystone to the entire edifice. Parallels to these three steps will be pointed to in the genesis and organisation of the *Cantos*, hinged as they are around an ambivalence of thematic content as well as of enunciatory polarities.

A. THE LOGICS OF DISCOURSE AND IDIOMATIC SYNTHESIS

Engrams of vestigial error

Pound obstinately argued that his words refer to some real object, be it in the actual world, in the past, or among historical records; he also drew the attention of his reader to the process of reading as writing, of writing as reading, leaving traces of his quotations, borrowings, allusions. Why are they so perversely elliptical; why is the parataxis epistemological as well as stylistic? Are we supposed to fill out the gaps, to correct the misquotes, to hunt for exact references? Even when Pound frustrates our goodwill and desire to follow his hints – in

Canto CI, for example, distorting the Na-Khi goddess Seng-ge ga-mu into a masculine god renamed 'Sengmer ga-mu', for no clearly discernible reason[4] – it would be premature to express our disappointment in unqualified rejection of the whole text.

Conversely, it would be misguided to attempt to erase all similar blemishes from the text, in the hope of reaching at the sacred core of vision; I would suggest Pound's very spelling-mistakes and inaccuracies have the function of reminding us that his writing is an act which possesses its own duration. Pound hates above all the patience of the academic who believes himself to be immortal and hopes to attain the pure essence of a faultless text. Pound's mistakes go along with his poetics, are inseparable from them, since they first of all provide the text with a certain sense of rhythm. As Joyce wrote, 'A man of genius makes no mistakes. His errors are volitional and are the portals of discovery.'[5] 'Volitional' is not 'deliberate' (as when Joyce takes a sly pleasure in letting the characters of 'Grace' in *Dubliners* heap up distorsions of dogma and history for a parodic effect): it is to be taken in the sense of 'economical' – and Pound's 'volitionist economics', which provide the subtitle for *Jefferson and/or Mussolini*, would apply to a theory of reading – in an economy of *arche* and *telos* which alone can lead to the Heideggerian sense of the fate of 'erring greatly'. The 'volitional' effect of such textuality is closer to the device used by Joyce in the second chapter of *Ulysses*, when Stephen's eyes skip rapidly over the contents of Mr Deasy's letter: we hear only fragments, but retain a sense of the live man reading and in a hurry. 'Man reading shd. be man intensely alive. The book shd. be a ball of light in one's hand' (*GK*, p. 55). The sentence would sound and read differently if Pound had typed 'should' in full. One has to account for this intoxication of speed, of velocity in the actual process of reading, a reading haunted by a flickering light coming from a 'jagged' paradise, or by the more obnoxious haste in putting certain ideas into action.

Joyce, to quote him once more, had remarked quite dryly that Pound's 'brilliant discoveries' were compensated by 'howling blunders', stemming from his quickness of mind ('He understood certain aspects of that book very quickly'[6]), but it is probably more important to understand Pound's blunders, inaccuracies and misprints as part of a general position of enunciation. First of all, it is clear that Pound generally quotes from memory, unless he is transcribing a document, as with the letters of Malatesta's mail-bag,[7] or the archives pertaining to the foundation of the Sienese Monte dei Paschi.[8] In the latter case, minor inconsistencies derive from faulty readings of Latin or Italian texts, or simply from an understandable hurry in conveying the major idea which attracts him.

However, most 'mistakes' in the *Cantos*, and earlier poems as well, have always puzzled a majority of critics, who may have missed the fact that Pound generally devises a pedagogy through 'errors' in order to incite the reader to a necessary self-education, schooling himself against error and finding his way in the dark forest. The matter of 'The Seafarer' and of 'Homage to Sextus Propertius' has been well studied; the way in which Pound provoked the scholars by his offhand treatment of translations has been shown to announce the strategies of the *Cantos*.[9] What stands out is that, even if his conceptions of the translator's task have varied from one text to another – so that he adhered to the shape of sound when rendering the literal equivalent of 'The Seafarer', while attempting to play on content and layering and interweaving conceptual motifs when adapting from Propertius – Pound has invented a technique of creative mistranslation by a subtle manipulation of near-misses and strained felicities. When he translates *wrecan* by 'reckon' instead of 'recite' in the first line of 'The Seafarer', he privileges the phonetic paradigm at the expense of the narrative flow; and when he produces the famous howler on *canes* in 'Homage', II.49, read as the plural of *canis*, 'dog', instead of the future of *cano*, 'I sing', thus writing 'night dogs' where the Latin text means 'You shall sing of the drunken signs of nocturnal flight', he may be totally misled by a poor knowledge of Latin, but he may also have considered that the following lines were explicit enough: indeed he adds, 'These are your images' to the original, in order to convey the main idea of the real *canes* and the theme of inspiration granted to the poet by the Muse Calliope:

> 'Obviously crowned lovers at unknown doors,
> 'Night dogs, the marks of a drunken scurry,
> 'These are your images . . .'
> Thus Mistress Calliope . . .   (*CSP*, p. 229)

What then might he have gained? First, an assertion of his right to dodge the scholarly limits of cribs, and secondly a subject rhyme chiming with the following poem in III, 20: 'and keep mad dogs off his ankle' (p. 230). The blunder plays therefore all the functions of a pun evoking a complex allusion. This is also the case of the most notorious solecisms, 'vote' instead of 'prayer' for *vota* (I, 38) or the famous 'devirginated young ladies' replacing '*touched* by the sound of music'.

Pound's verbal violence and playfulness aims at a direct re-creation of the force of the original in order to bring 'a dead man to life', presenting 'a living figure' (*L*, p. 149).

The sense of life comes from such unorthodox handling of language, which challenges the reader's expectations, wakes him from a passive consumption of texts by plunging him into the whirlpool of 'logopoeia', 'phanopoeia' and 'melopoeia' in constant and daring interaction.[10] There is but a short step from certain 'mistakes' to new coinings of names, and, when Pound fuses two male Egyptian gods into one female divinity, 'Princess Ra-Set',[11] his motive is a very serious one: the presentation of a complex intuition of the bisexuality of gods, just as when he links oriental and Egyptian gods in an invocation to Isis-Kuanon. Pound's personal pantheon has been built in this way, just as his idiom mixes snatches of frontier slang with elements of sacred prayers in Chinese or Greek.

Not only is the textual process literally undecidable – that is, one cannot ascribe it to the wilful perversity of the author, but one has to study the textuality to find reasons for such word-formations – but it is also related to the specific way Pound's text considers its own referentiality. When Pound justifies the technique of translation used in the 'Homage', he explains that his disruptive tactics aim at re-creating a direct relation to 'life' as experienced in our present times, in Europe: 'If the reader does not find relation to life defined in the poem, he may conclude that I have been unsuccessful in my endeavour' (*L*, p. 231). The reference is historical and political; the denunciation of British imperialism by the parallel with the Roman Empire proves the relevance of the plays with language. The obliqueness of language is the shortest way to get to ideological issues through poetic lyricism: 'I certainly omitted no means of definition that I saw open to me, including shortenings, cross cuts, implications from other writings of Propertius' (p. 231).

Hence three main areas of 'volitional' error can be distinguished. The first area is delineated by the strong belief in having to state in necessarily oblique ways a deviant corpus of 'mysteries'. 'Error' is thus the product of the interaction between a set of rhetorical strategies hinged around peculiar modalities of utterance, and the way dogma or othodoxy (from religion to economics) pictures heterodoxy or dissent. This would explain Pound's stubborn interest in the unknown author, the cranky theorician, all the by-paths of apocrypha and sectarian historiography. A second area is a more direct consequence of the division of the speaker, whose inconsistencies, contradictions and oscillations introduce the wedge of desire, of alterity in an otherwise well-formed ideological discourse, Ambivalence and duplicity will then be ascribed to the erratic or 'fading' nature of the speaking subject.

A third zone covers the ways in which such a subject attempts to recite his 'classics' just as he remembers them, wishing to 'COMMIT' himself 'on as many points as possible' (*GK*, p. 7), and, moreover, on points which are themselves 'committed verbally to [his] memory' (p. 28). His 'sweeping statements', abrupt generalisations and inaccuracies of detail enact the process by which a living intelligence shows its workings, vacillating between memory and forgetfulness. The older stale verities are rediscovered through the progressive adequation of a memory with a text being written in the present. It would therefore not only be caddish to correct the misprints and faulty transcriptions; it would also submit the text to the philological imperialism of the 'beaneries' it sets out to subvert.

The later Cantos abound in parentheses such as '(No, that is *not* philological)' (Canto LXXXV, p. 544) or '?that is a forced translation?' (LXXXVI, p. 566) or even '(this is a mistranslation)' (XCIX, p. 710), and Canto CII prints in upper-case letters a superb misquotation from Homer, 'OIOS TELESAI ERGON . . . EROS TE' ('a man to go to the end of his acts and words' – *Odyssey*, II, 272), which replaces *epos* (words) by *eros* (love), just at the moment when the factive personality of men of action such as Odysseus is precisely beginning to blend with neo-platonic contemplation of a pure mind identified with Love!

The best device to stimulate a reader's curiosity or indeed admiration is not to make him grudgingly rely on an all-knowing and infallible narrator, but to let him be lured into unknown paths by an unstable voice, liable to commit blunders, and which, blundering and thundering, enmeshes itself and the reader in the ramifications of an idiomatic and extemporised culture.

Since the ignorance Pound attacks is always an ignorance of fundamental issues (such as 'coin, credit and circulation'), and since the error is always referred back to a process of unconscious mystification ('The error has been *pecuniolatry*, or the making of money into a god' – *SP*, p. 318), the Poundian narrator who speaks in the *Cantos* is aware that he can combat the prejudices not by a pretence of possessing universal knowledge, but by being animated by the irrepressible desire to know more of the truth:

> I shall have to learn a little greek to keep up with this
> but so will you, drratt you.   (CV, p. 750)

And this is to be found in a Canto written just two years before the final silence.

This mode of allocution combines gruff priggishness of a sort and a humorous awareness by Pound of the limitations of his scholarship. Pound uses culture in a very different way from Joyce, who likes to mystify and bluff the reader, posing as a specialist of Aristotelian aesthetics, though never quoting the major source through which he had access to Aristotle, Bosanquet's Hegelian *History of Aesthetic* (1892).[12] Pound never parades erudition; he takes it as a tool to make the reader think: ' "You damn sadist!" said mr cummings, / "you try to make people think." ' (Canto LXXXIX, p. 603) Like Heidegger, who repeatedly asseverated that 'reason' as occidental rationality was the first obstacle on the way of thought, Pound states that

We think because we do not know.

    R O M A
    O   M
    M   O
    A M O R   (*SP*, p. 304)

The palindrome brings home the fusion between the point where knowledge transforms itself into its contrary, love born of lack, and the sacred *templum* needed for the foundation of a city.

From these rapid considerations, I shall pose one central question, to which I shall return in the course of this study: does this simply and immediately entail that Pound reduces the status of his text to that of purely oral literature? Are we to hear in this faltering voice but one mode of a living speech, faithfully recorded with all its hesitations on the paper?[13] I shall just give two provisory remarks to hint that it might be too simplistic to opt for unilateral orality. On the one hand, the example of Propertius has shown that all elements of textuality as written contribute to the management of 'blunders' and mistranslations. On the other hand, the undecidability of the process remains: as soon as it is accepted that certain errors may be intentional, no error can be corrected (and indeed the history of the successive corrections of the text shows that any decision to correct could bring about the risk of further mistakes[14]). For instance, a French reader will immediately wish to change 'Le vieux commode en acajou' (Canto VII, p. 25) to 'La vieille commode', which is correct, but then he will come to the long passage of Canto XVI in which an unmistakably idiomatic French voice is heard narrating dire experiences of trench warfare. Thus,

> O voui! tous les hommes de goût, y conviens,
> Tout ça en arrière.
> Mais un mec comme toi!   (p. 73)

sounds slightly strange ('en arrière' could be 'à l'arrière', i.e. not on the front, or 'par derrière'; 'y conviens' cannot be accounted for – is it 't'en conviens', 'ils conviennent', 'convenables', etc.?) but could nevertheless be uttered by a Parisian speaker using already dated colloquialisms in a certain situation of enunciation. The foregrounding of enunciation by the frame of the written text is therefore more important than the grammatical correctness of the utterance, so that even 'le vieux commode' can be reread as implying an American speaker, Henry James for instance, quoting Flaubert or de Goncourt from memory to an absent-minded American poet in Paris.

The first motif we encounter in the *Cantos*, the descent to Hades in the Nekuia passage, acquires a radically programmatic significance when we perceive that the interaction between Homeric heroes and the souls of dead men produces a whirling node of speeches and voices which intertwine around each other. At a first level of the resolution of the antagonism between oral and written literature we find we must come to terms with the implications of the 'voices' in the text. When William Carlos Williams describes the *Cantos*, he rightly points out that 'The thing that is felt is that the quick are moving among the dead',[15] and it is felt in the 'quickness' of their speech, in the rapidity of perception and the vividness of their delivery. Between oral and written, we should then find a certain sense of pace identical with a meaning: 'He has kept his plan fluid enough to meet his opportunities. He has taken, laudably, the speech of the men he treats of, and by clipping to essentials revealed its closest nature – its pace, its meaning.'[16]

Williams's praise is all the more useful as he later reproached Pound for having deliberately misused this idiom in a 'highbrow' way by making fun of it. When an interviewer asked Williams in the sixties whether he thought Pound had contributed to the formation of an American idiom, his reply was violent.

> w.c.w. But both Eliot and Pound rejected Whitman as a master. He didn't have anything to teach them. But they didn't *know* what he had to teach them. The idiom itself, which they did not acknowledge.
>
> w.s. Although Pound sometimes uses an exaggerated American dialect.

w.c.w. He tends to clown it as Lowell does, in a Yankee farm accent, but he doesn't do it well. He clowns it so obviously that – It's a kind of hayseed accent, which is entirely in his own mind. No one would ever talk that way.

w.s. Is this the voice you hear in the letters often?

w.c.w. Why, I think so. . . . He thinks he's smart, and he's not smart. He's inaccurate. He attempts to make fun of all American speakers, but he doesn't know what he's talking about.[17]

The force of this rejection, with the embarrassing tinge of paranoia (Williams insisting that 'it was personally directed toward making fun of me'), comes from the disappointment of a poet who had thought that his friend and mentor was working in the same direction: 'We seek a language which will not be at least a deformation of the speech as we know it – but will embody all the advantageous jumps, swiftnesses, colors, movements of the day . . . .'[18] For him, Pound has been caught by the lure of the written text, the 'Artemis thing' or the sacralising invocation of the gods.

Williams could not realise that Pound's 'map of misreading' had indeed already included this particular misreading in the vortex of mistranslations, and that it was the only way for the text to beome identical with the map of America: not simply the melting-pot of the 'Polish mothers' from which Williams's concept of idiom derives, but also a sense of the timelessness of rhythms of recurrence, and above all, space, space . . . .

Seeds of speed

> So slow is the rose to open.
> A match flares in the eyes' hearth,
>   then darkness.
>
>   (cvi, p. 752)

One of the most important statements about American literature was probably made by Olson when he decided to open *Call Me Ishmael* with the famous declaration, 'I take SPACE to be the central fact to man born in America, from Folson cave to now. I spell it large because it comes large here. Large, and without mercy.'[19] From such a central position, Olson is able to reach directly to the core of Pound's poetics of the voice:

Ez's epic solves problem by his ego: his single emotion breaks all down to his equals or inferiors (so far as I can see only two, possibly, are admitted, by him, to be his betters – Confucius & Dante. Which assumption, that there are intelligent men whom he can outtalk, is beautiful because it destroys historical time, and

thus creates the methodology of the Cantos, viz, a space-field where, by inversion, though the material is all time material, he has driven through it so sharply by the beak of his ego, that, he has turned time into what we must now have, space & its live air.[20]

Pound's wish to 'outtalk' great men he quotes is a very keen notion of what happens in the dialectical interaction of voices, since the best way to outtalk is to talk louder, more quickly, more persuasively, more beautifully, or simply to frame the other speakers' voices by the space of writing. Olson is here preaching for his own concept of Projectivist Verse, in which 'one perception must immediately and directly lead to a further perception',[21] but he provides a much better concept with which to approach the *Cantos* than Wyndham Lewis's complaints about the nature of time in Pound's poetry.[22] Olson's main merit is to displace the opposition between time and space, which affords so many opportunities for polarisation in *Finnegans Wake*, and also to ally the remarks on the 'ego' to the notion of the speed of utterances by which Pound intends to measure historical time against formal and poetical space. Speed results from the relation of time and space, and Pound articulates speed with enunciation when he transforms his poem into a series of traces of foregone speeches or 'verbal manifestations'.

Speed provides a relation, a ratio, which not only measures forms as determined by spatio-temporal continua such as cultures, but also relates this measure to the very foundation of poetry, metaphor defined by Aristotle – revisited by Pound, it is true – as 'the swift perception of relations'.[23] Speed has meanwhile another aspect, which pertains to politics and ideology, since 'ignorance' is generally nothing else than a delay in understanding, or, in Pound's recurrent tag, a 'time-lag'. The whole concept of economics is already implicit there, for Usura sells time and profits by time; hence the process of obfuscation which Usura triggers off: 'The enemy has been at work during these very twenty years of Fascism that you have lost to him through procrastination. Twenty years at five per cent in which he has doubled his capital while he goes on drawing interest. This sum that he pockets is your loss.' [24] If one admits Pound's axiom that 'the truth of a given idea' is 'measured by the degree and celerity wherewith it goes into action' (*GK*, p. 182), slowness will be equated with the evil forces, and rapidity will reveal intelligence. The larger rhythms of history and the smallest bits of speed available in language will then be found to keep a common time or beat; this may even justify the technique of parataxis: 'A man whose mind moves faster than a snail finds it tedious to have to explain the connecting links of his thought. If he has had the patience to do it once, say 1923, it is hard for him to realize that his reader of 1937 may have no idea of what he has been driving at for more than a decade.'[25] Between the divine speed of God's immediate intellection of the cosmos –

> But Gemisto: 'Are Gods by Hilaritas';
> and their speed in communication
> (xcviii, p. 685, see also p. 690)

– and the 'waste matter' which is caused to stagnate in the bogs of Usura, various degrees of speed measure verbal intelligence and levels of culture.

The idea of a voice is always linked with a concern for speed which is revealed by Pound's remarks on translation: 'Where the translation can be improved is in dimension of inflection of the voice. Possibly *no* change of vocabulary required, but the greater variety of intonation and of sentence movement. The indication of tone of voice and varying speeds of utterance' (*L*, p. 298). Rouse, the translator of Homer, followed Pound's advice to some extent in his modernised and rather colloquial rendering of the *Odyssey*, but he nevertheless stopped short of indicating the differences between certain 'speeds of utterance'. However, the accent on the speed of speech is not limited to stray remarks on translation, nor to literary theory in general, but informs the very project of the *Cantos*: 'Narrative not the same as lyric; different techniques for song and story. "Would, could", etcetera: Abbreviations save *eye* effort. Also show speed in mind of original character supposed to be uttering or various colourings and degrees of importance or emphasis attributed by the protagonist of the moment' (*L*, p. 322). This proves indeed that Pound saw his poem as a collection of utterances produced by diverse 'protagonists', each of whom is identifiable by idiom and rapidity of delivery.

One of the best commentators on the *Cantos* has pointed out that the poem is governed by different rates in speed when we read for the meaning and when we listen to the music (which could be superimposed on Pound's distinction between 'lyric' and 'narrative'): 'And so the verse-lines of the *Cantos* have to be read fast for their meanings, but slow for their sounds.'[26] And Davie quotes from the last paragraph of the chapter devoted to Dante in *The Spirit of Romance*, in which Pound defines poetic mastery as the control of rhythms or 'government of speed'. The effect of parataxis culminates in a kind of enunciative double bind, since the eye rushes forward to gather all the motifs in an overview as comprehensive as possible, while the lack of links, the sudden jumps from image to image in the absence of connectives, makes for a slow and halting melody. Such a double bind is the consequence of the strong awareness of the division of the subject between his series of signifiers and the lack he himself is, perpetually thrown forward into another disguise. The ambivalence of motifs will be shown to come from the same source, the same impossibility of reading the text straightforwardly.

Pound's typical restlessness and energy manages to transcend itself in moments of lyrical arrest and splendour (these are the passages the anthologies are fond of quoting), yet it would be misleading to read them in isolation; I shall develop this point when studying more closely the dynastic Cantos, and would like to take the example of a late Canto to show how the 'government of speed' can be the structuring device of particular passages.

Canto XCIII opens on a typical display of purely visual stasis by presenting an Egyptian hieroglyph, glossed by its translation from 'the Stele of Antef':[27]

'A man's paradise is his good nature'
sd/Kati.
'panis angelicus' Antef
two ½s of a seal
having his own mind to stand by him   (p. 623)

The Confucian or Mencian 'seal' is now reunited in Egypt, and this wisdom is borne by the Homeric persona, Odysseus, who never loses his mind. The reshuffling of themes from earlier Cantos continues in a staccato rhythm; Apollonius, Augustine and finally Dante appear; love is the object of a complicated and multifaceted approach. At one point Pound breaks his montage, including Mussolini, Goddeschalk and Beaumarchais, to address his reader directly:

> All ov which may be a little slow for the reader
> or seem platitudinous
>   und kein Weekend-Spass
> Mr Hoepli sent a small brochure to Svitzerland
>   and his banker friend replied '*urgente*':
> 'destroy it e farlo sparire'.   (p. 627)

The trick of stopping the flow of the narrative to underline some point takes on a different function from the usual 'underlinings' which come from ideograms or foreign quotations. Here, the slow meditation of the mind turning around beauty and love is contrasted with the usurer's wish to destroy the evidence, obviously some pamphlet containing new proposals for economic reform. Pound had spent some time commenting at length on Books II and III of Dante's *Convivio* and was reaching the fourth when all of a sudden the theme of speed was turned upside down, used by the enemy, which seemed to be confirmed by several unexpected deaths ('Grenfell's death was (like some others) / suspiciously sudden' – Canto XCIII, p. 627)). Thus ignorance reigns, is even spread out from schools and universities, according to Yeats's anecdote,[28] and this highlights another mode of lack of awareness:

> The Bard of Avon mentioned the subject,
> Dante mentioned the subject,
>   and the lit profs discuss other passages
>   in abuleia
> or in total unconsciousness
>   Four thousand years after KATI   (p. 627)

The repeat of the Egyptian cartouche ties in with the beginning of the poem and recalls the huge period of time which has been obliterated. Pound gives us a sense of duration and a major passion, a love which alone can make reading active and efficient because it works on our will. Possessed by this 'love', the reader will warm up to the subject, which is, of course, usury as denounced in Shakespeare's *Merchant of Venice* and Dante's Hell. By another modulation of the voices, which involve subtle shifts to foreign languages, the Canto turns into a litany-like incantation singing pity:

> Ysolt, Ydone,
>> have compassion,
> Picarda,
>> compassion
> By the wing'd head,
>> by the caduceus,
>>> compassion (p. 628)

'The Alchemist' had already provided the poet of the 'Pisan Cantos' with haunting repetition of names, and it leads here to a recall of 'Cantus Planus':[29] 'The black panther lies under his rose-tree./ J'ai eu pitié des autres./ Pas assez! Pas assez!' (p. 628). Pity develops a new mood inherited from the Pisan sequence, a new perception of the pure light, 'The light there almost solid'. All this blends into a sensation of magic and mystery, of a sleeping vortex whose immobility could also be the climax of speed:

> holding that energy is near to benevolence
> Au bois dormant,
>> not yet...! Not yet!
>> do not awaken.
> The trees sleep, and the stags, and the grass;
> The boughs sleep unmoving. (p. 629)

Behind the translucent visions, the reader is meant to ponder on the relative values of speed and slowness:

> Nec deus laedit
> and the Lorraine girl heard it in the fields.
> Tho' the skater move fast or slow
>> the ice must be solid
>> Pone metum, Cerinthe (p. 630)

The moment of waking from the magic trance has come, but the seasons are still mixed, spring should have come but ice covers lakes, and knowledge only opens onto new ambiguities:

> Shall two know the same in their knowing?
>> You who dare Persephone's threshold,
>> Beloved, do not fall apart in my hands. (p. 631)

Division and unity are always brought in an unstable balance, and the repetitive whirl upward simulates a movement of ascent which is founded on voices and speeds of utterances more than on visions; or, rather, the visions acquire a sense once they are related to the upsurge of voices:

> 'Blind eyes and shadows'
>> to enter the presence at sunrise
>> up out of hell, from the labyrinth
>>> the path wide as a hair
> & as to mental velocities:
>> Yeats on Ian Hamilton: 'So stupid he
> couldn't think unless there were a cannonade going on.'
>> the duration
>> in re/ mental velocity
> as to antennae
> as to malevolence.
>> Six ways to once
>> of a Sunday. Velocity.
> Without guides, having nothing but courage
> Shall audacity last into fortitude?
>> You are tender as a marshmallow, my Love,
>> I cannot use you as a fulcrum.
>> You have stirred my mind out of dust.
> Flora Castalia, your petals drift thru the air,
> the wind is ½ lighted with pollen
>>> diafana,
> e Monna Vanna...tu mi fai rimembrar.   (pp. 631–2)

The last line is taken from Dante's vision; he compares Matelda, gathering flowers over Mount Purgatory, with Proserpine about to leave for Hell, losing the eternal Spring of the Enna vales. Personal allusion and remembrance, an interweaving of mythological and literary themes centring on Dante, Guido and the troubadours, lead to an ambivalent threshold: the path to Paradise is almost identical with the road to Hell; what matters is the series of 'velocities' which make the vibrations of the words echo like the fragrant petals or the sacred pollen of an eternal nature: there Being or 'presence' speaks of itself, but in a foreign tongue.

Organic symptoms

Culture is for Pound the dominant link between education and
creation, writing and reading, production and distribution, and
moreover it is the result of multiplying of time by space, in the same
way as speed is space divided by time. The sense of speed or slowness
transforms itself into an understanding of the various systems of signs:
just as speed can tell you about a character's 'seriousness' – hence
Pound's admiration of Mussolini's '1930 disinvoltura and ease' (*GK*,
p. 182) – cultural formations exist on the map and in chronicles as a
condensation of time and place, set in motion by individual or
collective subjects. That the concept of 'sign' is inadequate will be
shown by an analysis of Pound's main source, Frobenius and his
Kulturmorphologie.

Pound explained to Eliot that there was no exact English equivalent
of *Kulturmorphologie* ('transformation of cultures', 'morphology of
cultures', 'historic process taken in the larger' – *L*, p. 336) and that
Frobenius did not work from documents like Frazer but 'went to
things', which put him on a par with Fenollosa and Fabre (ibid.). It is
basically Frobenius's organic and 'totalitarian' concept of culture
which appeals to Pound; already in the 1890s the German anthro-
pologist had started explaining that cultures were live organisms,
and he went to Africa to prove this. Cultures are measured on a scale
which distinguishes between infancy, adolescence, maturity and
decrepitude, which is not without its Viconian echoes. Pound read
through the seven volumes of *Erlebte Erdteile*[30] after 1928, and
devoted several articles to Frobenius in the thirties. He evolved at the
same time his problematics of 'ideology' and of 'organic symptom',
both seen as constitutive of a *paideuma* or active culture. 'Culture' is
too limited for Frobenius's conception of a *paideuma*, which Pound
sums up as 'the complex of ideas which is in a given time germinal' (*SP*,
p. 254): it embodies myths and institutions, social and artistic codes,
rules, laws and techniques of production. In the fourth volume of
Erlebte Erdteile, the term of 'symptom' begins to crop up in relation
with the death or survival of cultures: 'He who has studied the break in
cultural time and space in the year 1914 thanks to characteristic
symptoms . . . .'[31] The destruction of traditional values in Europe
made for an application of anthropological methods of analysis to all
cultural systems, and placed the 'monuments' created by cultures
within a system of unconscious production. This is acknowledged with
some reserve by Pound: 'Frobenius has left the term with major

implications in the unconscious (if I understand him rightly). I don't assert that he would necessarily limit it to the unconscious . . .' (*PR*, p. 254).

Pound wishes to assert the right for a creative individual to break with a dying *paideuma* in order to bring about the new cultural synthesis, which cannot be achieved without certain modulations of anthropological concepts.

While Frobenius only mentioned 'monuments' in his early work, where they are to be understood as organic signs of cultures, his *Monumenta Africana*, especially volumes IV and VI, sees cultures as 'sums of symptoms' (*Gesamtheit der Symptome*[32]) which must be organised in a general 'symptomatics'.[33] Thereafter Frobenius investigates *Kultursymptome* which map out the salient or diacritical marks of a *paideuma*: the shapes of bows, tumuli, dwelling-structures, taken together, define precise loci on the surface of the earth and are grouped in 'hamatic' or 'erythrean' symptoms. Pound looks perplexed in front of these multiple classifications: 'Whatever one thinks of his lists of symptoms, Hammite, Shemite, etc. he rhymes with Dante "che'l giudeo fra voi di voi non ride" ' (*GK*, p. 243). His reference to Dante, *Paradiso*, v, 81 ('That the Jew should not laugh at you among you'), is rightly glossed as a praise of cultural difference and not envy or hatred: 'It is nonsense for the anglo-saxon to revile the jew for beating him at his own game' (*GK*, p. 243).[34]

The terminology used by Pound here is closer to Gaudier's reinterpretation of Frobenius in his 'Vortex' printed in *Blast* than to Frobenius's own concepts, which shows that Frobenius was mediated by Gaudier's more artistic synthesis in Pound's personal *paideuma*.[35] In the *Guide to Kulchur*, Pound merely notes his own complicity with the 'nomadic' character of 'brother semite' (p. 243). In a text written in Italian at roughly the same time, Pound moves from the organicist world-view to a denunciation of symptoms as signs of an illness:

The importance of Leo Frobenius consists in that he has demonstrated that when arts are ill, the illness is not only there. Art can be a symptom. . . .
    To attack the symptoms of illness without identifying the cause is to act like a savage. One can study symptoms. . . . The great master of diagnostic, Leo Frobenius: he has created a whole Institute, a whole education of perception. . . . Frobenius indeed represents the crisis *of* – not *in* – the system.[36]

Pound rightly generalises the 'symptoms' to more than racial characteristics, and, whilst Frobenius has found a model of a living culture in Africa, which he opposed to a dying occidental culture (thereby radically influencing Spengler), Pound praises 'health' with more and more heavily ideological stresses: 'Health is more interesting than disease: health is total.'[37]

It is true that Pound had been using the term 'symptom' before he had read Frobenius (for instance, seeing in the First World War 'only a symptom of the disease' – *L*, p. 47), but the concept of *Kultursymptome* allows him to go beyond a limited empiricism to which he still adhered in the twenties. At the time of his association with the *New Age*, the division between creative artists and mere diluters or epigones was expressed by a distinction between the 'symptomatic' and the 'donative' works of art (*PR*, p. 25). The symptomatic artists merely reflect their times, the donative 'draws latent forces' and brings about a new concept of civilisation. But he could not yet link the distinction to a general survey of cultures in history, nor to the attention to verbal manifestations as betraying individual energy. When he found in Frobenius that a *paideuma* consisted in the dissemination of symptoms in race *and* language, as well as art, he could see that the symptomatology was determined by a series of causes which he would eventually situate in economics.

The main point is the reversal of a would-be Nazi tendency which identifies race and cultural heritage; instead the *paideuma* creates race and cultures, and this is coupled with a concept of 'totality': 'Economics can no longer be taught as a jumble of heteroclite statements. . . . In Economics one demands that text-books start with a clear definition of the terms . . .' (*GK*, p. 254). The symptoms can be shown to possess a logic of their own; they reveal not just the consequence of a cause, not just a part for the whole, but the systematicity of the system. In terms of illness, a cough is a sign that one has caught a cold, but it can also be a symptom that one reacts in a hysterical way to a trauma. A series of signs is organised as a syndrome, while a series of symptoms belongs to a discourse which articulates signifiers; the cold as sign will be cured by medicine, while the cough as symptom will be cured by a discourse in which it no longer features as a signifier of trauma.

In the *Guide to Kulchur* the division has been again displaced. Pound uses *Ulysses* as an example of the 'Monumental' because it merely provides 'the end, the summary, of a period' (*GK*, p. 96), a period called 'the age of usury', and decides to leave the retrospective element out of his new synthesis: 'The reader, who bothers to think, may now notice that in the new paideuma I am not including the monumental, the retrospect, but only the pro-spect' (ibid.). *Ulysses* is thus only a 'katharsis', both 'diagnosis and cure': 'The sticky, molasses-covered filth of current print, all the fuggs, all the foetors, the whole boil of the European mind, had been lanced' (ibid.). This is based on Pound's opposition between the 'analytic' work of prose and the 'synthesis' achieved by poetry in a more vital affirmation of prospective values.[38]

The Poundian concept of culture is thus an expanding whole, with widening axes of reference, as the project for a sequel to *Guide to Kulchur* shows: Pound proposes a long essay on

> criticism of Greek and Latin cultural heritage *confronted* by post-Renaissance knowledge of subjects not familiar to Pico della Mirandola. The Classics, not vs. 'the moderns' as in 18th Cent. shindy, etc., but their place in a plenum containing XIXth Century Europe, the Orient, prehistoric art, Africa, etc. In short, in a *full* culture, with cinema and modern mechanics.   (*L*, pp. 295–6)

The extent of Pound's range is bewildering, and yet a certain organisation appears: he starts from the Mediterranean world in general, which links Greece and Renaissance Italy plus the Provençal tradition, thus defining the Southern 'classical' pole, which may extend to Africa and finally includes Byzantium in the later Cantos. To the West, he obviously starts from America, balanced by China to the East, the youngest and the oldest civilisation moving toward some kind of mutual enrichment. And the Northern axis takes in Europe, which is not limited to the Age of Enlightenment, but reaches into the nineteenth century, before finding stabler roots in the England of Magna Carta and the first battles for civil rights.

In this complex whole, no 'donative' artist or thinker can be given a lasting pre-eminence, indeed Pound merely lists names to achieve the effect of a *rappel à l'ordre* of his cultural heroes; while voices were measured by their speed of utterance, cultural vortices are set in motion by the *Cantos* in rapid sequences of names: Dante, Confucius, Homer, Frobenius, Cavalcanti, Aristotle, Ovid, de Gourmont, Aquinas, Douglas, Gesell, Gaudier-Brzeska, Yeats, Brancusi, Joyce, Wyndham Lewis, Picasso, Gemisto, Ocellus, Plotinus, Erigena, Richard St Victor, Saint Anselm, Apollonius, Jefferson, Mussolini, Adams...The *Guide to Kulchur* starts by discrediting the mere list of ideas to be found in reference books ('I may, even yet, be driven to a chronological catalogue of greek ideas, roman ideas, mediaeval ideas in the occident. There is a perfectly good LIST of those ideas thirty feet from where I sit typing' – *GK*, p. 29) but ends up presenting 'examples of cultures' organised in series: for instance, Boccherini's Opus 8, no. 5, is given as embodying the same principles as the *Cantos*, being a 'record of struggle' (*GK*, p. 135); but the mere mention of the title has been enough, and nothing further is said. I shall come back to this strong drift in all of Pound's writings: the temptation to replace ideas in their logical conjunction by a sequence of names without conjunction – according to the principle of parataxis, but assembling a collection of differences, dissociations, disjunctions. At this point, the name has become a symptom, and requires a different type of logic, the logic of the signifier as articulated by a subject of the enunciation.

Thus the reduction of culture, in near-caricature, to a menu or a concert programme (Pound thought he could explain what a real musical renaissance was like only by reproducing the programme of his Rapallo festivals). The discontinuous nature of such statements reveals more, because the slow accumulation of cultural riches is condensed in a 'record' which still refers back to the subject who has created it. The 'total' concept of culture, organising the entire pattern of perception, defines a sense of proportion or rather 'structure' – Bach is praised for his invention of a firm 'total "structure"', namely lateral movement in time space' (*GK*, p. 154) – which has nevertheless to be founded, not on the void, like Joyce's universe, but on discontinuity: hence the gods, both outside culture and its only basis.

'Without gods, no culture. Without gods, something is lacking' (*GK*, p. 126). I shall endeavour to move backward, attempting to find behind the origin of speech and discourse, as measured by speed of utterance, behind the entire structure which integrates them into an organic cultural totality and gives them a meaning, the real ground on which the interpenetration of voices and symptoms can be achieved in a political and religious foundation.

B. ETERNAL STATES OF MIND AND THE STATE THE MIND

From Myth to the Real

The experience of the gods, upon which cultures find a foundation, is a matter of statement on the nature of reality. The best point of departure remains the deliberately naïve Catechism of 'Religio, or The Child's Guide to Knowledge':

> What is a god?
> A god is an eternal state of mind. . . .
> When is a god manifest?
> When the state of mind takes form.
> When does a man become a god?
> When he enters one of these states of mind. (*SP*, p. 47)

This short text, the first of the numerous 'Guides' written by Pound, presents us with a minimal set of beliefs, which gains by being completed by the 'Axiomata' written three years later:

(1) The intimate essence of the universe is *not* of the same nature as our own consciousness.
(2) Our consciousness is incapable of having produced the universe.
(3) God, therefore, exists. That is to say, there is no reason for not applying the term God, *Theos*, to the intimate essence.

(*SP*, p. 49)

From a confrontation between these two texts, it appears that the term of 'state of mind' implies no subjectivism, no aesthetic fallacy in the symbolist mode. 'State' is qualified by 'eternal' and thus one moves from the realm of the subjective into that of an ineffable ultimate reality, which words can attempt to describe at best by approximations; thus *Theos*, preferable to 'God' because the Greek word already suggests a plural in English. What is described by this is an experience which belongs to the category of 'ecstasy', a 'dis-placement' from mind to 'state' of mind, akin to the mystical fusion with the universe Pound alludes to in his Essays as *atasal*.[39] The movement of 'entering' is the same motion as that described by the first line of 'A Girl': 'The tree has entered my hands'.[40]

The mystical side of this experience leads nevertheless immediately toward the question of the arbitrariness of the name given to it; the Catechism had to explain why it followed the conventional usage and decided to retain the names of the Greek gods:

Are there names for the gods?
The gods have many names. It is by names that they are handled
  in the tradition.   (*SP*, p. 48)

Tradition is imposed by history and by a sense of place, since 'this rite is made for the West' (ibid.), and justifies both the naming-process and the reality of the experience; it cannot be reduced to hallucination, even in the positive sense it took with Rimbaud.[41] The names are not to proliferate in a vertiginous swirl of surreal impressions; they are bound to state as exactly as possible what cannot be normally expressed by symbols. In a way, it is an *a priori* foreclosure of all philosophic discussion, which relies on abstract statement: 'Cadmus, or any other myth, knows where to stop, in the sense that the maker of myth don't try to cut corners, he don't try to level out all differences and state what he doesn't know' (*GK*, p. 128).

The god's name is thus a 'statement' which discloses a lack at the same time. The account Pound gives of the way Greek myths took shape is here expressed in universal terms, yet it relies on an intense personal experience of loss and selflessness of which the very early San Trovaso notebook gives an idea. The fundamental lack in being that the ecstatic experience revealed has to be transformed into a desire to expand the self, until it becomes one with the cosmos: 'All art begins in the physical discontent (or torture) of loneliness and partiality. / It is (was) to fill this lack that man first spun shapes out of the void. . . . / Of such perceptions rise the ancient myths of the origin of demi-gods. Even as the ancient myths of metamorphosis rise out of flashes of cosmic consciousness' (*CEP*, p. 322). This is why in the famous passage from *The Spirit of Romance* Pound can say at the same time that myths manifest 'a permanent basis in humanity' and are 'explications of mood': 'I believe that Greek myth arose when someone having passed through delightful psychic experience tried to communicate it to others and found it necessary to screen himself from persecution' (*SP*, p. 92). Pound mentions 'persecution' as the first reason for the ineffability of the experience, which shows how potent the ghost of paranoid distrust of the 'enemy' already was in this early period, while, if we follow Lacan's conception of the 'real' as that which cannot be symbolised,[42] it is by virtue of a structural necessity inherent in language that these occurrences cannot be recounted.

Thus it is no surprise to see Pound immediately adding that the experience is only conveyed to the 'elect', those who have had it themselves: 'Certain it is that these myths are only intelligible in a vivid and glittering sense to those people to whom they occur. I know, I mean, one man who understands Persephone and Demeter, and one who understands the Laurel, and another who has, I should say, met Artemis. These things are for them *real*' (*SP*, p. 92). Even if we suspect that Pound himself is the several personalities he alludes to, it does not matter, for the concept of personality is by then exploded: what stands out is the direct, dramatic, intense confrontation of a speechless real 'state' and the heavily symbolical past of language and culture. The Poundian gods figure names which approach the division in Being Heidegger calls ontological difference; speech rebounds on its very limits to open up the subject, torn apart between the stock of names he can master and the violence of the exposure to blinding light.

The experience transforms the poet into a potentially subversive terrorist who may insist on the necessity of the return of the gods, and not content himself with his 'delightful' experience; many youthful poems show Pound in this role, posturing as the aesthete turned prophet. The juvenile and awkward Whitmanesque hymn 'From Chebar' provides a good example; it ends on,

> The order does not end in the arts,
> The order shall come and pass through them.
>
> The state is too idle, the decrepit church is too idle,
> The arts alone can transmit this.
> They alone cling fast to the gods,
> Even the sciences are a little below them. . . .
>
> It is I, who demand our past,
> And they who demand it.
>
> It is I, who demand tomorrow,
> And they who demand it.
>
> It is we, who do not accede,
> We do not please you with easy speeches. (*CEP*, pp. 271–2)

Ezekiel, who is identified by the title, provides a powerful persona for the poet and lends momentum to the eschatological promise of a return of the gods – the artists shall take over political and religious functions abused by irresponsible rulers. If Ezekiel, who saw the 'heavens' open and 'visions of God' by the river Chebar (Ezekiel 1:1), was in the 'thirtieth year' of his age (the reference is unclear in the Hebrew), he was a more active Mauberley or Pound. The arts provide both an end in itself, since it concentrates the most vital experience

available to man, and an end which transcends itself, since it is bound
to have repercussions in society and politics.

The vision cannot be explained: it belongs to the catechumen alone,
but, as soon as a shape for it has been found, the shape will burst out of
its formal frame and connect the vision with a desire for a better life, or,
indeed, a paradise on Earth. No explanation, no metalanguage is
adequate, because the experience provides both an initiation and the
transfer of the names into action.

In his Foreword to *A Quinzaine for This Yule*. Pound, who uses the
pseudonym of Weston St Llewmys, lays down once and for all the law
he will adhere to throughout his poetic career: never to explain
anything. We have William Carlos Williams's testimony that it was
indeed a favourite dictum of Pound at this period (the book is dated
1908). What is also fascinating is the connection between 'slowness' as
pertaining to beauty and the rapidity of flashes of illumination that this
little epigraph poses:

> Beauty should never be presented explained. It is Marvel and
> Wonder, and in art we should find first these doors – Marvel and
> Wonder – and, coming through them, a slow understanding (slow
> even though it be a succession of lightning understandings and
> perceptions) as of a figure in mist, that still and ever gives to each
> one his own right of believing, each after his own creed and
> fashion.   (*CEP*, p. 58)

This paragraph might indeed be kept as an introduction to the 'Pisan
Cantos', with their insistence that 'slowness is beauty' and their recall
of those flashes through which a jagged paradise appears, saving the
poet from utter despair.

The keywords 'Marvel and Wonder' are found in Sandalphon's
lament, in the poem by the same title; Sandalphon is 'the angel of
prayer according to the Talmud' and Pound chooses to treat this
legend as a 'reality' and not as a romantic story in the vein of
Longfellow:

> Marvel and Wonder!
> Marvel and wonder even as I,
> Giving to prayer new language
> and causing the works to speak
> of the earth-horde's age-lasting longing,
> Even as I marvel and wonder, and know not,
> Yet keep my watch in the ash wood.   (*CEP*, p. 68)

Sandalphon prays and does not explain why he cannot die while the other angels do die, one by one, and are metamorphosed into flowers. He does not explain because he 'names' and transforms what he names: clearly a figure of the poetic power ascribed to language, which by the intensity and clarity of its vision cannot broach any metalanguage, any commentary – futile additions which would destroy the intensity and break the pace of the 'works'. The words participate in a general process of transformation, heightened by a general 'exile': 'And though I seek all exile, yet my heart / doth find new friends and all strange lands / Love me and grow my kin, and bid me speed' (*CEP*, p. 69). There is yet a sense in which the poem is a metalanguage, a commentary on another text, Longfellow's poem taken as a point of departure for a 'real' experience which requires a 'mask' to be uttered.

The poem by Longfellow is to be found in *Birds of Passage* and follows close after a text celebrating 'The Fiftieth Birthday of Agassiz', a reference which at this time might have escaped Pound's notice, but which turns out to be more significant later. From a rapid examination of Longfellow's text, it appears clearly that Pound takes it as a point of departure for another exercise in creative imitation – the stanzas from 'Sandalphon' which treat the Talmudic legend as an opportunity for allegory:

> The Angels of Wind and Fire
> Chant only one hymn, and expire
> With the song's irresistible stress;
> Expire in their rapture and wonder,
> As harp-strings are broken asunder
>   By music they throb to express.
>
> But serene in the rapturous throng,
> Unmoved by the rush of song,
> With eyes unimpassioned and slow,
> Among the dead angels, the deathless
> Sandalphon stands listening breathless
>   To sounds that ascend from below;

This becomes for Pound's youthful and immature re-creation an exercise in voice control and in the elaboration of a new persona; his Sandalphon speaks in the first person ('Ye think me one insensate / else die I also' – *CEP*, p. 68). This is why Pound adds in his footnote that 'Longfellow also treats of this, but as a legend rather than a reality', for it corresponds to Longfellow's explicit statement at the end of his poem:

> It is but a legend, I know, –
> A fable, a phantom, a show,
> Of the ancient Rabbinical lore;
> Yet the old mediaeval tradition,
> The beautiful, strange superstition,
>   But haunts me and holds me the more.
>
>   . . .
>
> And the legend, I feel, is a part
> Of the hunger and the thirst of the heart,
> The frenzy and fire of the brain,
> That grasps at the fruitage forbidden,
> The golden pomegranates of Eden,
>   To quiet its fever and pain.[43]

Such aloofness is completely foreign to Pound's effort, who, although he cannot get rid of Victorian diction and archaisms ('And the autumn of their marcescent wings/Maketh ever new loam for my forest'), strives for an immediacy of utterance which is all the more remarkable. In that sense, Pound's technique, despite all its preciosity, is a test of his sincere belief in the presence of 'gods', from whatever pantheon they may be derived.

The masks of politics and art

The ineffable experience which alone the gods allow to name, and the role the arts have to play in the creation of a state – all this was the object of the poem, Browning's *Sordello*, that was to exert a lasting influence on Pound as he fought with recalcitrant material in an attempt at 'setting his ideas into order' for his own poem.

Sordello has always had a special significance and attraction for readers of Pound – first of all because he made no mystery about his debt ('Und überhaupt ich stamm aus Browning. Pourquoi nier son père?' (*L*, p. 218)) and also because much of what looks obscure in the *Cantos* appears almost normal in comparison with the word tangles of the Victorian poet. Although the dialogue between Pound and

Browning which marks the inception of the long project, the writing of a modern verse epic, has been well studied,[44] the reasons for Pound's early enthusiasm can be presented in the context of discussion of the poet's enunciation. When he discards the 'Three Cantos' of 1915–17, published in *Poetry*, to patch up the present Cantos II and following, Pound eliminates the posturing of the Browningesque poet as puppet-master, who poses and shows off on the stage he creates. His problem is, then, not so much the invention of a new genre as the discovery of a new manipulation of voices.

But, if he abandons Browning's mode of presentation, he deepens the problematics of *Sordello*, which he then comes to see as a complex meditation on the interaction of language and politics. In the first poem of 'Three Cantos' Pound admits that he has been tempted to mimic Browning's 'bag of tricks' in too servile a manner, exactly as he acknowledged in a letter: 'The hell is that one catches Browning's manner and mannerisms. At least I've suffered the disease' (*L*, p. 90).

> . . . say I take your whole bag of tricks,
> Let in your quirks and tweeks, and say the
>   thing's an art-form,
> Your Sordello, and that the modern world
> Needs such a rag-bag to stuff all its thoughts in . . . .[45]

Here Pound still practises a distinction which will be ruled out by Canto I: the dissociation between the search for a form and the intrinsic truth of a discourse; Sordello, the real troubadour he had presented in his essay through his *Vida*,[46] cannot be the same as the mouthpiece used by Browning in his offhand manner. The rather awkward admission, 'I stand before the booth, the speech; but the truth / Is inside this discourse – this booth is full of the marrow of wisdom', remains in the wake of the questions raised by 'Near Perigord'. Just as there can be only one real Bertrand de Born, one truth contained by his poems and his life, the original perspectives are diffracted by the 'broken bundle of mirrors' in Browning's art-form, and the fragments of fact are strewn on the ground like so many 'fresh sardines' caught in a net and arrayed on 'the marginal cobbles'.

In the *Cantos*, Pound stops strutting in front of the booth and plunges into the discourses and their specific voices, uttering their truth from within, as it were. However, when he abandons Sordello as an introduction to a modern 'Masque' and shifts instead to Odysseus, he both accomplishes the fusion between creative personality and empathetic selflessness which Browning dreams of in *Sordello*, and obeys the essential impulse of *Sordello*'s initial address to the audience. For Browning starts with a ritual sacrifice to the dead not so unlike Pound's own *Nekuia*; indeed, he draws aside Shelley's ghost in order to begin his song. His imaginary audience is composed of dead and living souls gathered for the occasion:

> So, for once I face ye, friends,
> Summoned together from the world's four ends,
> Dropped down from heaven or cast from hell,
> To hear the story I propose to tell.
> Confess now, poets know the dragnet's trick,
> Catching the dead, if fate denies the quick . . . .
>
> (*Sordello*, i.31–6)

In the *Cantos*, the 'rag-bag' replaces the dragnet, but the catch Pound dumps on his metaphorical cobbles really consists in dead and live men who all make themselves heard in a variety of accents.

Browning has already explained at the beginning of *Sordello* that he could have used direct dramatic presentation, letting his characters speak, 'myself out of view' (i.15), but that he has chosen another mode of portrayal to tell his story: that of the lecturer who 'chalk(s) broadly on each vesture's hem / The wearer's quality'. He will be present on stage and comment, like those who 'take their stand, / Motley on back and pointing-pole in hand' (i.25–31). The presenter shifts the scene at will, expands a long digression, indulges in a long purple patch such as the description of the castle of Goito Pound admired so much,[47] and even connects the story's complicated chronology to his own birth-day![48] Obviously Pound appreciated so much freedom, but thought that it needed paring down, as his comment on Browning as a model for literary reform indicates: '1. Browning – dénué des paroles superflus [*sic*]' (*L*, 218). The temptation of falling into the trap of a twisted verbosity for the sake of developing private conceits into a post-metaphysical romance was real for Pound as he started writing his first Cantos; for the only alternative to Browning was '2. Flaubert – mot juste, présentation ou constatation' (ibid.).

> Or shall I do your trick, the showman's booth,
>   Bob Browning,
> Turned at my will into the Agora,
> Or into the old theatre at Arles,

> And set the lot, my visions, to confounding
> The wits that have survived your damn'd *Sordello*?
> (Or sulk and leave the world to novelists?)[49]

In fact, as Daniel Stempel has shown, the freedom of which Browning availed himself belongs to the art of the Victorian diorama, and presents a guided tour of Verona, Mantua and the cities of the Condottiere.[50] It is only at another level that we can recognise the impassioned meditation on art: the 'morality play' showed a certain number of values which were examined by the poet in front of his audience. The ruptures of tone one finds in *Sordello* would not have been possible in a Victorian novel, for, even if novelists were fond of chiding or complimenting their characters, they at least adhered to a certain psychological verisimilitude. And here, for instance, we have the troubadour Eglamor, who is dismissed contemptuously in Book II and dies after having been humiliated by Sordello, coming to be seen at the end of Book IV as a more positive character than Sordello, thanks to the general progression of the political plot.

The showman's techniques come to the fore in the course of the *Cantos*: Pound too weighs his characters, approves and condemns, and, if he rightly refuses the Chinese-lantern technique of neat vistas displayed to the audience, if he makes fun of Browning's 'Appear Verona', heard several times in the first few pages of *Sordello*, he similarly plays on the theatrical mode of presentation, while discarding the more formal metalinguistic preoccupations with the search for an adequate genre. It is no coincidence that the main amphitheatre chosen by Pound as the 'scene' of his *Cantos* should be Verona:

> Across the Adige, by Stefano, Madonna in hortulo,
> As Cavalcanti had seen her.
> The Centaur's heel plants in the earth loam.
> And we sit here...
>   there in the arena...   (IV, p. 16)

This becomes one of the leitmotifs of the *Cantos* ('and we sit here / By the arena, *les gradins*' – XXI, p. 98) in order to present the frame of the historical perspective, the booth from which a collective subject witnesses the pageant of historical deeds as they are summoned up, until the scene is more fittingly repossessed by tragedy in the Pisan Cantos:

> The chess board too lucid
> the squares are too even...theatre of war...
> 'theatre' is good. There are those who did not want
> it to come to an end   (LXXVIII, p. 477)

But, at the end of this Canto, Pound acknowledges that he cannot remain on a balcony, as in the play by Lope de Vega, but is caught up in the play. The impersonality of the earlier Cantos is thus abandoned ('And we sit here. I have sat here / For forty four thousand years' – XI, p. 50), and the mythical abstraction of a Tiresias who has 'foresuffered all' breaks down. Pound's theatre has slowly moved from Verona to Rome ('Arena romana, Diocletian's – XII, p. 53) and then to Pisa, while Sordello had shifted his intrigues from Verona, split by the feud between the Guelph and Ghibelline families, to Rome, 'the shining city', which in his mind corresponds to the Pope, hence to the people's will or complete democracy: 'Rome typifies the scheme to put mankind / Once more in full possession of their rights' (*Sordello*, IV, 1023–4). For Sordello, the move from Verona to Rome is political because it represents a rejection of the aristocratic families of the north and an espousal of the democratic cause; it is also ethical, because entering the arena of real politics means an escape from the narcissistic seclusion of his ivory tower at Goito. Rome is therefore the ideal city to be built by the poet's dreams and the real city of a free humanity reconciled with belief.

The story of *Sordello* is simple enough: Sordello is a gifted poet whose desires for eternity forbid him to achieve any objective; he is crushed by the romantic longing for infinity, can never fit into the power game played by his real father, Taurello Salinguerra. Yet there is a moment when everything seems possible: Taurello decides to place his son, whom he has not recognised as such, at the head of the Romana family in Verona; he will champion him, marry him to the woman he loves, Palma. Then he realises that Sordello is his heir, and the poet's visions soar with more confidence; he describes his ideal poem to his father, a poem which would embody the best political ideal, in order to convince him to join the side of the Pope. Sordello describes, in fact, Browning's *Sordello* by a kind of daring perspectivist effect, as he opposes the 'synthetic' form of poetry to the 'epic' and dramatic modes. The synthetic mode corresponds of course to a general political reconciliation of the Pope's side with the Kaiser's supporters. It would achieve a fusion of the exterior moralisation of

Dante's *Commedia* and the dramatic liberations of individual and amoral energies one finds in Shakespeare.

> 'Man's inmost life shall have yet freer play:
> 'Once more I cast external things away,
> 'And natures composite, so decompose
> 'That' . . . why, he writes *Sordello*! . . .
>   '...Leave the mere
> 'Explicit details! 't is but brother speech
> 'We need, speech where an accent's change gives each
> 'The other's soul – . . .'   (*Sordello*, v.617–37)

The next ideal city which then stands for this 'synthetic' speech is – for Pound prophetically enough – Venice, because it has heaped up spoils from other countries and civilisations and manages to incorporate them under a common shape, a common *seal*; Venice is crowned by a Dome which works like a final symbol:

> '. . . till their Dome
> 'From earth's reputed consummations razed
> 'A seal, the all-transmuting Triad blazed
> 'Above. . . .   (v.648–51)

Sordello's attempt remains a failure precisely because everything seemed suddenly possible; when Palma and Taurello leave him with the badge of power around his neck, he dies, crushed by the weight of contradictory demands. He appears as a Hegelian *schöne Seele* unable to overcome regression and alienation by real action, and at the same time as a visionary prophet who holds the intense vision of a system in which religion and art, the State and the People, the Father and the Mother, would be reconciled.

The political and aesthetic drama enacted by Sordello can be read as a psychoanalytical conflict, for he is depicted as haunted by a 'fount' in his castle of Goito, which represents a Keatsian ideal of Greek eternity. Only at the end do we learn that his mother has been buried beneath it. Whenever he flees from politics he retires there to meditate. However, this feminine association explains Sordello's concern for the people, whilst Taurello, the paternal principle, is attached to the Emperor's legitimacy. Sordello discovers during his reveries that he and the people are one, 'The people were himself' (VI.120). This is why he must die, since his death is the only hope of achieving a symbolic action (and also because Browning cannot show Sordello's masterwork to the protagonists of the narrative: it is none other than the poem he is writing!). Death is the only way of 'producing deeds but not by deeds' (v.571). Pound was no doubt impressed by this confrontation with the pure man of action, the older Condottiere, who looks younger than his prematurely aging son at the end. Sordello's an example of an *'omniformis'* mind[51] who perishes by a complete 'decomposition' of 'natures composite'. Pound may well have found here a mirror to ulterior preoccupations with an ideal father and ruler, Mussolini, counterbalanced by the recurrent regressive wish to be encapsulated within the feminine bosom of Venice. Malatesta and Confucius will stand in much the same dialectical interaction in the Cantos.

The Temple with its Dome and Seal should mediate between the mythical font (Goito, Venice) under which the mother's influence is felt, and the ideal city (Rome, Ecbatan) of the political utopia. For Sordello's failure comes from the impossibility of mediating between the finite and the infinite:

> Thrusting in time eternity's concern, –
> So that Sordello...   (*Sordello*, I.566–7)

This is the 'So that . . .' which recurs in the *Cantos*, and which provides a sporadic link through the paratactic montage. It connects the world of ancient myth with the actualities of political synthesis. For Pound needs the concept of 'gods' and 'myth' precisely because he wants to avoid the tragic fate of Sordello; gods reconcile time and eternity's concern. The only way to avoid the invasion of the theatre of war by tragic actors lamenting the withdrawal of the gods or their cruel games is to unite the political will with the intuition of a terrestrial Paradise (not an aesthete's 'drowsy Paradise' like Goito). Thus Browning's affinities with Ovid become a little less strange, a little less arbitrary than when they are just stated without demonstration in *The Spirit of Romance*: 'The mood, the play is everything; the facts are nothing. Ovid, before Browning, raises the dead and disssects their mental processes; he walks with the people of myth' (p. 16). This new type of 'dissection' is also a 'dissociation', a decomposition leading to the affirmation of the discontinuous paradise of the gods. As such, it requires a completely new rhetorical strategy, based on the voice's speed and delivery, and not on 'speech figurative':

That's Wordsworth, Mr Browning. . . .
That should have taught you avoid speech figurative
And set out your matter
As I do, in straight simple phrases:
Gods float in the azure air,
Bright gods, and Tuscan, back before dew was shed . . . .[52]

'No logic of discourse'

The 'government of speed' on which Pound's poetics rely implies that the discontinuous perception of the flashes of godlike presence is both an arrest, a stasis, an ecstasis, and the maximum of speed, the 'speed of light'. How then can his poem be built on such a paradoxical movement; how can one even speak of a 'structure'? The interweaving of voices and themes will be the answer.

The most concise introduction to the structure of the early Cantos – for it is easier to keep the distinction between earlier, middle and later Cantos as a working definition, even if the break, contemporaneous with the events of 1945 and the subsequent redaction of the 'Pisan Cantos' rule out any ordered progression or general scheme – is probably to be found in Yeats's tract 'A Packet for Ezra Pound'. Yeats wrote this piece in 1928, after a visit to Rapallo, at a time when the Cantos numbered but twenty-seven (*A Vision*, p. 4). It is now taken for granted that this account is unfaithful because, as Pound himself said, Yeats misleadingly spoke of a 'Bach Fugue', whereas he had 'no idea' of what a fugue was like. But, despite such a hedging qualification, Yeats seems to pinpoint the very nature of the first Cantos when he reproduces, still a little mystified, and not without reservations, Pound's pattern of whirling letters:

There will be no plot, no chronicle of events, no logic of discourse, but two themes, the Descent into Hades from Homer, a Metamorphosis from Ovid, and, mixed with these, mediaeval or modern historical characters. . . . He has scribbled on the back of an envelope certain sets of letters that represent emotions or archetypal events – I cannot find any adequate definition – ABCD and then JKLM, and then each set of letters repeated, and then ABCD inverted and this repeated, and then a new element XYZ, then certain letters that never recur, and then all sorts of combinations of XYZ and JKLM and ABCD and DCBA, all set whirling together.[53]

I prefer to concentrate on the actual description quoted by Pound himself, rather than dwell on the cultural analogies with either Cosimo Tura's Schifanoia frescoes, or Balzac's *Le Chef d'oeuvre inconnu*, for they give a fresh testimony of the way Pound indeed rationalises a composition process which he has by then almost completed, before deciding to broaden the scope of his historical foundation. Both the main 'themes' – and this is the only traditional term that is not too determinate to deal with Pound's 'immense poem' – can be summed up by a series of letters which may then be inverted. If ABCD stands for the first theme, the 'Descent' (or the evocation of Homer's world and the Nekuia), the inversion of the theme, DCBA, might correspond to an 'Ascent'; however, the cypher used for the second theme, or 'Metamorphosis', does not seem to be repeated in the inverted form. What we find there is in fact just a simplified description of the first sixteen Cantos, which marks the affinities of the third with the first, of the fourth with the second, and points to the way one can read Pound's ideograms.

ABCD:	Canto I	Descent
JKLM:	Canto II	Metamorphosis
ABCD:	Canto III	Descent
JKLM:	Canto IV	Metamorphosis
DCBA:	Canto V	⎫
DCBA:	Canto VI	⎬ Ascent?
DCBA:	Canto VII	⎭
XYZ:	Canto VIII	New element (Malatesta)

Then the confusion is too great to allow for any poem-by-poem identification of themes, so that we must turn to the comparison with the Schifanoia frescoes, with their triple layer of events, to understand why precisely XYZ should be used for Malatesta himself, and not just the Malatesta Cantos:

He has shown me upon the wall a photograph of a Cosimo Tura decoration in three compartments, in the upper the Triumph of Love and the Triumph of Chastity, in the middle Zodiacal signs, and in the lower certain events of Cosimo Tura's day. The Descent and the Metamorphosis – ABCD and JKLM – his fixed elements, took the place of the Zodiac, the archetypal persons – XYZ – that of the Triumphs, and certain modern events – his letters that do not recur – that of the events in Cosimo Tura's day. (Yeats, *A Vision*, p. 5)

First it is important to note that the analogy with the painting rules out a purely Platonic or neo-Platonic pattern, with a hierarchy of eternal, recurrent and transient events in that order, since the zodiacal signs occupy the middle of the frescoes, and ensure the transition from the realm of the 'archetypal persons', such as Malatesta, to the 'modern events' which do not recur.

A second point is vital in establishing the relevance of this pictorial model: in the panels of the Schifanoia the whole room is divided into twelve months, each possessing its sign and also two accompanying figures which symbolise the decans of the Zodiac. Hence, it is perfectly fitting that Pound should wish to blend his two 'fixed elements' (ABCD and JKLM) when they mediate between archetypes and contingent exemplars.

Finally it is interesting to situate rigorously the use of 'theme' and 'archetype'. The themes stem from literary models (Homer, Ovid), while the archetypes belong to the domain of history ('mediaeval or modern historical characters'), which seems to be itself divided between the upper region of archetypes and the lower region of mere 'events'.

If we agree that the pattern conjured up by Yeats bears still some kind of relationship with the division between the 'ephemeral', the 'recurrent' and the 'permanent' Pound gives in one of his letters (*L*, p. 239), it follows that Heaven or the permanent functions between the ephemeral and the recurrent precisely because it is the point of intersection between gods and men, men and animals, matter and spirit, love and chastity, and so on. The function of the central section is both to pose opposites and to transgress limits; the descent into the world of the dead raises the question of the value of life and of the 'name to come' of heroes dead and alive; the brutal and swift transformations Ovid paints so well in his *Metamorphoses* show the uncanny presence of the gods in our world, and the latent and threatening possibility of bestial degradation.

Is such a state of whirl and flux really the main theme of the *Cantos*? Yeats had seemed to imply so when he presented Pound in his Introduction to the *Oxford Book of Modern Verse*: 'Ezra Pound made flux his theme: plot, characterization, logical discourse, seem to him unsuitable to a man of his generation. He is mid-way in an immense poem in *vers libre* called for the moment *The Cantos*, where the metamorphosis of Dionysus, the descent of Odysseus into Hades, repeat themselves in various disguises, always in association with some third that is not repeated.'[54] Despite the necessary simplification,

Yeats points out that repetition is the only structuring device, since a *tertium quid* which is not repeated allows for the musical audition of repetitions. What now remains to be demonstrated is that the concept of 'theme' cannot be understood as such without reference to a voice which posits the theme, and above all ensures that its ambivalence should be felt at different levels.

Sordello presented the model of an exciting chronicle revisited by a powerful voice which was able to unravel the tangle of perplexities the poetic language, the political situation and the metaphysical problematics created for an audience in need of help. As the first Cantos were rewritten, Pound abandoned the device of the authorial voice and left the commentary to mere repetition and metamorphosis: the metamorphosis of voices was to bring out its own hierarchy of values, its own political judgements. The succession of interlocking rhythms, the speed of the voices, the intonation of the utterances find a certain *ratio* between time intervals – the only important element of music, according to Pound's treatise[55] – and the form cut out in space, as determined by the page and the writing-process.

The elements Yeats brought to the fore can be connected with my remarks on speed and 'mistakes' to stress the ambivalence of the entire thematic design of the *Cantos*. Yeats underlined the possible reversals of themes, and the fact that they only find a meaning when they are set whirling among other particulars which are transient. Besides, Pound reaches his aim by a textual practice which is original, since he borrows his 'themes' and images from texts he translates.

The first Canto takes its point of departure from a Latin translation of Book XI of the *Odyssey* by Andreas Divus, and profits by its very inaccuracies. Divus provides Pound with a first guide, an unreliable guide, whose inadequacy is his main asset: 'and a crib of this sort may make just the difference of permitting a man to read fast enough to get the swing of his subject' (*LE*, p. 264). For instance, Divus uses a corrupt text which not only keeps a line which, repeated twice (lines 60 and 92), is now generally considered an interpolation (*diogenes Laertiade, polumekhan Odusseu*), but distorts the second *diogenes* into *digenes*; thus he correctly translates line 60 as 'Nobilis Laertiade, prudens Ulysse' (*LE*, p. 262) but gives for line 92 'Cur iterum o infelix linquens lumen solis'. This becomes in Pound's first version, 'Man of ill hour, why come a second time,/ Leaving the sunlight . . . ?' (p. 264), and, in the Canto, 'A second time? why? man of ill star'. This is the famous apostrophe by which Tiresias greets Odysseus before drinking from the blood for soothsaying. Thus a corruption of the text which appears as a double interpolation is translated by mistake into a puzzling and teasing line. Does this imply that Odysseus has already come to Hell? Has he already invoked Tiresias? Pound manages to place his hero's *iter* (voyage, way, perambulation) as an *iterum* (again, once more) – that is, as an original repetition.

Besides, this 'repetition' of a theme which appears for the first time enables Pound to link it with the second theme, the metamorphosis of Dionysus: the *iterum* hides indeed the main epithet used for Dionysus, *digenes* or *digonos*, 'born twice'. I shall have the opportunity of developing this point, and only remark here on the rich layering of textual maladjustments which inextricably underpin the conjunction of motifs. If repetition comes first, the absence of a full-blooded origin invalidates the attempt at identifying the mythical source with a primitive blood-rite. The transgression – that is, the descent of a live man among dead ghosts – has always already happened.

Pound no doubt wishes to link this strange duplication with the no less strange ellipsis made by Dante in his *Commedia*, when instead of having Odysseus come to the Nekuia in order to learn from Tiresias the way home, he has him meet his own persona, Dante accompanied by Virgil, in Hell, because he has decided to go on with his travels, and is found guilty of hubris! The Dantean Odysseus seems to have succumbed to the lure of Circe, who has left him with an irrepressible thirst for knowledge, who leads him to the pillars of Hercules and hence out of the Mediterranean world, until a wave covers him in a final shipwreck. He has nevertheless replaced the *pollon d'anthropon iden* by a desire to know men's vices and virtues ('e de le vizi umani e del valore' – *Inferno*, XXVI.99) which connects him with Pound's Alessandro in Canto VII ('Eternal watcher of things,/ Of things, of men, of passions' – p. 27).

As Pound's changes in his translation show, he is intent on conveying the sense of 'live men' speaking, and he emphasises this when he presents Elpenor's ghost and the surprise of Odysseus at encountering him there:

> Pitiful spirit. And I cried in hurried speech:
> 'Elpenor, how art thou come to this dark coast?
> 'Cam'st thou afoot, outstripping seamen?'
>   And he in heavy speech:
> 'Ill fate and abundant wine. I slept in Circe's ingle.

'Going down the long ladder unguarded,
'I fell against the buttress,
'Shattered the nape-nerve, the sould sought Avernus. . . .'

(I, p. 4)

It is of course difficult to appreciate the humour of the scene with its latent dramatic irony; what could be less heroic than a drunkard's death? Homer, Divus and Pound manage to render it poignant, thanks to the first misunderstanding of Odysseus, who thinks Elpenor is alive and has just been quicker; the difference in speed and status (alive or dead) is mirrored in the difference of speech rates; 'hurried speech' and 'heavy speech' translate *verba* quite faithfully, while suggesting the ironies of precipitation and drunkenness, and calling for rites which will dispel the ambiguities of the situation by re-establishing the order of language, founded on prophetic discourse.

Elpenor's name embodies the same dialectic of opposites, for he is the 'man of hope' (*elpis-aner*) and is thus 'unfortunate' but still hopes for a posthumous fortune or 'fame'. Divus has correctly translated *andros dustenoio, kai essomenoisi puthesthai* (*Odyssey*, XI, 76) by 'viri infelicis, et cuius apud posteros fama sit' (*LE*, p. 261), while Pound chooses to force the translation by a line he decides to italicise in the Canto (as if to put us on our guard): '*A man of no fortune, and with a name to come*'. Pound could have kept the phonic equivalent 'fame' to translate *fama*, which shows that this forced interpretation is deliberate; indeed, it will recur throughout the 'Pisan Cantos' because of its associations with the name of Odysseus as *Ou tis*, 'No one'.

The Elpenor motif of haste and repetition is itself repeated in history, for the first historical event narrated at some length in the *Cantos* is the murder of Alessandro de Medici by Lorenzo:

'Whether for love of Florence', Varchi leaves it,
Saying 'I saw the man, came up with him at Venice,
'I, one wanting the facts,
'And no mean labour . . . Or for a privy spite?'
Our Benedetto leaves it,
But: 'I saw the man. *Se pia*?
'*O empia*? For Lorenzaccio had thought of stroke in the open
But uncertain (for the Duke went never unguarded)
'And would have thrown him from wall
'Yet deared this might not end him', or lest Alessandro

Know not by whom death came, O se credesse
'If when foot slipped, when death came upon him,
'Lest cousin Duke Alessandro think he has fallen alone,
'No friend to aid him in falling.'

(v, p. 19)

The same fall precipitates Alessandro and Elpenor as it is mimicked by
the halting rhythm of a probing mind trying to disentangle fact from
fiction; the Duke was run through with a sword, so that he might know
the cause of his death, but the same ambiguity hovers around the
scene, whose motives are never made clear, especially as all this had
been told before:

And all of this, runs Varchi, dreamed out beforehand
In Perugia, caught in the star-maze by Del Carmine,
Cast on a natal paper, set with an exegesis, told,
All told to Alessandro, told thrice over,
Who held his death for a doom.
In abuleia. But Don Lorenzino
Whether for love of Florence...but
'O se morisse, credesse caduto da sè'
Σίγα, σίγα

(ibid.)

The echoes from Aeschylus's *Agamemnon* all point toward a similar
repetition, since lines 1344–5 jumble the injunction to be silent 'once
more and a second time'.[56] Pound effaces himself behind Varchi's
voice, merely adding '*Caina attende*' to suggest Dante and the fate
reserved for traitors;[57] he thus leaves the interpretation open, adding
another layer of silence to the original voices; he nevertheless seems
contemptuous of Alessandro's *abuleia*, which, if it does not justify
Lorenzo, shows a common destiny with a befuddled Elpenor. The text
is thus built up by the accretion of divergent discourses, divergent
voices, thriving on their contradictory echoes: 'Both sayings run in the
wind/*Ma se morisse!*' (Canto v, p. 20). Like Elpenor, Lorenzaccio
wished to leave a name, a name that can be written in the air.

Odysseus's function is thus not so much that of a voice as that of a
persona, through whom we see and hear – a passive persona as
paradigm of active experience. The first lesson his experience brings
home to us is that there can be no untimely hurry – especially if one
wishes to go through Hell:

And if you will say that this tale teaches...
a lesson, or that the Reverend Eliot
has found a more natural language...you who think you will
get   through   hell   in   a   hurry...   (XLVI, p. 231)

The spacing-out of the words on the last line indicates the necessary
length of the travel through a hell which has just been stigmatised as the
Inferno of Usura, while situating the process within language: no
language can come unsullied by the powers of darkness; therefore a
long work of undoing, of dissociation and new synthesis, is necessary.

When the reader has come to Canto XLVI, he has had access to the
key, so to say, of history, but he knows that everything depends on the
exact mode of access to the process. Thus he must be able to relate the
denunciation of the Bank's satanic creation of money 'out of nothing'
or, in Paterson's words,

> Hath benefit of interest on all
> the moneys which it, the bank, creates out of nothing
>
> (p. 233)

with the same metamorphosis, but seen in a positive light this time, in
Canto II:

> And, out of nothing, a breathing,
>   hot breath on my ankles,
> Beasts like shadows in glass,
>   a furred tail upon nothingness.   (p. 8)

The divine metamorphosis accomplished by Dionysus who reveals his
true nature to pirates by transforming their ship into a wild forest full of
lynxes is given as a moment of powerful illumination. The ecstasy is
brought about by the sudden reversal of speed into immobility and
silence – 'void air taking pelt / Lifeless air become sinewed' (ibid.) –
and then, 'The smooth brows, seen, and half seen, / now ivory stillness'
(p. 9). The divine transformation of speed into a slowness which is
pure beauty has its satanic equivalent in the 'Black Mass' of Usura,
which proceeds by obstructing the dissemination of knowledge and
blocks information on the one hand, while on the other it prospers
when art works are made 'to sell and sell quickly' (XLV, p. 229).

Creation *ex nihilo*, speed versus slowness – these first 'themes' have
to find their 'subject' who will enounce or denounce them – 'I,

Acoetes' of Canto II, pleading with King Pentheus, warning him against his own abuleia,[58] or a Poundian narrator engaged in a friendly contest with his colleague T. S. Eliot – until the very 'subject' becomes identical with the 'subject-rhymes' which relate theme to theme, Canto to Canto.

The whirl of voices which slowly or swiftly emerges from the series of metamorphoses attempts to weigh the characters taken from legend, myth or chronicle.

> 'Eleanor, ἐλέναυς and ἐλέπτο λις!'
>   And poor old Homer blind, blind, as a bat,
> Ear, ear for the sea-surge, murmur of old men's voices:
> 'Let her go back to the ships,
> Back among Grecian faces . . . .'   (II, p. 6)

The voices attempt to probe the person of Helen, who will later be identified with Usura in her destructive role:

>   Usura, commune sepulchrum.
> helandros   kai heleptolis   kai helarxe.
> Hic Geryon est. Hic hyperusura.   (XLVI, pp. 234–5)

But in the early Cantos, as we have seen, Helen served as a reminder of divine beauty and was opposed to the debilitated voices of old men, who appeared identical with those who had created the conditions of the First World War. Similarly, the image of gold, which is associated with woman's beauty, looks entirely innocent in the first series of Cantos; in Canto I, Circe is described with her 'golden girdles', 'bearing the golden bough of Argicida' (in the translation of the Homeric hymn to Aphrodite, which, as Hugh Kenner accurately noted, is probably more important than Ovid for the architecture of those Cantos[59]). Canto IV exploits the imagistic superposition of gold and gods to satiety ('Like the church roof in Poictiers / If it were gold. . . . Gold, gold, a sheaf of air, / Thick like a wheat swath, / Blaze, blaze in the sun, / The dogs leap on Actaeon' – p. 14) until the image is transformed into the myth of Danaë, waiting for the golden rain which brings her the seed of Zeus, a myth which links Canto IV ('Lay the god's bride, lay ever, waiting the golden rain' – p. 16) and Canto V ('The bride awaiting the god's touch' – p. 17), where gold finally connotes the work of the poet writing with care, or that of the mediaeval painter polishing his halo:

The fire? always, and the vision always,
Ear dull, perhaps, with the vision, flitting
And fading at will. Weaving with points of gold,
Gold-yellow, saffron... (ibid.)

But, after Canto XXVI, which denounces the vice of luxury through
the introduction of golden forks to the Doge's table, his wife being the
originator ('Sed aureis furculis, that is/with small golden prongs/
Bringing in, thus, the vice of luxuria' – p. 122), gold acquires mostly
sinister overtones, until the dynastic Cantos voice the unequivocal
condemnation of 'Gold is inedible' (and we shall see in the next
chapter the necessity of such execration). Gold becomes the symptom
of the 'money-fetish' and of reification of merchandise, while the
remnant splendour of Byzantine empresses such as Gallia Placidia at
Ravenna can still be expressed by the magical formula 'In the gloom,
the gold gathers the light against it' (XI, p. 51). The phonetic pattern
stresses the ambivalent and dialectical nature of the system of tensions
set in motion by Pound. Gloom and gold, light and darkness are
reconciled for an instant, in a 'weaving' with gold points accomplished
by the text: if *loom* can be said to be looming out of *gloom* through
gold, *gold* may still beget gods or demi-gods who will fight against
darkness. Their action will be identical with that of perceiving beauty
or reading the text, because a single *logos* will be set *against* dispersal:
'In the gloom the gold/ Gathers the light about it' (XVII, p. 78); 'Gold
fades in the gloom,/ Under the blue-black roof, Placidia's' (XXI, p. 98).
The subject rhyme has acquired an independent life; it organises its
own system of echoes and breaks decisively through the montage of
Malatesta's letters (XI) or mediates between the Medici's intrigues, the
legend of Midas and a sacred paean to spontaneous Nature (XXI).

In the same way, sexuality participates in this structure of reversals,
oscillations, paradoxical oppositions gathered by the vortex of voices.
For instance, we have come to learn from Pound that usury and
sodomy are linked – as they were for Dante in his Inferno, and for all
medieval theologians, because both fight against the natural reproduction of species:

Usura slayeth the child in the womb
It stayeth the young man's courting
It hath brought palsey to bed, lyeth
between the young bride and her bridegroom
CONTRA NATURAM (XLV, p. 230)

But the theme of sodomy is introduced in the *Cantos* in the negative, so to say, since the first mention of the 'sin against nature' is made by one of the arch-villains of Pound's historical gallery of rogues, Pope Pius II. In Canto X, Malatesta is depicted by the Pope's reports as guilty of all sins: he is incestuous, a sodomite, a fornicator, a killer:

> '*Lussurioso incestuoso, perfide, sozzure ac crapulone,*
> *assassino, ingordo, avaro, superbo, infidele*
> *fattore di monete false, sodomitico, uxoricido*'   (p. 45)

Malatesta is a counterfeiter and sodomite in the Pope's vehement anathema, and Pound amuses himself when he quotes Sigismundo's quip telling his troops that if they are less numerous they are superior to the Pope's army because 'there are more men in this camp'.[60]

It follows that the reader may be slightly disoriented when he comes to the anecdote of the 'Honest Sailor': the doctors play a practical joke on a sailor and make him believe that they found a baby, taken from a prostitute, in his belly, so that he stops drinking, becomes rich and leaves a fortune to his 'son' but refuses to be called 'father' when he dies: ' "I am not your fader but your moder", quod he, / "Your fader was a rich merchant in Stambouli." ' (XII, p. 57). We are, it is true, told the context of the joke; John Quinn, bored with a bankers' meeting, disgusted at 'the quintessential essence of usurers' (p. 55) decides to give them a lesson, and to illustrate by a bawdy vignette the unhealthy source of their money. But the Canto opens with a very positive presentation of Baldy Bacon and Dos Santos, two active and intelligent money-makers who are praised for their awareness of natural increase,[61] so that we are in doubt whether the Honest Sailor represents the 'quintessence' of usury, or a case of positive readjustment of a warped *directio voluntatis*.

Again, the meaning is not inherent in the story itself, but, like a Freudian joke, is derived from the situation of its enunciation; at the level of the enunciation, the joke condemns, satirises and establishes an important point concerning usury which will be developed much later. But, taken in the ideogrammic context of the Canto, the meaning is completely the opposite, the Old Sailor being, after all, a more moral figure than Dante's Odysseus. His youthful indiscretion can be condoned; he may have been literally abused by a 'rich merchant', who sounds as ominous as Mr Eugenides in *The Waste Land*.[62] We are, however, presented with a deceived 'father', whose 'son' takes him for his real father when he is not, although he acts accordingly, and who himself believes he is a mother, when he is not – this anti-natural position being reserved for poets, who, like Eliot or Pound, can beget and exchange sexes:

SAGE HOMME

These are the poems of Eliot
By the Uranian Muse begot;
A Man their Mother was,
A Muse their Sire.   (*L*, p. 170)

Again, any story, any myth or indeed any artistic collaboration will have to get back to some origin, knowing full well that it is out of reach; the story of the Honest Sailor is a tale of an impossible paternity (in a Horatio Algiers story, the son would finally discover that the Sailor had visited the prostitute before they were both taken to the same ward), Pound's main question remaining 'Who issues what?' But there is always a *mistake* about the origin: someone has shifted the baby, or mislaid the embryo, or coined a different coin. In spite of all that, the wish to go back to the root, to cut with the pen faster than the tongue can slip, to understand the nature of the error, is probably the only way of ever managing 'to let the light pour' (Canto xciv, p. 635): 'light fighting for speed' (xci, p. 616).

2 Ideogram and Ideology

'3 vols of Ideology' Pray explain to me this neological title!
What does it mean? When Bonaparte used it, I was delighted
with it, upon the common principle of delight in everything we
cannot understand. Does it mean Idiotism? The science of
non compos mentuism? The Science of Lunacy? The theory of
Delirium? Or does it mean the Science of Self-Love of *amour
propre*? or the elements of vanity?   (John Adams to Thomas
Jefferson, 16 December 1816[1])

Ideo-logos

A major feature of Pound's unique consistency, despite all contradictions, obscurities and ambivalences, lies probably in the
constant interaction between all his productions. In a reply to Yvor
Winters's objections that Pound had been guilty of an 'abandonment
of logic in the Cantos', he defended the method of his poem by a
reference to his prose writings; Winters could attack the paratactical
method 'presumably because he has never read Fenollosa or any prose
criticism and has never heard of the ideogrammic method'.[2] Thus these
other texts appear as prerequisites to an understanding of the *Cantos*,
and no reader can decipher the rapid succession of allusions, quotations and individual voices if he ignores the essays, the translations, the
various introductions and even the letters. If one is loath to be
disqualified, turned out of the club of the elect, it is necessary to start
reassembling the parts of the huge ideogram which can be named 'Ezra
Pound', so that a strange and new vitality starts animating the discrete
facets and elements, down to seemingly irrelevant details. The paradox
of such writing, which emphasises division, heterogeneity, disintegration in order to reassert the fundamental cohesion of the whole, is
implicit in the very terms by which Pound defines his ideogrammic
method or system.

In a recapitulation dating from the darker Fascist years, Pound sees this method as his main 'contribution to criticism': 'True criticism will insist on the accumulation of these concrete examples, these facts, possibly small, but gristly and resilient, that can't be squashed, that insist on being taken into consideration, before the critic can claim to hold any opinion whatsoever' (*SP*, p. 303–4). The 'hard' quality of these examples had long before been praised by Pound in connection with prose, as a rejection of the 'soft' values of post-Victorian poetry, and will attach itself to the political virtues celebrated in 'Thrones'; these thrones are introduced as early as 'Rock-Drill':

> Belascio or Topaze, and not have it sqush,
> a "throne", something God can sit on
> without having it sqush

(LXXXVIII, p. 581)

From the 'hard facts' to the seats of gods, one and the same active influence, one and the same adamantine resilience, an almost autonomous drive to make sense. The poet has simply to find the facts, so that the gods may find a seat or an altar, and this process of discovery is slow and exacting; Pound always reminds his reader that the name of 'troubadour' comes from *trobar* (to find), and that 'invention' derives from *invenire* (to find): his progression through myths and culture will be that of the poet–discoverer who patiently collects pebbles along his path.

Since 'invention' is restricted to the discovery of facts, the principle, system or theory will only have to generalise from the facts; the humble nature of science is opposed to syllogism, rhetoric and logic. Such an implicit humility is then turned into a principle of symptomatic reading, for it follows no less consistently that anyone who writes unwittingly constitutes an ideogram of his creeds, of his terms of reference, of his fundamental beliefs. Literature thus articulates a system of values, uniting sensibility, intelligence and will. 'The first credential we should demand of a critic is his ideograph of the good; of what he considers valid writing, and indeed, of all his general terms' (*LE*, p. 37). Pound tends to admit here that 'general terms' are part of the ideogram, which pushes a little further from his initially staunch empiricism. It would be misleading to exclude concepts from the ideogram; it is rather that no concept can be formed without recourse to the ideogram.

It is only in the 1930s that Pound started generalising and systematising what, by definition, should have been kept within the bonds of inductive and empiricist philosophy. Thus, if, as Ronald Bush clearly demonstrated, the ideogrammic method was not the formative principle behind the composition and remains a 'red herring' for critics,[3] it is remarkable that Pound should have created such a time gap between his early appreciation of Fenollosa, whose widow gave him her husband's papers to edit in 1913, and the application of these insights to verse composition in the late twenties and early thirties. A few chronological landmarks may help. January 1914: 'Fenollosa, as you probably know, is dead. I happen to be acting as his literary executor . . .' (*L*, p. 31). June 1915: 'Fenollosa has left a most enlightening essay on the written character (a whole basis of aesthetics, in reality) . . .' (*L*, p. 61). January 1917: 'I have just sealed up Fenollosa's "Essay on the Chinese Written Character", to send to them. It is one of the most important essays of our time' (*L*, p. 101). November 1927: 'Any question of method or interpretation of ideograph can wait for or be referred to Fenollosa's "Essay on the Chinese Written character". . . . At present it is the scattered fragments lent by a dead man, edited by a man ignorant of Japanese' (*L*, p. 214). This reveals that the 'method' had only taken shape after a few major ideological and political commitments had been made; the ideogram had to be related to Pound's increasingly economical and political angle of perspective, because the ideogram needs ideology to sussist as a 'system'.

Since the principle is so general that it had been widely used before acquiring its name, Pound had to explain that he had used the method before he had read Fenollosa. The first exhibit of *ABC of Reading* is a collection of five quotations which go back to 1913 and illustrate what the concept of a 'serious artist' was at the time. However, the difference between the text as printed in the *Literary Essays* and its ideogrammic version is striking, for Pound has left his quotations alone, without any commentary to link them, while in the original essay they all appeared as illustrations of an argument (which indeed tended to show the limits of rational demonstration: 'There is another poignancy which I do not care to analyse into component parts, if, indeed, such vivisection is possible' – *LE*, p. 53). This proves that the ideogrammic method merely replaces a critical terminology derived from de Gourmont's 'dissociation des idées'.[4] But the lack of critical concepts and connectives shows the quotations to be in themselves stylistic markers of excellence; Dante, Cavalcanti, Villon and Yeats stand out sharply as momentous landmarks of universal literature. The 'monumental' is still part of the principle of ideogrammic juxtaposition. The 1913 essay started from a distinction between the 'clear statements' of good prose, with Flaubert and Stendhal as models, and the 'passionate moments' of lyrical affirmation peculiar to poetry. In the new presentation, Pound attempts to bridge the gap he had opened, since poetry now catches up with prose by a radical application of the principle evoked earlier, 'Dichten = Condensare'.[5]

If one can only express the 'heart's movements' by striving toward greater clarity, as Stendhal says, then condensation becomes the first poetic asset. The 'higher potential' of poetry derives from its ability to condense a novel of the Jamesian type into five pages, or a general history of China into ten cantos. Besides, the ideogrammic elements are all quotations, and quotations referred back to their sources; thus their personae can reveal new voices, animated and magnetised by the emotional charge which survives, heightened, in the poetic montage. Its basic principle is the tension of text and voice.

Can this afford criteria which may help distinguish between an 'ideograph of the good' and, for instance, an 'ideology of beauty'? Is there a common process of unification in the harmonisation of differences which can lead to the overall perception of the ideogram, and in the necessarily political function of 'ideas going into action'? It would be idle to start criticising Pound for his half-baked notions of what an ideogram really is; and, if the famous analysis given in the *ABC of Reading* to show that the idea of 'redness' is created in Chinese by the juxtaposition of four 'pictures', for 'rose, cherry, iron rust and flamingo', is definitely wrong,[6] Pound was relatively early aware of the blunder committed by Fenollosa – 'Chinese by putting together concrete objects as in F's example / red / iron rust / cherry / flamingo / Am not sure the lexicographers back him up' (*L*, p. 333) – but for him this did not rule out the validity of the analysis. And indeed the conclusions of so eminent a sinologist as Marcel Granet are the same, although they start from a totally divergent analysis of the written character in Chinese:

Written signs and vocal signs which are named by the same term (*ming*) are equally forceful symbols which are considered entirely interdependent. This conception enables us to understand why the signs where we recognize '*phonic* groups' are no less *representative of reality* than the so-called ideographic characters, where we want only to see drawings. It is remarkable that the so-called *phonetic* part of these groups is often their most stable element. The radical, on the contrary, is unstable and is often suppressed. It is the least meaningful element. It plays, at best, the role of a specifier. Usually it scarcely has more than the purely practical function of facilitating the (technical) classification of signs (not a classification of notions). These would-be radicals seem to be superfluous elements. On the other hand, each group of strokes, which is often treated as 'phonetic', forms a symbol which is complete in itself and normally corresponds much better than the radical to what we might be tempted to call a root. Interdependent with a vocal sign we insist on seeing an emblematic value, the written sign is itself considered as a sufficient representation, or rather, if I might say so, an efficient designation.

Writing, given these attitudes, need not be ideographic in the strict sense of the word. However, it cannot be other than representative. A consequence of that is that the fate of speech is linked to that of writing.[7]

Thus, in a way, Pound had grasped the fundamentals of the Chinese character, even if, following Fenollosa's distorted intuitions, he thought that all characters are 'drawings'; however, he had the example of Confucius, who said, according to certain traditions, that the sign for a dog was the perfect drawing of a dog.[8] The sign relates speech and writing because it stylises a conventional picture or gesture:

The written sign shows the way to a sort of *general idea* by evoking first of all an *assigned gesture full of diverse consequences*. . . . The graphic emblem records (or claims to record) a stylized gesture. It possesses an *appropriate* power of suggestion, for the gesture which it portrays (or claims to portray) is a gesture of *ritual* value. . . . It causes the appearance of a flood of images which allows a sort of *etymological reconstruction* of the notions.[9]

The etymological reconstruction has to be linked in his theory to the function of the subject, who becomes a 'serious character' ('a man's character apparent in every one of his brush strokes' – *L*, p. 333) when he can underwrite the complex gesture; this time, we move from the ritual perception of etymology to the economics of the character.

The *ABC of Reading* explains how the 'general statement' works like a cheque: 'Its value depends on what there is to meet it. . . . In writing, a man's name is his reference. He has, after a time, credit' (p. 25). The correspondence between ideogram and cheque is simple: the arbitrary connection between four objects emphasises their

common property (redness) in so far as it is warranted by a certain state
of society (an English speaker might not see a flamingo as primarily
red, but a robin assuredly, while a French speaker sees a flamingo as
pink). The social consciousness of language outlines a basis for 'belief'
and 'credit'. In the same way, a cheque can be faked or a hoax, a joke, if
it does not correspond to any security or cover. This entails a first
displacement: instead of posing a static relation between words and
referents in the real world, Pound adheres to a conception of dynamic
exchange between statements and the 'delivery of something you
want', thereby opening the space for need, wants and desires. The
'cover' of cheques is not restricted to representation, but is relayed by
communication, and, more importantly, by transformation in a process
of exchange.

In literature, you can never be sure of what is immediately good or
sound; the question of the interrelation between name and reference
acquires a strategic value. For, just after having written that a writer's
'name' is his 'reference', Pound reverts to the classical use of the word:
'A general statement is valuable only in REFERENCE to the known
objects or facts' (*ABCR*, p. 26). Whilst I shall develop the problem of
'references' in Chapter 4, here I should just like to point to the
inscription of a name within the literary ideogram: a name's credit
comes from his underwriting, covering of his reader's expectations by
true meanings, true references (not referents, of course, as will be
demonstrated later). And, the stronger Pound stresses the natural
character of this operation, the deeper he has to commit Nature itself
to some kind of similar underwriting, so that things appear capable,
like men, of 'signing' their name, of inscribing their living ideograms on
the surface of the Earth, without any need of speech:

> 'We have', said Mencius, 'but phenomena.'
> monumenta. In nature are signatures
> needing no verbal tradition . . . .
>
> (LXXXVII, p. 573)

It is only when names can be dissociated from their bearers that the
whole economy of signs and signatures is disrupted; the splitting of
signature in 'nature' on the one hand and 'sign' on the other is always
threatening, but the ideogram is enriched by this underlying tension
when it attempts to marshal facts so as to compose a name. History and
economics will both need to be founded on this general analysis of
credit and circulation of atomic facts. Language and money, culture

and science function all according to the model of a 'critical' selection and combination of facts. Thus the critic not only 'invents' as he finds symptoms; he 'chooses' (from *krino*, to choose – *ABCR*, p. 30) and selects the 'luminous detail': 'Any fact is, in a sense, "significant". Any fact may be "symptomatic", but certain facts give one a sudden insight into circumjacent conditions, into their causes, their effects, into sequences, and law. . . . These facts are hard to find. They are swift and easy of transmission. They govern knowledge as the switchboard governs an electric circuit' (*SP*, pp. 22–3). The harder they are to find, the more easily can they be transmitted, for Pound's quest is haunted by the utopia of some root facts, which must have been covered by the dark mass of historical sedimentation, obscured by the powers of usury. Once they are dis-covered or found, they may be set back in circulation within the circuit of knowledge and distribution. But they organise a vital pattern which can remain inert, latent, demagnetised writing – 'dust' to the 'fountain pen' one hears in the 'fountain pan':

> This liquid is certainly a
> >   property of the mind
> nec accidens est   but an element
> >   in the mind's make-up
> > est agens and functions   dust to a fountain pan otherwise
> >   Hast 'ou seen the rose in the steel dust
> >   (or swansdown ever?)
> >   so light is the urging, so ordered the dark petals of iron
> we who have passed over Lethe.   (LXXIV, p. 449)

The condition of truth lies in this ordering, and its chief effect is that of revelation, truth as *a-letheia* according to Heidegger in the de-concealment of Being. That such a writing can be read in Nature is a proof of its ontological quality, and its evanescence is founded on a sense of the discontinuity of the universe and of the gods.

The tension between order and chaos is but the dramatisation of the act of intellection, especially when history is the object, since the historical field is one in which meanings are not pre-given, even if facts abound. A voice is needed to give the surplus of meaning which can tilt forward the ideogram toward its volitional aim. The problematics of utterance and enunciation has to be placed in the gap between typographical fragmentation and ideological assertion, in the oscillation between a centre, an axis, and the ever-recurrent risk of dismemberment.

Confucius is Pound's major asset in what he evokes as his 'ideological war', a war which acquires more sinister overtones in some of the radio speeches. At one point, in a broadcast of 1941, Pound calls up Brooks Adams 'prophesying a 30 years' war, an IDEOLOGICAL war': 'And let me remind you that the notion of ideological war is FORWARD, not backward. . . . A new idea rises in Europe.'[10] In a broadcast written in March 1942, he attacks the British newspapers which 'keep so gingerly OFF all the ground where there is ideological COMBAT'.[11] This shows an acute consciousness of his role in politics, for his economic theories are clearly understood as pawns in a general ideological war. This takes a shriller form during the war, but the preceding decade had seen multiplying signs of this ideological pressure. When Chan Kai-shek failed in China, it was because he had used 'Confucian slogans a little too late' (*SP*, p. 109). Thus a study of Confucius is essential to ideological commitment: 'The proponents of a world order will neglect at their peril the study of the only process that has repeatedly proved its efficiency as social coordinate' (*Con*, p. 19).

It is therefore of the highest importance that the *Cantos* should be able to prove the legitimacy and the existence of such an ideological war. It might appear advisable to show that the term 'ideology' is used without any negative connotations, and indeed in its etymological sense. The term is introduced in the *Cantos* through the voice of John Adams, who heard it pronounced by Napoleon: 'Napoleon has invented a word, Ideology, which expresses my opinion' (XXXIII, p. 160). We do not know what the opinion of Adams was, or about which subject, but we do gather an impression of unreliability from Napoleon's imperialist manoeuvres and economic failure: ' "En fait de commerce ce (Bonaparte) est un étourdi", said Romanzoff' and 'After the peace of Tilsit, where cd. I go but Spain?' / For he must always be *going*' (XXXIV, p. 165). Up till the fifth decad of the *Cantos* (XLII–LI), Napoleon appears as a negative figure, while Jefferson tends to be on the side of the *idéologues*.

For, indeed, Adams was in a way mistaken when he thought that Napoleon had coined the word 'ideology' (he was simply referring to the group of philosophers whose doctrine was the *Idéologie*), but he was right in ascribing the Napoleon the modern and now current sense of the term – indeed, from Napoleon's usage to Marx's there is but a brief step to take, and it is not by coincidence that Marx is quoted in Canto XXXIII: Pound's montage of letters and citations, including one from the *Capital*, aims to situate the word 'ideology' against a historical background.

In 1815 Napoleon had been engaged for at least fourteen years in a denunciation of the *idéologues*, because most of them, such as Cabanis, Destutt de Tracy and Volney, were initially in favour of the last constitution (the *Constitution de l'an III*) and were opposed to the restoration of a monarchical rule. They led the opposition of the intellectuals and liberals, and, whilst Napoleon could do nothing directly against them, he tried to throw disrepute on them by calling them 'dreamers and metaphysicians' and always using 'ideology' in a context where it meant ineffectual abstract thinking.

Pound knew the word as early as 1918 in its historical sense, and he was able to make the connection with Remy de Gourmont, who in a way now appears to literary historians as the last of the *idéologues*; thus it is striking to meet de Gourmont at the origin of the ideogrammic method and at its end, if ideology is really its end. When praising Jules Romains as the only successor to de Gourmont's intellectual pre-eminence in Paris after the first World War, Pound writes, 'Jules Romains is idéologue, and undoubtedly mars his work by riding an idea to death. . . . He seems to me about the only "younger" man in France whose head works at all' (*L*, p. 133). From de Gourmont's sensualism to the economic theories of the *idéologues*, Pound could be sure to find himself on familiar ground, which covered all that he cared to salvage in nineteenth-century philosophy. Besides, he could not ignore Stendhal's early devotion to the circle of *les idéologues*, and his imitation of Destutt de Tracy's book on love in *De l'amour*.[12]

Ideology was first of all a theory of the human mind which tried to replace the word 'soul', which smacked of metaphysics, by that of 'ideas'; and the ideas were traced back to their origin in a sensationalist way, on the model of Condillac's analysis of perception. Destutt de Tracy explained in his 1796 *Mémoire* that 'ideology' would be the new science of ideas and sensations, since it was the 'discourse' (*logos*) about visual images and perceptions (*eidos*).[13] Ideology was radically scientific, and would cure of metaphysical abstract terms. Thus it had ramifications in physiology (especially of the brain), logic, grammar and pedagogy, with the ultimate aim of 'regulating society in such a way that man finds there the most help and the least possible annoyance from his own kind'.[14]

Destutt de Tracy had been particularly noted for his proposals for a new system of education, which would have been adopted by the young French Republic had not Bonaparte seized the power. For him, public education was essentially an economic matter:

The first condition of public morality is a well balanced budget and just taxes which distribute equitably the burden of imposts among the citizens. The second condition is a judicial system which protects good citizens from bad ones. If the people have good taxes and good laws, no laws will be necessary to force them to study. It will suffice that the State affords the means towards education.[15]

Destutt takes up positions that will be held by Pound in 'Rock-Drill' and 'Thrones', especially when he adds, 'The least abatement of taxes will much more raise the number of literate people than a squad of schoolmasters.'

In a way, for all his opposition to and disparagement of *les idéologues*, Napoleon would probably have concurred on this point, and this is how Pound starts seeing him after Canto XLIV, praising him for having left a sound *Code Civil* ('monumento di civile sapienza' – p. 227), until eventually he grafts him onto the Chinese chronicle.[16]

Pound heard of Destutt and the other *idéologues* through their correspondence with Jefferson, who was very close to them, to the extent of translating or having translated works by Destutt (such as his commentary on Montesquieu, published anonymously for fear of censorship in France[17]). Meanwhile, Adams looked more reserved, for his aristocratic leanings made him view the spirit of the French revolution with more misgivings than Jefferson. However, Adams and Jefferson agreed on one point, the economic philosophy they took from Destutt's *Economie politique*, which contained a radical criticism of paper money. In 1818 Jefferson saw the 'flood of nominal money' invading the United States, which 'by interpolating a false measure is deceiving and ruining multitudes of our citizens'.[18] He asked Adams if he might use some letters of his in broad agreement with Destutt de Tracy in a pamphlet. The subject recurs at the end of the Adams Cantos:

> Gold, silver are but commodities
> Pity, says Tracy, they ever were stamped save by weight
> They are commodities as is wheat or is lumber. (LXXI, p. 420)

This theme is the line of the arguments of the Physiocrats, and we shall see that it has immediate relevance for the ideological war waged by the Chinese Cantos, even if Pound takes the completely opposite position in economics.[19]

Thus the ideological war which was brewing through the middle Cantos finally finds a fit 'theatre' in China:

> Oulo of Kin, greatest of Kin, under him were books set
> > into Nutché
> > in his reign were only 18 beheaded
> > but his brat was run by his missus
> > and they had an ideological war   (LV, p. 299)

The *Guide to Kulchur*, which comes from roughly the same pre-war period,[20] provides a prose explanation of the ideological conflict enacted by the Cantos. Ideology is seen as the product of history, a history which does not exist in itself, but has to be relived by the observer and commentator, and appears determined by economics and social forces. At times, especially when he discusses ideology, Pound sounds like a Marxist, since for him the 'science of ideas' invented by the *philosophes* finds its true basis in the 'production of ideas':

> History that omits economics is mere bunk, it is shadow show, no more comprehensible than magic lantern to savage who does not know what causes the image.... From sheer force, physical prowess, craft, jaw-house, money-pull, press to radio, government has undergone revolutions of modus and instrument. / Ideologies float over this process. Emotions, appetites, are focussed into political forces.   (*GK*, pp. 259–60)

According to Pound, ideologies exploit irrational drives and serve as masks in a wrong sense; they disguise the real fights for power. Pound starts by linking ideology with the omission of the economic factor from an analysis of history; but, unlike Marx, he is ready to acknowledge the political use of ideology as a positive force (Mao would be inclined to such a position). He develops this point in greater detail in the chapter entitled 'Government', which lists certain means to achieve political supremacy: 'Government has been based on fact, fancy, superstition, folk-ways, habits, ideas, ideologies' (p. 241). In Pound's view, ideology is the weapon of the democratic state, since he opposes the 'fact' of pure physical strength, the 'fancy' of the Condottiere, and the regulating function of language in smaller assemblies. The inherent corruption of the democratic system will then be particularly revealed by the language symptoms it produces. They are discernible by a loss of clear lines: 'Superstitions merging into ideas, ideas cloaked or camouflaged as ideologies' (ibid.). From there on, he concludes that it is necessary to control the press and radio, just as Lenin or Roosevelt did, in order to find the minimal base to enforce monetary reform.

What can possibly be achieved by a writer, by someone who has not yet hit upon the availability of radio broadcasts to convey his 'ideas' to a vast audience? He maps out first of all the interaction of forces dominating the current ideological fray, then uses the ideogrammic method as a way of controlling writing through his voice, and of disseminating his voice through writing. The author as 'speaker' must add his voice to the latent force or energy of the *gramma* or written sign. Could it be that Pound's ideological stress on the pictorial origin of the Chinese character came from the ineluctable necessity of reintroducing a voice into a sign, a sign which had come increasingly to lack a voice the more it became the signature of China?

Voices and Chinese history

> Run your eye along the margin of history and you will observe great waves, sweeping movements and triumphs which fall when their ideology petrifies.   (*GK*, p. 52)

Pound aims at showing that 'serious history revives, bit by bit, in our time' (p. 277) through his own re-elaboration of dynastic chronicle. The project is explicit enough: we are to read a detailed exposition of the evolution of China from its mythical origins to the eighteenth century, at which point it is replaced in the economy of the *Cantos* by the America of John Adams. The source is one single series of books, so that one can follow step by step the notes taken by Pound from de Mailla's monumental *Histoire Générale de la Chine*, founded on Zhu Xi's *Mirror of History*, itself a compilation of Sima Guang's *Zizhi Tongjian*, *The Complete Mirror for the Illustration of Government*. The main factor to be kept in mind is that the history classic belongs to the great texts of the neo-Confucian school, which arose at the end of the eleventh century and attained pre-eminence in the fifteenth century.[21] The summary made by Zhu Xi stresses a moralistic and indeed ideological conception of history. When de Mailla translated it, adding his own sources for the period that had not been covered by the chronicle, he prepared the official version of China for the *philosophes* of the Enlightenment, but was regarded as subversive by the Church.[22] The extraordinary influence of the work on the French Physiocrats, who then exported it to America, where some of them, such as Du Pont de Nemours, lived, links it indeed with Jeffersonian ideals of democracy.[23]

An editorial note which shows clearly the Physiocrats' preference for agriculture has been underlined by Pound in his copy of the seventh volume of the *Histoire*. Ouang-Ngan-ché had reformed the regulations concerning the lending of grain to peasants; and, while the reforms were heavily criticised by the people, the editor sides with Ngan, praising the idea of lending grain in the spring that did not have to be paid for till autumn, after the harvest. This project, he adds, and this is the sentence marked in the margin, 'must have been hateful to usurers who only feed on poor people's blood' (VIII, p. 305, n. 1). The link between the *Histoire* and the later Cantos becomes explicit when we see that the general editor, M. Deshautesrayes, deliberately cut out the long speeches which de Mailla had translated from the *Chou King*, which had by then been separately translated into French.[24] Pound's source admits of several grafts, such as interpolations from the Latin edition of Lacharme's translation of the *Book of Odes*, and also the *Book of Rites* or *Li Ki*, but in the main Pound limits these interpolations.

One of the 'lessons' in Chinese history the *Guide to Kulchur* wanted to give was the need to acquire a sense of 'balance in NOT mistaking recurrence for innovation' (p. 274); indeed some sense of balance is needed for the reader, who shifts from the abrupt statements of the *Guide* to a long chronicle spreading over ten Cantos. These do little to inform the lay reader about the history of China: the blunt transitions and lack of elementary explanations would suffice to frustrate the reader's desire for knowledge. On the other hand, sinologists would be horrified by these bold vistas over vast and heterogeneous periods, condensed at a third remove. But the reader has to cope with a totalising insight into a study of 'social texture' which remains foreign and yet yields practical maxims applicable to the present. Despite his highly individual style, Pound tries to add nothing to the elements he finds in de Mailla's book, but feels obliged to stress salient points or enliven the at-times drab lists of names.

How can we connect the spoken style, with its imitations of American or English dialects, with the will to play a role in a synthesis which must be totalitarian? I should like to build up a model capable of posing the problem of the musical voices in the text, assigning them less to real history or economy than to the way the reading–writing subject is involved in ideological discourses which he creates at the same time. For instance, Pound notably displaces the question of historical truth, since he decides to work from a single source, which he never checks against others. The Chinese tradition of keeping annals of daily affairs, written down 'on a loose leaf', each historian 'for himself, without communicating anything to anybody' presents a model of 'impartial severity' (*Histoire Générale*, i.iii). According to de Mailla's idealised model of probity, impartiality 'must be History's main attribute if it is to check the Princes and to prevent them from committing mistakes' (ibid.). Pound echoes this in 'History is a school book for princes' (Canto LIV, p. 280), which leaves out the cautionary slant, and he knows he must condense because his ideological model had condensed before him: 'He [Confucius] had 2000 years of documented history behind him which he condensed so as to render it useful to men in high position, not making a mere collection of anecdotes as did Herodotus' (*Con*, p. 19). Thus Pound decides to be partial, and subordinates the historian's disinterested pursuit of truth to his will to rationalise and introduce order.

The dynastic Cantos begin by a general recapitulation of the teachings discovered in history:

> And I have told you of how things were under Duke
> > Leopold in Siena
> And of the true base of credit, that is
> > the abundance of nature
> with the whole folk behind it. (LII, p. 257)

Soon enough the tone becomes more violent, attacking 'big jews' and *neschek* (usury in Hebrew), so that with the second recapitulation, made through the mouth of John Adams, the whole oral force of the utterance resounds:

> IGNORANCE, sheer ignorance ov the natr ov money
> > sheer ignorance of credit and circulation. (ibid.)

The fight against ignorance cannot be accomplished by the disclosure of the initial truth alone. Pound has started modifying his sources ever so slightly (the original sentence had 'downright ignorance...') to show that if one 'can't move 'em with a cold thing like economics'[25] one can 'move and teach' at the same time. A command of voices is the main rhetorical tool used in the ideological fight. And, as if to display his virtuosity, after having stated elliptically the central motif 'Between KUNG and ELEUSIS' (p. 258) Pound transforms his economic proselytism into a peaceful evocation of ritual. The *Li Ki* provides a solemn new overture:

> Know then:
>   Toward summer when the sun is in Hyades
> Sovran is Lord of the Fire   (p. 258)

This new knowledge consists in the cyclic return of seasons, each marked by a peculiar rite, so as to weave a network of correspondences between colours, foods and activities, thus pointing to an ordered and centred cosmos. The shift toward the ritual introduces at the same time a new tone, a new scansion, modifying, stretching out and spacing out our hearing. An earlier instance of the same dimension is to be found in Canto XLIX (p. 245):

> Sun up; work
> sundown; to rest
> dig well and drink of the water
> dig field; eat of the grain
> Imperial power is? and to us what is it?

The anonymous folk-song opens onto the 'dimension of stillness' which binds rites, work and peace. Rites are not just codified ceremony: they organise know-how, similar to Hesiod's poem. Truth is implicit: one must respect the rhythms of a Nature which alone creates riches. Truth then speaks of itself and is better heard in this way: 'Call things by the names. Good sovereign by distribution / Evil king is known by his imposts' (Canto LII, p. 261). The 'sense of proportion' which music alone can afford (*GK*, p. 283) as a 'sudden clearing of the mind of rubbish' is indeed differential – one needs the shriller voices of racial hatred to appreciate the desire for stillness, order and contemplation. The system of tensions belongs to the rite itself ('Month of the longest days / Life and death are now equal / Strife is between light and darkness' – Canto LII, p. 259), but the ways in which they are solved is different when we move to the chronicle proper.

Canto LII began with a strong assertion of an authorial voice apostrophising the audience. This voice reveals soon its spoken character: it alternates between the rural American voice Williams described, with its sometimes caricatural excesses ('sojer', 'millyum', 'iggurunce'), and chauvinistic prejudice (the Mongols become 'mongrels' and the Portuguese 'Portagoose', which affords opportunities for outrageous puns: 'for the Portagoose boss who had sent him / i.e. he wuz honoured but cdn't spill proppergander' – LXI, p. 337), and a more English accent, which can mimic Cockney mannerisms:

And the Emperor TAÏ TSONG left his son 'Notes on Conduct'
. . .
The 10th a charter of labour
and the last on keepin' up kulchur
      Saying 'I have spent money on palaces
        too much on 'osses, dogs, falcons
but I have united the Hempire (and you 'aven't)   (LIV, p. 287)

Pound's own twang (of which the *Letters* give a fair selection) takes possession of the chronicle from time to time, and I shall try to understand when and why. Against this, the hieratic tone of the 'record of rites' offers a homogeneous appearance, the '-th' endings ('winter ruleth', 'cricket bideth') stressing the aspect of ritual psalmody in a sacrificial calendar.

Between these extreme and opposed voices a third tone appears, the second Canto of the series, when it attempts to narrate the linear chronicle: 'Yeou taught men to break branches . . .' (LIII, p. 262). This voice recites the names and actions, slightly oscillating between the dry technique of shorthand notes from the French text, as in:

      the FIVE grains, said Chin Nong, that are
           wheat, rice, millet, *gros blé* and chick peas   (ibid.)

and the more vocal dramatisation of some episodes:

      Hia! Hia is fallen
          for offence to the spirits
      For sweats of the people.   (p. 265)

It may even show that the need to abbreviate imposes abridgements, compressions and ellipses which probably no historian would allow:

Wars,
wars without interest
boredom of an hundred years' wars.   (p. 272)

However, the recitation is often interrupted by puns in foreign languages (Greek, French, Chinese characters, Italian, and so forth). These are not just written word-plays intruding into an otherwise oral chronicle, but rather a means of both tightening the web of allusions and broadening the chronicle's horizons. The Chinese sacred herb *tsing-mo* calls up *molu*, written in Greek characters, (p. 263), in a phonic superimposition of Odysseus and mythic Chinese emperors, while Pound uses a French quotation just after – 'que vos vers expriment vos intentions / et que la musique conforme' – which looks like a literal quotation from de Mailla, but is not exactly; the text of the *Histoire* says, 'Que vos vers expriment votre intention; et que la musique y soit analogue: qu'elle soit simple et naturelle' (vol. I, p. 93; Pound's copy shows a mark in the margin). Pound has chosen to condense the sentence, at the cost of a slight impropriety, in order to have it sound even more like his definition of the exact 'conformity' between words and music he praised in the troubadours ('motz el son'). This last stylistic level is that of the 'foreign words and ideograms' which 'enforce the text but seldom if ever add anything not stated in the english' (p. 256, note). These 'underlinings' help to build the system of echoes, self-quotations and self-references of the *Cantos*.

In addition to the four stylistic levels distinguished here – the ritual, the chronicle, the spoken voice, and the foreign insertions – we can distinguish four levels of spatial and temporal references. The essential reference is of course to China, and occasionally Japan, from '2837 ante christum' to the Manchu dynasty. The chronicle stops in 1735. Then, France and enlightened Europe are perceived through the Jesuits and de Mailla: a key period, since it brought about the discovery of Confucius in Europe. The Jesuits play an important role in China itself (Cantos LVIII to LXI). Moreover, the history of China tends towards the history of the United States, which starts with Adams, and finally contemporary Italy ('anno seidici' – LII p. 257) rediscovers trends forgotten since the Malatestas and abruptly resurges in Canto LIV with an allusion to a submarine manoeuvre: '(Pretty manoeuvre but the technicians / watched with their hair standing on end / anno sixteen, Bay of Naples)' (LIV, pp. 279–80). To the main areas of study there correspond different historical and ideological models: to the Chinese dynasties, Confucius; to Enlightened Europe, the curiosity of the

Jesuits; to the United States, the compounded will of Jefferson and Adams; and, to contemporary Italy, the improvising artistic genius of Benito Mussolini.

If we admit that the following axes of equivalence hold true for most of the stylistic medleys of voices –

American/British spoken idiolect	farce, distortion, poignancy of utterance
historical chronicle	ellipsis, dramatisation
impersonal ritual	high, hieratic style
intertextual level	unexpected plays on signifiers in several languages

– the fact remains that the multiple interactions of different levels produce the more striking effects.What is more, a passage in French can grow out of the Chronicle itself, connote the Europe of the Enlightenment, and also point to the limitations of Pound's version as a translation. When he interposes '(piquée de ce badinage)' in an account of the debauched life and death of Tçin Hiao –

> TçIN HIAO told a girl she was 30
>   and she strangled him
>   (piquée de ce badinage) he drunk at the time
>
> (LIV, p. 282)

– this is all we shall ever learn about this prince, who leaves a grotesque and almost surrealist image which comes to relieve the boredom stemming from a monotonous roll-call of names. At times, Pound seems to be writing in a strange frenchified idiom, as if he wished to convey the Gallic lilt of the original phrases (and also the truth that 'Our European knowledge of China has come via latin and french' – note on p. 254):

> thereby relieving the poor of all douanes
> giving them easy market for merchandise
>   and enlivening commerce
>   by making to circulate the whole realm's abundance.
>   and said he knew how hard it wd/ be to find personnel
> to look after this . . . .   (LV, p. 296)

Generally, pure paraphrases are rarely unbroken, other stylistic markers are added, or they are replaced by long or elliptic snatches of quotations, which generally provide subject-rhymes with other Cantos or earlier poems. Such is the case of the passage in French which concludes Canto LVI:

> HONG VOU declined a treatise on Immortality
>   offered by Taozers, Et
> En l'an trentunième de son Empire
>   l'an soixante de son eage
> HONG VOU voyant ses forces s'affoiblir
>   dict: Que la vertu t'inspire, Tchu-ouen.
> Vous, mandarins fidèles, lettrés, gens d'armes
>   Aidez mon petit-fils à soutenir
> La dignité de cest pouvoir . . . .   (p. 310)

The echoes of Villon, and therefore of Villon as quoted in *Hugh Selwyn Mauberley*,[26] give a sort of foreign grandeur to this emperor's death. These subject-rhymes can be very playful, as when a list of Chinese towns and provinces triggers a certain rhythm which becomes that of an old French folk-song, the 'Carillon de Vendôme':

> Han, Lang, Ouen, Kong,
> Mie, Kien, Tchong, King,
> Fou, Pong, Chun King
>   gone
> Vendôme, Beaugency, Notre Dame de Clery
>   (LVI, p. 303)

Pound, who probably knew the song from hearing it sung in France, could also have found it in the *Ballades Françaises* of Paul Fort (Fort was a friend of Remy de Gourmont).[27]

If the allusions to France sound carefree, almost childish, the references to Italy conjure up an atmosphere of war, of prison, and of economic experiments: *fondego*, *ammassi* and *confino*[28] manage to create a bleak-enough ideogram of the Fascist country Pound was living in, in spite of the supposedly dynamic exchange of ideological models.

The style of the Chronicle fulfils therefore a precise function: it uses all the stylistic means at its disposal to lead back the reader's mind to an understanding of recurrence, both in the vast corpus of texts produced up to this point by Pound, and in the relatively limited corpus from which he quotes or translates. In a way, the Chinese Chronicle is absorbed by the ideological montage of the *Cantos*, instead of coming there as a refractory element. Besides, the interrogation on the sense of history is not primarily philological, as it will turn out to be with 'Rock-Drill' and the later Cantos.

Two passages in the *Cantos* deal with the same historical event, the revolt of Wu-Wang against Cheou-sin, or Chou Hsin, which led to the collapse of the Shang dynasty. In the first Canto of *Rock-Drill*, Pound quotes Couvreur's translation in Latin and French of the Book of History, which mentions the huge army levied by the despot:

Cheóu's host was like a forest in Mu plain,

林　　　quasi silvam convenit

jo lin

'Liking some, disliking others, doing injustice to no man.'

(LXXXV, p. 553)

Cheóu's army 'looks like a forest (because of the number of soldiers)' according to Couvreur's text, which gives the ideogram of 'the wood', *jo lin*;[29] Pound thus decides to leave the character, the Latin translation, and omits completely the story of the victorious issue of the battle, adding simply a moral description of the new emperor which does not come from Couvreur, but manages to splice in an allusion to Odysseus ('no man') and a very general portrayal of the universal moral qualities needed for a good emperor.[30]

The same scene presented in Canto LIII is not much more lively, but the philological exercise gives way to a condensed narration:

In plain of Mou Ye, Cheou-sin came as a forest moving
　　Wu Wang entered the city
gave out grain till the treasures were empty
by the Nine vases of YU, demobilized army　　　(p. 266)

In both passages, events are sparse, and one is just given a canvas, not a full scene. The connections are left out, but the dynastic Cantos stress the alternation between good rulers and tyrants; the good ruler distributes what he takes from his enemy to the people. In 'Rock-Drill', the linguistic speculation on radicals and ethics has been stripped of any informative value, and what stands out is an ideogram which Pound is fond of glossing for its almost metaphysical value: *jo lin* is the origin of a Confucian anecdote involving a raft and logs, and is thus connected with the Greek concept of *hulé*, matter or substance as uncut forest. (*SP*, p. 97.)

The type of ellipsis used by the Chronicle of the dynastic Cantos is different, and it is only when it turns into a litany of rites or of names that all narrative links are missing. For instance, during the recitation of the rites to be observed in spring –

> RITE is:
> Nine days before the first moon of spring time,
> that he fast. And with gold cup of wheat-wine
> that he go afield to spring ploughing
> that he plough one and three quarters furrows
> and eat beef when this rite is finished,
> so did not Siuen
> that after famine . . .   (LIII, p. 271)

– the relationship between the Emperor's failure to keep the rites and the famine is none too clear, precisely because the stylistic difference has not allowed for the voice of the Chronicle to be heard explicitly.

In another case, the montage is highly successful, when Pound rapidly evokes the drought in Tching Tang's time:

> For years no water came, no rain fell
> for the Emperor Tchin Tang
> grain scarce, prices rising
> so that in 1760 Tching Tang opened the copper mine
> (ante Christum)   (LIII, p. 264)

The creation of money cannot by itself bring back abundance: 'gave these to the people / wherewith they might buy grain / where there was grain'. But Pound then links the distributive function of money, the piety necessary for a sound government in harmony with natural order, Frobenius's trick of magic in Biembe when the African tribes thought he had brought rain and thunder, and the fundamental motto of Confucian wisdom:

> The silos were emptied
> 7 years of sterility
> der im Baluba das Gewitter gemacht hat

> Tching prayed on the mountain and
> wrote MAKE IT NEW
> on his bath tub   (pp. 264–5)

The ideograms *hsin*[1] *jih*[4] *jih*[4] *hsin*[1] enforce the sense of the whole evocation, and, even if we do not learn whether the prayer was successful (it eventually was), we fully understand how rites and monetary proposals move in the same direction: the teachings of Confucius.

The function of the subject's voice

The style of the chronicle dominates Canto LII, which is devoted to covering the period from the mythical emperors to Confucius. There is an echo of the ritual with the foundation rite of Sié:

> RITE is:
> Nine days before the first moon of spring time,
> that he fast. . . .   (p. 271)

If we make an exception of the usual abbreviations ('wd/', 'shd/', 'yr', etc.), we must wait until Canto LIV to see plays on the American voice, which crop up along with intertextual references and graphic super-positions. The names of some emperors tend to get blurred, and are the pretext for visual echoes:

> The Prince of Ouei put out hochangs
> put out the shamen and Taotssé
> a.d. 444, putt' em OUT
> in the time of OUEN TI   (p. 283)

The pun on 'OUT' and 'OUEN TI', followed by 'OU TI' on the next page, calls up the puns on *Ou tis* (Odysseus) in the 'Pisan Cantos'; this also emphasises the existence of two kings named Ou Ti, one who brought about the ruin of the Sung dynasty, and one who founded the Leang dynasty: 'OU TI / collecter of vases . . . So OU TI of LEANG had a renaissance' (pp. 283–4). But the second Ou Ti manages to bring back the Buddhists who had been expelled by Ouen Ti, and he becomes a monk himself. In this way, all the visual puns appear as not playful so much as condensations creating a kind of musical shorthand enabling the reader to gain valid historical insights.

It is also at this point that the Buddhists intervene, and embody the principles of anti-Confucianism; just after the mention of the second Ou Ti we read,

> And the 46 tablets that stood still there in Yo Lang
> were broken and built into Foé's temple (Foé's, that is
> goddam bhuddists.)

(LIV, p. 284)

'Foé' is the transcription given by de Mailla for the Buddhists, and Pound puns on 'foe' in English (in his copy he has underlined 'un ennemi déclaré de la doctrine des Foé et des Tao-ssé, il en méprisait les distinctions subtiles et frivoles' – VIII, p. 309). In addition, these pages reveal such expressions as 'Emp'r'r huntin' and the Crown Prince full of saki' (Canto LIV, p. 284), 'halls were re-set to Kung-fu-tseu/yet again, allus droppin' 'em and restorin' 'em' (ibid.), and 'jobs for two millyum men' (p. 285). The progressive introduction of the American voice, which would have been quite discordant some pages earlier, when Confucius's life was presented for instance, follows now close upon the enigmatic allusion to the writer's situation in Italy: 'Pretty manoeuvre . . .' (pp. 279–80). These lines have no relation whatsoever with their context: no similarity of date or action is there to create an echo. The interpolation is deliberate, necessarily evoking surprise. Here, then, as in other Cantos preceding this 'decad', the play of voices begins to be effective through a system of displacements, of abrupt shifts. It is precisely when this voice – the personal idiom – comes into play, that history undergoes modifications, is cut in a more arbitrary and conspicuous fashion. Pound's voice as 'idiomatic voice' has then three main functions, bearing on historical selection and temporal rhythms; the role of Confucius and of Buddhism; the parallels between China and Italy or America.

From Canto LIV onward, Pound shows that periods follow each other in cycles, that Chinese history has a tempo of its own, different from the mere succession of dynasties. The American idiom stresses the Chronicle so as to give it a rhythm it could not acquire by itself, and this rhythm is marked by effects of acceleration or deceleration. I have just quoted 'allus droppin' 'em and restorin' 'em', and we find in the next Canto, 'The hen sang in MOU'S time, racin', jazz dancin'/and play-actors, Tartars still raidin'' (LV, p. 291), or again, 'Y TSONG his son brought a jazz age HI-TSONG' (p. 292). Only this singular idiom could hint at a jazz rhythm, insisting on the decadence of the Empire confronted with the Tartars.

On the other hand, in Cantos LX and LXI, Pound wants to enhance some aspects of the relations between the Jesuits and the Chinese, and this same voice intervenes to slow down the action, to show Captain Tching Mao's distrust of the Europeans: 'and the Dutch are the worst of the lot of them,/ poifik tigurs' (LX, p. 331), or to convey the warning of a mandarin:

> 'You Christers wanna have foot on two boats
> and when them boats pulls apart
> you will d/n well git a wettin'' said a court mandarin
> tellin' 'em.   (LXI, p. 336)

The idiomatic voice also helps to emphasise the role of Confucius in the history of China. First, Confucius is systematically opposed to Buddhists from the moment that they prevail in the administration: 'And now was seepage of bhuddists' (LIV, p. 280). They become all that Pound execrates: 'last TçIN down in a Bhud mess' (p. 282). When everything goes wrong, they are not far away, or the Confucianists face too stubborn an opposition: 'Students went bhud rather than take Kung via Ngan' (LV, p. 298); 'HOEÏ went *taozer*, an' I suppose/Tsai ran to state usury' (p. 299).

Finally, this popular and individual voice draws continuous parallels with the history of the United States. The most characteristic example is when in Canto LX we learn about the embargo decreed by Lord Kang: 'so our lord KANG layed an embargo/ (a bit before Tommy Juffusun's)' (p. 330). The leading voice animates the Chronicle, enlivens the details and shows their contemporaneity. China and the United States become superimposed; the mentions of 'woikinmen thought of' (LXI, p. 335) or the fight against corruption ('And they druv out Lon Coto fer graftin'' – p. 336) or the praise of honest peasants who are rewarded only for their merits ('Chiyeou didn't do it on book readin'/ nor by muggin' up history' – LXIV, p. 358) show that we might well be speaking about America: the Chinese Chronicle has conjured up the first settlers and their descendants, who remain there, in the background. They are the 'original' Americans whom Pound wishes to protect against the monopolies. This is, then, the theme of the following Canto: 'Came KIEN, 40 years before "our revolution"' (LXI, p. 338), 'Encourage arts commerce an' farmin'' (LXII, p. 342).

At that point, only two pages after the last dynastic Canto, Pound's voice has acquired such a rhythmical momentum that its importance is multiplied: Pound, like a ventriloquist, speaks through Adams without our perceiving a real hiatus. The authority of the 'I', which compresses, selects, restrains, speeds up, beats different rhythms, interprets and mimes all the characters' voices, becomes then overwhelming, and I shall try to understand the general structure which makes this evolution necessary.

But the main difference in the traditional pictures of China and of the United States consists in the Chinese sense of reverence, not only for a hierarchy, but also for one's elders and superiors:

> Urbanity in externals, virtu in internals
> some in a high style for the rites
> some in humble;
> for Emperors; for the people
> all things are here brought to precisions   (LIX, p. 324)

The layering of voices has a social function; indeed it may reflect the division of society; and Pound's identification with the ideological basis of his 'source', Confucius, implies that what the *Chi-King* says is valid for his *Cantos*:

> That this book keep us in due bounds of office
> the norm
> show what we shd/take into action . . . .   (ibid.)

And yet, in these Cantos, ideology is more clearly revealed through the strategic domination of the subjective voice than by the presence of formed blocks of pre-given 'truths' which would intrude upon histori-cal narration in order to orient it. Chinese wisdom is, for instance, pronounced by authentic Chinese characters who replace it in the historical context; the general maxims are always backed by some voice situated in the Chronicle: 'Zinkwa observed that gold is inedible' (LVI, p. 303), or 'Said TAI-TSOU: KUNG is the master of emperors' (LV, p. 294). The Chronicle is indeed a compilation of successive utterances:

> Ruled SIUEN with his mind on the 'Gold Mirror' of
> TAI TSONG
> Wherein is written: In time of disturbance
> make use of all men, even scoundrels.

> In time of peace reject no man who is wise.
> HIEN said: no rest for an emperor. A little spark
>   lights a great deal of straw.   (p. 292)

Thus we see Chun Tchi commenting on the *Chi-King* (Canto LIX), or Lieu-yu-y organising a system of *ammassi* approved by the Emperor. The major exception is to be found in the case of Taï Tsong's *Notes on Conduct* already quoted, in which the 'keepin' up kulchur' shows that the utterance has shifted towards the idiomatic voice. However, at this point the selection becomes obvious, since Pound only retains rules 3, 5, 7, 10 and 11 from a whole series, bringing to the fore the maxims concerning the maintenance of unity in the Empire.

The 'wisdom' of Chinese emperors and Confucian ministers is thus conveyed by incremental repetition; little items are piled up and at times pasted together through the intervention of the American voice. While a classic representational ideology takes for granted a cultural universality which it then 'naturalises' and camouflages in general statements (the ideological blocks being disguised as descriptions or remarks on the 'eternal truths' of 'human character'[31]), in Pound's *Cantos* it is the universality of Nature which is given at the outset, and a sense of the natural order of language and institutions pervades the whole history. The position of the individual voice in this order is rather tricky, because it must appear both as an organic offshoot and as the constant pedagogical reminder of a *rappel à l'ordre*. This is probably why Pound cannot integrate the cornerstone of Confucian thought in his Chinese Chronicle, namely the *cheng ming* or principle of rectification of names. De Mailla's *Histoire* does not fail to expose it at length: the first maxim given by Confucius is the 'Cheng Ming'. When asked by King-Kong what good government means, Kung replies that it means that 'the master be master, and the subject, the subject; That the father be father, and the son, the son' ('Il consiste en ce que le maître, soit maître, & le sujet, sujet; que le père, soit père, & que le fils, soit fils' – *Histoire*, II, p. 201). And King-Kong comments, 'Nothing truer, said King-Kong; for if the master is not the master, the subject is not a subject; if the father is not the father, the son is not the son. Whatever riches one may possess besides, one cannot find any rest' (ibid.).

What is embodied here is a concept of order which cannot so easily fit into European ideologies; as Jacques Gernet explains, taking his cue from Xunzi's philosophical school, the link between 'the heaven' (*tian*) and Nature is so close that no prince can claim to *impose order*:

One of the best explanations of the theory of the 'Rectification of Names' (*zhengming* [= Pound's *cheng ming*]) can be found in the works of Xunzi. Arising from the circles of scribes and annalists who saw in the use of terms in conformity with ritual tradition the means of expressing a moral judgement, the theory of *zhengming* became the instrument of a new order based on merits and demerits. By labelling people, that is by granting titles and ranks, the prince produces order which guarantees the smooth running of the whole society. By so doing, he does not intervene in disputes, but simply sets up a mechanism which averts them because it is based on the consensus of all. . . . The prince does not give orders, he does not intervene directly, remaining completely impartial, he is the source and the guarantor of universal order.

The idea which seems in some way to underlie Western thought, that order is based on the power of constraint and individual authority, is no more in evidence in Xunzi than among other Chinese thinkers. Order which has its origins in the Chunqiu period in the whole of the ritual rules and the hierarchies of family cults is in Mencius the spontaneous result of the conduct of a prince called to become universal ruler, the effect of the virtue of the saint in Zhuangzi, the product of objective forces created by life in society for Xunzi or of general rules set up by the heads of State for Han Fei. The idea that order can only result from a spontaneous, almost organic, adjustment is found in the conception of the universe. No individualised power can command Nature, whose balance is guaranteed by the interaction of opposite and complementary forces and virtues, whose growth and decline is to be seen in the changing of the seasons.[32]

This general concept of a natural order explains Pound's daring innovations in stylistic discrepancy, and his timidity, even his subservience, in face of a text he quotes and uses as universal source. The wish to go beyond the opposition between knowledge and ignorance by the introduction of ritual and natural reverence has to be achieved through the hesitant introduction of a subjective voice which can nevertheless never assert itself fully; it only gives a sense of rhythmical scansion, showing that the path of Chinese history is as cyclical as the succession of the seasons, defining cycles of order and disorder. Since Confucius himself praised the return of Yao and Chun ('Yao and Chun have returned'/sang the farmers . . . ./'I am/"pro-Tcheou" said Confucius five centuries later./With his mind on this age' – Canto LIII,

p. 268), Pound can feel justified in attempting to give a sense of the return, if not of the gods, at least of the sound principles based on myth. A stylistic feature of these dynastic Cantos suggests that they have a circular pattern: the first two and the last two are the only ones to be headed 'Canto no.—' in the original version, while the remaining eight are numbered only.[33] The first two culminate on Confucius, while the last two praise the achievements of the Jesuits; the four intermediate Cantos (LIV–LVII) deal with the original chronicle proper, while the four concluding Cantos slow down the rhythm to deal with modern times.

LII LIII / LIV LV LVI LVII / LVIII LIX *LX LXI*

Confucius is opposed to Buddhists in LIV–LVII, to Christians in LVIII–LXI.

History is retrospective, dissolved in returns and restorations: this movement gives unity to the tedious montage of anecdotes, and provides a constant 'ideo-logical' wisdom. Moral analysis becomes the purpose of historical writing: Adams will confirm this later, 'IF moral analysis/be not the purpose of historical writing' (LXII, p. 346) – completely omitting the 'economical analysis' which was supposed to found it. For instance, Pound never mentions the T'ang emperors' creation of state – not bank – notes. These notes are often mentioned in Pound's prose writings (he dates the event either 'A.D. 840' or '856' – *SP*, pp. 260 and 313), but are not integrated into the history of the period (Canto LV). Likewise, French terms, Italian terms or Greek tags relate the histories to basic principles of language, economics and policy, while remaining outside the scope of the ritualisation of Chinese historiography. When King Wang changes the currency, the Greek quote from Aristotle serves as a warning:

> And King Wang thought to vary the currency
> μεταθεμένων τε τῶν χρωμένων
> > against council's opinion   (LIII, p. 273)

We are indeed, in keeping with Pound's fascination for cyclical voyages, embarked on a periplus:

> all order comes into such norm
> igitur meis encomiis, therefor this preface
> > CHUN TCHI anno undecesimo
> > > (a.d. 1655)

> periplum, not as land looks on a map
> but as sea bord seen by men sailing.   (LIX, p. 324)

The most arbitrary punning link ('anno' – Hanno's periplus of Canto XL) shows nevertheless how the dialectical progression of history can be made to fit a circular map, in a progression which can only be perceived from Pound's own moving and central perspective.

The increasing ritualisation of history, which ends by the pure assertion of recurring order – order as recurrence and recurrence as order – very uncritically mimes the historical movement by which Confucius has been sanctified, promoted to the rank of official sage, and invoked to conceal or initiate all the dynastic restorations in China. Pound does not attempt to dissociate Kung's teachings from more 'legalist' applications of his views by tyrannical emperors.[34] Kung, now master of rites, consecrates the ritual of history which only adores order, its 'totalitarian' nature ambiguously fusing a religious and agrarian concept with the new 'ideological' concept born in nineteenth-century Europe.

The legalist overthrows the literato, or rather annexes him, reducing the implications that could be drawn from the intertextual play to a few traces from other texts already written, to be translated in the new idiom. 'All order comes into such a norm': the ethical norm of Confucian morals now appears as written *for* the prince, from his point of view – since 'History is a school-book for Princes . . . .' The tension between truth and ideology, between intertextuality and the idiomatic voice comes from the fact that the discourse of order cannot help ordering around the other discourses, at the expense of the polyphonic play. One has to wait until the 'Pisan Cantos' to hear this polyphony again. The actual trauma of the incarceration brings about not just a redistribution of ideological positions, but another economy of the voices: the rapid shifts of tone, the discovery of a new kind of 'truth', through the unceasing dialogue with oneself and one's past, disentangle the tight net of codified discourses and restart the craftsman's main study, a study of the relationship between words and money, symbols and names. At that moment, the whole discourse about Confucian China, passing to the level of intertextual reference and constituting the dense textuality of the poet's memory itself, and being conveyed by a discontinuous and exploded texture of multiple allusions, functions in a richer and more economical way.

Then, and only then, can another *eidos* – on whose difference from the *eidos* of *ideology* I shall comment – come to the poet as a surprise, or indeed divine apparition:

> Saw but the eyes and stance between the eyes,
> colour, diastasis,
> > careless or unaware it had not the
> > whole tent's room
> nor was place for the full Ειδὼς   (LXXXI, p. 520)

Thus the ideological subject can meet his own signature in a new *ideogram*, which may even turn into an *idiogram*. [35]

3 Ezra Pound and Pecuchet: the Law of Quotation

> mens sine affectu
> > that law rules
> > that it be
> > > sine affectu. . . . (Canto LXII, p. 343)

In most studies of the sources used by an author, the attempt to retrace the way a novel or a poem works by reference to other texts seems radically misplaced: it generally appears as a game of pure scholarship, presupposing that the critic by definition knows more than the author, perhaps believing that he is in possession of more valid information than a writer who unwittingly refers to complicated documents; in more sympathetic cases, the critic assumes he can find a key to the hidden intentions of the author, to his unconscious even, if he exposes the creative project lurking behind his choice of literary models. His hermeneutic approach will attempt to understand the author better than he understood himself. But with Pound the picture changes, for the desire to go source-hunting, even with the somewhat perverse motivation of checking his poem against possible or necessary errors of transcription, is one of the most fundamental critical responses induced by the text. The problems of reference appear as the major issue, posing the twin problematic of the 'credit' which can be given to Pound and his text, and of the historical relevance of his *Cantos*.

I have shown that the poetic art of the *Cantos* tended to reduce itself, in the dynastic Cantos, to a montage of citations underwritten by a voice. However, these ten Cantos testify to an epic spirit, because the material is expanded to include a vast empire, spanning centuries, interwoven with illustrations, flashbacks and prophecies. In the second

106

part of the diptych, the sequence of poems literally turns into a series of quotations extracted from the ten volumes of the *Works* of John Adams. One cannot help being impressed by the strange self-abnegation of a poet who limits his role to the oral impersonation of some characters mentioned in American history. However, this process, far from betraying a lapse in creativity, systematises many principles elaborated during the work on the Chinese material, and finds an answer to the dilemma created by the interaction of voices and discourses within the ideogrammic montage.

Pound is playing the 'scissors-and-paste man', rather like Joyce, who once said, 'I am quite content to go down to posterity as a scissors and paste man for that seems to me a harsh but not unjust description.'[1] Joyce, whom Pound was the first to recognise as the true successor to Flaubert,[2] counted on securing his own immortality by setting generation after generation of scholars, researchers and professors on the tangled tracks of his encyclopaedic references: according to one famous quip, he wanted to keep the universities busy for more than 300 years. Pound's interest was no more aroused by this type of literary immortality than by that of the artist who remains divine and infallible, both transcending and immanent to his creation. Pound wished to burrow to the heart of a vortex of energies, through which to promote the constant renewal of the idioms, values and visions of the gods he advocates in his critical writings. Hence the 'Make It New' motto applies to politics and to literature, to cultural economy and to economic thought. This is why the *Cantos*, the logbook of an ever-shifting exploration, the depository of knowledge and techniques gleaned among Homeric heroes and Confucian emperors, presents such a formidable obstacle to our reading-habits; the sight of the blocks of quotations culled from obscure textbooks and heaped rather haphazardly on the page to form a superb erratic chaos is at times utterly bewildering.

Pound does not ask us to compete with him in erudition, nor does he attempt just to lead us towards the framework which will supply the text with its hidden key. He simply teaches us to read in a different way – where 'read' is an intransitive verb, possessing none of the transparency so often associated (by Pound himself) with the essential activity it connotes. I shall endeavour to map out the chart of such a reading, starting with the Adams Cantos, which follow on from the dynastic Cantos. We have seen how this chronicle spans several millennia and ends in 1735, a date which marks both the death of the Emperor Yong Tching and the birth of John Adams. The second panel of the diptych is devoted to the saga of John Adams, whose life will appear in its entirety as an exact counterpart of the whole history of the Chinese and Manchu dynasties.

The textual strategy is thus hardly able to remain the same, and Pound chooses in these ten Cantos to radicalise the principle of assembling quotations. The series of poems becomes literally a string of quotations, almost every word originating from the main source; according to F. K. Sanders, who edited Pound's original sources with the most useful commentary, 'nearly all of the more than 2500 lines that make up the "Adams Cantos" have a clearly recognizable source, identifiable by volume and page number, in the *Works* of John Adams'.[3] Hence the generally unfavourable reception of the sequence, exemplified by Leon Surette's wholesale rejection:

> In the Chinese and Adams cantos Pound seems to have forgotten what he was doing. It was his task to condense history so as to fit it into his poem. But the Adams cantos are not a condensation of the American revolution, nor of the career and life of John Adams. They are simply a condensation of the *Life and Works* of John Adams. The revolution and the man can indeed be found in those ten cantos, but they are not the true subject of the section as they ought to be. The true subject is that ten-volume edition which massively interposes itself between the reader of the *Cantos* and John Adams.[4]

Indeed, where is the 'subject' when one faces such a zeal for copying? How can Pound allow himself to be carried away by such compulsive repetition, by such relish for playing the understudy of Adams, that generally his additions are limited to vocal changes in the phrases he knits together, or short parenthetical statements to condense yet a little more his condensation? What ethics, what logics of communication are presupposed by such a procedure? And, above all, how should one set about recognising the separate units? Are the quotations broken up according to set rules, with attention to the individual word, or to the single volume? Is the principle underlying this dazzling montage to be found in the quirks or flights of fancy which unexpected connections reveal, or in a sterner ideological incitement?

Abbreviations

Pound's key word appears as early as the first of the Cantos:

19th March 1628
18th assistant whereof the said Thomas Adams
(abbreviated)
Merry Mount become Braintree, a plantation near Weston's
Capn Wollanston's became Merrymount.   (LXII, p. 341)

The lines are part of an evocation of John Adams's genealogy, which ends with the mention of the eighteen assistants to the Governor of the Company of Massachusetts Bay in New England, the last of whom was Thomas Adams. The *Works of John Adams* simply states: 'of whom Thomas Adams was the last' (*WJA*, I, p. 4). The original sentence read 'of whom'; Pound has deliberately given his verse a more 'original' ring than the original, inverting but slightly the order of items which follow. They refer to the naming of the town of Braintree and to Captain Wollaston, who began a plantation near Weston's (p. 4). This plantation changed its name from Mount Wollaston to Merry Mount. Pound's obviously enjoys the idea of quoting, even obliquely, the name of Weston, which is linked with the origins of his family, on his mother's side. But, besides this 'signature' hidden in the text, his intervention stops at the parenthesis, and at the selection of certain bits of sentences taken from a larger context. Thus, for instance, the date quoted does not refer to this legal decision, but belongs to the first deed of the Plymouth Council. The question is, then, to define the limits of each quotation so as to ascertain its meaning, while the operation at work is explicitly stated: *abbreviare*.

The abbreviation permits a powerful condensation of meaning and also facilitates maximum poetic impact. Pound has reminded his readers of the 'Dichten = Condensare' principle in the *ABC of Reading*, and he continues to do so throughout his work. Pound explained to his American publisher, who was not a little disturbed by the demands and audacities of the text, that he had no intention of writing a preface or an explanatory introduction. Nor was he prepared to annotate the poem: to annotate amounts to paraphrasing, for one either adds a commentary or one summarises to communicate the essence of the work. Now, these two approaches are impossible. On the one hand, one cannot summarise a text which is already a laconic *tour de force*: 'Nobody can summarize what is already condensed to the absolute limit.'[5] On the other hand, adding a glossary to a text would presuppose a metalanguage, whose function would be to specify, with the same latitude given to the subject who is rewriting the story. The Confucian ethics of communication lies, however, in opposition to such textual aids. Confucius identifies a good historian as one who only condenses history and adds nothing: 'Kung said he had added nothing' (note to Canto LXXXV, p. 559).

Compilation may authorise omissions, but not an overload: in Canto XIII, Confucius praises the historians of earlier times because they had left gaps for the things they as yet did not know; Aristotle only becomes a 'serious character' in the *Guide to Kulchur* when Pound notices that he had had the compilation of the constitutions of 158 cities carried out (*GK*, p. 342; see also Ch. 6 below). The self-denial of the chronicler, the discipline of the sage's utterance: are we moving towards the goal of Mallarmé's 'absolute poem', which entails 'la disparition élocutoire du poëte, qui cède l'initiative aux mots, par le heurt de leur inégalité mobilisés'?[6]

A new rigour reveals itself in the Adams Cantos, and one only needs to compare these ten Cantos (LXII–LXXI) with the *Eleven New Cantos* (published in 1934), which are contemporaneous with the essay *Jefferson and/or Mussolini* (written in 1933, published in 1935). In the first series, 'Jefferson – Nuevo Mondo', Pound seeks to provide a polyphonic interpretation of American history: he lays together extracts from the correspondence of Jefferson and Adams, which involves cross-references to the second group of Cantos, and he adds extracts from Van Buren and Jackson (see Cantos XXXI–XXXIV, XXXVII, XL and XLI). Their determination to create a 'new world', as well as a new culture and a new civilisation, is in opposition to the cultural decadence which, according to Pound, has followed on from the War of Secession; this war is in turn connected with the financial traffic of groups of corrupt politicians, such as those led by Hamilton, the supporter of the banks.

Pound's chronology implies a clear division between 'civilisation' and 'decadence', which falls into two periods of degradation: from 1760 to 1830 there still existed an American culture, which slowly died away between 1830 and 1860, during the conflicts between the 'people' and the bankers. The nadir was reached from 1870 to 1930; therefore Pound openly affirms his hope and belief that 1930 will mark a renewal, especially since the events in Italy can provide a relevant example for the United States. An American 'Renaissance' seems possible. In the Cantos of 1934, Adams is seen as only one of the founders of the American Republic, which Jefferson dominated by his encyclopaedic learning and his force of character. The question which Pound was wrestling with at the time was the following: what would Mussolini have done in Jefferson's position and vice-versa? The answer was that they would have behaved in exactly the same way. The composition, alternating letters from Jefferson, Adams and Van Buren, is further varied by quotations from Marx and the poem by Cavalcanti. But after the dynastic Cantos the function of montage alters fundamentally: it is no longer a question of projecting a multiple light across intersecting periods, but one of showing how Adams really stands out as the last of the great emperors, the founder of the one American dynasty.

Following the first American Cantos, two key ideas emerge, related to Adams's personality: that the revolution was not primarily of a military nature, but above all moral and political; and that the Battle of Lexington was but a symptom of a deeper evolution of thought. All the syndical groups, the associations and the corporations, were concerned with their own interests to the detriment of the community. So Adams seemed more conservative than Jefferson, with whom Pound's sympathies initially lay, for he provided more than anything a counterbalance in his experience and puritanism to Jefferson's generous enthusiasm and latent contradictions. And in Cantos LXII–LXXI Jefferson is curiously absent (he is directly referred to only fifteen times or so in almost ninety pages); he has already, in fact, been replaced by an all-too-real 'symbolic Father', Mussolini. Now, the essential difference between Adams and Jefferson comes not from their political divergence, but from their concepts of heredity, and the idea of the foundation of order.

Jefferson has perhaps left only ideas, too many ideas; Adams, as perceived by Pound between 1937 and 1939, had attempted to set up a dynasty, thereby selecting from among the new American ideas those which could be borne out by facts. This is only glimpsed in *Jefferson and/or Mussolini*:

> I mean to say T. J. had a feeling of responsibility and he knew other men who had it, it didn't occur to him that this type of man would die out.
>   John Adams believed in heredity. Jefferson left no sons. Adams left the only line of descendants who have steadily and without a break felt their responsibility and persistently participated in American government throughout its 160 years.   (p. 19)

The value of a man's thought is only attested by his putting these ideas into action: the principle is taken literally here, and implies that ideas have to be 'embodied', become flesh and word in an organic heritage.

Descent proves the validity of the origins. Pound does not remain as eulogistic on this point concerning the Adams family, since in a text dating from the war he questions its ability to keep the founder's virtue intact. It is worth noting that these reservations emerge at a time when Pound finally responds to Eliot's severe criticism in *After Strange Gods*, when he accused him of falling into modern heresy. For Eliot, Confucius has always been the philosopher of the 'Protestant' rebel in Anglo-Saxon countries: 'But Confucius has become the philosopher of the rebellious Protestant.'[7] Eliot cites Irving Babbitt, I. A. Richards and Pound. Heresy is opposed, in Eliot's thesis, to tradition; tradition is a matter of *unconscious* heritage going through generations, while orthodoxy or heterodoxy implies the exercise of 'conscious intelligence'.[8]

Pound replies by accusing Eliot in turn of Protestantism; he even insinuates that he may have been contaminated by the Jewish poison (which is involuntarily ironic, since *After Strange Gods* is one of Eliot's most outspoken testimonies of anti-semitism):

> It is amusing, after so many years, to find that my disagreement with Eliot is a religious disagreement, each of us accusing the other of Protestantism. . . . But what Eliot says about Confucius is nonsense, or nearly so. He has renounced America ever since the time of his first departure, but if he would consider the dynasty of the Adamses he would see that it was precisely because it lacked the Confucian law that this family lost the Celestial Decree. (*SP*, p. 291)

And Pound stresses the fact that the last heirs of the family are now 'anonymous officials, absolutely outside public life' (ibid.). The Celestial Decree refers to the Chinese concept of the legitimacy of a dynasty; when the Emperor became tyrannical, he lost his divine investiture, and it was right to overthrow him, as the *Chou King* set out to illustrate from concrete cases. We shall see how Brooks Adams himself, the author of *The Law of Civilization and Decay*, a work which Pound greatly valued at the same time as he was attacking Eliot, failed to understand the fundamentals of economics, and above all, failed to see himself as committed to putting his ideas into practice (see Ch. 5 below). Pound does not realise that there is a complete contradiction between the idea of the Celestial Decree or Mandate of Heaven, which consecrated a new ruler notwithstanding family relations, and the mystical possession of a 'law' by a family. It takes the elaboration of a whole system of symbolic economy to attempt to bridge this gap.

Heritage refers to an organic 'culture', since the main issue is 'issue' itself – that is to make things and people grow, to keep the ground free from weeds and other degenerations or miscegenations. Mussolini's subsequent drama is highlighted against the history of the Adamses, for he too was unable to form a dynasty, a physical and spiritual line, which explains Pound's bitterly sarcastic remarks about Ciano.[9] The question of the 'law' of the name and of a fair economic doctrine crops up again with the question of technique: how can one, with no additions and no commentary, present an organic tradition, which, by definition, must be complete? Pound has already begun tackling this problem in an introductory article calling the Jefferson–Adams Letters 'a Shrine and a Monument' (*SP*, pp. 117–28). The project of transmitting an organic *paideuma* immediately comes up against insurmountable difficulties, and it would seem that the technical difficulty and illegibility of the Adams Cantos correspond to this aspect of the problem: 'Two methods of turning in the evidence of the Adams letters are open. I could quote fragments and thereby be inadequate. The letters are printed. Or I could assert the implications, or at least the chief implications. The MAIN implication is that they stand for a life not split into bits (*SP*, p. 122).

How might one avoid the 'splitting into bits' aspect of collage if the most important consideration is to put across as vividly as possible the impression of totality and unity? The article in question opens with a reminder of the Frobenius project: that of defining the fundamental components of a culture or *paideuma* by an analysis of its 'monuments'. These 'monuments' are thus signs and symptoms at the same time; they function independently of the awareness of the subjects who produce them, but they manifest none the less a specific intention, an ideal goal. Now the burning question Pound poses – 'If we are a Nation why have we not kept our national culture?' – demands a complex solution. The poet as heir cannot keep any distance, any aesthetic aloofness – similar to that which is reproached in Eliot – with regard to his own culture. As inheritor, every utterance of his has to grow out from the true 'roots' of the *paideuma*, yet will inevitably reproduce, mimic even, the very uncertainties, hesitations and contradictions of his culture. In short, whenever he produces signs, he may expect them to be read as symptoms, and conversely. As the shrill bard of an aphasic culture or as the schizoid propagandist praising an allegedly totalitarian health he will have minimal room for manoeuvre. Hence the adoption of such a minimalist strategy.

The dynastic Cantos terminate by encompassing the Chronicle with a rhythm of mythical recurrences: this essentially conservative gesture was required to transmute the indefinite progression through wide spans of historical contingence into a meaningful epic yielding definite values. The paradigmatic opposition between order and chaos slowly becomes the only possible reading of the Chronicle, just as Confucian thought is contrasted with any Buddhist or mystic decadence. The new monument discovered by Pound in the *Works* of John Adams serves primarily as proof that at certain periods an American civilisation existed and was contained in a few privileged depositories. Adams henceforth is distinguished from Benjamin Franklin, who, for instance, 'had not integrity of the word' (*SP*, p. 118). Adams will thus be in charge of defining an organic doctrine, one that is coherent and totalitarian, and reveals itself in thousands of symptomatic gestures, in myriads of details which all cast light upon whatever in the total vision is not expressed by a metalanguage.

Order and unity in the quotations

The total vision possesses an intrinsic order which can radiate through all the splinters of paideumic blocks: such is Pound's thesis. But who or what gives coherence to this vision? Is it the man Adams, as hero and founder? Is it the sense of transcendent values? What does the unity of each block or Canto consist in? The issue of textual unity can be split into two major areas: every unit is a unity belonging to a larger whole, and is significant as such; the overall vision is generated by Adams as relived from within, re-enacted as it were, by the poet's voice.

It is first of all necessary to show that this unity is not determined by that of a given 'narrative' but derives from the subject at play in the text. Pound allows a certain ambiguity to persist there, since, when he writes to his publisher rejecting accompanying notes and explanations, he adds that he has only followed the chronological order: 'Plain narrative with chronological sequence.'[10] Like the ten dynastic Cantos, which are put together chronologically, the ten Adams Cantos appear to follow a chronology. An index provided by Pound as the unique concession to his publisher stresses the thematic logic and the historical progression. I shall examine these here, giving attention to the relevant dates, which I affix to Pound's list of themes treated in each Canto (p. 256).

1. 'JOHN ADAMS': general presentation of his life.
2. 'Writs of assistance': 1761.
3. 'Defence of Preston' (and the Boston massacre followed by the trial): 1770.
4. 'The Congress (Nomination of Washington)': 1775.
5. 'Voyage to France': 1778.
6. 'Saving the fisheries': 1778–82.
7. 'Plan of Government': 1780.
8. 'Recognition, loan from the Dutch, treaty with Holland': 1782.
9. 'London': 1785–7.
10. 'Avoidance of war with France': 1800.

From this table of contents, indeed, Pound's objective seems fulfilled: he has managed to transform the ten Cantos into a single narrative. But only a superficial examination would take these ten 'subjects' for the main theme of each Canto; and the pattern does not hold true if one compares each of the Cantos with the real contents, much as Pound has done with the Chinese Cantos. Then enormous discrepancies start appearing. (The page following the title or 'subject' is the one Pound uses in the contents.)

LXII (pp. 341–50)	'John Adams' (p. 341)
LXIII (pp. 351–4)	'Writs of assistance' (p. 354)
LXIV (pp. 355–62)	'Defence of Preston' (p. 359)
	'Congress' (p. 364)
LXV (pp. 363–79)	'Voyage to France' (p. 371)
	'Saving the fisheries' (p. 377)
LXVI (pp. 380–6)	?
LXVII (pp. 387–94)	'Plan of Government' (p. 392)
LXVIII (pp. 395–402)	'Recognition, loan . . . , treaty . . .'
LXIX (pp. 403–8)	(pp. 400–5)
LXX (pp. 409–13)	'London' (p. 412)
LXXI (pp. 414–21)	'Avoidance of war with France' (p. 418)

The chronological order seems to hold for the first and last Cantos, if one works from Pound's classification. The themes do no wholly follow the division into Cantos, but it is still possible to see an ordered chronicle, with a beginning (c. 1760) and an end (c. 1800). But in the Cantos themselves, as the reader encounters them, the texture is more chaotic than Pound would wish to suggest.

Each theme is taken up several times, implying that the index tries to impose an arbitrary chronological order. For, if we reread the Adams Cantos looking only at the dates Pound mentions, we can see that from Canto LXVI (the fifth in the series) onwards, the notion of a chronological order wears thin. Up till then, Pound only gives dates which follow on.

LXII   1628, 1735, 1770, 1774, 1782, 1795, 1796, 1854, 1938 (this Canto traces the genesis of the dynasty and extends to the spiritual descendant at Rapallo)
LXIII   1801, 1825, then 1758, 1760 (chronological order is already interrupted, but Pound clearly explains that he is moving backwards)
LXIV   1752, 1768–9, 1769, 1771, 1773, 1767–9
LXV   1775, 1777, 1804 (the year when Adams starts his auto-biography, not of the events mentioned), 1780, 1782, 1783
LXVI   1783, 1768 (with Adams's *Dissertation*, p. 402), 1768, 1772
LXVII   1773, 1754, 1819, 1814, 1787

Then the order of the dates become really confused. And it goes without saying that the confusion would have been much greater if Pound had given each time the exact date of the letter quoted or of the historical event referred to. Thus, despite an appearance which Pound tries to preserve, the unity of each Canto is neither thematic nor chronological. History is grasped as a series of concentric eddies which discloses its real source: a book.

Each Canto is a collection of quotations and Pound's aim is for the reader to experience each quotation as an adventure or as a piece of music. The Adams Cantos are of varying lengths, ranging from the nineteen pages of Canto LXV to the four of Canto LXIII. The first one introduces Adams and gives a summary of all the themes which are later developed: it is thus analogous to an overture in music, a procedure which has already been used in the Chinese Cantos. For this introduction, Pound relies solely on the first volume of Adams's *Works*, which consists of his biography written by Charles Francis Adams, using fragments from an intended biography by John Quincy Adams. He ends this Canto on the opposition declared between Adams and Hamilton: good and evil, justice and corruption come face to face to establish one axis of American history.

Pound has not yet begun giving references, when on the second page of the second Canto, one finds:

Vol. Two (as the protagonist saw it:)
       No books, no time, no friends
Not a new idea all this week   (LXIII, p. 352)

This follows on directly from:

      friends, sectaries,
Eripuit caelo fulmen
and all that to ditch a poor man fresh from the country

Pound clearly indicates that he is passing from volume I to volume II of the *Works*, the Latin quotation stemming from the appendix to the first volume and referring to Benjamin Franklin and Turgot, who exchange revolutionary mottoes and make fun of the young Adams, who is too upright to accept involvement in their plans. The contrasted motif of 'friends' and 'no friends' mixes two historical periods, the first referring to Franklin (1811) and the second to John Adams in his youth and early manhood (1757). Thus Pound underlines the solitude of his hero, who refuses to compromise once he is in France – a solitude which is nourished by his autodidactic energy in learning. When twenty-one, Adams stated his desires and ambitions: 'I long to be a master of Greek and Latin. I long to prosecute the mathematical and philosophical sciences . . .' (*Diary*, 24 Apr 1756, *WJA*, II, p. 13). Pound decides to show these intellectual ambitions in action, and dramatises the position of his 'protagonist' who is both 'actor' and 'author' of the quoted fragments. Quotation as such presents Adams as the protagonist in a play of which Pound would be the director, and at least arranges the material in a striking way (he refuses to have his second Canto start with the early autobiographical material, but links this with the rest of Adams's career as President). There is a constant superimposing of times and roles, so that, while the reader can never forget the historical importance of Adams, he can follow his progress and especially find his own reading-activity mirrored in that of the 'protagonist'.

For this Canto introduces us to Adams's own readings, and reading is a preparation for his future activity (the 'theme' indicated in Pound's table, the 'Writs of assistance', only takes up the last six lines). Pound presents Adams at a time when he is giving himself a culture, quoting Scott, Byron, Mrs Savil's *Ars Amandi* and Shakespearean plays – all this starting from the sad avowal of 'no books'. Indeed, we see that for

Adams, as for Pound, reading is an intense activity which makes man a complete being:

> Exercises my lungs, revives my spirits opens my pores
> reading Tully on Cataline quickens my circulation
> . . .
> Read one book an hour
>   then dine, smoke, cut wood
> . . .
> read Timon of Athens, the manhater
>   must be (IRA must be) aroused ere the mind be at its best
>   (LXIII, p. 353)

This Canto presents in a remarkable fashion both the early seeds of culture which will remain active throughout Adams's career and the constant beliefs concerning ethics and politics:

> Scott's fictions and even the vigorous and exaggerated
> poetry of Ld/ Byron
>   when they wd/ not read him anything else
> property EQUAL'D land in J. A.'s disposition   (p. 351)

The judgements do not come from Pound, but he has chosen to juxtapose the slightly old-fashioned taste of Adams with his agrarian bias: a whole ideology, which both appeals to Pound (his connection with the Physiocrats needs no further emphasis) and has a conservative ring, is thus depicted in minimum space.

Adams is presented in his attempts to give himself 'a language to think in' and a general method to rule his life:

>   . . . Gridley
> enquired my method of study
> and gave me Reeve's advice to his nephew
> read a letter he wrote to Judge Leighton: follow the study
>   rather than the gain of law, but the gain
> enough to keep out the briars, . . .
>
> you must conquer the INSTITUTES
> and I began with Coke upon Littleton
>   greek mere matter of curiosity (in the law)
>   (LXIII, p. 352)

Pound does not yet realise the full significance of Coke's *Institutes*, but only after 'Rock-Drill' returns to this major reference in the later Cantos, following the lead given by Adams several decades earlier. The slightly ambiguous dismissal of Greek law acquires a deeper significance when Pound begins emphasising the fundamental importance of *curiosity*: this is what facilitates his reading of the Byzantine laws or of the Chinese Edicts in 'Rock-Drill' and 'Thrones'.

The logic of discourse and montage is dependent on the chronicle of the reading itself, which intensifies the slightly unsynchronised parallel between the author and protagonist, Pound and Adams. There is no longer a division between the poet who picks out certain phrases and notes, and the man of action whose exploits are being recounted. The chronology of the reading itself acquires as much importance as that of the events, with Pound placing his own dating of events alongside that of Adams. He dates his condemnation of Hamilton as the arch-fiend of American history from 11 January 1938 (Canto LXII, p. 350), and amuses himself with the parallel between the fact that Adams at one point kept night vigils with several senators and his own late night readings of the *Works*, which have to stop somewhere:

> Says Gridley: You keep very late hours!
> > End of this Canto.
> > > (LXIV, p. 362)

As soon as the quotations are referred back to the volumes themselves in a direct way, Pound feels able to proceed much faster, quoting references by page number only, as with

> > alum   (p. 432)
> Suppose yr/ladyship has been in the twitters
>
> > > > I
>
> oated at the Red Lion   (LXV, p. 365)

During a visit to Brookfield, Adams was shown how alum was produced from a stone they had there. The cryptic allusion to the product should by itself immediately trigger the reader's curiosity, and, reverberating across the *Cantos*, bring him back to the lines devoted to the papal alum mines in the third Malatesta Canto: 'And they struck alum at Tolfa, in the pope's land,/To pay for their devilment' (X, p. 46). This unexpected source of riches for Pope Pius II may find its equivalent in America, if an enlightened ruler is interested. The text incites the reader to be possessed by a similar unflagging curiosity whose scope knows no bounds, relating microcosmic details to the wider scheme of the universe. In this way, the opposition between division and totality acquires a methodological function, and Adams can rightly state (in a political context, but with the metaphysical perspective in mind), 'I am *totis viribus* / against any division' (LXXI, p. 415). He refuses all threats to the American Union, and attests the spirit of independence and resistance.

The struggle against division suggests a work which tunnels into its sources and stimulates at the same time a reading in action, as well as an action rooted in a reading. Knots of meaning draw together the divergent strands on the surface studded with thousands of precise details. For example, Pound refers to a visit T. S. Eliot made to Rapallo, which he inserts into his text because of another semantic coincidence. For the *Diary* mentions a visit from the Duke de la Rochefoucauld to Adams in Paris, to obtain some explanations of the Connecticut Constitution, and this becomes mixed with a poem by Lady Lucan copied in Adams's *Diary* a page before this. Pound then executes an astonishing piece of montage:

> Nor where who sows the corn by corn is fed
> (Lady Lucan's verses on Ireland)
> > The Duke de la Rochefoucauld
> made me a visit
> (Lady Lucan's verses on Ireland)
> made me a visit
> > and desired me to explain to him some
> passages in the Connecticut constitution
> > (at which point Mr Eliot left us)
>
> > > > (LXVI, p. 378)

Eliot's visit can, in a rather oblique fashion, be taken as having the same function as de la Rochefoucauld's, since both have come to ask for technical explanations in areas where both Pound and Adams have a certain competence. The reference to the verse is repeated to suggest a more poetic medium in the presentation, while Pound selects the line which fits in with his economic creed and omits the conclusion going in a different sense: 'Open our ports at once, with generous minds, / Let commerce be as free as waves and winds' (*WJA*, III, p. 351). These passages suffice to prove how strongly Pound wants to achieve the superimposition of his own reading-experience upon the multifarious experiences of John Adams.

Readers may grow a touch suspicious, for they may rapidly attempt to locate the sources of each Canto in each of the ten volumes of the *Works*, allowing for minor overlappings only. However, Pound's mode of quotation and of presentation is not mechanical at all, and the correspondence between the number of Cantos and the number of volumes quoted is purely a matter of chance. For example, Pound does not use the fifth volume of the *Works* at all (which contains one part of Adams's *Defense of the Constitutions*). I shall briefly compare the *Cantos* and the volumes quoted by Pound:

LXII   *WJA*, I, pp. vi–578 (Introduction and *Biography*)

LXIII   *WJA*, I, p. 583–II, p. 124 (autobiographical writings, and travels and negotiations)

LXIV   *WJA*, II, pp. 129–331 (political writings)

LXV   *WJA*, II, p. 332–III, p. 380 (idem)

LXVI   *WJA*, III, pp. 381–539 (idem)

LXVII   *WJA*, III, p. 540–IV, p. 381 (idem)

LXVIII   *WJA*, IV, p. 383–VII, p. 348 (this Canto uses vol. IV, omits vol. V, moves on to vol. VI for a page – p. 416 – and then uses the letters of vol. VII)

LXIX   *WJA*, VII, p. 348–IX, p. 573 (this Canto ends with the notes condensing different passages from the official correspondence and Pound settles his score with Hamilton)

LXX   *WJA*, IX, p. 573–same (this Canto uses letters from vol. IX, extracts of papers from vol. VIII, beginning and ending with the same letter, though not the same words)

LXXI   *WJA*, IX p. 588–X, p. 376 (private correspondence)

As can be seen, Pound generally moves from one volume to another in the middle of a Canto, while often taking up his notes from the same page, or even the same line, which has the effect of linking Cantos LXIV, LXV and LXVI, for instance.

The question of unity within a Canto paradoxically does not refer to anything outside the Canto, when they are made up only of direct quotations. Their unity stems from the drama of reading, through which we picture the adventures of an American subject grappling with the history of the origins of his country and, in the writings of a symbolic founding 'Father', trying to discover the source of subsequent degeneration and the remedy for it. However, the unity of these

Cantos does not derive from an 'internal' or formal principle. One can discern circular Cantos, such as Canto LXX, which opens and closes with quotations from the same letter from Adams to John Trumbull (23 January 1791).

> 'My situation almost the only one in the world
> where firmness and patience are useless'
> J. A. vice president and president of the senate 1791
> (p. 409)

The end of the Canto links this letter to two others (*WJA*, IX, pp. 569 and 571), addressed to Brand-Hollis, in which the common feature is the use of Latin phrases:

> DUM SPIRO
> nec lupo committere agnum
> so they are against any rational theory
> DUM SPIRO AMO   (p. 413)

Pound transforms the classical tag used by Adams at the end of his letter (*'dum spiro* etc.') into a complex blending of rational theory and of love. Adams speaks of efforts to build a theory of government, but by removing the sentence out of its context Pound highlights Adams's double-edged preoccupations, for he affirms his rationality and a sense of ethics which finds expression in this invocation to an omnipotent love; in this, Adams closely resembles Dante.

But the majority of the Cantos in this series are 'open', which does not mean that they are linear, since they all contain cross-references to different parts of the *Cantos* and to other periods of history. The forms cannot be said to alternate systematically. The unity of a Canto comes from the writing hand which decides upon certain notes rather than others, working at times in minute detail, at times limiting its action to the relatively random culling of expressive items. But through this diversity of form a logic is created, which comes from the way Pound's voice intervenes in the text, transforming as it were the pure shorthand notes into a more symphonic longhand.

Pound's voices and the quotations

As with the dynastic Cantos, Pound's voice comes into play whenever allusions to a current historical situation are to be emphasised, or when a main idea needs to be stressed. The style then becomes more spoken, more American, even slangy. The voice lets itself slide into this dialectical process of reading/writing, as if from time to time to release certain affects or drives which have been repressed for too long by the Confucian ethic which insists, 'let nothing be added'. It is not coincidental that the vocal additions take on parodic inflections. The pulsions – now violent, now irresistibly comic – are used in conjunction with the mimicry of accents, just as the Boston Massacre is related in a pastiche of a Boston accent:

> so about 9 o'c in the morning Lard Narf wuz bein' impassible
> was a light fall of snow in Bastun, in King St.
> . . .
> so Capn Preston etc/
> lower order with billets of wood and 'just roving'
> force in fact of a right sez Chawles Fwancis
> > at same time, and in Louses of Parleymoot...
> so fatal a precision of aim,
> > sojers aiming??

> > > (LXII, p. 342)

The original simply said, 'At about nine o'clock of the night on which Lord North declares himself impassible to menace . . .' (*WJA*, I, p. 97). Pound's more 'popular' voice becomes a weird mimicry of the movements of the crowd on the point of insurrection, and modulates into Charles Francis Adams's own educated and hyper-refined accent when he condescendingly dismisses the crowd as men 'of the lower order of town's people' (p. 98). But, when John Adams has agreed to defend the British soldiers and Captain Preston, and proposes that they should not be hanged and should receive a fair trial, Pound transcribes this peroration into a strange idiom which sounds like his own:

> Gent standing in his own doorway got 2 balls in the arm
> and five deaders 'never Cadmus...' etc
> > was more pregnant
> patriots need legal advisor
> > measures involvin' pro-fessional knowl-edge
> BE IT ENACTED / guv-nor council an' house of assembly
> > (Blaydon objectin' to form ov these doggymints)

Encourage arts commerce an' farmin'
. . .
till then let us try cases by law IF by
                snowballs oystershells cinders
                was provocation
                reply was then manslaughter only
in consideration of endocrine human emotions
unuprootable, that is, human emotions –
                merely manslaughter
                brand 'em in hand
but not hang 'em being mere human blighters
                common men like the rest of us
                subjekk to
                                passions
                                        (LXII, pp. 342–3)

The increasing number of 'etc.s' does not show impatience or
off-handedness; on the contrary, what is rapidly sketched here is the
rest of the *Cantos* as mythical memory which can be added to this
specific instance of discourse. Although Adams (Charles Francis)
develops the momentous backlash of such a trifling incident, he
indulges in hackneyed rhetorical formulas: 'The drops of blood then
shed in Boston were like the dragon's teeth of ancient fable – the seeds,
from which spring up the multitudes who would recognize no
arbitration but the deadly one of the battle-field' (*WJA*, I, p. 99). Pound
deflates this image and condenses it into a single reference to his own
poem: 'I sailed never with Cadmus, / lifted never stone above stone'
(Canto XXVII, p. 132). The five unhappy martyrs of Boston file into the
rank of the 'tovarisches' who labour for nothing, and have let
themselves be deprived of the gains of their 'revolution'.

In the same way, John Adams's defence speech is rendered faithfully
in its content (John Adams explains that, if the assault against the
British soldiers was not so serious as to endanger their lives, the
missiles received were a 'provocation, for which the law reduces the
offence of killing down to manslaughter, in consideration of those
passions in our nature which cannot be eradicated' (*WJA*, I, p. 113),
but gains a bantering tone and an idiomatic simplicity of expression
('endocrine', 'mere human blighters' are Pound's transposed terms)
which underlines the universality of these 'passions', shows Adams's
humanity, and above all manages to reconcile the theme of an abstract
law with the basic feeling of pity for human beings.

Pound's voice both cuts through the quoted text's initial rhetoric and amplifies the motives by placing them in a wider context. If the allusion to Colonel Bladen is far from clear to anyone who has no source-book beside his *Cantos* (Pound refers to the opening sentence used in court, which Colonel Bladen judged restrictive to the King's authority, and which was later reinstated by the House of Representatives at the initiative of John Adams), we realise that Adams's competence is not only grounded on technical expertise, but also includes wider concerns, 'arts commerce and farming'. The overall humanity of Adams already bears the stamp of political prudence, for he needs to reassure international opinion by appearing as an arbitrator rising above the crowd's desire for vengeance, and this in turn denotes the grandeur of his ultimate designs.

Now this considerably more idiomatic accent is not arbitrary here, for the 'subjekk to/ passions' echoes another 'subject to passions', pronounced in Canto xxxvii by Martin Van Buren with reference to the High Judges of the Supreme Court:

> High judges? Are, I suppose, subject to passions
> as have affected other great and good men, also
> subject to esprit de corps.   (p. 181)

The expression 'subject to passions' is coined by Pound in condensing two clauses of Van Buren's ('are subject to the same infirmities, influenced by the same passions'), and, by an unexpected felicity of language, the suspicion that supreme judges may not be impartial is here used to defend common soldiers and to highlight Adams's supreme impartiality!

Adams is thus defined as possessed by a higher kind of passion, the passion for justice, which becomes identical with a Dantescan *Amor*. This is why he can represent the apex of individuality and reconcile subjectivity with law. This is the ideal towards which Pound himself strives. Adams is aware of his passions, but transcends them, for he symbolises both an impersonal memory and the acme of volition aiming at order and beauty. This is why Cavalcanti's 'Donna mi Pregha' can be fused into his efforts at expression:

> *in quella parte*
> *dove sta memora*, Colonel Chandler not conscious
> these crude thoughts and expressions
> are catched up and treasured as proof of his character.

. . .
read Timon of Athens, the manhater
          must be (IRA must be) aroused ere the mind be at its best
la qual manda fuoco   (LXIII, p. 353)

Adams knows the significance of words (and this is why Pound adds
the *cheng² ming⁴* three times to his remarks) and is aware that speech
has a symptomatic nature: he knows what a 'character' means, both as
verbal expression and as imprint on his audience. He links words and
utterances as well as words and things. As impassioned memory of
laws, constitutions and history, he belongs to the memory of the
Cantos, and is grafted onto it without effort. He alone can reconcile
Confucius and Cavalcanti (or Dante) for he relates moral judgement
to the creation of the new republic:

          most accurate judgment
                    about the real constitution
          which is not of wind and weather
                    what is said there
          is rather a character
                    than a true

 ching
          ming

          definition. It is a just observation.   (LXVI, p. 382)

Adams is at this point meditating on the difficulty of exactly defining
the Constitution, which cannot consist only in the power of Parliament,
or in the role of the High Judges, or in a combination of elements: 'This
[last attempt at a definition] is rather a character of the constitution
and a just observation concerning it, than a regular definition of it . . .'
(*WJA*, III, p. 477). This is proof of a singular intellectual rectitude, and
shows a demanding and inquisitive spirit. The foundation cannot be
reduced to a technical device, although it requires the technical skill of
an encyclopaedic mind to approach it:

          foundation of every government in some principle
          or passion of the people
                    ma che si sente dicho
          Locke Milton Nedham Neville Burnet and Hoadly
          empire of laws not of men   (LXVII, p. 391)

The interpolation of the phrase from Cavalcanti's love-poem 'Non razionale / mà che si sente dicho', which Pound translates as 'Not by the reason, but 'tis felt, I say' (*LE*, p. 156; and Canto XXXVI, p. 178) comes strategically between apparently irreconcilable statements, both made by Adams on the same page: that the Constitution must be founded on some passion, a nobler one, he hopes, than fear; that the right definition of a republic is 'an empire of laws, and not of men' (*WJA*, IV, p. 194). It is thus quite fitting that only a strong assertion of the speaking voice – *'dicho'*, I say – should unite Cavalcanti, Adams and Pound in the same movement tending towards the full recognition of passion and the acknowledgment of the rule of law.

At times, indeed, the passion which animates Adams is pushed to a higher pitch by Pound's own voice. It is, for instance, no coincidence that the Boston Massacre passage is announced by a reference to Rapallo, hence to the poet's position as an utterer ('Boston about the size of Rapallo' – LXII, p. 342). This recurs in an even more violent mode at the end of the same Canto:

> wont to give to his conversation
> full impetus of vehement will,
> charged course of Ham and his satellites
> to disappointment that they hadn't
> got us entangled with Britain
> defensive and offensive
> Snot, Bott, Cott left over from
> Washington's cabinet
> and as for Hamilton
> we may take it (my authority, ego scriptor cantilenae)
> that he was the Prime snot in ALL American history
> (11th Jan. 1938, from Rapallo)   (p. 350)

The rhetoric of insult distorts proper names (if 'Cott' is probably Oliver Wolcott, a close collaborator of Hamilton's, who are 'Snot' and 'Bott'?[11]) and gathers speed until it devours Hamilton, renamed 'snot' to show he sums up the defects of the three accomplices. This acceleration of rhythm permits the equally passionate words of encouragement 'ARRIBA ADAMS' (bottom of p. 350). The Spanish expression comes, no doubt, from the proximity of the war in Spain.

In the *Biography*, Adams is simply depicted as unfailingly hostile to Hamilton, able to slip into passionate ways of expression when he was not speaking in public ('Then it was, that he would give to his language the full *impress* of his vehement will' – *WJA*, I, p. 578; Pound has significantly changed *'impress'* into 'impetus', which is in keeping with his practice). The same relationship exists between the public and the private man Adams as between Pound, the chronicler, and Pound, the moralistic commentator. When he comes to sign his own name, to handle his pet themes in his own voice, Pound reduces Adams to the role of a megaphone, manipulating as he will the puppets of this American morality play which opposes the good guys and the bad guys of history. It is at this point that Pound derives maximum enjoyment, rediscovering the Dantean tones of his Hell Cantos XIV and XV:

> In this matter of redeeming certificates
> > that were used payin' the sojers
> > > vignette *in margine*
> > > King, Sam Johnson of N. Carolina
> > > Smith (W.) S. Carolina, Wadsworth (Jeremiah
> > > J. Lawrence, Bingham, Carrol of Carrolton
> > > gone piss-rotten for Hamilton
> > > Cabot, Fisher Ames, Thomas Willing
> > > Robt Morris, Sedgwick
> > > > > *natural burella*
> > > squad of the pink-haired snot
> > > traitors blacker then Arnold
> > > > blacker than Bancroft
> > > *per l'argine sinistra dienno volta*
> > > behind that mask Mr Schuyler (Filippo)
> > > these the betrayers, these the sifilides
> > > advance guard of hell's oiliness
> > > in their progeny no repentence
> *quindi Cassio, Cassio membruto*
>
> > > > > > > (LXIX, p. 407)

The voice which brings to bear the vehemence of violent passions, either love or hate, on the quotations it selects and pushes forward in such an 'impetus' needs at times a space of its own: this is the function of such vignettes 'in the margin', marginal landscapes of execration or even excretion, before reaching paradisiac visions. In a well-chosen gap between two quotations, Pound's voice allows itself an incursion and an improvisation, and indulges in slightly hysterical comments which use the shriller note of the frontier idiom:

ov the 64 members ov the House of reppyzentativs
        29 were security holders.
                lappin cream that is, and takin it
off of the veterans.
                an' Mr Madison's move wuz DEE-feated.
Maclay and Jim Jackson stood out against dirtiness'
                                        (LXIX, p. 408)

The linguistic plays are dominated by this scale of values, which is at times directly stated by Pound. For the sake of condensing, texts quoted are torn away from their contexts and find another context defined by the memory of the *Cantos*. Thus the intertextual play and the ideological impact tend toward the same organisation of meaning: its absolute centre is a subject fighting against his division and his contradictions, trying to untangle a complex system of historical signs.

'Le personnel manque'

The essence of Pound's strategy is not exhausted by the previous example, and, indeed, it does not generally consist in affirming straightforward meanings on the surface. Meaning is constantly felt to be wanting, and is only provided for the reader who agrees to identify with the text, to decipher its gaps and blank spaces. The reading-act of the reader has to be superimposed onto the reading–writing act of the poet; we have to embed ourselves in the notes included by Pound, to read again and again this strangely punctuated string of pulverised unities, and only gain access to a full meaning when our deciphering pierces through the poet's enunciation. One of the first consequences of this process consists in the disappearance of personal pronouns.

Pound often seems, in his American chronicle, only to mention historical events and never to describe the participants. Of course, he cannot encumber his texts with all the proper names cited by Adams. But one encounters passages as perplexing as the following:

Mrs Rops, fine woman	1
very pretty and very genteel	2
Tells old stories of withcraft, paper money and	3
Governor Belcher's administration	4
Always convinced that the liberties of the country	5
had more to fear from one man (Hutchinson)	6

> than from all other men whatsoever   7
> which have always freely and decently uttered   8
> Rich seldom remarkable for modesty, ingenuity or humanity   9
> (LXIV, p. 361)

Is not this the portrait of a beautiful woman according to Pound's criteria? Beautiful, cultivated, ready to tell ghost stories or political anecdotes, sharing Adams's ideas on finance, and also bearing an incomprehensible grudge against a certain Hutchinson? But is she convinced of this, or is it Hutchinson who expresses a belief similar to Adams's to 'I, the few'? If, and only if, one checks the source, one discovers that only lines 1 and 2 are concerned with her; the others describe a certain Colonel Pickman, who is not named here at all, with John and Samuel Adams speaking again in lines 5–9, criticising Hutchinson, then the rich. The ambiguity of the parenthesis with a proper name is total, for it is Pound's habit to associate the subject or agent of certain actions or phrases in a parenthesis which follows on from the reference: ' "America" (Wythe) will hardly live without trade' (LXV, p. 367); or,

> He (Adet) announced to the President the entire
>   annihilation of factions in France (18 June '95)
> He (Jay) returned yesterday to N. York   (LXII, p. 348)

But even more frequently the real subject is not discernible from what Pound quotes. When one comes across

> So there is no drop not American in me
> Aye we have noticed that said the Ambassador
> Sends to Morocco no marine stores
> sends 'em *glaces* and other things of rich value
> Said Lord Carmathen wd/ present me
> but that I shd/ do business with Mr Pitt very often
> (LXVI, p. 380)

only the word *glaces* gives some sort of indication: the French Ambassador speaks to Adams of the policy of the King of France, and this is relayed by the Duke of Dorset, who mentions Lord Carmarthen (misspelt by Pound). The form of the *Diary* allows for such a rapid succession of different speaking subjects, but more often than not one is tempted to believe that, whenever there is a doubt, it must be Adams who is speaking. This is not even true in the majority of instances: ambiguity remains the order of the day. In the passage which presents Routledge, the hesitation may well be intended:

> no word, orationem, probably not elegantissimam
> > Routledge was elegant
> 'said nothing not hackneyed six months before'
> > wrote J. A. to his wife
> I said nothing etc/ letter to Chase from John Adams
> > > (LXII, p. 345)

What matters for Pound in that case is to create the 'binding matter' needed by the self-referencing of the *Cantos*, so as to refer back to Malatesta, who was even admired by his arch-enemy, the pope Pius:

> I mean after Pio had said, or at least Pio says that he
> Said that this was elegant oratory *'Orationem*
> *Elegantissimam et ornatissimam* (x, p. 45)

The subject and addressee are not so clear, but does it really matter whether it is Adams or Routledge who is felt to be a bad orator? Pound has probably inserted 'wrote J. A. to his wife' by mistake, since it is only in a letter to Chase that Adams declares that he felt the debate, in which the very brilliant Routledge was on the opposite side, had been a waste of time, 'for that nothing had been said which had not been hackneyed in that room for six months before' (*WJA*, I, p. 229). It would have been logical to assume that this elegant adversary, Routledge, only mouthed banalities, whereas what finally stands out is the impression that Adams made on the public, which indeed corresponds to the facts and not exactly to the quotations in the original.

The verbs whose subject it is impossible to decipher are numerous; and, even for Adams, the 'I' of the autobiography or letters and diaries alternates with the 'he' in the biography, in newspaper-articles or in correspondence. For instance, the text moves from 'His literary connections sans which was no opening' to 'in fact one bookseller said to me', which then leads to several subjectless verbs, as in 'Found archery still being practiced' (Canto LXII, pp. 346–7). Pound seems aware of this constant ellipsis of the subject, and no doubt expresses this in:

'mope, I muse, I ruminate' *le*
personnel manque we have not men for the times   (p. 344)

It is striking that in the line where the first 'I' is missing, Pound should add a 'le' in French, which creates a strange enjambement. The oblique hint at an earlier passage in the *Cantos* – 'and here the placard EIKΩN ΓΗΣ,/ and here: THE PERSONNEL CHANGES' (XIV, p. 62) – allows him to translate into French Adams's desultory remark 'We have not fit men for the times' (*WJA*, I, p. 148) and at the same time to add another meaning. For in French 'le personnel manque' refers as well to the lack of the personal pronoun.

The personal pronoun is missed out then, and the grammatical subject is lost; this is a loss which can only be compensated for by the introduction of a strong subject, of the reader who gradually pieces together the salient details under the direction of the Poundian *ego scriptor*. Reading then turns into a drama, quotation into a performance, and reference into a complex act of homage. The technique of abbreviation has found its precise focus: what is left out is the grammatical subject, the last trace of enunciation in the statement; but, as this lack is represented, or even duly notified, to the reader, the reader may now appear as a subject, provide his own missing links, and at times opt for a solution which Pound had not expected. The construction of the American monument is inseparable from the potential deconstruction of the speaking subject – in the name of America!

The first problem the disappearance of an explicit subject raises is deciding with which word a quotation will start and finish. Sometimes there is collage within the same line, and without recourse to the original text the reader does not know to whom roles should be attributed. When one reads,

17th of September:
America will support Massachusetts
'that nation
now avows bribery to be part of her system'
Mr Henry, American legislature   (LXV, p. 364)

the lines provide units of complete meaning which have to fight for their attribution; one cannot be certain how they should be linked up. The logical inference one draws from such parataxis is that America has a corrupt system. But in fact it is Great Britain which is intended, and the well-trained reader will have grasped it on the force of Pound's mental associations: only Britain could have a corrupt system at that time!

The reader quickly learns to develop this kind of reflex and to propel himself into a world of values which will allow the decoding to take place. If the reader refuses these values, he is disqualified. Once his curiosity has been aroused, he reaches the conclusion that in its succession of events, as well as in its deeper causes, history affords such a multiplicity of perspectives centred around a single polarisation. But, thanks to the free play of the reader's invention, which may at will fill certain gaps and not others, history is never closed to whatever the ideology retains of an oversimplification, for, like a text, it opens itself to an infinity of rereadings.

Pound 'cuts' into in quotations to such an extent that the historical context of a given period seems to evaporate, and in this way he believes that he has found a universal truth based on the American experience of a 'symbolic father':

> pater patriae
> the man who at certain points
> made us
> at certain points
> saved us
> by fairness, honesty and straight moving
> ARRIBA ADAMS
> (LXII, p. 350)

Adams appears at times as a compound of the Creator and his creature, the first specimen of 'humanity'. This is why Pound slightly distorts an anecdote related by the *Diary* ('The indian preacher cried, Good God! that ever Adam and Eve should eat that apple, when they knew in their own souls it would make good cider' – *WJA*, II, p. 289) by omitting Eve's name:

> said Indian preacher: Adam! Adam when you knew
> it wd/ make good cider!   (LXIV, p. 361)

The credit given to Adams is immense, and Pound tries to prove to us that he is 'covered' by an immense richness. Adams is the founder not only of the Fatherland but also of justice: 'THEMIS CONDITOR' (LXXI, p. 417) is Pound's typical Greek and Latin coining. And the prayer to Adams which marks the end of Canto LXII, quoted above, finds an equivalent at the end of the ten Cantos. A final phrase of Adams is, 'Ignorance of coin, credit and circulation!' This is bound to re-echo through the *Cantos* as the ultimate summary of his teachings. And it is fittingly followed by Cleanthes' 'Hymn to Zeus', of which Pound translates the first two lines he quotes as 'Glorious, deathless of many names, Zeus aye ruling all things, founder of the inborn qualities of nature, by laws piloting all things' (p. 256). The connection between the multiplicity of names (*poluonome*) and the domination by law (*nomou*) finally relates Pound's sense of filial obedience and the double sense of 'citation': calling someone before a court; quoting people by their words. And, as Walter Benjamin remarked, in an insight which will be developed in the next chapter, 'to quote is to call a word by its name' ('Ein Wort zitieren heisst, es beim Namen zu rufen'). But the whole passage is necessary for a full understanding of Benjamin's theory of quotation, and, besides, deserves to be quoted at length; Benjamin discusses Karl Kraus's polemical style of quoting other writers:

'The closer you look at a word, the further away it winks back.' This is platonic love for language. But the proximity from which the word cannot escape is only rhyme. Thus the original erotic relationship between distance and proximity manifests itself in his language as rhyme and name. As rhyme, language soars away from the created world, as name it attracts all creatures to itself. . . . Quotation, the fundamental polemical device used by Kraus, derives only from the language of the man. To quote a word is tantamount to calling it by name. . . . He calls the word by its name, takes it away destructively from its context, but in this very movement calls it back toward its origin. The word then appears as not unrhymed, it is chiming and full of voices in the structure of a new text. As rhyme, it assembles similar words in its aura; as name, it remains isolated and expression-less. As regards language, the two domains – origin as well as destruction – reveal themselves through quotation. And conversely: it is only when they are fused – in quotation – that language is accomplished.[12]

Benjamin identifies the fundamental motive behind Pound's fascination for condensation, parataxis and quotation: it is only in this double movement of language, fusing the energies of political will, and organising the destruction of older, worn-out vocables, that poetry can measure itself against the essence of language. And the essence of language is a *Dichten* which inscribes a Name.

In the Law of the Name

Is, then, the law of quotation as much the law of names as of imitation? Pound chose to stop his quotation from Cleanthes at the end of the second line, but the text goes on, 'and our voice is in the image of your voice'. To imitate the voice of a Father, be he Zeus or Adams, does this mean to make one's voice in the likeness of his voice? Besides, how can a voice be an *image* of another voice? The easiest answer would be to say, when it is written, but the Greek text is more ambiguous, since in place of the version which is generally accepted (line 4: *ek sou gar genos esmen, isou mimema lachontes* – 'We are truly of your race [family], our voice is in the likeness of you') has also been read, . . . *echo mimema lachontes*; in one case man imitates the image of Zeus, in the other he imitates his voice, his reverberating echo: 'our voice is in the image of your voice'.[13]

But such a radical adequation is impossible, because history continues; indeed, if the terrestrial Paradise were now possible, then all language could become quotable. This is how Benjamin expresses it:

> A chronicler who recites events without distinguishing between major and minor ones acts in concordance with the following truth: nothing that has ever happened should be regarded as lost for history. To be sure, only a redeemed mankind receives the fullness of its past – which is to say, only for a redeemed mankind has its past become citable in all its moments. Each moment it has lived becomes a *citation à l'ordre du jour* – and that day is Judgement Day.[14]

It is true that only a Judgement Day of some sort could show Pound that his dream of an infinite *citation à l'ordre de l'ordre* was doomed. Pound's voice travels a more complex journey, traces out a more dislocated circle before discovering the movement which places the law in the text.

Adams is a symbolic Father because of his respect for law. In the introduction to the Jefferson–Adams correspondence I have already mentioned, Pound still places Jefferson in the central position of an authority on matters of money and justice:

But Europe went blind into that war [the First World War] because mankind had not digested Jefferson's knowledge. They went into that war because the canon law had been buried, because all general knowledge had been split up into useless or incompetent fragments. Because literature no longer bothered about the language 'of law and the state', because the state and plutocracy cared less than a damn about letters.   (*SP*, p. 123)

In the course of the dynastic Cantos, Pound found that what America wanted was a true dynasty. And it is at this point that one must turn back to the last Canto of the series, and understand why Adams is the true successor of Yong Tching, who dies when he is born. Yong Tching decides to expel all Christians, and then changes his mind, but refuses to let more missionaries into China and, more importantly, to allow a legal status for their institutions:

> and he putt out Xtianity
> chinese found it so immoral
> his mandarins found this sect so immoral
> 'The head of a sect' runs the law 'who deceives folk
> 'by pretending religion, ought damn well to be strangled.'
> No new temples for any hochang, taoists or similars
> > *sic in lege*
> False laws are that stir up revolt by pretense of virtue.
> . . .
> . . . nothing personal against Gerbillon and his
> > colleagues, but
> Xtians are disturbing good customs
> seeking to uproot Kung's laws
> seeking to break up Kung's teaching.

> > > > (LXI, p. 334)

What stands out as the direct link from Yong Tching is therefore less a coincidence of chronology than the transmission of the same concern for law. The main passion which animates Adams' public actions is his respect for a pure law which nevertheless takes into account the irrational aspect of humanity:

law not bent to wanton imagination
>> and temper of individuals

mens sine affectu
>> that law rules
>> that it be
>>> sine affectu in 1770, Bastun.

Bad law is the worst sort of tyranny.   (LXII, p. 343)

The main objection made by Yong Tching against Christian morals
was that they destroyed filial reverence and the cult of the ancestor,
two elements of primordial importance for the connection of Law with
the name of the father. But his successor added to the necessary
reverence for Law the literary qualities needed for Adams:

>> so his son Kien Long came to the throne
>> in the 36th of that century –
>> and as to the rise of the Adamses –   (LXI, p. 339)

He cared for law and for letters ('literary kuss, and wuz Emperor / fer
at least 40 years' – p. 340), and Pound no doubt remembered that Kien
Long had been praised by Voltaire as the equivalent in China of the
enlightened ruler Frederick the Great,[15] but above all he embodied the
very principle of poetic composition of the Adams Cantos: 'and
condensed the Ming histories' (p. 340).

I have shown how the Adams Cantos obey no other legislation than
that of the volume quoted, condensed, cut up at times to be taken as a
point of departure for 'para-odes' – songs alongside the original,
strange parasitic echoes which finally interweave with the rest. In so far
as each Canto opens not only onto a vast historical chronicle, but also
onto another intertextual network, progressing towards the centre of
enunciation constituted by Adams himself, perceived through his
letters, meetings, readings and decisions, the multiplicity of references
places Pound in the following dilemma: he must either use a compact
montage, welding firmly together all the *énoncés*, utterances, produced by Adams and his acquaintances, or he must generalise the use
of dots, points of suspension giving additional space to the receptacle
of the text.

A first degree of difficulty in deciphering stems from the conflict
between the desire to communicate all without distorting or adding
anything, to convey all these fragments of a total truth owned by the
Father, and the imperious need to condense, to abbreviate. On the one

hand, the text would aim for pure transitiveness; on the other, it would inscribe itself in the opaque zone of a signifier inseparable from its signified. This dynamic tension still seems to leave a place, a position for the writing subject: if the unity is broken, a time for scansion is required, a pause for the author jotting down notes and for the reader decoding, pauses in a perpetual *décalage*, taking advantage of the possible discrepancies between their respective rhythms. A kind of music can then be heard, composed of conflicting centres of enunciation, allowing for happy 'points' when they overlap: 'at certain points / made us' (LXII, p. 350).

But this indecipherability very quickly leaves the writing subject only the choice of two profoundly antagonistic modes of utterance: he can either explode into sudden, passionate, idiomatic eruptions which break through into the text and allow the uncontrollable passage to political act to be foreseen; or he can keep silent, disappear as enunciator, play the part of the squatting scribe who remains the faithful but mute caretaker of sacred hieroglyphics. And it is here that the law reposes, transcendent in its function and immanent in its 'character'. Adams intervenes as the voice of the Father who does not so much possess the law as found it. He bears it with his name, which any shrine or monument will disclose to the gaze of the passer-by:

> Came not by usura Angelico; came not Ambrogio Praedis,
> Came no church of cut stone signed: *Adamo me fecit.*
>
> (XLV, p. 230)

Adams as seen by Pound is the one who was in a position to lay down the law, to give a Father's name to America, and this cannot but fail because he discovers eventually that the law is double. Adams shows the reverence and the literary understanding for a unique and transcendent law, *themis*: 'THEMIS CONDITOR' (LXXI, p. 417). But *themis* gives way to *nomos*, the law of the city condensed in its money, which cannot help multiplying, disseminating into *nomina* and *nomisma*, names of the god revered under many appellations (*poluonome*) by someone whose name rings just like anyone, *Ou tis* or 'No one'. Multiple names for multiplied laws, decrees, bills, pamphlets, circular letters – all to be rewritten, passed along, endlessly reread. Of course, this proliferation cannot possibly be subsumed under a 'general statement' or an 'idea'.

This does not yet appear too clearly to Pound when he writes these Cantos; he needs the shock of the actual war – and the 1942 prose text shows this first awareness of the splintering of the evidence, the questioning of the model; but a shriller voice covers this immediately – and also the incitement to go back to one of the more important sources used by Adams, Coke's legal works.[16] The law is the backbone of Adams's strict position, of his unswerving determination, of his incorruptible sense of justice, as for instance when he opposes Franklin ('the ethics, so called, of Franklin / IF moral analysis / be not the purpose of historical writing – Canto LXII, p. 346). Pound cannot yet see that such a phrase as 'law is the subject's birthright' (LXIV, p. 356), which Adams quotes from Coke's second *Book of Institutes* ('The law is the subject's birthright' – II, *Inst.* 56, quoted in *WJA*, II, p. 158), entails a definition of what a 'subject' is – not only in the grammatical, nor simply in the political, sense, but fundamentally the subject in language, who reads and writes in order to be alive, and who becomes more and more problematic. Earlier in the same paper of Adams is another quotation from Coke: 'Common law is common right' (I *Inst.* 142a). Coke thus appears to give Adams the whole weight of his experience as defender of parliamentary freedom. He allows Adams to transplant to American soil the English heritage of the Common Law, which, from the Magna Carta onward, denounces all abuses, all monopolies. This is precisely the basis which the French philosophers lacked, a lack which undermines all their theories:

> common lay* of England, BIRTHRIGHT of every man here
> and at home
> (LXVI, p. 384)

and:

> the 41st section repeals MAGNA
> CHARTA the 29th chapter
> as follows the words: NO FREEMAN...to...by his peers
> and the law of the land
> Whereon said Lord Coke, speaking of Empson and Dudley,
> the end of these two oppressors
> shd/ deter others from committing the like   (ibid.)

---

* The 1975 Faber edition gives 'lay' here, but this is a typographical error and it should read 'law'.

Adams's strength comes from the discovery that he is perhaps 'more English than the English', since he uses the Common Law as a legal pivot to fight British tyranny, in much the same way as Coke had to fight against royal power. Thanks to this relentless effort, the nation is founded not only in fact, but also in law. The relationship of the subject to law will then be the dominant theme of the following Cantos; they show that to be 'subject' one has to be master over the issue of money. The Common Law is based on previous procedure, and this legal search for evidence, clues and trials is parallel to the ideogrammic method piling up historical examples: infinite reading of myriads of bills, decrees, codicils, gloses and commentaries. Set adrift in an everlasting epigraphy, the text abandons any hope of closure.

The paternal law defining a 'birthright' is also, in itself, a splitting up of the subject, torn apart between contradictory injunctions. The Confucian law, or the just Decree of Heaven identical with natural growth and abundance, first lost by the British, then by the Americans too in the course of the degradation of their history, can only be recovered by a subject who can bear being split asunder in the very act of naming.

Here again, Adams provides a model in his assimilation of the principle of Kung's pivot, the axis around which all enunciation revolves, since Pound will eventually gloss it as a mouth rifted by a vertical dash (see Chapter 4). Adams, in favour of the balance of power in the Constitution, and keen to keep laws which have demonstrated their efficacy, declares,

> aim of my life has been to be useful, how small in
> any nation the number who comprehend ANY
> system of constitution or administration
>   and these few do not unite.
> Americans more rapidly disposed to corruption in elections
>   than I thought in '74
> fraudulent use of words monarchy and republic

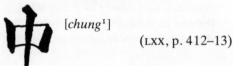

> I am for balance   [*chung*¹]
>   (LXX, p. 412–13)

While already showing a disquieting presentiment of latent corruption, he points to the unity of all founding principles, from Chinese dynasties to America.

4   The 'Pisan Cantos': Between Reference and Reverence

Pisa: the crisis-point of the word. The redistribution of discourses in a new mode of utterance and nomination could only have been brought about by a tragedy, in the intense and painful proximity of death, a historical and ontological tragedy, coupling exclusion and division for the anathematised voice which remains that of the 'ego scriptor' after the 'wreckage of Europe' (Canto LXXVI p. 458).

Anathema

> . . . the blessed things that have taken on what is cursed and the profane things that somehow are redeemed . . . Things set up, lifted up, or in whatever manner made over to the gods.
> David Jones, Preface to *Anathemata*[1]

To remark abruptly that Pound was anathematised seems either a convoluted way of expressing a truism – namely, that he was secluded in St Elizabeth for thirteen years – or to hint at yet another committed and argumentative defence of his sanity. I should like to suggest that the very preciosity of the Greek term affords an original way of manoeuvring around the problematic of exclusion, if it centres on the question of utterance. The 'case' of Ezra Pound, labelled traitor and criminal, found 'schizoid' or 'paranoid' by a panel of four psychiatrists, has already been acutely denounced by Thomas Szasz, who rightly points out the incoherence of the diagnosis, the inextricable confusions between a medical examination and a judicial power. Eva Hesse has more recently referred Pound's position back to the general analysis which Foucault makes of the great ideological containment of madness.[2] I could just add that, if indeed Pound was not actually straight-jacketed, the result of his incarceration was to shut him up, first, in a place where every new event had to be filtered by books, letters and a special set of friends, thereby defining particular strategies of survival; secondly, in a situation in which the question of insanity was so insistent that it continued to be excluded or reversed. As Olson reports, Pound once or twice said, 'I guess the definition of a lunatic is a man surrounded by them.'[3]

He of course alluded to the Jewishness of Kavka and other psychiatrists at St Elizabeth, but the vague qualification of 'them' can stay without further precision: the wry remark, getting at the continuous reversals between sanity and madness Foucault emphasises, and coming in Pound's case from the fact that these concepts were defined and enforced by those who were the prejudiced 'enemies' of what he represented, at least testifies to his buoyant sense of humour – a humour probably missed by Olson, who at first did not seem so adverse to the idea of leaving Pound in St Elizabeth: if he could only translate Confucius in peace, and not bother the world with his pernicious proposals for action![4]

Pound was held responsible for the risks he knew he was taking when speaking in his Radio Rome broadcasts – is this fair enough? But I wish to show that the modalities of exclusion and inclusion, of power and submission, are already at work in his poetry, in a system based on contradictions from which no critical point of view can be sure to free itself, since the abstract impartiality of any critical theory is questioned by Pound's linguistic process. My reading of the Pisan Cantos will be double, then: it will allow itself to be captured, captivated by Pound's vehement insistence on writing and speech, and will attempt to follow their disarticulations; and I shall read the text without refraining from calling up the usual picture, or rather faded photograph, of the American Disciplinary Training Centre, known as the DTC, in Pisa, of the cage in which the poet walked round and round, reliving in his mind three decades of literary activity, railing at the bureaucrats in Washington and Mussolini's executors, and above all quoting his classics, muttering Ovid and Kung to perplexed US Army sergeants. Whether this leaning Paradiso or Inferno of Pisa obliquely brought about a renewal of the ancient lyrical mode submerged behind ideological discourses in the thirties, reawakening the thrill of creating and fixing a vanishing order in a testament, or led to the inception of the oncoming breakdown and ultimate silence, I shall at any rate observe a certain amount of caution when tackling Pound's self-dramatising vignettes of the anathematised poet.

Writing from the gates of death a diary and a threnody, he nevertheless keeps conjuring up universal history as well as trivial anecdotes so as to ward off the Other – an Other all the more dangerous as it inhabits the Same and devours it from within, be it a multiple-faced Usura, the Hydra of semitism, or the barbarity of a botched American civilisation. 'Pound anathema' has this double meaning – defines the excommunicated prophet who, cursed and rejected, still castigates the opprobrium of those who have attempted to force him to silence when he only wanted their redemption and rebirth. If this double sense couples an active and a passive exclusion, it might yield a further *coincidentia oppositorum*, akin to the opposed meanings of primitive words which people the felicitous misunderstandings of Karl Abel, so influential for Freud's linguistic conceptions.[5] *Anathema* was originally, as is well known, a votive offering placed before the gods, and only later came to refer to something banned or cursed. The striking reversal is similar to the genealogy of the word *sacer*, meaning both sanctified and put to death, while the ambivalence of the curiously idiosyncratic religion of Pound (' "not the priest but the victim" / said Allen Upward' – Canto LXXVIII, p. 479) should, no doubt, be related to another *Gegensinn* noted by Freud when he ponders on the proximity of the German terms *stumm* (mute) and *Stimme* (voice).[6]

The object of my inquiry thus becomes this nodus or nexus of a 'mute voice' insisting to be heard from within the plural writing of the 'Pisan Cantos', for I hope to avoid certain traps set in place for the critic who engages with this superb and 'sacred' text, a landmark of contemporary poetry: he generally hesitates between a mimetic homage absorbed by the spellbound hunt for sources and allusions, and a thematic analysis based on whatever phenomenology of reading he happens to adhere to. Underlying this alternative is a common assumption about the practice of reading which is not so much treated as an activity as either considered to be the mere collocation of information, or felt to be the transparent link between two subjectivities. On the one hand, there is the fallacious utopia that all obscurities can be dispelled, as if they were so many veils masking some hidden core of meaning; on the other hand, the model of a projection from a 'full', i.e. not divided, self towards another, easily located self, functioning on the model of intentionalities consciously mastering their worlds.

Now, if there is such a thing as a Poundian text – a contention that might well have to be proved – my point is that it will only be read in all its *ana-themes* or *ana-semes*, the anathematised and idiomatic signifiers which exceed any direct meaning, any thematisation of sense, in the necessary opacity forbidding transparence when translating from language to language, code to code, discourse to discourse, signature to signature. The term 'anasemes' has been used by Nicolas Abraham and Maria Torok when they deciphered key-signifiers deduced by playing on the different languages used by the Wolfman's dream as analysed by Freud.[7] In Derrida's words, they investigate the 'desire for an idiom and the idiom of desire'[8] which the Unconscious incorporates in a 'crypt'. The idiomatic roots they discover as constituting the key to the Wolfman's dreams, hallucinations and psychosis are multilingual translations of pure signifiers playing on Russian, English and German rhymes. Pound's idiom attempts to inscribe itself in a similar way, starting from the anathesis of a split subject who signs himself in hieroglyphs and characters, all marked by an anasemic or anasemantic feature.

I shall try to show how the mouth of a caged Pound encloses the cage of words, and only opens to quote long strings of facts, gestures, names, all salvaged from the dungeon of official history. The retaliation of the past will be brought to bear on the future dream of immemoriality, and be uttered by a locked, barred, blocked voice, which, absorbing the contraries, oscillates between clatter and silence, congestion and liquidity. The plural names rely therefore on a writing which repeat its silence, in a proleptic trope – to express the name of the Name it just says, 'that the name be the Name'; this is how the aphasic voice can be sealed by a hieratic signature.

The opening of the 'Pisan Cantos' introduces the climax of the tragedy which has passed for current history: a *débâcle*, a general collapse which forecloses any political illusion of a just government, since the *Duce* is dead. The curve of fate bends down once more back to the Earth, to the anonymous, simultaneously choric and chthonic, presence of the labourer: 'The enormous tragedy of the dream in the peasant's bent shoulders'. Such a 'catastrophe' is literally enacted by the overturning of Mussolini's corpse:

> Manes! Manes was tanned and stuffed,
> Thus Ben and la Clara *a Milano*
>   by the heels at Milano

> That maggots shd/ eat the dead bullock
> DIGONOS, Δίγονος, but the twice crucified
> > where in history will you find it?
> > > (LXXIV, p. 425)

The double execution, first real, then symbolic (alluding to Mussolini's death and exposure) exceeds even the Christian pattern of crucifixion as a prelude to resurrection ('I believe in the resurrection if Italy quia impossibile est' – p. 422). It leaves Pound orphaned, torn asunder in a world which can no longer reconcile the real with the symbolic, thus cutting name apart from bearer, son from substitute father. His drifting quest, a periplum, is triggered by the duty to resume a descent into Hell, so that he may recapture the essence of his Homeric persona: Ou Tis as Noman.

> ΟΥ ΤΙΣ, ΟΥ ΤΙΣ? Odysseus
> > the name of my family. (p. 425)

The 'family name' links Odysseus with Elpenor's mention of a 'name to come', which etymologically links 'name' with 'fame' and 'speech' ('Cuius *fama* apud posteros sit'), since *fari* (to speak) and *fatum* (fate) are connected in *fama*. Now the real effort is in the attempt at a synthesis of speech, in order to become adult, not an *in-fans* any more, and writing, in the erection of a stele by seaboard, with phallic oar up. This entails a dialectical overcoming of the Christic situation, or indeed radically rethinking the paradigm of exclusion (Pound repeated for instance in his Rome broadcasts that Christ had been the first victim of the usury racket.[9])

> Absouldre, que tous nous veuil absoudre[10]
> lay there Barabbas and two thieves lay beside him
> infantile synthesis in Barabbas
> minus Hemingway, minus Antheil, ebullient (p. 427)

Villon's *Testament* only heightens the dramatisation of the poet as Christ deprived of the assistance of his friends, refusing the false synthesis which leads to easy discharge. For Jesus was crucified by the Jewish priests because they accused him of blasphemy for pretending to be God's son, while Barabbas signed with his name the premature fusion of the Son (*bar* in Aramaic) with the Father (*abba* in Aramaic). The paradox is that, in order to achieve the symbolic synthesis, the poet must be anathematised and somehow put to death. This focuses around his speaking-capacity, which is rather nicely conveyed through the Camp's slang: 'if we weren't *dumb*, we wouldn't be here' (p. 428, emphasis added).

Naming, speaking, writing are then the only weapons left to fight against the powers of darkness and ignorance:

Sponsa Cristi in mosaic till our time / deification of emperors
but a snotty barbarian ignorant of T'ang history need not deceive one
nor Charlie Sung's money on loan from anonimo   (pp. 425–6)

The tension between the subjective Noman and the objective drive towards usury is inherent in the loaded term 'anonimo'. These elements reappear but with different emphasis in the first pages of 'Rock-Drill':

止   chih³

a gnomon,
Our science is from the watching of shadows;
That Queen Bess translated Ovid,
Cleopatra wrote of the currency,
Versus who scatter old records
ignoring the hsien² form   (LXXXV, p. 543)

In 'Rock-Drill', Pound's voice mimes the collective recapitulation of dynastic memoirs and calls up the urge to search for the absolute sign or seal:

not a lot of signs, but the one sign
etcetera
plus always Τέχνη
and from Τέχνη back to σεαυτόν   (p. 546)

His assertion is safely located in the trace of a sign functioning as a signature, a signature which nevertheless remains cryptic, and the almost derisive 'etcetera' comes as a weird reminder that the process of naming is endless. In the 'Pisan Cantos', the loss of a symbolic father obliges him to invent a new myth and to place his *techne* in the very rift between name and bearer.

This defines the periplum for which no sextant is available, because it is but a string of names, exactly as Odysseus's periplum had to enact the toponomy of a map. Victor Bérard can help one to understand the function of real names, referring to real places in the linguistic games of the poem:

> Our poem is a portrait gallery. The names of the periplus have become the characters of the poem. . . . Each episode is built on the actualisation of a toponomy. The land of the Sardes, the Fugitives, is the theatre of the flight of Ulysses; the land of the Sikeles, the Orphans, sees him isolated. . . . The static periplus is turned by the poem into the dynamics of a *nostos*; it puts into human actions what the periplus gave as geographical descriptions.[11]

And Bérard adds elsewhere, 'The Greek onomastics and the nomenclature of the *Odyssey* appear to us as the double translation of one single topography.'[12] In the same way, Pound draws the map of his personal progress among names, retracing his past adventures in lands of different cultures (America, England, France, Italy, a literary China, the Africa of Frobenius, and so on), and the map of his present agony, juxtaposing these with names of fellow prisoners and sympathetic camp guards.

> and Rouse found they spoke of Elias
> in telling the tales of Odysseus   ΟΎ ΤΙΣ
>   ΟΎ ΤΙΣ
> 'I am noman, my name is noman'
> but Wanjina is, shall we say, Ouan Jin
> or the man with an education
> and whose mouth was removed by his father
>   because he made too many *things*
> whereby cluttered the bushman's baggage
> vide the expedition of Frobenius' pupils about 1938
>   to Auss'ralia
> Ouan Jin spoke and thereby created the named
>   thereby making clutter
> the bane of men moving
> and so his mouth was removed
> as you will find it removed in his pictures
>   in principio verbum
>   paraclete or the verbum perfectum: sinceritas
>   (LXXIV, pp. 426–7)

The passage condenses many themes, which are connected by a powerful montage-technique using a lilting rhetoric as vocal basis to construct their anasemic fusion. The *Guide to Kulchur* already presented the legends fusing Elias and Odysseus; the Greek hero and the prophet announcing the arrival of Christ fade into a more primitive figure, that of the Australian fertility god Wanjina or Wondjina. Pound had seen the pictures brought back by the pupils of the Frankfurt Forschungsinstitut, who had stopped in Rapallo and narrated him these legends, still current among aboriginal tribes today.[13]

Elias paradoxically announces the second coming of a Christ whose crucifixion is transformed into the multilation of the mouth: the mute Christ gives way to the Comforter, the Paraclete, or Holy Ghost. The series of substitutions allows Pound to blend the literato (*wen jen* in Chinese), the Australian god of fertility and Odysseus. He also puns on 'move' and 'remove', opposing the nomadic drive (with which he said he identified himself in the *Guide to Kulchur*) to the creation 'at a remove' from reality in the traditional Platonic criticism of art as a shadow of a shadow (when it does not refer to 'things'). The removal of the mouth (how can one remove a mouth, which is already a hole? – by sewing it, or sealing it, of course) permits the progression of the people. Such a progressive movement comes from a balance between overflow and castration; the naming-process is stopped so that the Name may come and be one with his people. The per-fection of the Word requires the disappearance of the subject who utters it.

The ideogrammic heaping-up of myths affirms the shift from utterance to mute writing; only in writing can the *verbum* be made perfect: 'consummatum est' – it is completed, abolished and realised. The Word is not only made flesh, but also perfected in an apotheosis uniting him with the Father's law. The removal of the mouth is the condition for the life of written texts. The Paraclete is called forth, he is named (*kalein*) beside (*para*) the heroic uttering subject, and as such he embodies the name of Christ as living memory. He is a name sent by the Father in the place of the Son. Thus *para-kalein* has the same root as the *calare* of *nomen-calare*, which gives 'nomenclature', pointing to some sort of living memento, who will recall everything that has been said. It is necessary that Christ should die, so that the nomenclature or *para-kalein* should be enacted among men ('it is expedient for you that I go away' – John 16:7). This absolute sincerity will later be identified with silence, since it is only the removal of the mouth which can give eternal life to the Name. The Paraclete is both the absolute witness and the proof that the Spirit can live through the letter as a real signature of a proper name.

The meaning of uttered words cannot impose itself in presence; it lives in the reverberation of a derived voice, which does not speak of itself, but quotes in the name of some other instance of enunciation ('for he shall not speak of himself; but whatsoever he shall hear, *that* shall he speak: and he will show you things to come' – John 16:13).[14] The mediation of another voice functions here as the 'citation form' or 'quotation noun' which some linguists call 'hypostasis'. That the term denoting one of the three persons of the Trinity should also refer to a citation can link the different performatives implicitly used here: the legal citation as the summoning of someone to the bar, asking him to appear in person 'in front of the law' (as Kafka would say), and the reproduction of another's words when he is elsewhere, or anywhere if they are printed. Absolute sincerity (the man standing by his word, as in the Confucian ideogram 信, is relayed by the intercession of the divine power as depicted by the sun's lance 'coming to rest on the precise spot verbally' – *Con*., p. 20 – in the ideogram of *ch'êng*, 誠) can then be perfected:

 the word is made

perfect (LXXVI, p. 454)

Pound comments in his *Terminology*, 'The righthand half of this compound means: to perfect, bring to focus.' I shall try to show that the risk such a sincerity has to accept is that of an utter loss or deprivation: for castration is the way towards truth.

There is nevertheless no pathos of self-sacrifice on the part of the literate man, who accepts castration and the removal of the mouth so that society may continue on its march forward. But the refusal of any clutter has a bearing on economic theory, whilst the exact implication of the superposition is none too clear in Pound's case: is he awaiting his execution because he said too many things? Is he rather playing the part of the Paraclete to Mussolini and other crushed leaders in history, as well as to martyred precursors such as Gaudier? How can he hope to select the right 'sieve' to avoid overflow, clotting or scarcity (in the terms of the Postscript to *The Natural Philosophy of Love*[15]) so that a satisfactory fluidity of words, things and actions may be achieved? The term 'clutter' will diffract such massive overdetermination, as the following passage bears out:

Tempus tacendi, tempus loquendi.
Never inside the country to raise the standard of living
but always abroad to increase the profits of usurers,
   dixit Lenin,
and gun sales lead to more gun sales
 they do not clutter the market for gunnery
  there is no saturation
Pisa, in the 23rd year of the effort in sight of the tower
and Till was hung yesterday
for murder and rape with trimmings plus Cholkis
 plus mythology, thought he was Zeus ram or another one
  Hey Snag wots in the bibl'?
  wot are the books ov the bible?
  Name 'em, don't bullshit ME.

莫 ΟΎ ΤΙΣ

a man on whom the sun has gone down

        (LXXIV, pp. 429–30)

The interaction of substitutes is endless: the corpse of Mussolini has now become a castrated bull, a bullock eaten by maggots, from which vital power has been substracted in the same way as for Wondjina. The cult of Dionysus used a bull instead of the tragical scapegoat, and this bull is once more echoed in the Camp slang: 'Don't *bull*shit ME' (emphasis added). Mussolini, both Boss (Pound refers to Confucius as 'Boss' in some of the dialogues of the *Analects*) and *bos*, the bull, is implicitly evoked by the angry Till, whose fate links him with Christ. Pound may remember Dante's equation between Christ and Jupiter (*Purgatorio*, VI.118–19), a Jupiter who later transforms himself into a bull when he rapes Europa (*Paradiso*, XXVII.84): Christ is a sacrificial bull for a long mediaeval tradition, going back to Augustine, because he takes upon him all the sins of humanity, called here 'Europa'.[16]

 Europe has been 'cluttered' more than raped, and for Pound Mussolini's aim had been precisely that of raping the continent so that efficient action might once more be possible; he too had to get rid of 'clutter':

Mussolini found himself in the cluttered rubbish and cluttered splendour of the dozen or more strata of human effort: history, the romanesque cluttered over with barocco, every possible sort of refinement, dust-covered, sub-divided, passive, sceptical, lazy, caressed by milleniar sun, Rome, Byzantium, Homeric Greece still in Sicily, *belle au bois dormante*. . . . (*J/M*, p. 66)

But Mussolini's 'effort' would be misread as a pure affirmation of will-power, and Pound rails against Nietzschean 'will to power' (Nietzsche becomes an 'ill-balanced hysterical teuto-pollack') only to praise 'will toward order' in terms which show the dangerous proximity of the evil motive and of the good objective (order as such): 'The greatest obstacle may well be just simple bossiness, bos, bovis, the bull, likes to order some fellow-human about' (p. 99). For 'the great man is filled with a very different passion, the will toward *order*' (ibid.).

Order starts with the order of seasons, and the scansion of speech by silence embodied by the Chinese concept of natural growth finds an exact equivalent through the motto of the Malatesta family. The clutter is indissociable from a perversion of natural rhythms, and Pound links this with the role of commercial and bellicist imperialism, coming back to Lenin's analysis of imperialism, for indeed 'the selling of guns and powder differs from ALL other industries in that the more you sell the greater the demand for the product' (*J/M*, p. 72). A generalised war economy is the only possible outcome of the clutter of words and things. In the absence of a Father who would cut out proliferating tissues, weapons continue to be manufactured, ships are sunk so that ships continue to be sunk (to rephrase an expression used in the broadcasts), in a confusion which is so inextricable that no one can assign an origin to it; or, rather, the constant overlapping of economic and linguistic processes renders any denunciation of the system desperate, since it is a mere waste of words to accuse without reaching to the origins, and since the origin is lost among conflicting myths: 'I suspect I talk in a what-is-called incoherent manner: 'cause I can't (and I recken nobody could) tell where to begin.'[17]

Exactly as the aboriginal tribes supposed that, if Wondjina recovered his mouth, he would plunge the world into a kind of universal flood, the capitalistic market is organised in such a way that nobody can denounce its abuses without being condemned to silence. Such a mechanism leads to perpetual wars, wars all the more unjust as everyone thinks he is on the right side. Usury breaks with the rhythms of the seasons by substituting a constant and mechanical clatter to the regular alternation of speech and silence, of production, distribution and consumption. The exchange of words, objects and women is caught within the bad infinite of the clutter/clatter, an *apeiron* fragmenting the organic wholeness of the cosmos because it makes time, which should be free, ever-given in its superabundance, pay.

But in the case of the passage from Canto LXXIV commented on here, the failure of the Fascist regime to stop the mechanism is mirrored in Till's condemnation: Till is a case of *hubris*, the totems he has elected for himself prove it, and his unquenchable thirst for knowledge (on the eve of his execution, he keeps asking for information about the books of the Bible) is the positive side of this excessiveness. He is on the side of Zeus, while Mussolini was earlier on related to Dionysus by the epithet *Digonos*.[18] The Dionysian rituals used bulls for their sacrifices, which links here Zeus and Dionysus. The bull can turn into a bullock, phallic becomes castrated, in a language which plays with such puzzling polarities and records the 'intellectual interests' of criminals. The wish to know more of the Bible rebounds as the question of the name: Till hopes to receive a definition of his name through sacred books, which is why the palindrome ' 'em / ME' is transformed by the play on the Chinese character *mo*[6], which means 'not, not to be'. Eva Hesse has shown that it was not gratuitous to see 'a man on whom the sun has gone down' in it.[19]

The sun has gone down on Ou Tis or everyman, so that his mouth is now sealed up. A whole Canto is hinged around the permutations between different Chinese characters, in all of which Pound believes he sees the square meaning 'mouth' (口 *mou*, the mouth, 中 *chung*, the privot, 日 *dji*, the sun, and 曰 *üe*, to say, speech).

> Chung   中
>
> > in the middle
> > whether upright or horizontal
> >
> > (LXXVII, p. 464)

> > Bright dawn   旦   on the sht house
> > > next day
> > > > with the shadow of the gibbets attendant
> > ...

> > nothing counts save the quality of the affection

> > mouth, is the sun that is god's mouth
> or in another connection   (periplum)   口
> > in the studio on the Regent's canal
> >
> > (p. 466)

All the elements of the *mo*⁴ ideogram are there, but scattered like the broken fragments of the tally-stick reproduced on p. 467 and glossed on p. 476. The sun has now become the god's mouth, through the shifter of *mo*⁴, and the barring line must pass through it in the middle, but can be either horizontal or vertical. The axis of truth is centred on the absolute light and brightness of the sun, a light which, when reconstituted in the effort of intuition becomes the risk of blinding *eidos*. The great acorn of light is never far from the castrating gesture of the Father.

Thus the question of the names of the books in the Bible opens onto the question of the nature of each utterance; the collective dream of a political utopia and the ritual of tragedy with its series of scapegoats are placed in the context of an *apocalyptic* utterance. Apocalyptic implies that truth is understood as dis-closure (and not adequation simply with the real), for *gala* (title of the Revelation in Hebrew) means 'to uncover', and is used to depict the uncovering of Adam and Eve's nakedness in Genesis.[20] This is why, whenever the apocalyptic tone is muted towards the elegiac, it nevertheless borrows the recurring device of the roll-call of names, in the stringing out of long litanies referring to individuals. The growing importance of names bears witness to the dissolution of all other possible discourses. A series of silhouettes is etched out against the background of a particular myth, which adds a layer of sense to the hermeneutic process and not to the individual concerned by the reference; when Till is related to Jason and the theft of the Golden Fleece, this does not describe a quality of his own ego, but reveals Pound's way of structuring his chaos, of making sense by the interconnection of two levels of names (soldiers, and gods or demi-gods, heroes). As for Till, he remains labelled by his specific utterance, which comes back like a tag: 'What are the books of the Bible?'

```
        – niggers comin' over the obstacle fence
                    as in the insets at the Schifanoja
    (del Cossa) to scale, 10,000 gibbet-iform posts supporting
                    barbed wire
    'St Louis Till' as Green called him. Latin!
        'I studied latin' said perhaps his smaller companion.
    'Hey Snag, what's in the bibl'?
                what are the books of the bibl'?
    Name 'em! don't bullshit me!'
```

                    . . .
            and Tom wore a tin disc, a circular can-lid
                    with his name on it, solely:
            for Wandjina has lost his mouth   (LXXVII, pp. 473–4)

By the submerged pun on 'solely', Tom wears a name which is a sun
too, and he is related to Wandjina because he is an aboriginal servant,
and his story is told by the same source in 1938:[21] a written name
replaces an utterance forbidden by the Father. Such a real and
metaphorical sun is also latent in the allusion to the Schifanoia
frescoes. Pound alludes to the panels depicting March and April; for
March, the lower section represents peasants who are grafting, cutting
and binding trees while Borso d'Este hears justice. The actual Camp
inmates jump over similar fences. The astrological symbol is the Ram
in the middle section, a ram which has a sun shining under its belly, just
at the place of the sexual organ, and a girl surmounts it to picture forth
spring. The April scene presents a bull with a bright sun glittering in the
same place: the metonymic transfer of the sexual properties to the
shining sun under the belly is all the more fitting here as the upper
section deals with the triumph of Venus; it enables Pound to fuse her
with the Cytherea of Malatesta's Tempio.

    These structural patterns enable Pound to shift from memory to
memory while keeping a certain progression, which was initially to
mirror the main project of the *Cantos*, from tragedy to contrition and
final assertion in spite of everything to the contrary. But the breaks are
so frequent that it is difficult to find the scheme adhered to faithfully;
as Pound wrote to the Camp Censor, 'The form of the poem and main
progress is conditioned by its own inner shape, but the life of the DTC
passing OUTSIDE the scheme cannot but impinge, or break into the
main flow.'[22] The sequence exhibits moments of intense despair and
redeeming visions of Paradise, but I should like to suggest that the
function of the names, along with a fluctuating but intense meditation
on the act of naming, provide the exact link between the 'inside' and
the 'outside', or more precisely the point at which the 'outside' is
turned into the 'inside', and conversely.

    As the Pisan Cantos gather momentum, the lists of names are longer
and more frequent, and they point towards the reconciliation between
history and nature, between subjective despair and objective comfort.
Just before the beautiful evocation of England in the twenties, a list of
names is transformed into a thanksgiving litany:

    if calm be after tempest
that the ants seem to wobble
    as the morning sun catches their shadows
    (Nadasky, Duett, McAllister,
    also Comfort K. P. special mention
    on sick call Penrieth, Turner, Toth hieri
    (no fortune and with a name to come)
Bankers, Seitz, Hildebrand and Cornelison
    Armstrong special mention K. P.
    White gratia Bedell gratia
    Wiseman (not William) africanus.
with a smoky torch thru the unending
            labyrinth of the souterrain
or remembering Carleton let him celebrate Christ in the grain
and if the corn cat be beaten
    Demeter has lain in my furrow
    This wind is lighter than swansdown
    the day moves not at all
    (Zupp, Bufford, and Bohon)

men of no fortune and with a name to come
                                    (LXXX, pp. 513–14)

Pound both voices his gratitude, indicating those who deserve a
'special mention' in his praises, including 'culture' heroes such as
Carleton, mentioned as having improved American wheat (*LE*,
p. 76[23]), and implies that he serves as the *fama* of those who otherwise
would remain unknown. Their names, interwoven with the names of
the gods (Christ and Demeter curiously united), point toward the same
natural utopia as the concluding note of hope:

            Under white clouds, cielo di Pisa
        out of all this beauty something must come
                                    (LXXXIV, p. 539)

This is the answer to the 'names to come'.

Each in the name of . . .

Reminiscing is the lyrical modulation of a fundamental urge to name,

which often takes the form of the figure of preterition (I shall not name
x, while naming it) or of rhetorical questions such as

> and now Richardson, Roy Richardson
>   says he is different
>   will I mention his name?   (LXXXIV, p. 537)

If the reference to actual people, quoted by name, stresses their
difference, it is because naming people or places has a certain weight,
even a political responsibility. At times, Pound sees his periplus as
mapping out the cartography of past allegiances, literary battles and
contemporary issues. To name is an action which remains present, and
this is why it engages a movement of celebration and denunciation at
the same time. Certain passages show that Pound is aware of this
complex achievement:

>   Roma profugens Sabinorum in terras
> and belt the citye quahr of nobil fame
>   the lateyn peopil taken has their name
> bringing his gods into Latium
>   saving the bricabrac
> 'Ere he his goddis brocht in Latio'
>   'each one in the name'
> in whom are the voices, keeping hand on the reins
> Gaudier's word not blacked out,
>   nor old Hulme's, nor Wyndham's,
> *Mana aboda.*
> The touch of sadism in the back of his neck.
> tinting justice, 'Steele that is one awful name.'
>   sd/ the cheerful reflective nigger
> Blood and Slaughter to help him
>   dialog repartee at the drain hole
> . . .
> 'definition can not be shut down under a box lid'
> but if the gelatine be effaced whereon is the record?
> 'wherein is no responsible person
>   having a front name, a hind name and an address'
> 'not a right but a duty'
>   those words still stand uncancelled,
>   'Presente!'
>   and merrda for the monopolists
>   (LXXVIII, pp. 478–9)

The passage unites the three main levels of action in the 'Pisan Cantos';
Pound appears in his personal history, his flight from Rome enhanced
by the parallel with the translation of Virgil by Gavin Douglas (*ABCR*,
p. 115), his defence of aesthetical values stressed by the allusion to
Hulme's poem with a Hebrew title, 'Mana Aboda'.[24] The political
motif then recurs with the reference to Mussolini's sentence often
quoted by Pound before the war: 'We are tired of a government in
which there is no responsible person having a hind name, a front name
and an address' (*SP*, p. 231). And the overheard dialogue interweaves
the present situation with the jumble of Fascist slogans. Thus the
personal and the mythical, the cultural and the political, the divine or
permanent and the anecdotal or transient are fused.

But the main link between all these levels is the consideration of the
power of names and definitions, of language's capacity to preserve the
past and orient for future action. The motif taken from Micah 4:5 ('For
all people will walk every one in the name of his god'), cut off from its
context, brings the surprising warrant of the Bible for polytheism, and
is turned back against the main monotheistic drift of a 'Jewish Bible'
which Pound had 'read daily' as a child but finally rejected for
ideological reasons. The context would have supplied, 'But we will
walk in the name of YHWH for ever.' Pound has spotted the one
sentence which can be reconciled with his cult of discrete and
discontinuous gods, and uses the quote from Micah as a *Leitmotiv* in
the Pisan sequence, until he blends it with the Greek divinities: 'Tellus
$\gamma\acute{\epsilon}\alpha$ fecunda / "each one in the name of its god" / mint, thyme and
basilicum' (Canto LXXIX, p. 487). It may be noted that the Septuagint
had tried to erase this sentence because of its polytheistic implications,
replacing it by 'for all the peoples will walk each *in his way*'.[25]
Nevertheless, even the completed passage in Micah can suit Pound:
Micah promises that the future Temple in Jerusalem will see all
peoples converging towards it, the particular affirmation of religious
idiosyncrasies tending to fuse in a sort of ideal synthesis of all religions.

We know that the 'Hebrew Scriptures' which a Camp cat was
tempted to swallow along with Confucius (p. 498) were, along with the
book of poems found in the toilets, among the few texts which helped
Pound to survive morally.[26] The uncancelled force of Mussolini's and
Hulme's words can borrow Micah's voice to make itself heard.

Pound's fulminations against the 'Jewish' part of the Bible, which
according to Zielenski had corrupted the sound portions,[27] are well
known, and Pound's thesis has on the whole remained unchanged: a
people can survive only if it is capable of creating a cult, a rite, a

religion. The Bible is dangerous only because of its staunch monotheism, and should be read 'after the reader is literate' (*L*, p. 345). Read too soon, the dogma will prevent people's imaginations from creating their own ecstatic syntheses of visions and names of gods. 'Xtianity a poor substitute for the truth, but the best canned goods that can be put on the market immediately in sufficient quantity for general pubk.??' (*L*, p. 345). Pound's strategy of reading has managed to find the weak spot, the little nugget of verbal wisdom which enables him to turn monotheism against itself.

The Bible cannot be used as 'reading-matter', since to borrow from a central bank is the economic equivalent of bowing down to a central god: both result in the same oppression or usury. Thus, in place of the 'Ersatzreligion' he denounced in his letters, Pound now advocates his 'Ezra-religion', which is rather a 'Micah-religion'; indeed, the two prophets fight for an underground theological supremacy in the *Cantos*, and they take positions quite close to those of their historical namesakes. Micah stands for the wider syncretism which found a kind of natural outlet at the time of the pre-Christian diaspora; Ezra is on the other hand the scribe who reads the Law to his people, then manages to rebuild the Temple in spite of all sorts of opposition, and finally forbids intermarriage with non-Jewish persons. His books ends when he gives the long lists of all those who had committed the sin of marrying non-Jewish wives and who recanted and were purified when they agreed to send them away. In that respect he is like Apollonius, hostile to the 'melting-pot' (but I shall come back to Apollonius), and like Pound, who apparently draws up lists in the same way. He writes to the censor:

> A very brief allusion to further study in names, that is, I am interested to note the prevalence of early American names, either of whites of the old tradition (most of the early presidents for example) or of descendants of slaves who took the names of their masters. Interesting in contrast to the relative scarcity of melting-pot names.[28]

The Micah–Ezra tension is perhaps more relevant to the general dynamics of the *Cantos* than it could appear at first sight, and would especially fit in with Pound's wish to see Jews obey their own law, which is very strict on matters of usury.[29] It might also throw some light on the obscure statement he made to Olson about the Jewish question in St Elizabeth: 'It's too bad, and just when I had plans to rebuild the Temple in Jerusalem for them. ....'[30]

Pound plays his role of the Paraclete for friends whose words will survive through his voice, but only if he achieves a mode of writing which can hold out and fight back the monopolists who will try to blot it out. Thus the names must be made to radiate, to convey their energies; this is why they are likely to be reduced to the status of exclamations such as 'Presente!' The Fascist salute becomes the more active mode of the Fascist evocation in the suppressed Italian Canto (Canto 72), whose title is 'Presenza'). While the political force of Canto 72 attempted to be heard through an elaborate interplay of masks and characters, now the pugnacious call to arms is introduced in a complex scrutiny, now active, now reflexive, of the evocative power of names. This may be exemplified by the jarring juxtaposition of the following two passages:

> I surrender neither the empire nor the temples
> > plural
> nor the constitution nor yet the city of Dioce
> each one in his god's name   (LXXIV, pp. 434–5)

and

> all of which leads to the death-cells
> each in the name of its god   (p. 441)

The 'god' in the second quotation functions as a misleading general idea, as an idol in short. But a proper name is not a particular object, nor is it a generality. The real role of a proper name is to describe without using a class. Hence the clue provided by the lines following the second quotation, which help to reconcile the positive and negative aspects of the 'god's name':

> lord of his work and master of utterance
> who turneth his word in its season and shapes it (p. 442)

The name implies first an utterance, or, in my terms, an enunciation apparently governed by the subject, but which might well lord it over him, and secondly a reference, that which is intended by the 'shape' of the word. Pound believes somehow that the situation of enunciation comes first, and the *Guide to Kulchur* shows it repeatedly: 'An imperfect broken statement if uttered in sincerity often tells more to the auditor than the most meticulous caution of utterance could' (*GK*, p. 129). In the same way, the *Analects* provides myriads of precise situations; each maxim must render 'the sense of the live man speaking' (*Con*., p. 194). This is all the more relevant as we know that Pound drafted his Pisan Cantos on sheets on the verso of which he was translating the *Analects*. This is how he presents them: they 'should be considered as definitions of words, and a number of them should be taken rather as lexicography, as examples of how Kung has used a given expression in defining a man or a condition' (*Con*., p. 194). Similarly, in the 'Pisan Cantos', if we do not find much 'lexicography', the sense of a living utterance is preserved till the end. As Confucius wished to 'fix the meaning and usage of the words' (*Con*., p. 277), so Pound strives for a total mobilisation of meanings, usages and utterances.

What matters is not so much sense, in terms of conceptual ideation or intellection, as reference, to use Frege's distinction between *Sinn* and *Bedeutung* (reference). Words can have different senses and a single reference (as is the case of the famous 'morning star' and 'evening star'). Proper names have no sense at all, taken strictly, if one understands by 'sense' the description of characteristics. But they do have a sense in that they are logically, even if loosely, connected with the objects or persons to which they refer.[31] Reference is played off against sense in the present of an enunciation which will be doubled by the reading-process, and I shall attempt to demonstrate its particularities in the 'Pisan Cantos'.

The mute fervour of tragic utterance haunted by silence or by erosion lurks behind the names Pound decided to include in his poem. While even asserting the magical power of the living voice, Pound transforms himself into the temple of his own writing, and this can be shown in the coupling of the clatter and the clutter. For indeed Pound knows that his personal tragedy is the logical outcome of a combat he had situated on the level of communication. He had decided to express himself publicly, using every medium available. And at a time when the Radio Rome officials were uncertain whether the broadcasts would be allowed to continue, Pound wrote Cornelio di Marzio a very revealing letter (28 December 1941): 'It seems to me that my speeches on the radio must continue IN MY OWN NAME, and with my voice, and not anonymously. . . . I can't write anonymous letters !!! and much less etc/ etc/ Either one fights, or one does not fight.'[32] 'Free radio speech' turns out to be the only way of signing one's ideas, and, in a

doomed but sublime utopia, Pound hoped that he could write his
signature in the air. But in Pisa the *ego scriptor* who is assured of having
gathered 'from the air a live tradition' (Canto LXXXI, p. 522) has gone
beyond the limitations imposed on EP speaking. And Pound's utter
consistency and sincerity (the word made perfect) has to be stressed;
he constantly denied the charge of treason because he knew he was not
giving 'Axis propaganda' in his broadcasts; he was only giving his own
propaganda – of course, fabricated from odds and ends gleaned from
Italian newspapers – and doing so in his own name. The radio seemed
to be the last medium open to a free individual, and Pound gave the
fact that he was allowed to speak as a proof that Radio Rome was really
free.

His idiosyncratic style in his broadcasts derives from the same
feeling, the impression he has that to make himself heard he must fight
against incredible odds, such as the lack of interest on the part of his
audience: 'Nothing solemn or formal will hold the American auditor.
If I don't sound a bit cracked and disjointed, they will merely twirl the
button and listen to the next comic song, dance or ballyhoolah
"soapopry". Hence the indications of American dialects etc. in the
spelling.'[33] The calculation in the tactics appears very rational,
although he more often than not sounds as if the mastery of his idiom
escaped him. However, he is quite self-conscious in this respect: 'Dearly
beeloved brevren, this is ole Ezry speaking. You probably do not
doubt it. You probably have derived that belief from the intrinsic
nature of the discourse, even if you tuned [in] after the announcement
of what was comin'.'[34] But at other times, Pound becomes excruciat-
ingly aware that the idiom and the discourse itself may hinder
communication: 'I am perfectly aware that I might as well be writing
Greek or talking Chinese with a foreign accent, so far as making this
statement clear to the hearer or reader is concerned.'[35] Here, the
hesitation between 'hearer' and 'reader' is all the more arresting as
Pound no doubt describes his *Cantos* as part of a general effort to
convey his concept of money.

Pound therefore never idealises the radio as a medium, seeing quite
well that the advantage of immediacy and broad diffusion is counterbalanced by the impossibility of connecting different points – in short,
of reassembling the facets of the ideogram as they are written in the air:

That is the disadvantage of the radio form, and heaven knows when I
shall be able to print the text in book or books available to the
American and English public. Book implying that the reader CAN,

when he wishes, look back, take up the statement of the Preface, see where Chap. x hitches on the Chap. I. Nevertheless you may as well make the effort to grasp at least the fact that there IS a sequence in what I am saying, and that the conversation of February coheres with that of April.'[36]

The recourse to the radio derives from the belief that usury has already taken over the press, and most of the printing-houses, and the voice aims at freeing print from the encroachments of finance; the *Leitmotiv* of the broadcasts refers back to Canto XIV:

> And the betrayers of language
> . . . . . .n and the press gang
> And those who had lied for hire;
> the perverts, the perverters of language,
>   the perverts, who have set money-lust
> Before the pleasure of the senses;
>
> howling, as of a hen-yard in a printing-house,
>   the *clatter* of presses,
> the blowing of dry dust and stray paper . . . .
>   (pp. 61–2, emphasis added)

The automatic 'clatter' calls up the 'clutter' of words, since the mono-polists are 'obstructors of knowledge, / obstructors of distribution' (p. 63). Whether the capitalist obstructs or overproduces, the result is the same: the system prints 'two lies at once' so that no one recognises the truth. A control of issue is the only solution, an issue which condenses the notions of just price and *le mot juste*: 'History without econ. is just gibberish. . . . Wherever one looks – printing, publishing, schooling – the black hand of the banker blots out the sun' (*L*, p. 263). The pure white light of the sun identified with absolute truth may nevertheless have to be filtered, but only by the hand of the honest printer. Thus is the 'man on whom the sun has gone down' or Ou Tis transformed by a series of displacements into the American patriot Otis, who attempted to revive printing in the early days of the young American Republic, but could not find a printer for his treatise on Greek metrics:

As long as the socialists use their accessories as red herring
to keep man's mind off the creation of money
many men's mannirs   videt et urbes πολύμητις
ce rusé personnage, Otis . . .   (LXXVIII, p. 482)

Otis then becomes associated with Soncino, an Italian printer of the
Renaissance, and Basinio, the author of a poem to Isotta, Malatesta's
mistress and wife: 'Otis, Soncino,/ the "marble men" shall pass into
nothingness' (LXXXII, p. 524). The phrase 'marble men' alludes not
only to the great figures of American independence, but also to
printers, with reference to the French expression le marbre, which
denotes the typographical slab or bed of stone. Although these printers
are bound to be forgotten, they have at least retained their names,
which can be memorialised by Pound, who did not deign to mention
the usurers' names in Cantos XIV and XV, because that would have
honoured them too much: 'In his edtn. he (Bird) tried to get the
number of . . . . . . correct in each case. My "point" being that not even
the first but only last letters of their names had resisted corruption' (L,
p. 293). The names, like works of art, reveal; they signal a vanishing
instance of utterance, thus of resistance: this does not imply pure
'presence', but rather the energy of enunciation which says 'Presente!'
Speaking subjects who keep their names in the Cantos escape from
oblivion, whilst the insignificance of noble women who attach too
much value to their fetish of a name is mocked by:

              Her Ladyship arose in the night
        and moved all the furniture
                  (that is her Ladyship YX)
        her Ladyship Z disliked dining alone and
            The proud shall not lie by the proud
                amid dim green lighted with candles   (LXXXII, p. 524)

This is also why the Cantos re-enacts the story of Pound's fight against
censorship by leaving a gap for Cantos LXXII and LXXIII.

Reference to conquer diffidence

        Proper names explain themselves and can be found
        in books of reference.
                                        (Basil Bunting[37])

Basil Bunting told Pound, according to Hugh Kenner, 'You allude too much and present too little',[38] or, in Pound's words, 'Basil Bunting told me that the *Cantos* refer, but they do not present.'[39] Like Basil Bunting, but with a positive appreciation, Hugh Kenner has consistently defended the thesis that the *Cantos* indeed 'refer' and do not 'present'. He interprets this referential quality as implying a trust in the purely denotative qualities of language, based on a belief in the reality of the exterior world, and as opposed to Eliot's web of 'post-symbolist' allusions. Kenner defines Pound's poetics as antagonistic to the 'poetic of the cave', 'the post-symbolist signification of ineffabilities, controlled by allusion and acoustic nuance':

> It is mimetic in one of the old senses of mimesis: its referents exist 'out there', in a place to which a Michelin map will guide you, perhaps two hours by car from Montségur. A system of words denotes that verifiable landscape. . . . The words point, point, and the arranger of the words works in trust that we shall find their connections validated outside the poem: connections he imitates on the page by the rhythmic and acoustic binding.[40]

I have attempted to situate Pound's poetry of reference in a system of *deixis* which equates saying with 'showing', implying that the signification of a designator is inseparable from what it refers to, in a dialogical situation which links speaker and addressee, or rather enunciator and coenunciator. If it follows from this analysis that reference rules out any poetics of 'presentation', does this mean that we have to submit the text to a test of empirical verification of the kind suggested by Kenner? If one has to agree that much obscurity is elucidated when a referent is located, it does not however follow that, once the obscurity has been cleared away, the sense of the poem is constituted by a superposition onto an actual map, for instance. To investigate the question and thereby sketch Pound's strategy of 'differential reference', I shall take an example from a well-known passage of the 'Pisan Cantos' which finds a precise locus when contrasted not with Eliot's post-symbolist poetics, but with William Carlos Williams's *Paterson* and his poetics of 'no ideas but in things'.

> Ed ascoltando al leggier mormorio
>   there came new subtelty of eyes into my tent,
> whether of spirit or hypostasis,
>   but what the blindfold hides

or at carneval
                    nor any pair showed anger
        Saw but the eyes and stance between the eyes,
colour, diastasis,
        careless or unaware it had not the
    whole tent's room
nor was place for the full Εἰδὼς
interpass, penetrate
        casting but shade beyond other lights
            sky's clear
            night's sea
            green of the mountain pool
            shone from the unmasked eyes in half-mask's space.
What thou lovest well remains,
                            the rest is dross
What thou lov'st well shall not be reft from thee
What thou lov'st well is thy true heritage
Whose world, or mine or theirs
                        or is it of none?
First came the seen, then thus the palpable
    Elysium, though it were in the halls of hell,
What thou lovest well is thy true heritage
What thou lov'st well shall not be reft from thee

The ant's a centaur in his dragon world.
Pull down thy vanity, it is no man
Made courage, or made order, or made grace,
    Pull down thy vanity, I say pull down.
Learn of the green world what can be thy place
In scaled invention or true artistry,
Pull down thy vanity,
                        Paquin pull down!
    The green casque has outdone your elegance.

                            (LXXXI, pp. 520–1)

At the end of the previous Canto, Pound had managed to overcome a
vehemently expressed despair ('Je suis au bout de mes forces/' –
p. 512); the image of a drowning Odysseus saved at the last moment by
the redeeming power of lyrical poetry was succeeded by a nostalgic
evocation of England culminating in the surprisingly grandiose or
flippant conclusion, 'sunset grand couturier' (p. 516). This stemmed

from the mention of 'her green elegance', connecting Nature as Gea-tellus in her spontaneous artistry with the conventional world of fashion suggested by the evocation of London. Thus it is no real surprise to find the name of Paquin, a well-known dress-designer at the turn of the century, spliced into the famous penitential hymn to the real source of love, contrition and atonement. Anyhow, the biblical rhetoric of lustration, taking its impetus from a private vision of eyes in the Camp's tent, has so much grandeur in its obsessive repetitions that Paquin's name has struck certain commentators as being slightly irrelevant. For my part, I knew of Paquin only through a popular bawdy song of the 1910s, 'Je suis biaiseuse chez Paquin', increasing the negative connotations of lust, luxury and vanity,[41] while Pound's American pronunciation of the name with a strong plosive 'p' would make it sound almost like 'faquin' (meaning cad, knave).

When we manage to learn more about Paquin, relevant features may be found, some of which destroy the web of speculative associations each reader is likely to spin for himself; for instance, the fact that she opened a house in London in 1912, at a time when Pound lived there but felt attracted by whatever came from Paris (' "We" in London 1911–14 were subsequent to a great deal of Paris' – *SP*, p. 427), strengthens the connection between the end of Canto LXXX and Canto LXXXI. But, on the other hand, she was the wife of a rich banker, Joseph Paquin, and exploited her entries into the higher echelons of Parisian society. Did Pound know of this, and is she meant to represent beauty bought by usury? Besides, she was not only a gifted designer, but also her own mannequin, and knew how to promote, advertise and manage her house in a very modern and efficient way.[42] Is she a symbol of grace and elegance, or of corruption and decadence? The only other explicit mention of her by Pound seems to go in the direction of a negative view: 'the mode Paris 1892–1910 is over. It is as uninteresting as a Paquin model for 1894.'[43] Is Paquin's name a kenning for what Williams calls 'obsolete'? Or is she a symptom of pure complacency and idolatry, since we learn that she exhibited a wax figure of herself at the Paris Exhibition of 1900? Pound seems to have known that green, along with white and gold, was one of her favourite colours for her much-admired evening gowns.

In the *Cantos*, the 'green casque' of Paquin has been undone by the elegance of nature, just as the pink casque of Stuart Merrill's 'baladines' assert hope and resilience.[44] And we thus are brought back to the text itself in order to ascertain the full impact of Paquin's association with Pound, and the real intention of the forceful

anaphoric link 'Paquin' – 'Pound' – 'Pull down'. The passage opens
with a description of a vision which may have been real or dreamt,
since the atmosphere is suffused with a half-light, a chiaroscuro
bordering on hallucination. Pound may allude to Dorothy's visit to the
DTC, or may wish to fuse the three women who haunt him ('Tre donne
intorno alla mia mente' – LXXVIII, p. 483). The subtle conceptual
framework situates 'stance' between the two antagonistic terms
'hypostasis' (meaning foundation, support, to stand under) and
'diastasis' (meaning separation, division, disintegration, displacement). An earlier passage had already introduced the scene with
almost mystical overtones:

> ... nor is this yet *atasal*
>   nor are here souls, nec personae
>   neither here in hypostasis, this land is of Dione
> and under her planet
>   to Helia the long meadow with poplars
> to Κύπρις   (LXXVI, p. 458)

Reticence and denegation manage to call up a scene which is not there,
since it is in the negative, although here as elsewhere the rhetorical
impetus of the verse transforms negation into affirmation: thus
invocation replaces the absent 'presentation'; the hymn and prayer are
the logical outcome of such a process. 'Hypostasis' takes on the clearly
neo-Platonic sense of fusion with the *nous* or world-soul, just as
'atasal' hints at full reunion with the divine.[45] However, a separation of
the eyes is necessary as the real condition for the sublimation of love
and reunion, just as the interpenetration of glances binds Donne's
lovers in 'The Ecstasy', a poem on which Pound commented:
'Platonism believed' (*ABCR*, p. 140). The *nous* is seen in spite of
obstacles, but also because of the obstacle of division.

And Paquin? Her presence acquires greater justification as soon as
we are alerted to the intertextual overtones, which derive from the
relatively strange orthography of *eidos*: *eidos* is grammatically a noun
in Pound's sentence, but he spells it with an omega (ω), which
dissociates it from the normal form with an omicron (o), meaning
form, vision, beauty. We have therefore moved away from the Platonic
eidos and are confronted with *eidōs*, a participle meaning aware,
knowing. Indeed, Pound is quoting from the Homeric 'Hymn to
Aphrodite', which stresses that the union between a mortal and a
goddess can never be achieved in full light, in the full knowledge of the

action; when Anchises sleeps with Aphrodite, she disguises her divine nature: 'Then by the will of the gods and destiny he lay with her, a mortal man with an immortal goddess, not clearly knowing what he did.'[46] *Ou sapha eidōs*, which implies semi-consciousness, is reserved for mortals, while in the following hymn to Aphrodite the gods can be 'amazed at the beauty [*eidos*] of violet-crowned Cytherea'.[47] The omega makes the difference between awareness, knowledge, perception and pure form or beauty. The lyrical impulse behind Pound's purgatorial prayer starts from an awareness of the limits of physical beauty, be it human or divine. The phenomenology of consciousness outlined here ('first came the seen, then thus the palpable') acquires its full importance when related to the conditions surrounding it ('Elysium, though it were in the halls of hell'). Paquin appears then as the necessary mediator between Nature and culture, man and goddess, above all between the poet's lonely fight and the forces of adversity, directly embodied by the victorious American armies (for whom she might pose as a dated pin-up).

There are clearly two worlds, the world of the 'live tradition' mastered at the cost of a life's dedication to beauty, and the world of anonymous barbarians: 'Whose world, or mine or theirs/ or is it of none?' The suggestion that the goddess might only appear to a 'No one', or blinded–castrated–mute *Ou tis*, has been explored before, but here the dialectical turn of the lustration brings back the vision and the awareness to the poet's own eyes:

> A fat moon rises lop-sided over the mountain
> The eyes, this time my world,
>> But pass and look *from* mine
>> between my lids
>>> sea, sky, and pool
>>> alternate
>>> pool, sky, sea   (LXXXIII, p. 535)

In Pound's unequal struggle, Paquin has to be punned into the feminine complement of 'No one', since she is *pas qu'un*, 'not just one': a feminine hand extended from the heavens or a tent's canvas, reawakening desire only to lead to sublimation, expiation and purgation. This is why the ending is so surprisingly triumphant:

> But to have done instead of not doing
> this is not vanity

> To have, with decency, knocked
> That a Blunt should open
>> To have gathered from the air a live tradition
> or from a fine old eye the unconquered flame
> This is not vanity.
>> Here error is all in the not done,
> all in the diffidence that faltered . . .   (LXXXI, pp. 521–2)

In the same way as a name was necessary to illustrate the point about beauty and fashion, a poet's name is given as another example of moral integrity (Pound alludes to Blunt's strong pacifist position during the First World War). The pairs of feminine eyes have taught other eyes to master their diastasis and find the 'old flame' of a tradition conveyed through glimpses and conversation. The substitution of Blunt's eyes for women's eyes reveals Pound's masculine bias, but also overcome the position of an aesthete such as Mauberley, who had remained 'inconscient' (like Anchises) of the 'diastasis' of 'wide-banded irides'; his belated connection between eyes and sexuality, crudely invoked by the pun on 'orchid',[48] flower and testicle, has been replaced by the latent play on 'casque', helmet, and flower of the genus of the orchis; the 'green casque' has indeed 'outdone' both Paquin and Mauberley.

The error would only have been not doing, not acting – Mauberley's sin of 'drifting' to an estrangement; here this is expressed by a complicated mixture of negatives and positives: 'all', 'not done', 'all', 'diffidence that faltered'. The error would have consisted in maintaining a modesty, a lack of confidence which hesitates, wavers: if the way to reference leads through difference, the way to difference leads through conquered diffidence, or, in other terms, reverence. For, while Williams wrote that there were 'no ideas, but in things', Pound could state that there is 'no presence, but in Names'.

A similar movement towards the conquest of diffidence is to be found in the core of Williams's *Paterson*, the famous key to the epic of the Passaic Falls, in which its author claimed to have discovered the seminal pattern of his 'variable foot'. The echoes linking *Paterson* and the 'Pisan Cantos' are numerous but have not been stressed as much as the more obvious references to *Finnegans Wake* or *Four Quartets*. But it seems to me that the main insight in Williams's poem, as for instance condensed in the magnificent phrase 'and no whiteness (lost) is so white as the memory / of whiteness', owes its conceptual rigour and its rhetorical force to Pound's meditation on time and memory in the Pisan sequence, and to his translations from Confucius: 'Washed in the

Keang and Han, bleached in the autumn sun's slope, what whiteness can one add to that whiteness, what candour?' (*Con*., p. 194).

In the following passage, Williams concentrates his gaze on the present, symbolised by the rock at the point where the water, both literal and metaphorical of time and history, rushes down to a kind of annulment:

> Look for the nul
> defeats it all
>
> the N of all
> equations   .
>
> that rock, the blank
> that holds them up
>
> which pulled away –
> the rock's
>
> their fall. Look
> for that nul
>
> that's past all
> seeing
>
> the death of all
> that's past
>
> all being   .

> But Spring shall come and flowers will bloom
> and man must chatter of his doom   .   .

> The descent beckons
>   as the ascent beckoned
>   Memory is a kind
> of accomplishment
>   a sort of renewal
>   even
> an initiation, since the spaces it opens are new
> places

> inhabited by hordes
> > heretofore unrealized,
> of new kinds –
> > since their movements
> > > are towards new objectives
> (even though formerly they were abandoned)
>
> No defeat is made up entirely of defeat – since
> the world it opens is always a place
> > formerly
> > > unsuspected. A
> world lost,
> > a world unsuspected
> > > beckons to new places
> and no whiteness (lost) is so white as the memory
> of whiteness   .[49]

The rock and the sudden absence of the rock, taken together, are the Falls: the perception of this identity relates the eye to memory, necessarily uniting past, present and future at the point where they converge in death. Memory nevertheless reaches a real foundation, a surface capable of resisting death and annihilation, the 'N of all equations'. This letter calls up in its very materiality the zigzagging triadic pattern of ascent, descent and upsurge of hope. The sign thus elaborated is a 'beckoning', or a waving-gesture which invites in a wink, bringing back eternal survival. In this version of a Joycean 'fortunate fall',[50] Williams discovers the perpetual ambivalence of terms usually treated as end-concepts, such as 'death', 'forgetfulness', 'lack of desire'; it is no mere metric grid that he discovers, but the conceptual movement which marks the best work of his later period, such as 'Asphodel', in which concepts and moods whirl up in an endless dialectical spiral.

The intricate syntax, which allows for multiple constructions through polyphonic enjambements ('look for that nul/that's past all/seeing/the death of all/that's past/all being'), leads to the assertion of pure process, uniting being and nothingness, all and null. The almost ironical rhyming-couplet singing of spring, of the return of Koré, or Persephone, deflates metaphysical anguish, reducing it to seasonal moods. Memory becomes the only dialectical engine of the process, since desire itself has vanished, in order to herald the triumph of life. Thus the self-revising, self-correcting and 'experimental' character of the poem finds a philosophical justification, since the movement of life and the evolution of form lead to the same breakthrough, inscribing 'what thou lov'st well' as the true heritage.

Accomplishment, renewal, initiation: these terms are almost synonymous with Pound's successive insights into the 'perfection of the word', 'making it new', and finding 'hypostasis' or true contemplation, yet in their dialectical rotation one cannot help feeling swept away a little too quickly, as if the process were asserted too confidently, with too great an allegorical onus. After Pound's bold use of breaks and parataxis, Williams almost appears as striving for a classical balance of concepts and feelings in this majestic sweep of reversals. The final transformation is no metamorphosis; it jumps over the particular intensity of statement to discover broad universals:

> The descent
> > made up of despairs
> > > and without accomplishment
> > realizes a new awakening:
> > > > which is a reversal
> of despair[51]

Form and content may well be completely fused in the triadic organisation of rhythms, themes, concepts and lines, but Williams cannot achieve the same 'poignancy of utterance' as Pound in the 'Pisan Cantos'. A very long 'even' will no doubt carry an incredible weight; the movement from 'accomplishment' to 'initiation' belongs more to a comfortable reassurance that life is worth living than to an intense agony leading to survival and light. One reason for this is that the theme of 'memory' has been stated, not enacted; Pound's strategy of reference, while doing away with any presentation (we have no 'scene', like *Paterson*'s masterly evocation of a Sunday crowd in the park) and replacing description by invocation or evocation of real persons (Paquin, Blunt) or hymns to mythical beings (Demeter, Aphrodite), makes us follow his struggle: the struggle for survival, which is also a struggle for enunciation and naming, bringing the light to the reader as an unexpected but logical triumph of poetry.

In spite of his credo that only 'particulars' and a sense of 'locality' can create the new poetic idiom, Williams succumbs in *Paterson* to the symbolic mode of representation.[52] With Pound's *Cantos*, the reader may constantly be nagged by the fear that he has lost sight of Pound's referents – all the more so as he guesses that no position of mastery is allowed to the author either; mastery has to be won, diffidence surmounted in the very act of uttering, of writing, of reading. The truth of the poem thus appears not just in the adequation with an exterior world, of whose reality no one, not even Berkeley, has ever doubted, but in the process by which someone or something becomes present, for a while, on the background of a structure made up of absence, before the long loop of reference curves back on itself, to complete itself on the blankness of the page.

That the name be the Name: ploce against catachresis

I have tried to situate Pound between a philosophy of reference and a philosophy of difference by relating his writing to a concern for *deixis*, showing and uttering in a given situation at the same time; this would point to what might be termed Pound's constitution of a 'nomenclature' – not merely, in Joyce's parodic distortion, a 'nomanclatter',[53] the clatter/clutter leading to the double bind through which Odysseus as 'No one' writes his idiom, but rather in the sense defined by Vico:

> Among the Greeks, 'name' and 'character' had the same meaning, so that the Church Fathers used indiscriminately the two expressions *de divinibus characteribus* and *de divinibus nominibus*. 'Name' and 'definition' have also the same meaning; thus, in rhetoric, under the head of *quaestio nominis*, we find a search for a definition of the *fact*, and in medicine, the nomenclature of diseases is the head under which their nature is defined.[54]

Thus Pound's marked drift towards nominalism in the later Cantos (under the influence of Coke and of his philological researches) – 'Si nomina nescis perit rerum cognitio' (CIX, p. 772) – still accompanies the affirmation and the invocation of the gods:

$$\delta\ \theta\epsilon\acute{o}\varsigma$$

runs thru his zodiac,
        misnaming no Caledon,
not in memory,
            in eternity
                and 'as a wind's breath
that changing its direction changeth its name',
                                Apeliota
                                    (CVI, p. 752)

As winds veer, names change to adapt to shifting conditions of enunciation:

> and the sheep on Rham plain have different names
> according to colour
> nouns, not one noun plus an adjective
>
> (CV, p. 747)

The genesis of this effort to link gods and names in a prelogical system of 'primitive thinking' can be traced back to a process of reverence for nature, as Vico suggests in the same analysis: 'In Roman law, *nomen* signifies right. Similarly, in Greek, *nomos* signifies law, and from *nomos* comes *nomisma*, money as Aristotle notes; and, according to etymologists, *nomos* becomes in Latin *nummus*. In French, *loi* means law, and *aloi* means money.'[55] This connection is observed by Pound:

> Mons of Jute should have his name in the record,
> thrones, courage, Mons should have his name in the record.
> Vasa klipped for the people, Lycurgus, nomisma,
> and 'limitation is the essence of good nomisma'   (XCVII, p. 672)

The montage of monetary history revisited by Del Mar and historical heroes forgotten by official chronicles will be examined in the next chapter; what matters here is the problematic of naming as self-consciously exhibited, used in a new reflexive mode. Courage has to do with the risk of a name endures (' "Ten men" said degli Uberti "who will charge a / nest of machine guns / 'for one who will put his name on a chit' – p. 676), because the cultural symptomatology inherited from Frobenius culminates in the sacred writing of a signature which can then underwrite one's 'reference': in Latin, *nomen* also means the inscription of a name in an account-book, designating a sum of money owed by the bearer of the name. To have a good *nomen* thus means to be free from debt. This is, as we shall see later, the one condition for the transmutation of *nomina* into *numina*, of names as nouns into Names as invocations of divinities.

This is why Basil Bunting's strictures about 'reference' may now be integrated into the general scheme of the *Cantos*. Indeed, Pound never wishes to 'present', to render the illusion of a scene taking place: he never has in mind to 'reproduce reality', as in a mirror-image; this trite sense of 'mimesis' he leaves to the novel. But does he obey the original sense of 'mimesis', so often recalled and stressed by William Carlos

Williams: to imitate the process, the workings, of reality?[56] 'To invent, not to copy!' But Pound does not try to 'invent' in that sense, as I have shown; for him to invent is to find, to dis-cover. But finding does not imply reproducing in a picture, and even when the *Cantos* 'show' Malatesta and Adams, they never stop long enough on a scene; the result of the montage of quotations is to force a whirl of details, particular objects, points of interest, clashes of utterances onto the reader. The real is not given 'in' the text – it remains outside; but it is as 'jagged', as unreadable, as the text. It is 'given' in a kind of eternal abundance in which everything is copresent – past, present and even future evoked by prophetic utterance; but it withholds itself as sign, the transparency looked for vanishes as soon as the operation of reading and of writing has begun.

Ultimately, the poet's voice cannot cover such a mass of whirling references, and he can merely point to the names themselves, in a movement of refer*a*nce (obliquely reminiscent of what Derrida calls 'differ*a*nce'), that is more homage than conjuration. The two dominant modes of utterance ushered in by the 'Pisan Cantos' are, on the one hand, the evocation of friends, enemies, important rulers, historical figures grasped through privileged sources, and, on the other, the invocation of gods and synthetic divinities. As a matter of fact, invocation is quite the opposite of 'suggestion', for references are all part of the jagged surface of the poem. What names may suggest is generally wrong, and Pound is amused at times by the anti-Cratylism of proper names: 'no soldier he although his name is Slaughter' (LXXXIV, p. 537). A proper name discloses an absolute reference because it embodies an absolute difference, a designation which loses all 'sense' in order that reference might become reverence. At best, names disclose a forgotten link with the numinous; they are symptoms of civilisations which kept their gods, their rites. The gods are immortal because we have retained their names, as so many traces which seem to say: 'They do not know they are dead', thus making them live on.

Reverence is best of all expressed in writing, in a different writing; thus names can remain traces, hieroglyphs, characters, palimpsests. This is why Pound wished to use a different type of writing as often as possible when he invoked the names of his favourite divinities: Athena, Dionysus, Persephone, Aphrodite, the Sun as Helios, the Earth as Gea are such numinous figures that not only are their names untranslatable, but they must retain their original characters; in this way, an English-speaker will not be able to pronounce them easily, will almost stumble on the obstacle. The names should not be pronounced in the same system as they are read; Pound's use of Chinese is here paradigmatic, since up to 1938 he had 'no idea' of the 'sound' of certain ideograms sent to him (*L*, p. 319).

The different foreign characters, Greek and Chinese, which are set in parallel in some instances, organise two modes of invocation. The Chinese characters introduce first a sense of decorative stress, then a mystique of numinous repetition, of enlightened tautology; the Greek letters compose lyrical burdens, submerged in the ancestral ear, closer to a chant or an hymn. As Pound explains, the *Cantos* are written in 'American', 'but the Greek, ideograms, etc., will indicate a duration from whence or since when. If you can find any *briefer* means of getting this repeat or resonance, tell papa, and I will try to employ it' (*L*, p. 322).

Pound was eventually to find a *briefer* mode of repetition – and no one would have thought to suggest it to him: the simple duplication of an ideogram on the page. This derives of course from the problematic of names:

> I speak of Sir William Pulteney.
>   Name for name, king for king
>
>   王   wang
>
>   王   wang
>
>   (LXXXIX, p. 591)

To enforce the principle of the *cheng ming* ('That the King . . . should be King . . .') Pound uses direct repetition, in which *wang* can be taken as noun and as name, as function and part of a proper name. This device recurs in the montage depicting the travels of Apollonius of Tyana:

> ANTONINUS reigned 138 to 161
> SEVERUS and Julia Domna about 198
>
>   王
>
>   王

. . .
not baffled by terror,
    and wanted to keep Sparta, Sparta,

        that the king   王   shd/ be king

王

μὴ ἐνομιλούντων
    not a melting-pot

                (XCIV, pp. 640–1)

In discussion with Egyptian sages, Apollonius praises Sparta for having kept intact the purity of its institutions and race (*me enomilounton* means 'from mingling'[57]). The rectification of names has consequences for the rejection of mingling, intermarriage, and 'melting-pot' names.

But then Pound embarks on a new voyage, this time through the *Sacred Edict of K'ang Hsi*, in which he attempts to discover an *arche* (Canto XCVIII, p. 686). The Salt Commissioner in Shensi translated an edict written in formal and official style so that he might make it accessible to the people, which meant that he used proverbs, homely sayings and repetitions of everyday idioms. The editor of the colloquial version of the *Edict*, F. W. Baller, concludes his introduction by saying that 'The Chinese think in quotations', and Pound uses this:[58]

        Iong-ching republished the edict
But the salt-commissioner took it down to the people
      who, in Baller's view, speak in quotations;
      think in quotations:
'Don't send someone else to pay it.'
Delcroix was for repetition.
      Baller thought one needed religion.
Without ²muan ¹bpo ... but I anticipate.
      There is no substitute for a lifetime.
The meaning of the Emperor,
      ten thousand years heart's-tone-think-say,
he had reigned for 61 years

敬　　　reverence

and τὸ καλόν

孝

'Parents naturally hope their sons will be gentlemen.'

正　　　cheng

經　　　king

The text is somewhat exigeant, perhaps you will consider the
meaning of

cheng　　正

king　　　經

(pp. 690–1)

The visual repetition is used as a direct appeal to the reader's attention;
Pound takes his cue from Baller's note which glosses the *Edict*'s phrase
quoted literally by Pound with 'Cheng-ching = "upright" in a
Confucian sense. Here it applies rather to individual deportment than
to rectitude between man and man' (p. 5, n. 9). The repetition is
nevertheless encapsulated within a general conception of man and
language, which takes the reader directly to the set of attitudes implied
by Confucian morals while this happens in his/her reading-act. But
Pound does not add a comment to the character, as Baller does; he
merely requires his reader to see and ponder.

And, when he comes to chapter VII of the *edict*, Pound finds his
technique confirmed; for the Emperor, in defining 'orthodoxy',
explains that no one should be led astray by Buddhist or Christian
'heresies': 'If you recognize that reason is true, and know that the mind
enlightened is heaven, the mind in darkness is hell – you will then as a
matter of course have a ruling principle . . .' (VIII.15, p. 87). Looking
up to find the ideograms used to express a maxim so close to his own
belief, Pound sees two characters repeated:

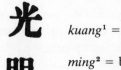

kuang[1] = light, brilliance, glory,
a man with a torch
ming[2] = bright, light, the sun and
moon together, intelligence

The significant repetition does not immediately trigger off a visual equivalent, for Pound just notes it, adding also Khati's maxim, 'A man's paradise is his good nature / (Khati) / doubled kuang[1] ming[2]' (Canto XCIX, p. 699). After this, the connection is made between Khati and the doubled characters:

Kuang
Kuang
Ming   Saith Khaty
Ming   (p. 702)

In Canto C, the repetitions become visual: we first find the 'white light' repeated (p. 718), and then the double *kuang ming* (p. 719). The accretions are endless, for this time it is Ford's maxim ('Get a dictionary and learn the meaning of words!') which is added to this peculiarly literal light:

'A DICtionary
                and learn the meaning of words!'

                    Kuan   光

                    Ming   明

Double it
                    Kuan   光

                    Ming   明   (p. 719)

Repetition is seen as structuring the ideogram, even devouring it. Pound uses the classical Chinese device of repeating a character, which transforms an adjective or a noun into a verb (not in the case of *wang*). The intensive repetition of a radical transforms nouns into names and names into verbs. The distinction Fenollosa made between the

Chinese character, which imitated the process of nature in rendering a faithful design of a sequence of actions, and Occidental abstraction, has now been overcome: through ploce, the principle of *cheng ming* ('That the King, who should reign, should be King indeed') has invested the whole field of names. Any name, repeated, will take on the added meaning of the 'indeed' which marks the figure of ploce (as in 'a woman who is a woman indeed'). Repetition becomes synonymous with 'putting a *name* – not an idea – into action'. In the case of the King, the name will be identical with the function: the proper name will be proper or fitting. This is the main mode of 'reference' Pound wishes to reactivate. As it is, it conveys a whole ideology (as one can see in the case of the 'melting-pot') while subverting all the common terms which would be needed to articulate the subject of ideology: for such an ideology of naming turns into a radically new way of writing.

Rhetoric and music blend in a strange polyphony made up of repetitions, the didactic passages alternating with the paradisiac moments of elevation. Pound all the time asserts that he only says what he says; he quotes Chinese classics or edicts which apparently only state the obvious:

> Gt. is gt. . Little is little;
> With friends one is one
> 2 is 2   (XCIX, p. 705)

But, when he repeats that he adds nothing or just means what he says, he does so in such a clipped, elliptical way that the reader is either led to the source (and then reads Baller's footnote, for instance) or wishes to see, out there, what happens or happened in the real world, or in history. Armed with a little key, the reader goes back to the text, which remains as impenetrable; one may at times feel as baffled as when, following up the hint provided by the index-heading 'To recapitulate' in the *Guide to Kulchur* (p. 348), which refers to the entry 'Food' on p. 111, one merely finds, 'No place to stay for any time, but food every ten miles or fifteen or twenty. When I say food, I mean food. So, at any rate, it was.'

We should be wrong to voice our disappointment: this entry might have been the point of departure for the wonderful catalogue of restaurants and cafés which the 'Pisan Cantos' holds in store. Besides, the injunction to repeat, the imbrication of whirling *Leitmotive* and the repetitive sequences of the later Cantos indicate the need for a new conception of signs. Repetition sets off a rhetoric of its own, but first presents itself as the destruction of all rhetorics. To repeat 'that the name be the Name' in so many broken half-quotations is tantamount to realising the particular force, violence or wisdom contained in each word.

> Wisdom lies next thee,
>   simply, past metaphor.   (LXXXII, p. 526)

A new economy of the sign should bypass conventional rhetorics by replacing metaphors, either too formal or too worn out, by ploces. The ploce as intensive repetition eradicates the perversion of language which Pound calls metaphoric but is in fact catachrestic – since a catachresis refers to an impropriety of language, especially whenever a proper term is lacking and has to be supplemented by a tropological denomination. The 'arm' of a chair, a 'sheet' of paper are thus dormant metaphors which have been included in everyday language. The normal tendency of language-use moves towards a loss of differences, a dwindling of energy, entropy finally. Thus, according to Pound, or to Mallarmé for that matter, language is contaminated by usury. Against language as used and abused, against the erosion of tropes, Pound wishes to promote a new political economy of the sign.

This is why the question of signs, wider than that of names, situates itself between *catachreses* as they tend to dominate and proliferate in the usual chrematistics of language (the same root links both words: *kata-chrestai* meaning to mis-use, *chrema-chrestai* to use things, possessions, hence to make money and do business) and the *ploces* articulated in numinous repetitions of names. By the use of ploces, the frontiers between names and signs break down, while the new economy attempts to define the synthesis relating signs and objects, names and bearers, production and distribution in a general circuit of exchanges. This will be the subject of the next chapter.

The question of naming leads inevitably to that of the structure of paternity, and from the first Canto to the last the horizon of the periplus remains the same: the quest for a name. This is the main subject of the *Odyssey*, since Telemachus wants to find a father, dead or alive, in order that his fame, his *kleos* (meaning both memory and glory), should survive him. Only once he has found him can the real competition between Telemachus and the suitors start, and the legitimate son be in a position to claim the kingdom on the strength of his father's name. In the same way, the entire life of Homeric heroes is spent in the hope of acquiring a name in order to escape from the dire and pitiful fate of the 'nameless' victims who crowd the corridors of Hell. The sea is, of course, the privileged place for an anonymous disappearance; not all the heroes have the good fortune of having Leucothea's veil extended to them, or even Elpenor's posthumous rites:

> 'What gain with Odysseus,
> 'They that died in the whirlpool
> 'And after many vain labours,
> 'Living by stolen meat, chained to the rowingbench,
> 'That he should have a great fame
>> 'and lie by night with the goddess?
> 'Their names are not written in bronze
>> 'Nor their rowing sticks set with Elpenor's;
> 'Nor have they mound by sea-bord.
>
> (xx, pp. 93–4)

The still anonymous sailors, like the tovarish sown by Cadmus, all ask for their difference to be inscribed in a ritual space. Pound believes that even if 'toujours le beau monde gouverne' and 'gli uomini vivono in poci',[59] the entire system of values and of signs can be bettered for all. The reconstruction of an entire architecture of myths, values and words entails that the difference of 'proper' names should be founded on reverence, or on respect for the symbolical structure.

Once more, Confucius demonstrates this: 'Tze-Yu asked about filiality. He said: Present day filial piety consists in feeding the parents, as one would a dog or a horse; unless there is reverence, what difference is there?' (*Con.*, p. 198).

5 Poundwise: Towards a General Critique of Economy

> What is the meaning of 'useful'? . . . What is capable of use in the hands of some persons, is capable in the hands of others, of the opposite of use, called commonly 'from-use' or 'abuse'. . . . Thus, wine, which the Greeks in their Bacchus, made, rightly, the type of all passion, and which, when used, 'cheereth god and man' (that is to say, strengthens both the divine life, or reasoning power, and the earthly, or carnal power of man); yet, when abused, becomes 'Dionusos', hurtful especially to the divine part of man, or reason. And again, the body itself, being equally liable to use and to abuse, and, when rightly disciplined, serviceable to the state, both for war and labour; but when not disciplined, or abused, valueless to the State, and capable only of continuing the private or single existence of the individual (and that but feebly) – the Greeks called such a body an 'idiotic' or 'private' body, from their word signifying a person employed in no way directly useful to the state; whence, finally, our 'idiot', meaning a person entirely occupied with his own concerns. (John Ruskin, 'Ad Valorem', *Unto this Last*[1])

Pound's 'obsession' with money and usury has been well documented, and is generally dismissed as the main root of all his 'aberrations'. I should like to show that, on the contrary, his lifelong concern with money and economics not only provides a key to his system of thought – in which, indeed, it rationalises certain important delusions – but also reveals an attempt to inscribe the moving and complex signature of his name in the world of history and art. An ultimate self-reference underlies the scattered allusions to actual facts and theories and ties up

183

his 'voice' to an idiomatic writing. Although it sounds a little too complacent to agree wholeheartedly with Allen Ginsberg that Pound's economics are 'right',[2] one can asseverate that they stimulate an understanding of our world in a manner both novel and perplexing; moreover, if they are at times inextricably confused, they are never boring, and the source-books to which the reader is directed prove worth reading. Obviously, one never reads Pound for his economic theories only, but any reading which would try to discard them as an unnecessary adjunct to the gems or lyrical purple patches would fail by Pound's own standards: it would overlook the wish to create a totalitarian synthesis of culture, and remain blind to the particular strategies dictated by the nature of the text.

The crucial role of money, which so much haunts Pound, is revealed by an essential difference around which all subsequent definitions revolve: the difference between usury and interest. Since the terms 'usury' and 'interest' escape the formal barriers set up by professional economists, what appears to be at stake is the status of difference in writing, a difference valorised positively, as we shall see, in Pound's conception of interest. I should thus essentially wish to question the link most critics still establish between interest and usury, as if they were synonyms in Pound's views – a mistaken assumption which is expressed by Kurt Heinzelman, for instance: 'Pound hated the idea of interest because, as the essence of usury, it represented the self-perpetuating power of money.'[3] If, on the contrary, the difference between a just interest and usurious practice opens up a new reading of cultural history, it is because difference as such is generated by the writing- and reading-process.

The interpretation of history is conceived by Pound from the start as hinged around some fraction which embodies irreducible difference: 'I offer another axis of reference: the difference between maritime and agrarian usury, the difference between 30 per hundred and 6% average Roman usury' (*GK*, p. 34). From such a perception of a quantification of fractional processes can the totalitarian effort tend towards a grasp of all parameters at work in history: thus will critics be able 'to tell from the quality of a painting the degree of tolerance or intolerance to usury extant in the age and milieu that produced it' (p. 27). Symptomatic readings of this type will then have to be generalised, in the hope that percentages and fractions may add up and disclose the totality of a symbolic order.

An analysis of usury is the ideal foundation for a new synthesis, assembling the pure and radiant nuggets of the past. The fact that

Pound's public and private Inferno should have been associated with a prophetic denunciation of the occult power of finance and the devotees to Mammon should not postpone the main affirmation: the agonised re-creation of a religion and a culture after the apocalypse has come – be it the Quattrocento, the American Civil War, the First World War, or the Second World War and the end of the Fascist utopia at Saló. After the fall, the task of salvaging remains to be executed. In order to relate Pound's critical effort to the writing of the *Cantos*, one has to follow his economic arguments and take seriously his theses on money. They cover a wide range of motifs, from sexual instinct to politics, from ethics to writing, since the ultimate goal of these interlocking chains of thought is the constitution of a general science of signs, or semiology. Pound's critique aims at founding a new signifying-activity of language and money in a system which accounts for the logics of linguistic, sexual and commercial exchanges. A genesis of the sign will be sketched from its origin to its distribution, a distribution which will have to bear the onus of the argument when it appears that it not only is opposed to production, but completely replaces production in the system's economy.

Ruskin, Dante and the Bible

Considering Pound's intense preoccupation with money and economy from the end of the 1910s onward, what strikes one is not that monetary themes recur throughout the *Cantos*, but rather that no consistent technical vocabulary is mastered – in short that there is no autonomous Poundian economic theory. On the other hand, his signature and idiolectic mark is unmistakable on all the theories he borrows from. Thus Pound's peremptory assertions have sometimes misled commentators who attempt to place him within the series of unconventional economists without situating his point of departure among classical writers such as Dante and Ruskin. It is from such a firm basis that one can understand his association with Douglas and the Social Credit reformers, his enthusiasm for Gesell and certain daring experiments.

Ruskin, whose life took a parallel course to Pound's, provides the first essential link between Pound's aesthetic expertise and his commitment to monetary reform. It was not until the 1940s that Pound found confirmation of this link (which he was to qualify with important reservations) in Brooks Adams's *Law of Civilization and Decay*, which provides a complete survey of the monetary history of Western civilisation and states clearly the belief that art reflects economics: 'In an economic period, like that which has followed the Reformation, wealth is the form in which energy seeks expression; therefore, since the close of the fifteenth century, architecture has reflected money.'[4] However, Ruskin's views had long been available to Pound, from the *Stones of Venice*, which yields most of the insights on which Canto XLV is based,[5] to the concept of an organic totality of life, of 'wholeness' which has been impaired by usury. The 'integrity of being' has been destroyed by malevolent powers, which entails that aesthetical treatises have to be completed by a theory of economics.[6] The similarities of tone between *Munera Pulveris*, *Unto this Last*, *Fors Clavigera* and the *Cantos* are so striking that one ought to go back to the inception of Ruskin's attempts at mastering the concepts of political economy in *The Political Economy of Art*.[7]

Ruskin and Pound share the same fundamentalist approach, blending naïvety and philological subtlety, sweeping generalisations and astute concrete projects. Ruskin, like Pound, addresses a wide and unspecialised audience, explaining that the first principles of political economy ought to be understood 'by all who mean to take the responsibility of citizens' (*Political Economy*, p. vii). The terms 'political' and 'economy' are referred back to their origins in the *polis* and *oikos*, for the city and the house stand in dialectical combination. The competence of specialists or professional men is of little use, and completely misses the point, which lies in the interdependence of the two domains: 'a large number of our so-called merchants are as ignorant of the nature of money as they are reckless, unjust, and unfortunate in its employment' (p. viii). Ruskin disowns most classical economists, Adam Smith excepted, because 'the authors themselves had been not unfrequently prevented from seeing to the *root* of the business' (ibid.). From Adams to Ruskin, the insistence of unprejudiced analysis of the 'root' or 'nature' of money in fundamental.

The etymological procedure entails one consequence: Ruskin refuses to distinguish between the economy of social exchanges and domestic economy, since the 'administration of a house' and 'the wise management of labour' are founded on the same root and the same natural, or rather familial, order. Thus the 'mistress of a household' is presented as the 'perfect economist', for she has to balance economy and luxury, sparing and spending. And, by the introduction of the theme of luxury, Ruskin manages to relate his analysis of political economy to an element which he feels to be neglected by economists:

the production of art. Ruskin insists that, if a nation cannot produce 'pleasant luxury', which means good art, it decays and perverts the 'serenity and morality of life' (*Political Economy*, p. 17). Among the basic needs of a population are food, clothing and art, while the laws deduced from the sane management of a farm can apply to a whole country. Ruskin is so eager to reconcile the oppositions he starts from that he bypasses the question of production as such, and when he defines the management of labour he only sketches three moments: apply your labour rationally, preserve its produce carefully, distribute it reasonably (p. 15). For him, indeed, only peasants and artists appear as producers, which is echoed by Pound (in an article written before any contact was made with Major Douglas or other economists): 'The nation is profoundly foolish which does not get the maximum of best work out of its artists. The artist is one of the few producers. He, the farmer and the artisan create wealth; the rest shift and consume it' (*LE*, p. 222). In the same manner, Ruskin explains that 'men of genius' can not be 'produced' but only discovered (*Political Economy*, p. 24); once the real artist or producer is found, the state should take care of him, help him to refine himself and progress. Thus for Ruskin, as for Pound, the process is always 'sifting, melting, hammering, purifying – never creating' (ibid.). The 'gold' of genius cannot be created *ex nihilo*, but should thrive in an organic system.

The economics of culture are underlain by an ontology of creation, which has to be developed by an ethics of communication. If the analogy between domestic and political economy holds true (and Pound will find a confirmation in Confucius), this presupposes an exact correspondence between the rights of the paterfamilias, the duties of a teacher and preacher, and the sovereignty of a head of state. Ruskin advocates a sense of fraternity and filial deference that will permit all the metaphorical 'farm hands' to be taken in charge by a 'paternal government': 'The real type of a well-organized nation must be presented, not by a farm cultivated by servants who wrought for hire, and might be turned away if they refused to labour, but by a farm in which the master was a father, and in which all the servants were sons' (*Political Economy*, p. 20). Such a paternalistic and agrarian community relies on a theological model of the world, and Pound is critical of its excesses, especially when it leads Ruskin to a global rejection of the machine: 'Ruskin was well-meaning but a goose. The remedy for machines is not pastoral retrogression' (*SP*, pp. 194–5). A more precise definition of money and circulation is required.

Pound's definition of money starts, like Ruskin's, from a demarcation between a domain in which the familial model applies to the state and a domain in which anarchy reigns, or, more precisely, between real 'economy' and 'chrematistics'.[8] 'Economy' follows an end, just distribution and consumption, whilst 'chrematistics' aims at making money for its own sake. The Greek conception of this radical opposition falls back on the metaphysical division between a closed and ordered *cosmos*, and the threatening infinity of an *apeiron*, a disharmonious in-finite which brings about chaos and disorder. In an interesting way, Pound has grasped that the concept of infinity did not belong to the Greek vision of the world, and that, if usury appeared as the indefinite proliferation of an intermediary, as the endless reproduction of money attacking natural prodiction, it had to be expressed in terms foreign to the Greek equation of *cosmos* with beauty and order – namely, in the terms left to us by Judaeo-Christian theology. This is why the antagonism between usury and wholeness is often dramatised by Pound as the struggle between Jewish *neshekh* and Classical *to kalon* – not for superficial (or ideological) and racialist reasons, but for a conceptual reason. A passage from an Addendum to Canto c, published in 1942, will allow us to situate all these terms:

> The Evil is Usury, *neschek*
> the serpent
> *neschek* whose name is known, the defiler,
> beyond race and against race
> the defiler
> Τόκος   hic mali medium est
> Here is the core of evil, the burning hell without let-up,
> The canker corrupting all things . . .
> . . .
> Poisoner of the fount,
>   of all fountains, *neschek*,
> The serpent, evil against Nature's increase,
> Against beauty
>   Τὸ καλόν
>   formosus nec est nec decens
>   (Addendum for c, p. 798)

Aristotle's denunciation of chrematistics in the *Republic* is spliced in with an appeal to the law of the Bible, while *tokos*, meaning 'born' and 'usurious interest' is set rhyming with *to kalon*, 'the beautiful'. I shall come back to a fuller examination of the term *tokos*, and wish only to underline the use of a Jewish concept, which goes along with a refusal to identify usurers with a given race: 'Usurers have no race. How long the whole Jewish people is to be sacrificial goat for the usurer, I know not . . . It cannot be too clearly known that no man can take usury and observe the law of the Hebrews. No orthodox Jew can take usury without sin, as defined in his own scriptures.'[9]

In the *Guide to Kulchur*, Pound explains that he wants historians to study the rates of interest in antiquity, and even to go back to the Scriptures:

> I wd. go back even further and suggest that the forbidden fruit of Hebrew history is a usury parable. At least that wd. make sense, the distinction between *neschek*, corrosive usury, and *marbit* (or pronounce it marbis if you prefer) is clear in the pentateuch. If you take it that the age of abundance ended when the *marbit* swelled out into *neschek* you wd. avoid a number of contradictions. (*GK*, p. 42)

Pound has had access to precise sources, for indeed in several places (such as Exodus 22:25, Leviticus 25:36, and Deuteronomy 23:19–20) the *neshekh* is forbidden, and can be distinguished from *tarbit* (*marbit* in Pound's transliteration). However, the distinction is more semantic than legal: *neshekh* (literally 'bite') is advance interest, and corresponds to the exaction of interest seen from the debtor's point of view, while *tarbit* is the increase or recovery seen from the point of view of the creditor;[10] *both* are explicitly condemned: 'Take thou no usury of him, or increase' (Leviticus 25:36). Even the minimal interest on crops was forbidden; but, of course, the interdiction did not apply to dealings with foreigners: 'Unto a stranger thou mayest lend upon usury; but unto thy brother thou shalt not lend upon usury' (Deuteronomy 23:20). When the Catholic Church declared in 1179 that the taking of interest was forbidden by Holy Scripture, it made money-lending the main Jewish business. Not only did Canon Law not apply to Jews, but they had few other opportunities for lucrative trade.

This historical evolution is well-known, and it is fascinating to see how Pound forgets the lesson of real history to construct his own myth of origins; using his skill as philologist and reader, he attempts to come to terms with the Law, never surmising that the Law might not be the same for all, or that it could differentiate between peoples. Whereas the Mosaic Law differentiated between the chosen people and the others, Pound situates the division within mankind as a whole, between natural increase and the venomous bite of the serpent. Thus the Garden of Eden is a world free from usury; the serpent is the arch-usurer, persuading Eve to eat of the fruit in order that together their 'bites' should endlessly 'gnaw' at the perfection of life. Pound thus feels free to go back to the original Word which forbids sin and opens the door to a prelapsarian Paradise; this is how he hopes to 'rebuild the Temple', and this notion recurs all the more in the 'Pisan Cantos' in that this Temple is now the only one he can erect.

The few quotes from the Bible he found in Pisa, especially Isaiah 1:27 ('Zion shall be redeemed with judgement, and her converts with righteousness'), blend together to compose the Jewish ideogram of Justice in these Cantos:

> to redeem Zion with Justice
> sd/ Isaiah. Not out on interest said David rex (LXXIV, p. 429)

This becomes a *Leitmotiv* of the earliest Cantos in the sequence, and is developed in a vignette:

> and there is also the XIXth Leviticus.
> 'Thou shalt purchase the field with money.'
>   signed Jeremiah
> from the tower of Hananel unto Goah
> unto the horse gate $8.50 in Anatoth
> which is in Benjamin, $8.67
>   For the purity of the air on Chocorua
>   in a land of maple
>   From the law, by the law, so build yr/ temple
>   with justice and meteyard and measure
>   (LXXIV, p. 440)

Pound associates the interdiction of usury in Leviticus with the story of Hanamel, who buys a field in Anathoth (Jeremiah 32:7–9). The passage insists on the right sum, 17 shekels, transposed into US dollars by Pound, and on God's commands to buy the field with money: 'Fields shall be bought for money, and deeds shall be signed and sealed and witnessed . . .' (Jeremiah 32:44). This sealing is the sign that the Law is the same for all, and, in Pound's logic, if the Jews did not follow their own Law, he was entitled to feel more Jewish than the Jews – which, by the way, is an excellent recipe to learn to continue persecuting oneself.[11]

Pound does not realise that it is contradictory to enforce Canon Law and the Jewish Law at the same time, although they both say the same thing; but they leave free play for the Other. For Pound, the Other is already within, silently gnawing, destroying the fruit from the inside. Nevertheless, Canon Law succeeded in establishing a synthesis between the Greek concepts derived from Aristotle and the teachings of Judaeo-Christian revelation, and this is why Pound constantly returns to it, especially as he finds it backed by Dante's allegories of Hell.

Dante puts the usurers in Hell in Canto xvii of his *Inferno*, but, if Pound decides to situate his own Hell in Cantos xiv and xv, it is a pointer to Dante's own Canto xv, which accuses certain famous literati of the time, such as Brunetto Latini, or of the past, such as the grammarian Priscian, of homosexuality and blasphemy; the link between Phlegeton (Canto xiv) and Geryon (Canto xvi) is achieved by the denunciation of 'la trahison des clercs', or in Dante's view, of those who either abandon their maternal language[12] or attempt to rectify it by depriving it of life. The progressive link established by Dante between blasphemy, sodomy and usury is condensed by Pound into the term 'perversion': the perversion of language and of money attacks the root or fount of all things.

The 'fount' is of course the root of the 'mysteries', or the sacred nature of fertility as enacted in coition. The intense light of the orgastic fusion is attacked by the necessary barren nature of money; or, if any offspring stems from money, it is perverted at the root, like the Honest Sailor's son. Dante's *Inferno* and Pound's Hell list philologers and perverters of language as directly contributing to the general conspiracy: the 'pets-de-loups, sitting on piles of stone books, obscuring the texts with philology' are like Brunetto, who sold his *Livre du Trésor*, a compendium of tropes and expressions in usage, to another tongue and culture. This leads to sterility both in a literary way and in a concrete way, and Pound no doubt remembers, when he accuses Usura of having lain *'between* the young bride and her bridegroom' in Canto xlv, that the Epilogue of Christopher Hollis's pamphlet on economics, *The Two Nations*, concludes with a parallel between 'the age of usury' and 'falling birth-rates'.[13]

'Tokos' as 'son' and interest

The questions of generation and of usury appear from the start as inextricably confused, for interest is the 'offspring', the 'son', of money. Can it be reconciled with the father in a just system, or must it always bear the responsibility of perversion, division, fragmentation? In its ambiguous role of *pharmakos* – a role notably played by the Jews, as Pound keenly noted – the son may often take the guise of a rival threatening to usurp his father's place. Hence its ambivalent nature, acting both as poison and as remedy, as Derrida's reading of Plato and of the 'metaphysical' attacks on writing have so well shown.[14] What nevertheless stands out for Pound is the undeniable economic fact that interest is born organically from exchange and may pervert it from within. Can it belong to 'economy' without being produced by a mechanism similar to capitalism; can it be fostered by natural production?

Pound's denunciation of chrematistics, which destroys the order of the city, is consistent with the theme of perversion and dual origin; for, in the unlimited cycle whereby money breeds money, reversing the natural order of wares–money–wares, the 'offspring', or *tokos*, takes the place of the 'father' or principal. In a way, the usurious interest duplicates the pattern of Oedipus, who discovers he is both son and husband, offspring and origin. If Pound's conception of montage in his *Cantos* rules out any ordered exposition of economic themes, he nevertheless knows that he has to bring about a *peripeteia*, a brisk reversal of perspective, a sudden flash of light disclosing a blinding truth. The structure of the 'detective story', which follows the pattern of the discovery by Oedipus that he is both sleuth and villain, and thus must act out his punishment himself by putting out his eyes, underlies much of the quest for truth that the *Cantos* dramatises so powerfully. And the fact that Pound seems to accept a little too uncritically the mediaeval coupling of usury with sodomy stems in fact from a deeper insight of the Oedipian tale; for the original curse of Laios's offspring derives from his seduction of a young boy. Laios, according to certain legends, had raped the young Chrysippos, who had then committed suicide. His condemnation was then pronounced by the oracle at Thebes, dooming him to be killed by any son he might get from Jocasta. Jocasta herself was a great-grand-daughter of Pentheus, who, as the *Cantos* tells us repeatedly, had been slaughtered by the Maenads when he tried to oppose the cult of Dionysus.

All these motifs are linked by Pound in the *Cantos*, in a way which shows that the theme of *tokos* inheres in a historical and cosmic tragedy. Let us now reread the famous statement by which Paterson founds modern banking:

> Hath benefit of interest on all
> the moneys which it, the bank, creates out of nothing.
>
> Semi-private inducement
> Said Mr RothSchild, hell knows which Roth-schild
> 1861, '64 or there sometime, 'Very few people
> 'will understand this. Those who do will be occupied
> 'getting profits. The general public will probably not
> 'see it's against their interest.'   (XLVI, p. 233)

In quoting from Hollis's *Two Nations* the famous declaration which exposes the trick by which the Bank of England cheats the people of its own money, Pound not only triggers the important associations William Carlos Williams develops in his American-based epic, but also immediately plays on the same type of 'Joyceian riddle' as *Paterson*.[15] Paterson, who creates out of nothing, becomes the real Pater–Son, father and son of credit, thereby obeying the strange logic of the *tokos*, the supplement of interest which usurps the function of the father. Such a perversion of paternity attacks the real 'interest' of the community, and gnaws into the natural increase from which money should be derived. Pound's anti-semitism crops up when he chooses to juxtapose the names of Rothschild and of Paterson, since he splits the name, first with an upper-case S, then with an hyphen, to stress the derivation of 'child' from the emblem of 'semitic excess' (instead of merely emphasising the original meaning 'Red Shield', for instance). What is then suggested in a rather devious way is that all those who would have had access to information have already been caught up in the swindle, have become 'children' of the linguistic and capitalistic process. The phrase 'occupied/getting profits' thus represents the inclusion of Aristotelian chrematistics within a more sweeping satanic inversion of values, since 'Hell' alone knows who is who in that almost obliterated history of usury. Indeed, chrematistics appears as mere obfuscation, while the infinite cycles of *tokos*-breeding spiral up and down inside one another.

This is confirmed in Canto XLVIII, which starts with a characteristically unanswered question:

> And if the money be rented
> Who shd pay rent on that money?
> Some fellow who has it on rent day,
>   or some bloke who has not?

. . .
                    Was put in the cellarage
Van Buren having written it down
'deface and obliterate' wrote J. Adams
'become fathers of the next generation' wrote Marx
..tuberculosis...Bismarck
blamed american civil war on the jews;
particularly on the Rothschild
one of whom remarked to Disraeli
that nations were fools to pay rent for their credit
Δίγονος
DIGONOS; lost in the forest; but are then known as leopards
after three years in the forest; they are known as 'twice-born'.
                                                            (pp. 240–1)

Pound manages to reintroduce a quotation from Marx's *Capital* in a very telling context. Earlier on, in Canto XXXIII, he referred to Marx's analysis of the exploitation of children as the outcome of the violent transformation of British industry, and quoted directly, 'report of '42 was merely chucked into the archives and remained there while these boys were ruined and became fathers of this generation' (p. 162). They are here juxtaposed by a deft splicing of motifs with abandoned children who have turned wild, and who, because of their association with wolves and leopards, are devoted to the god Dionysus; Dionysus, as inventor of wine, which symbolises rapture and frenzy, stands for the *pharmakos*, the Other who is potentially destructive as well as regenerative. These children are born a second time, just as Dionysus, born a first time from his mortal mother Semele – who died on perceiving the full thundering stature of Zeus, who had impregnated her – was born a second time from the thigh of his immortal father. The epithet *digonos*, usually reserved for Dionysus, is here applied to these waifs, just as money as *tokos* is born 'twice' because it is created out of nothing and because people have to pay for it.

The Greek legends blend with Marx's impassioned denunciation of the brutal drudgery of these poor working-class children, sold by their parents, forced to work like slaves day and night in factories. The calvary of such forced labour had also been denounced by the Children's Employment Commission, at the time of the several Factory Acts which were never enforced. Marx shows how the shift from small factories towards large-scale industrial exploitation destroys the structure of the family, since the first enemies of these children were their parents. Capitalism has done away with the traditional *patria potestas*, Marx explains.[16] The inversion of traditional values is, however, not attributed to the parents themselves but to the system of capitalistic exploitation. Thus, children deprived of 'education, morals, religion or familial love'[17] become the 'fathers of this actual generation'. They enact in their tortured bodies the fate of the *tokos*, the offspring sacrificed to the production of alienated work which, as it were, creates them anew, as fathers of their fathers, and heirs to the creation *ex nihilo* of money and capital.

The passage from Canto XLVIII links, in a fascinating layering of images, the picture of the European industrial revolution, with Germany following hard on the heels of Britain, and the American Civil War, depicting at the same time the dialogue between the three Jews, Marx, Disraeli and Rothschild, who dominate the second half of the nineteenth century. They point to the foolishness of nations which are willing to be gulled by a system which replaces natural generation by the autonomous production of capital. The true heritage of creative personalities such as Van Buren is forgotten (his memoirs are put aside 'in the cellarage', since they were written in 1854 and published in 1918), just as official reports can be 'shelved' for more than twenty years. Instead, one finds the overwhelming power of capitalistic reproduction, as summarised by Marx in the context of the creation of central banks:

> The Bank of England began lending its money to the government at 8%; at the same time it was empowered by Parliament to coin money out of the same capital, by lending it again to the public in the form of bank-notes. It was allowed to use these notes for discounting bills, making advances on commodities, and for buying the precious metals. It was not long ere this credit-money, made by the bank itself, became the coin in which the Bank of England made its loans to the state, and paid, on account of the state, the interest on the public debt. It was not enough that the bank gave with one hand and took back more with the other; it remained, even whilst receiving, the eternal creditor of the nation down to the last shilling advanced.[18]

The whole thrust of Marx's analysis is, then, to reconstruct the complete mechanism which produces such an inextinguishable debt; such is also the aim of Pound, who, although he disagrees with the concepts used by Marx, agrees on the principle: namely, that one needs

to make an *ethical* decision in favour of economics against chrematistics, and that this moral step has to be achieved through a sense
of the right filiation. Only then can the perpetual debt which leads to
wars be fought, and *interest* eventually become a weapon against usury.

This is demonstrated by two passages which again link the Adams
family with, on the one hand, a denunciation of the national debt and,
on the other, a sense of positive 'interest':

> ....but the vice-presidency is –
> to call things by their proper names – in the market.
> 'Defective in elementary knowledge and with a very
> undigested system of *ethics*, Mr Clay (Henry)'.

> After conversing with Mr Calhoun, Adams reflected:
> Paper currency...reductions of fictitious capital....
> Accumulation of *debts* as long as credit can be strained....
> Mr Noah has a project for colonizing jews in this country
> And wd. like a job in Vienna....
> Xmas, 1820, read aloud after breakfast
> From Pope's 'Messiah'. Not one of my family
> Except George,
>   appeared to take the least *interest*,
> Nor is there any one of them
>   who has a relish for literature.
> . . .

>   ...we have neither forefathers nor posterity,
>   a few years will efface them.
> . . .

> England more by her *interest* than
>   from principle of general liberty...
> We shd. separate from all European concerns.
> . . .

> Interfere with official duty? I said
> I thought that it wd. as the U.S. was *interested* in
> the Canal Company by their subscription of one million dollars.
> . . .

> I called upon Nicholas Biddle...and recd. two dividends
> of my bank stock.....as I might be called to take part in
> public measures.....I wished to divest myself
> of all personal *interest*....Nov. 9. '31.

(XXXIV, pp. 168–9, emphasis added)

The last of the Adams Cantos concludes with a similar montage of conflicting senses of interest:

> were our interest the same as theirs
> we might better trust them, yet not entirely
> for they do not understand even their own.
>   I have hitherto paid the Dutch interest out of capital
>   (London'85 to Art Lee)
> . . .
> that there were Americans indifferent to fisheries
>   and even some inclined to give away
>   this was my strongest motive
>   for twice going to Europe.   (LXX, p. 412)

The constant effort of Adams is to rouse interest, find the right interest, and dissociate interest from national debt. Could it be that just as Pound seems to hope that he can turn the Law against itself, the Jews against themselves (even by using their thinkers against themselves), he is now using 'interest' against interest? Is this just a case of unconscious ambivalence, such as I have tried to sketch in Chapter 1 in relation to several themes and images'? In fact, Pound seems well aware of his manoeuvres, and, even if he never thematises the opposition, it is obvious that it functions constantly. In *Jefferson and/or Mussolini*, for instance, he says, 'The main line of American conflict for the first half of the last century was the fight between public interest and the interests' (p. 79). The shift from singular to plural makes all the difference; no qualification is needed, for the juxtaposition alerts the reader to the necessity for a correct definition. Parataxis is here the main locus for a distinction between ploces and catachreses. Interest links directly the question of economics with that of the ambivalence of language, as, for example, when the picture of the London hell of usury is summed up by 'the invisible, many English,/ the place lacking in interest' (Canto XIV, p. 62), which also chimes with 'without dignity, without tragedy' (p. 63).

Language has to convey this interest in living, an interest which can almost be quantified, as shown by passages from the Rome broadcasts in which Pound is desperately trying to tell American college students that they must immediately read Aristotle, Demosthenes and Confucius; the 'INTERlexshul revolution' he advocates thus takes the form of, 'Which would be both an adornment in the conversation and of use in their business. Business of LIVIN', I mean, cent per cent, gettin' something out of life by the process of puttin' their interest, mental interest, into it.'[19] The full interest means 'living at 100%', while the evil sense of interest would be 'selling out' to a soulless business. And, of course, one can translate 'that the king should be King' into 'let the king be a hundred per cent King'.

Mussolini's revitalising-effect always lay for Pound in the immediate perception of interests: 'The secret of the Duce is possibly the capacity to pick out the elements of immediate and major importance in any tangle; or, in the case of a man, to go straight to the centre, for the fellow's major interest' (*J/M*, p. 66). For Pound himself, it meant inquiring directly 'why do you want to put your ideas into order?'[20] This is also why the Fascists always attracted Pound more than the Communists: 'The fascist revolution is infinitely more INTEREST-ING than the Russian revolution, because it is not a revolution according to preconceived type' (*J/M*, p. 24). Thus, to have been able to interest someone in economics is always a potential threat for the usurers; when Pound starts gathering elements about Metevsky, he finds his informers reluctant to go on as soon as he states his interest:

> So I said to the old quaker Hamish,
> I said: 'I am interested.' And he went putty colour
>
> (XVIII, p. 82)

Pound has definitely perceived the link which, according to Habermas, constitutes interest: the connection between work, language and power.[21] Thus, if interest is useful, necessary even, one can never forget that the word is ambivalent, and the real edge is kept when it functions as a wedge: that is, when it allows the interested subject to go on with his questions, to progress by dissociations, to distinguish between difficult notions. If economics as science is not 'interesting', it is because, as Griffith said, 'Can't move them with a cold thing like economics' (*SP*, p. 209). But, conversely, the 'cold thing' moves of itself by the actual exploitation of 'interests' in the creation of capital, and it can be 'moved' or displaced by intelligent men who are interested. They enact their interest by differentiating:

> And to know interest from usura
> (Sac. Cairoli, prezzo giusto)
>   In this sphere is Giustizia.
>
> (CXIII, p. 789)

or: . . . Fanatics do not understand
interest. (LXXXVII, p. 576).

For the root has been lost, the initial difference which should interest
everyone: 'Somewhere in the time of Medici tropism, the distinction
between *partaggio* and *usura* was muddled' (*SP*, p. 251). The inquiry
starts from such a quest for the just division.

Interest between use and abuse

Pound's economics do not aim at being a pure science; they aim at
'moving' man by self-discovery of his vital interests, his entire position,
the axis of his being. Economics have to be related to will – thus the
'volitional economics' – because taken in itself the science of economics is not interesting: 'No intelligent man will be content to treat
economics merely as economics, and probably no writer could write
anything of interest in so doing' (*SP*, p. 250). Pound's method fuses
Fenollosa's ideogrammic montage and de Gourmont's dissociation of
ideas. 'You can study economics almost entirely as dissociation of
ideas' (p. 251). This introduces an entire ideological strategy, a
complete system of rhetorics, and the distinction between certain root
concepts.

The origin of the error lies in a conceptual tangle, the confusion
arising because people were abused by words: 'The Church slumped
into a toleration of usury. Protestantism as factive and organized may
have sprung from nothing but pro-usury politics. And the amazing
history of the XIXth century is summed up in: "Marx found nothing to
criticize in money" ' (*SP*, p. 243). The last sentence, quoting Gesell's
Natural Economic Order,[22] implies that Marx's interpretation of the
conditions of production leading to the concept of surplus value is
flawed at the root because it misses the real nature of money and relies
on false distinctions: 'The nineteenth century, the infamous century of
usury, went even further, creating a species of monetary Black Mass.
Marx and Mill, in spite of their superficial differences, agree in
endowing money with properties of a quasi-religious nature' (*SP*,
pp. 316–17). Marx indeed takes money to be the 'general equivalent
of value', a concept which Pound strangely understands as an
'accumulator of energy' (p. 277). What does Pound's criticism attack
here? First of all, it is very doubtful whether he knows more than the
tenth chapter of *Capital* already quoted: 'Best chapter in Das Kapital
so far as I am concerned.'[23] However, he seems fully to agree with

Marx's theses, and to believe that, if Communism failed, it was because his followers did not read him well enough. 'After all Marx was pretty good at history and diagnosis. Nobody on the Axis side denies that Marx discovered several genuine faults in the usury system. All we ask is a way to CURE 'em. . . . ECONOMIC first. Of course the Bolshies didn't.'[24] Marxism has found a right diagnosis but no real solution, a little like the novel (Joyce) which stops short of a real synthesis of the will. 'Because the Marxist diagnosis was pretty near right. The remedy did NOT work. AND the revolution was betrayed.'[25] This is why the Pisan Cantos move from praise of the Wörgl experiment, which attempted to put Gesell's idea of stamp scrip into practice, to an explicit criticism of the New Economic Policy, by which Lenin put an end to the hope of achieving a really Communist economic programme:

> But in Russia they bungled and did not apparently
> grasp the idea of work-certificate
> and started the N. E. P. with disaster
> and the immolation of men to machinery
> and the canal work and gt/ mortality
> (which is as may be)
> and went in for dumping in order to trouble the waters
> in the usurers' hell-a-dice
>
> (LXXIV, p. 441)

This reveals a precise analysis of what went 'wrong' according to Pound: he does not condemn dumping; he sees the root of the perversion of the Russian system as lying in a desire to compete with capitalist powers, thus following the same path. This of course leads back to Marx's diagnosis; could it be that he describes too uncritically the system he has called 'Capital'?

When Marx tackles money directly in *Capital*, he uses certain expressions which for Pound must ring curiously: 'The intrinsic relation of capital to itself by which it presents itself, when one perceives the process of capitalistic production as an organic whole, when capital appears as money generating money, seems to be without the mediation of an intermediary movement . . . .'[26] This comes from a passage which bitterly and scathingly attacks Proudhon's 'romantic dream' of free credit as presented in his *Gratuité du Crédit*.[27] Marx explains that Luther was better informed than Proudhon because he knew that one can make a profit by lending as well as by selling. Pound, who always said that he was a Proudhonian at heart,[28] would have been horrified at Marx's cynicism. Marx's mystification, to use Pound's term, actually derives from his acceptance of the metaphor 'money breeds money' ('Geld heckt Geld'), which obviously appears as catachrestic.[29] All subsequent muddles on 'creation' follow from this misunderstanding of the real barren nature of money: 'The imbecillity of the XIXth century stemming from misuse of word "creates". Both Mill and Marx and dozens of other loathsome individuals contributed to the muddle. Work does not create wealth, it *contributes to the formation of it.* Nature's productivity is the root' (*GK*, p. 357). It is in this sense alone that Pound writes, 'The Production IS the beloved' (Canto CIV, p. 742). Production is directly opposed to the satanic creation, the creation *ex nihilo* of credit by banks.

But, whenever Marx gives the example of Paterson, he presents him as a representative of the budding English industrial capital which wishes to curb usury and transform the purely financial capital into government-controlled banks: 'The Scotsman William Paterson . . . is by all odds Law the First'[30] – which is quite ironic when one sees what praise Law receives in the later Cantos![31] For, indeed, Marx draws a sharp distinction between usurer's capital and industrial capital, since for him the former does not modify the mode of precapitalistic production, while the latter not only brings about its destruction but also provides a key whereby the mechanism which produces surplus value may be understood.

By contrast, Pound's entire effort is directed at collapsing production and nature into a single concept; and he goes so far as to say that overproduction itself appears as a natural phenomenon: 'Nature habitually overproduces. Chestnuts go to waste on the mountain side, and it has never yet caused a world crisis' (*SP*, p. 203). Obviously, for any Marxist, to handle overproduction in this way sounds like utter nonsense; yet there is a certain pathetic consistency in the tenacity with which Pound denies the specificity of industrial capital. But what is more striking is the fact that Marx entirely confirms Pound's intuitions – with the qualification that their convergence only lasts while they talk about purely monetary capital. Marx's development on 'usurer's capital' is strangely congruent with Pound's analysis.

Marx explains that usury 'does not alter the mode of production, but attaches itself firmly to it like a parasite and makes it wretched. It sucks out blood, enervates it and compels reproduction to proceed under ever more pitiable conditions.'[32] Usurer's capital attaches itself like a vampire to a given mode of production, and attacks the owner of his means of production – that is, the small landlord or the poor labourer, in a society dominated by private ownership; peasants, craftsmen, farmers are its more likely preys. 'Usurer's capital as the characteristic form of interest-bearing capital corresponds to the predominance of small-scale production of the self-employed peasant and small master craftsman' (*Capital*, p. 581). Usury is a cancer, then, because it intervenes in times of unforeseen disaster, or during the difficult period after the stock of crops has been consumed: 'Usury lives in the pores of production, as it were, just as the gods of Epicurus lived in the space between worlds' (p. 585).

The derivative nature of usury lies in its exploitation of a type of production (small-peasant and petit-bourgeois) with methods which are characteristic of capital while remaining outside the sphere of capitalist production. It nevertheless allows for the transition from one mode of production to another: 'this complete expropriation of the labourer from his conditions of labour is not a result which the capitalist mode of production seeks to achieve, but rather the established condition for its point of departure' (*Capital*, p. 582). In itself, however, usurer's capital does not tend towards the dissolution of the system it exploits, since it thrives upon it:

> Usury, like commerce, exploits a given mode of production. It does not create it, but is related to it outwardly. Usury tries to maintain it directly, so as to exploit it ever anew; it is conservative and makes this mode of production only more pitiable. The less elements of production enter into the production process, the more does their origination from money appear as a separate act. The more insignificant the role played by circulation in the social reproduction, the more usury flourishes.   (p. 596)

Marx thus confirms Pound's basic belief in the possibility of finding a solution within the cycle of circulation alone, since Pound's model of economics never extends beyond this 'ancient world where ownership of means of production by the producer himself was at the same time the basis for political status, the independence of the citizen' (p. 583). In this limited world, indeed, the attempt either to speed up circulation with Gesell's *Schwundgeld*, or, following Douglas, to control the issue of money and the market itself, stems from the idea that *circulation* can show the right function of *production*. Then money does not 'create' wealth, and the circulation of goods and coins can stabilise itself at a fair mean.

Pound's definition of usury is thus to be understood in this context: 'a charge for the use of purchasing power, levied without regard to production, sometimes without regard even to the possibilities of production' (*SP*, p. 325), although the terms 'use' and 'production' acquire a different meaning from those Marx evolves in *Capital*. Pound's war against usury retains something of the revolutionary accents of Marxism, and a certain amount of confusion is at times possible, as for instance when Pound says, 'But the monopolies, the sanctions, the restrictions imposed by the guilds were, at least, monopolies of producers. The various monopolies which culminate in the monopoly of money itself, key to all the other monopolies, were, and are, monopolies of exploiters' (*SP*, p. 146). This passage written in 1944 echoes throughout the *Cantos*, which derives its ethical impetus from such concepts:

> Bellium cano perenne...
> > (end of Canto LXXXVI, p. 568)
> ...between the usurer and any man who
> wants to do a good job
> (perenne)
> without regard to production –
> > a charge
> for the use of money or credit.
> > (beginning of LXXXVII, p. 569)

It is here that one can see most clearly the link established by Pound between his praise of production and the theme of *use*, which could be confused with Marx's distinction between 'use-value' and 'exchange-value', from which he evolves the genesis of capital and the creation of surplus value. Marx starts from the hypothesis of a simple distinction between the use of objects and their exchange; such a process is perverted in the economic phase which sees the domination of interest-bearing capital (which is the rule of 'money breeds money' and of the *tokos*): 'As with the case of labour-forces, the use-value of money is here its capacity of creating value, an exchange-value superior to the one its embodies.... Money then acquires the property of generating value, exactly as it is in the nature of the pear-tree to give pears.'[33] This is called 'fetishism' by Marx, because, in the movement of inversion, industrial profit appears as a derivative profit, while usurious profit is taken for granted; money a *thing*, represents the whole process of production, which in fact becomes all the more enigmatic. The simple attempts to understand its genesis has the effect of destroying this fetishism. Marx's analysis is no doubt more sophisticated than that of Pound, who doggedly asserts that usury is the sale of the *use* of money, while Marx sees in usury the use of a sale, so to speak, or the use of a mystifying multiplication of value. Pound is closer to St Thomas, for whom the use of money was already a consumption of money. Usury necessarily comes to an end when use dominates in the circuit of exchanges:

> 'No longer necessary', taxes are no longer necessary
> in the old way if it (money) be based on work done
>> inside a system and measured and gauged to human require-
>>> ments
>
> inside the nation or system 道、
>
> and cancelled in proportion
>> to what is used and worn out
> à la Wörgl.   (LXXVIII, pp. 481–2)

To 'use' in Pound's proposal has the double meaning of wearing out (in the material or symbolic depreciation of the coins or notes, for instance) and the full appropriation of nature in a balance between needs and goods; any tax is a false intermediary, even when it is aimed at redistributing wealth:

> As to tax on non-cultivated land: why not go fascist and merely *cultivate* the damn land when the owners of latifundia fail to do so? All taxes or fixed charges are from hell. A division of fruits is the proper mode. . . . Tax? In money?? The answer is *cultivate* the land; right of ownership shd. imply obligation to *use*'   (*L*, p. 342).

Any tax participates in the usury system because of its mechanical application and because it implies a lack of respect for natural rhythms. All of Pound's proposals, whenever they are concretely formulated, go in the direction of some division, whether of the produce (a division of the fruits here) or of time (a recurrent scheme in Pound's pamphlets is the reduction of work-hours: if every man could be convinced that he would use his time better when accepting to work less, he would first provide work for someone else, and then be able to cultivate himself). There lies the root of *partaggio* as lawful interest based on use and productivity: an interest in one's leisure time (free time devoid of anxiety) and the possibility of attaining a 'better life' offered to all.

The Scholastics share this assumption and concentrate on the link between *use* and *interest*; for pure interest without a vital use leads to usury, while the use of time or products without interest leads to idleness or hoarding. For them as for Pound, the idea could be grasped by a simple division, or rather a verbal subtraction: it was enough to eliminate the *-ura* suffix from *usura* to find *usus* as the true basis of life. This on the whole is what Aquinas achieves in the *Summa Theologica* in his celebrated condemnation of usury: he distinguishes between two categories of 'use'. There are certain things which are consumed by their use, such as bread and wine; if their use is allowed, it turns into a right to property. One could not sell wine a first time, and then sell the use of wine: this would mean selling the same thing twice. This rule applies to the lending of such things: 'Et simili ratione injustitiam committit qui mutuat vinum aut triticum petens sibi dari duas recompensationes, unam quidem restitutionem aequalis rei, aliam verò pretii usus quod *usura* dicitur.'[34] Now there is a second category of things which are not used up when their use is sold, as when a house is let for a period of time, and these may require a specific form of payment; but, even so, money has been made to promote exchange, as Aristotle states in his *Ethics*, to which Aquinas refers in the article just cited: 'est illicitum pro usu pecuniae mututae accipere pretium, quod dicitur usura' (it is unlawful to receive a payment in money for the use of money which is called usury).

For the Scholastics, therefore, following on from Aristotle, interest was illicit whenever it occurred as a tax, or any kind of fixed payment stipulated in advance for the use of money, but it was tolerated if there was any risk of loss, in which case 'interest' would make up for the loss, or for the difference in gain. The word 'interest' embodies the sense of a difference: ' "Quod interest" means "that which is the difference" between the injured party's present position and the position he would be in if he had not been injured.'[35] This difference, which remains hypothetical, includes the loss of profit the lender might have suffered: the compensation required is then a supplement of value based upon a fictive time, a conditional setting. All this had already been defined by Roman Law, but when the twelfth-century schools took over the term referring to this difference – *intersum*, *interest*, 'it is between' – they turned the verb into a noun. This move was made to adapt to the increasingly complicated commercial realities of their time, but nevertheless opened a gap in Aquinas's prohibitions. Whereas the verb *interest* was restricted to sentences such as 'in his rebus nihil interest' (there is no difference between these things) or 'hoc pater ac dominus interest' (this makes the difference between father and master), the Scholastics turned it into a substantive, *interesse*, which as early as 1220 is found opposed to *usura*.[36] In short, *interesse* is not a gain nor a tax, but a differential compensation which avoids loss in the case of default.

The distinction is quite tricky, since *interesse* involves lost profit in the conditional (*lucrum cessans*) and such a potential loss of profit may open the door to usury if one accepts that money can in itself become the cause of gain, which even Aquinas seems to admit in certain texts, thus contradicting his general assumptions.[37] But the established 'difference' was finally founded on a theory of will and a system of ethics; for the main sin consisted in the intention, in the desire to get rich through money, and intention has to be called upon as the last recourse in case of doubt. This is also why Pound opens his Adams saga by clearing him of any such bad motives: 'Acquit of evil intention . . .' (Canto LXII, p. 341). For Pound, this means linking the 'system' of differential economics with a general theory of will, and a respect for 'Justice' in its individual as well as collective aspect. Interest could be reconciled with *just price* if one took care of the *just time*.

Just price and just time

Pound's commendation of the 'just price' theory has often been associated with his concern for *le mot juste* as exemplified by Flaubert;[38] however, his economic views on the matter may at times ring more ominously than his denunciation of usury, with which any 'liberal' might easily agree. Moreover, a hesitation is perceptible when it comes to the choice of a political order which will enforce 'just prices'. When Pound advocates Fascism because Mussolini is the only ruler capable of putting economic reforms into action, or when he exclaims in his Rome broadcasts that 'Every reform, every lurch toward the Just Price, toward the control of the market is an act of homage to Mussolini and Hitler',[39] he stresses the authoritarian solution to economic problems, solving the tension between an agrarian model of economics and highly developed industrial states by a fixation of 'just prices'. Now, Pound's position becomes clearer when we see that the maturation of his theories between 1918 and 1935 is exactly contemporaneous with the economic evolution of Fascist Italy as it moved towards autarky and state control of the market and prices. A short summary will suffice. Whereas most nations were still suffering from unemployment after the financial collapse of 1929, Italy rapidly recovered after 1935; productivity and employment were, paradoxically, stimulated by the need to adjust to the closure of foreign markets in the wake of the Ethiopian war. Autarky, which was imposed by the retaliatory measures taken by the neighbouring democracies was transformed into an ideology, a credo, and gave the impulse to daring monetary reforms. In June 1934 Mussolini insisted that the state should control the money and foreign-exchange markets, and in December 1934 it was decreed that all foreign transactions had to be made through the Instituto Italiano.[40] The main transformation occurred early in 1935, when Thaon de Revel replaced Jung as Finance Minister and instituted a series of bilateral treaties with other countries; clearing and compensation took the place of free trade, which implied by July 1935 that the lira could not be kept at par with Italy's gold reserves. The myth of the obligation to keep 40 per cent of reserves in gold was still dominant at the time, as was gold parity. To counteract this, a Fascist theoretician such as Einaudi could send a note to Mussolini urging him to create 'another myth' to replace the myth of gold: 'The lira is a merchandise. . . . But why should its price vary? . . . It is more useful to have 6 billions of wares or machines than 6 billions of sterile gold buried in the sacristy of banks.'[41] The currency was to be valued not according to the reserves, nor according to the simple process of circulation, but in line with the level of liquidity determined by the state to meet the current needs of the market. Pound had real grounds for believing that the reforms he had sought to popularise for some years would finally be experimented with by the Fascist regime, and because of this new hope he even refused to leave Italy when offered a teaching-job in America. But, if Pound's model of autarky was definitely agrarian, he was not deceived by nostalgia, and the 'Laws' he had written down for his daughter reveal his awareness of basic problems of survival: 'Autarchia. The ideal is that everyone should be bauernfähig. The moment a family is separated from the land everyone must be able not only to DO something, or MAKE something, but to sell it.'[42] All the themes considered up to now are summed up in this short note: the family taken as the basic production-unit, the need to produce in order to meet demands, and the determining-function of time, for the note went on, 'When the land is no longer there, nothing will WAIT. People not peasants must think QUICKER than peasants.' 'Nothing waits' when land has lost its status as the true basis of abundance.

The link with Scholastic theories of money and prices is clear. The real point of departure is a description of the logic of exchanges fixing average prices as defined by custom; from this description a standard is erected, then made into the 'just price'. On the other hand, money cannot be sold, because this would entail selling the measure. If money is a conventional measure (as with Aristotle), to make someone pay for its use means to sell time. Tawney sums up this analysis quite well:

> To take usury is contrary to Scripture; it is contrary to Aristotle; it is contrary to nature, for it is to live without labour; it is to sell time, which belongs to God, for the advantage of wicked men; it is to rob those who use the money lent and to whom, since they make it profitable, the profits should belong . . .[43]

This seems directly to contradict Einaudi's suggestion that money is a 'commodity', and Pound makes every effort to resolve this contradiction.

The thesis of a 'natural law' has theological foundations, and William of Auxerre, for instance, utters the most striking denunciation when he writes,

> Nothing, however, so naturally gives itself as time: willy-nilly things have time. Because, therefore, the usurer sells what necessarily belongs to all creatures, generally he injures all creatures, even the stones; whence if men were silent against the usurers, the stones would cry out, if they could . . . .[44]

The definition of usury is now 'the selling of time', and the aim of Pound's poem is indeed to make the stones cry out against usury (almost achieved in Canto XLV), for usury perverts the natural bounty of time, given by God and Nature. For the stones do cry out when men are mute, because they speak of stonecutters' skills, of concern for art and decoration, of clear outlines.

Now, it is no surprise that the remedies Pound derives from the economists he quotes most, Gesell and Douglas, centre around an appreciation of the time-factor in economy. Since the basic duplicity of money derives from the fact that it functions both as a vehicle of exchange and as a standard of value, usury perverts the natural rhythms of exchange while selling the measure defined by law. In Pound's words, 'Time is not money, but it is almost everything else' (*SP*, p. 211). The alternative value of time in the new model of circulation is exemplary. The first solution is to speed time up, since 'nothing waits' in the modern circuit of exchange, cut off from 'land'. Time is turned towards the future; money looks for an acceleration which will beat usury at its own game, as it were. Hence Gesell's idea of taxing money itself by obliging all owners to stick a stamp on the paper notes every month. The experiment proved a success in the small town of Wörgl in Austria, until the government, perhaps afraid it might spread, forbade it. 'All the slobs in Europe were terrified', concludes Pound in Canto LXXIV (p. 441). Gesell has thus invented 'counter-usury', since 'taxation was fixed on the money itself, and accelerated the circulation of money, whereas all other forms of taxation weigh on, cramp, sabotage exchange' (*SP*, p. 246). Pound is not blind to the difficulty of applying this scheme on a large scale, nor to the fact that, if the reform were limited to the prohibition of hoarding, it would not prevent people from using other tokens of value. Nevertheless, the 'general equivalent' would have been 'money that cries to be spent within a given period of time' (p. 247).

Pound only 'discovered' Gesell around 1935, and acknowledges in 'The Individual and his Milieu' (1935) that his *ABC of Economics*, written in 1933, was incomplete since it relied only on Douglas. For Douglas stressed precisely the opposite element in the time-factor inherent in the cycle of production and distribution: the role of the past as the reserve of inventions, cultural values, scientific progress – the combination of all the efforts of mankind to improve productivity. This is summed up as 'increment of association' and is opposed to its negative perversion, usury, with which it has been confused: '*Usury* and the *increment of association* under unobservant eyes were confused one with the other' (*SP*, p. 235). Thus, around 1935, Pound could believe he had found the exact formula, the just proportion between an awareness of the past as a source of values, and of the future as the goal for an ideal civilisation, freed from all blocks caused by ignorance and monopolism; and, moreover, he could believe that the formula was going to be applied in Italy. The synthesis was only a matter of adjustment:

So long as Douglassites refuse to consider . . . the unjust privileges of money above any other product, so long as the Gesellites refuse to consider the cultural heritage (the increment of association, and the possibilities inherent in a right proportion in the issue of fixed money and Schwundgeld, monnaie fondante, stamp scrip) for just so long will both groups sabotage each other and delay economic light. (p. 246)

The past crystallises as 'culture', a culture which determines our behaviour from the outside, preconditions thoughts and language, and points to the 'unconscious' quality required by Frobenius for his *paideuma*. The past and the future must be synthesised by a law – what Lacan would call the place of the Other – so that money may embody the right symptom. But symptoms always disclose a 'gap', a 'loss', a hole which cannot be healed.

With a relatively sure grasp of the evolution of monetary thinking, Pound sees the common root of the diverging economic theories of Major Douglas and Gesell in the hidden influence of Proudhon: 'Proudhon will be found somewhere in the foundations of perhaps all contemporary economic thought that has life in it', he writes at the opening of his obituary of Orage, the ardent advocate of Social Credit ('In the Wounds', *SP*, p. 410). For Proudhon attempted to solve the problem of credit and distribution through typically non-Marxist solutions, and in Pound's mind both Gesellites and Douglasites posit a similar distrust of conventional money: the former forbid hoarding by affixing a stamp to the note itself; the latter wish to replace inadequate certificates of wages by national dividends.

National dividends should be paid directly by a state which masters its credit and thus bridges the gap between prices and money, or, in the last words Pound heard Orage deliver on the radio before he died, 'in the gap between Price-values and Income is enough gunpowder to blow up every democratic parliament' (*SP*, p. 410). As Orage puts it elsewhere, still commenting on Douglas's economics, there are two 'streams' which flow out into the world, 'a stream of goods and a stream of money to claim the goods', but 'their rates of flow are different. The rate at which money prices are generated is always in excess of the rate at which monetary tickets are distributed.'[45] In his conception, money remains trapped within an incomplete and perverting synecdoche, since the part never catches up with the whole it is supposed to represent. Money can never 'stand for' goods: first, because everything flows in this twin current of merchandise and token; and, secondly, because their velocities are different – 'Now the part is never as great as the whole, and if wages, salaries and dividends form the only stream of purchasing power, it can never keep pace with the other stream of prices.'[46]

It is no surprise to find a similar synecdochic movement working through Gesell's image of a 'shrinking money' (*Schwundgeld*) which does not so much represent wealth as point to its absence, to a lack and even a loss. In the *Schwundgeld* theory, money is not possessed but hastily exchanged; Gesell imagines what a merchant or a banker would do in a system using 'Free-Money' as its only legal tender. The gold he might have kept would be deprived of any exchange-value, and he would be ill advised to buy more: 'The uselessness of the demonetised gold forced them to consent to exchange it for Free-Money, and the loss inseparable from possession of the new money forces them to get rid of it in order to transfer the loss as quickly as possible to others.'[47] This becomes, in a more paradoxical formulation, 'He will endeavour to pass on the loss connected with the possession of money by passing on the money.'[48]

Nevertheless, Pound trusts the 'system' to be capable of recuperating all gaps and losses, which are necessary for the metonymic circulation of desire as interest, of interest as difference. But conceptually the systematisation is a failure, and one need not be a professional economist to realise the illogical and utopian nature of Pound's *coincidentia oppositorum*: 'I offer the proposition that with a just proportion between *Schwundgeld*, res moneta, monnaie fondante, stamp scrip, and a fixed money not needing a monthly stamp, you would have the simplest possible system for maintaining a monetary representation of extant goods, i.e. a "money-picture" of extant goods' (*SP*, p. 247). Pound simply forgets that Gesell's *Schwundgeld* can only achieve its aim if it remains the *sole* means of payment, thus disqualifying any attempt to hoard or to barter. In fact, the exact proportion of liquidity to be liquidised and the justice of a 'just price' defined by law must depend on the people's will, understood as its 'good will'.

The system cannot be corrected by reforms only, for intellect has to rely on will and honesty:

> No intellectual system of economics will function unless people are prepared to act on their understanding. . . . No economic system can be effective until a reasonable number of people are interested in economics; interested, I should say, in economics as part of the problem: what does and what does not injure others.   (*SP*, p. 208)

Thus Pound's starting point is almost the same as Marx's: that is, he finds a 'first instance' of how the economic factor determines everything else, only then shifting the emphasis towards questions of consciousness, of dealienation and of ethical values. What Pound was still groping for in his *ABC of Economics* is reached through Gesell after 1935: a positive notion of interest, later to be rewritten as 'curiosity', an active care for the setting-off of natural production against the perversion of money and values. This is precisely the point emphasised by Keynes in his discussion of Gesell's ideas, since he elects him as one of his neglected precursors. His *General Theory of Employment, Interest and Money* devotes six illuminating pages to Gesell.[49] For Keynes, Gesell's idea of stamp -scrip paved the way for a new and sounder definition of money, and when he looked for a formula with which to balance the 'return on money loans' with the 'return to active investment', he dissociated interest from usury (pp. 355–6):

> The rate of interest, which depends on constant psychological characters, has remained stable, whilst the widely fluctuating characters which primarily determine the schedule of the marginal efficiency of capital have determined not the rate of interest but the rate at which the (more or less) given rate of interest allows the stock of real capital to grow.   (p. 356)

Thus the rate of interest can be kept low while the marginal efficiency of capital is high; this dissociation is of tremendous consequence for an economy not yet ready to suscribe to full nationalisation.

Keynes adds an important reservation: Gesell had only outlined one half of a theory of interest, for the notion of 'liquidity preference' had escaped him. Liquidity preference is synonymous with 'hoarding', but can apply to a whole nation, as India proved when it allowed itself to be impoverished by its liquidity preference (*General Theory*, p. 337). The advice against the hoarding of gold and jewels in palaces instead of letting them circulate is of course a strong point in favour of China as compared to all other empires. This again corresponds to the age-old view that the scarcity of coin increases usurious rates of interest and credit: 'Ob pecuniae scarcitatem', quote the Cantos now and then. Thus, in Keynes's view, which completes Gesell's intuition, the rate of interest is the just reward for parting with liquidity. Interest is the 'price' which is paid to equilibrate the desire to hold wealth in the form of cash with the available quantity of cash. It is only in that sense that there can be a 'just price' of interest, on which the 'just price' of the market has ultimately to be founded.

For Keynes, then, Gesell, who appears initially closer to the spirit of mercantilism, because he encourages circulation even at the risk of dumping and imperialism, and who advocates competition instead of state control of the market, can be the real 'answer to Marxism'

(*General Theory*, p. 355). On this basis, Pound finds no contradiction in agreeing with Lenin and Stalin on the need to control banks and credit, but he rejects Marxist proposals for a complete takeover of the means of production:

> and but one point needed for Stalin
> you need not, i.e. need not take over the means of production;
> money to signify work done, inside a system
> and measured and wanted.   (LXXIV, p. 426)

Pound would not have been in a position to appreciate the value of Keynes's praise of Gesell (for, owing to an early misunderstanding, he consistently attacks Keynes as being a 'classical economist'[50]), but he would concur with him that the main problem is no longer 'production', but sound management of 'distribution': 'But in 1918 we knew in London that the problem of production was solved, and that the next job was to solve distribution, and that this meant a new administration of credit' (*J/M*, p. 48). What Keynes states in scientific and exact terms of economic analysis was found by Pound in a more mythical language, exploiting certain simplified definitions, in Orage's *Alphabet of Economics* (1917). Orage stated plainly that money derived its power 'by virtue of the credit attached to a Symbol'[51] and situates this within the process of exchange:

> By means of money, capital which cannot be moved can be exchanged as if it were carried in the pocket. The solid capital becomes as light as air! . . . The liquefying of solid capital being necessary, men undertake the work; but they charge for the product exactly what they can get for it. And this charge or price for the use of liquid capital or money is called Interest.[52]

We have seen that this 'interest' has to be related to the subject's own desire, to a general system of circulation, and to the efficiency of symbols. It is now possible to grasp the unconscious logic of such a circulation of symbols in a system founded on differential rates or ratios.

The circulation of liquidities: money, sexuality, language

From the preceding discussion, it is easy to see why Pound asserts that one can 'study economics almost entirely as dissociation of ideas' (*SP*, p. 251). The difference between *usus* and *usura* is not merely semantic, but relies on an active concept of difference; philology points to the need for an economic basis, without which, for instance, one cannot understand why in sixteenth-century English, at the time of the rise of mercantile capitalism, the term 'use' or 'usance' meant 'usury' and not 'usage' (it is still to be found employed thus in Locke's and Hume's attacks on usury). De Gourmont's methodology is helpful here, for he distinguishes between 'clichés' which are only words, and 'commonplaces' which fuse ideas together.[53]

De Gourmont's vocabulary is precise and might entail confusions if his distinctions are overlooked; for him, an 'idea' is almost always opposed to a 'truth', 'idea' being positive – this is the heritage of the *Idéologues* – whilst 'truth' is negative, a worn-out image which must be split up, dissociated, in order that the submerged sensation might regain its clarity. 'Along with commonplace, one could almost always use the word "truth", thus defined once for all: a commonplace not yet dissociated; dissociation being analogous to what is called analysis in chemistry.'[54] Pound practises similar dissociations (especially in his *ABC of Economics*), while de Gourmont never went very far with concrete examples of 'analysis'.[55] Both share the belief that differentiation leads to a world of forms, of figures, and not of abstractions.

> For the modern scientist energy has no borders, it is a shapeless 'mass' of force; even his capacity to differentiate it to a degree never dreamed by the ancients has not led him to think of its shape or even of its loci. The rose that his magnet makes in iron filings does not lead him to think of the force as floral and extant (ex stare). (*LE*, p. 154)

The mind must fight against 'unnecessary idea-clots' to recover the sanity of a world 'where one thought cuts through another with a clean edge' (ibid.). The plea for dynamic difference is foremost in the concern for terminology in metaphysics and morals: 'unless all attempt to unify different things, however small the difference is, is clearly abandoned, all metaphysical thought degenerates into a soup' (p. 185). History has proved how vital the sense of distinctions was, since the loss of the difference between usury and interest opened the way to capitalism. If usury is defined as the sale of 'use' or the sale of the 'use of time', it becomes fundamental to know what 'use' means. Even the attempt at reconciling heterogeneous doctrines points in the same direction, the reinscription of difference within the system or totality. What Pound finally derived from Major Douglas's complex calculations was the perception that there remained a 'gap' in the 'A + B theorem', a widening difference between prices and purchasing power; what mattered was to reinscribe this difference in a system of 'interests', thanks either to the 'loss' of money Gesell's stamp script implied, or to the fixing of a 'just price' by the ruler. Pound's complete reversal of tactics, from the 1918 theories of Social Credit – which rejected state control of money, Douglas sternly criticising 'the deadly nonsense regarding the "sole right of the State to issue Money" ' [56] – to his recourse in 1950 to Del Mar's *History of Monetary Systems* which identifies 'sovereignty' with the state's right to issue money,[57] obeys in fact a complicated personal inscription of difference in the economic and symbolic system.

Pound's refusal to deal with production leads him to a very ambivalent position on the matter of surplus value. If the system is founded on men's interests and their 'use' of the land, the surplus can attack the root; this becomes clear in certain rather hysterical passages in the Rome broadcasts:

> There is enough purchasing power based on labor, and on labor only, to run all the culture, to keep all the studies, arts, all the amenities, the good life in toto. The extra purchasing power does NOT create these things, it corrodes them. It does NOT create what makes life fit to live, it attacks it. It spoils it. It rots it.[58]

Now the problem seems to be set out in its simplest formulation: if all the surplus value is bent towards usury, how does one reconcile pure use and interest defined as an active participation in nature's increase? Pound does not advocate 'small is beautiful', nor is he to be confused with Malthusians. The difference between surplus and interest bears also heavily on sexual systems and moral codes; a passing remark in an essay of 1934 connects these fields:

> By 1934 Frazer is sufficiently digested for us to know that opposing systems of European morality go back to the opposed temperaments of those who thought copulation was good for the crops, and the opposed temperaments of those who thought it was bad for the crops (the scarcity economists of pre-history).   (*LE*, p. 85)

Pound is of course in favour of the first party, as the evidence of the

Cantos indicates, not simply because of his pagan and polytheistic leanings, but also because magic, money and sexuality ultimately lead to the same affirmation of fecundity.

The magical element is not the reverse of the economic obsession, as some of the best commentators continue to assert. Bacigalupo's major exegesis of the *Cantos* is one fair example of this unwarranted prejudice: when he mentions this 'sort of complex centering around the notion of money, which is the negative of Pound's world, the positive one being the magic world',[59] he does not stress the interdependence of the two sides, and when he goes on to write that 'there is little doubt that the meditation of the word is the source of the poet's deepest intuitions, whereas all his obsessions center upon what he once referred to as the "toxicology of money" ', he practises a distinction which Pound's effort at creating a general semiology of signs and coins refuses. True, Bacigalupo notes the importance of the 'pun linking his name to the monetary unit', but does not conclude that, if, as we have seen, a meditation on names is the source of a theory of signs and of money, the two domains must be identical; the object of Pound's quest is the ultimate symbolic system which will unite the writing of a name, the definition of economic justice, and the radiance of life within a paternal law.

After the 'Pisan Cantos', Pound thought he had found such a 'law' in the history of money as he found it studied by Del Mar. He thus accomplished a move which can be described in Freudian terms as the shift from the infantile urge to link money, faeces and gift in the anal phase to the full sublimation posterior to the Oedipus complex. Or, to be more exact, Pound's case is a good example of a writer's fate being parallel to the development of psychoanalytical theory, from Freud's early texts on the anal character of money, to Lacan's concept of a symbolic law.[60] This general drift of Pound's writing is witnessed too throughout the *Cantos*, starting with the early attempts in the twenties, which are contemporary with de Gourmont's book on natural sexuality, and moving on to the later poems of 'Thrones', in which a study of ancient legal texts, Chinese edicts, Coke's commentaries and early coinage brings all the elements together in the Temple of the text.

When Pound settled in Paris in 1920, after having been instrumental in bringing about the publication of *Ulysses* and *The Waste Land*, he still needed to 'digest' the modernity of these two masterworks, and to fuse their technical innovations with his growing awareness of social and financial problems. The rejection of England, as expressed in *Mauberley*, was coupled with a first denunciation of 'usury age-old and age-thick' (*CSP*, p. 208), and when Pound expressed his views just after arriving in Paris, he devoted most of his remarks to a discussion of credit-control in an interview with the *New York Herald*. He blamed England for its 'insensitization', adding, 'I suppose the word sensitive gives an impression of femininity. And yet any scientist is anxious to have his instruments highly sensitized.'[61] The Postscript to his translation of Remy de Gourmont's *Physique de l'Amour*, *The Natural Philosophy of Love*, rationalises and radicalises both the opposition between masculine and feminine, and the attempt to reach a balance of the sexual and economic circuits. The first step is a transformation of his relationship to London into some kind of sexual act: 'Integration of the male in the male [*sic*, for female] organ. Even oneself has felt it, driving any new idea into the great passive vulva of London, a sensation analogous to the male in copulation.'[62] The key to the knot of themes Pound then develops is triggered by a random remark that the brain might be nothing but a clot of genital fluid.

Pound uses a 'hypothesis' to launch a sequence of para-scientific speculations which replace the process of thought in the framework of chemistry. The alchemy of imagination boils down to a spermatic chemical reaction: 'Thought is a chemical process, the most interesting of all transfusions in liquid solution. The mind is an upspurt of sperm' (*Natural Philosophy*, p. 172). While critics have often marvelled at the unguarded and daring flights of fancy Pound indulges in in this weird text, it has not been recognised that he only developed de Gourmont's proposal to study man's imagination, his images of love, his erotic reveries as having a foundation in nature, or more precisely in the sexual habits of other animals.[63] Pound does not feel hampered by the formal pretence upheld by de Gourmont of being scientifically sound, and elaborates a whole myth, which has the same status as Plato's myths, for instance. The legend of the brain as a 'great clot of genital fluid held in suspense or reserve' (p. 169) intervenes because it is the only type of discourse Pound can produce at the time so as to fuse sexuality with economy.

Pound plunges headlong into a store of very ancient fantasies, which range from the mediaeval trope of the spiritual 'seed' to Chinese theories of sexuality. For most mediaeval thinkers, indeed, the mind appeared to consist in a kind of sperm, and copulation was seen as the passage of this fluid from the head down to the medulla into the future embryo. Alain de Lille does not hesitate to develop the parallel, the question being to ensure total fertilisation: 'Verbositas est semen quod fructum non facit.'[64] This underlies Dante's discussion of the components of the soul in *Convivio*, IV, which postulates a *semente*, a seed in man which comes from God.[65] Chinese conceptions of sexuality, especially in certain Taoist doctrines, ascribe the same relationship to brain and sperm, and Needham quotes the maxim that 'the father sows the white, and the mother sows the red',[66] which means that the brain and nerves come from the father's semen, while muscles and blood come from the mother's menstrual blood. Pound harps on the point: 'People were long ignorant of the circulation of the blood ... Gourmont speaks of a "circulation nerveuse", but many people still consider the nerves as at most a telegraph wire, simply because it does not bleed when cut' (*Natural Philosophy*, p. 178), and he implicitly alludes to Berman's work on glands to prove his more rambling figments.[67]

But then, from the assuredly mythical physiology of this curious mass of intellectual spermatozoids, Pound jumps to a generalisation which is all the more striking as he has not yet broached the subject of anality: 'Three channels, hell, purgatory, heaven, if one wants to follow yet another terminology digestive excretion, incarnation, freedom in the imagination ...' (*Natural Philosophy*, pp. 178–9). Pound gives a systematic formulation to his early rejection of Joyce's use of scatology in *Ulysses*, which has been introduced in the letter by which he expressed his annoyance at finding Bloom's fart in the place of the resolution of a fugue: 'I am much milder and far less indecent = au moins = je suis peut-être un peu plus phallique, mais m'interessent moins les excrements et les feces humains [*sic*].'[68] Pound appears almost shy of voicing his position in English, and his broken French, which nevertheles stresses 'interest' as a main motive, states that he is less interested in excrement than in the phallus. Two months later, he adds a footnote to an article on Henry James which defines prose as analytical or symptomatic, whilst poetry turns to the 'emotional synthesis' (*LE*, p. 324, n. 1). Prose corresponds to disgust, rejection, anality, refuse, excrement, and the task of poetry is to transmute these inferior elements into a phallic drive toward heaven, aesthetic imagination and paradise. Analysis and anality go along together, and the 'arsethetic' (*P/J*, p. 158) is always related to Hell.

All these elements are well-known, as the 'excremental vision' of the Hell Cantos has been the object of many commentaries.[69] I would only stress the need for an 'economic' analysis of these cathexes, and underline the parallel with historical structures. For instance, in *Jefferson and/or Mussolini*, Pound notes that he was slow in perceiving that there was a Fascist revolution at all in Italy, and adds that he never saw any of the violence or disturbance mentioned by the press: 'nobody hit me with a club and I didn't see any oil bottles' (p. 51). Such a denial of practices frequently reported, but surely not observed by a tourist in Piazza San Marco (the place Pound writes 'from'), testifies to Pound's willing blindness, but can also be linked with the unconscious motive underlying the terror-tactics of the *squadristi*; they did not shoot, like Hitler's SA or SS (at least, not so much), because the compulsory purgation of 'reds', suspects or trade-unionists was seen as an equivalent of the catharsis through which a city was purged of violence and opposition. In a way, the work of *Ulysses*, as Pound sees, it is not too far from what Mussolini achieved in the first stage of his conquest of power: a cleaning-up of the body politic, swept free of unhealthy passions, so that a new harmony between men and gods might be re-established. Only thus could a sense of 'interest' and a sense of 'tragedy' be reconciled.

In the *Cantos*, the excremental vision is never too far from the picture of an incestuous *Mitteleuropa* – dominated by the Jewish attachment to the family, seen as a close circle of passions – for much the same resons as made Stephen Dedalus attempt to 'prove' that Shakespeare was a Jew, with reference to Aquinas.[70] The enemy is for Pound the soft mass, the bloated flesh, and the striking feature is that phallic assertion needs the 'cutting' quality of thought, which dissociates, dissects the 'clots' which become clogs. As Pound wrote jocularly to E. E. Cummings, 'At any rate buggar the castration complex'!(*L*, p. 268). For Pound, therefore, castration opens the way to phallic drives, and similarly money becomes positive when it is fluid, when circulation is swift and easy; a liquidised money loses its bad smell, it detaches itself sufficiently from the anal gift in which it found its origin. The flow of magnetised money then figures the equivalent of sperm in its orgastic and phallic dynamic. The creation of forms is achieved when it goes back to a Madame *hulé*, or matter, or 'female chaos'.[71]

This is the root of Pound's consistent refusal to identify money with condensed labour, as presupposed by his reading of Ricardo and Marx. When money condenses value, it tends to be the prey of speculators and usurers. It congeals, stagnates, sticking to the fingers, stacked in safes and banks – thereby providing usury with its amorphous mass, on which the satanic transubstantiation is achieved. An act of discernment or dissociation alone can eliminate the anal side and let the gold be gold, so that money can shine again, like the golden rain awaited by Danaë, or the liquid light of the gods, or the impulse nourishing creative works of art. Liquidity is posed as the mediator between the phallic and anal poles, nevertheless needing the castrating operation of critical intelligence before being set in motion.

All these underground motifs explain the curious logic of Pound's economics, and find a concise expression in the Postscript, especially when Pound explains that he aims at harmonious polarisation:

> A sense of balance might show that asceticism means either a drought or a crowding. The liquid solution must be kept at right consistency; one would say the due proportion of liquid to viscous particles, a good circulation; the actual qualities of the sieve or separator counting perhaps most of all; the balance and retentive media. (*Natural Philosophy*, p. 180)

The same attempt to reach a satisfying compromise in circulation as presided over the synthesis of Gesell and Douglas can be observed here, fifteen years earlier. And the financial motif is delineated by the recurring signature of the 'balance' which can be read as the Roman *libra* or Pound. But an even longer period of time is involved before Pound manages to underwrite the entire system of exchanges with his signature.

Circulation and just price are harmonious because the function of surplus value has not been perverted by fetishism. The male thrust forward yields inventions, while the female principle obeys 'utility' and 'extreme economy' (*Natural Philosophy*, p. 171). Woman keeps a record of the 'useful gestures', thereby constituting instinct, while the male's prodigality aims at extravagant combinations, 'merely because in him occurs the new up-jut, the new bathing of cerebral tissues' (ibid.). Pound is intent on dissociating this spontaneous production by sudden overflow from actual labour: 'The dead laborious compilation and comparison of other men's dead images, all this is mere labour, not the spermatozoic act of the brain' (p. 179). The rapport between positive surplus and negative overproduction is to be found in a passage which prefigures the argument that 'Nature usually overproduces':

> In its subservience to the money fetish our age returns to the darkness of mediaevalism. Two osmies may make superfluous eggless nests, but do not kill each other in contesting which shall deposit the supererogatory honey therein. It is perhaps no more foolish to go at a hermit's bidding to recover an old sepulchre than to make a new sepulchre at the bidding of finance. (p. 171)

The allusion to the osmies is instructive, for, thanks to de Gourmont's rich lore of actual observations based on Fabre's works, Pound can prove that 'Nature overproduces' among animals. The osmies provide a model of 'workaholics'; these overactive solitary bees are described 'having exhausted their ovaries, but not their muscular force, building extra nests, provisioning them with honey . . . thus showing a real craziness for work' (p. 155). Such deviant behaviour poses a problem: how can Nature pervert the law of economy which instinct apparently observes? Pound, following de Gourmont, has to imply a wider sense of 'instinct' than is generally understood; de Gourmont derides the conventional opposition between instinct and intelligence, sides with instinct as being more 'useful', and decides that it is consciousness itself which is an 'extra' (p. 152), while a fantastic footnote of Pound's emphasises the 'wonders' which make larvae repeat the same useful gestures as soon as they are born, leaving time for 'contemplatio', since the long period spent in the cocoon is a preparation 'for the acts of its desire' (p. 156). Therefore, if nature and the movement of capital are not separated by a conceptual barrier, if there is but one ontology of production, the entire weight of dissociation between use and usury will rely on the intellectual surgery of man's interest; only there will one find an active and positive sense of 'intelligence'.

Ascetic men may well mismanage their liquidities, just as luxurious men do, but the discharge, retension or 'castration' is never negative in itself. At times Pound seems inclined to praise courtly love, following de Gourmont's idealised notions of 'Platonic love'; at times he indeed favours the illumination gained in coition. But the hermit or the saint whose contemplation results in a crusade is not worse than a capitalist who spares a surplus to build an empire on exploitation, and needs more wars and markets so that the demand may increase.

The intimate connection between the domains of sexuality, economics and history is observable throughout the *Cantos*, and helps throw some light on relatively obscure passages. For instance, in Canto CIII, Pound advocates:

Monetary literacy, sans which a loss of freedom is consequent
cunicoli, canalesque
     and the people (min) ate
     caelum renovabat,
       animals dance,
         manes come.   (p. 732)

Del Mar's injunction that no one can be free without being able to understand financial history is connected to a reminiscence of the *Chou King*, and linked with the discovery of Roman drains or 'canals' (*cunicoli*) by a friend of Pound's.[72] The Canto ends on a surprising note, with a 'repeat' from the chronicle of the Lombards which opened the sequence of 'Thrones':

> Lupus comes itineris, Rothar arianae haeresios –
> > edicti prologo
> dope already in use
> 'Puteum de testiculis impleam clericorum'
> > dixit Alchis
> would fill full a well with priests' balls,
> > heretics', naturally
> Das Leihkapital.
> And there is, of course, the Mensdorf letter
> > that has had (1958)
> > > no publicity.
> > > > (p. 737)

Rothar, being related to Pound's son-in-law, interests him primarily, along with the religious struggles and the heresies which marked his succession. Pound has come back to Migne's *Patrologia* and covers ground which had already been used, thus looking for some kind of anecdote to tie in with the economic theme. He thus manages to splice in a story of castration, a reference to Marx's *Capital*, and an allusion to the letter he and Mensdorff had sent in 1928 – which stresses the anniversary, and the time-lag owing to adverse forces – to the Carnegie Endowment for Peace, suggesting that overproduction and the manufacture of armaments would inevitably lead to wars.[73]

The story of the fight between Alachis (not Alchis) and Cunibert shows a cruel tyrant who hates priests and monks promising that, if God grants him the victory, he shall have all priests castrated ('si mihi Deus iterum victoriam dederit, quod unum puteum de testiculis impleam clericorum' – *Patrologia*, vol. 95, col. 620). Pound is mistaken when he assumes that Alachis is a defender of orthodoxy, but nevertheless right to see him fighting against the line of Rothar and Cunibert, touched by Arian heresies at the time. Alachis's terrible threats of castration are indeed reiterated, but he is defeated and killed by Cunibert. Castration leads on directly to 'das Leihkapital', an expression which is used by Marx to describe purely financial capital, loaned in the form of money, coin and notes, and which recurs in his discussion of Proudhon and the analysis of the apparently spontaneous generation of capital ('Geld heckendes Geld')[74]). Capitalism is superimposed on emasculation and religious perversion; it thrives between sodomy – as the story of the Honest Sailor attempted to tell – and castration – and Pound never forgets that the downfall of Chinese dynasties and the loss of Confucian values happened at the time of the domination of eunuchs. The swift historical montage, juxtaposing a battle in 688 AD, Marx, and 1928/1958, is bound to be more tantalising than explicatory; nevertheless the new focus of 'Thrones' on Byzantium allows a sound notion of interest (6%) to be related to a consciousness of 'Justice' which destroys any unholy associations with a perverted Stambouli.

Intellection and sexuality remain as two poles which magnetise the particles, coins or sperm, and keep the circuit at a correct degree of liquidity:

> The organization is functional
> and to maintain a liquidity...
> > begin at the precinct level...
>
> > (XCIX, p. 696)

Pound blends here in a general 'system' the contribution of Gesellite reforms and Social Credit, and the terms of *The Edict of K'ang Hsi*, which says that 'wealth is like water'[75] and forbids the exaction of interest at over 3 per cent.[76] From this synthesis alone can Pound claim to have rediscovered the 'phallic heart' (glossing the ideogram *sin* 㣺 which looks a little like a picture of male genitals, while the fact symbolising the heart[77]):

> Wang: that man's phallic heart is from heaven
> > a clear spring of rightness,
> Greed turns it awry   (XCIX, p. 697)

By law, not by nature

The phallic value of money forbids misreading it as a 'condensation' of value: money does not condense value, it represents it within a system; or it represents the system for those who toil in it and use it. Money is the locus of the conjunction between Nature and Law, *nomos* and *cosmos*, custom and will. Philology and differential analysis backed by an ever-renewed 'interest' need the confirmation of history, a history which will be read with microscopic attention, in the drabbest of its minutiae. When one says that money signifies value, what kind of signification does this imply? The answer Pound gives during the war is that it is a 'symbol' of the system: 'It is not enough to say of the new money that it is a "symbol of work". It is a symbol of collaboration. It is a certificate of work done within a system, estimated, or "consecrated" by the State./State or imperial money has always been an assertion of sovereignty' (*SP*, p. 281). This is entirely confirmed by Del Mar after the war, when he distinguishes between the intrinsic value of the gold or silver which may compose a coin, and the value as representation of the law:

> Value is not a thing, nor an attribute of things; it is a relation, a numerical relation, which appears in exchange. Such a relation cannot be accurately measured without the use of numbers, limited by law, and embodied in a set of concrete symbols, suitable for transference from hand to hand. It is this set of symbols which, by metonym, is called money. In the Greek and Roman republic it was called (with a far more correct apprehension of its character) nomisma and nummus, because the law (nomos) was alone competent to create it.[78]

Del Mar points out the link between symbol and metonymy in this dense analysis: money is a symbol, because its representation is not arbitrary, nor mimetic, but purely conventional; it bears the insigne of the whole structure which creates it; it is also a metonymy, because one coin is enough to lead back to the series of coin: the singular can at will be transformed into a plural, and conversely – 'The unit of money is all money.'[79] Del Mar's main theoretical source, quoted several times, is of course Aristotle, whose definitions in the *Politics* and *Ethics* serve as a point of departure for rejecting all theories which attempt to calculate the value of money by the costs of production, the ratio between silver and gold, or the operation of labour; value is intangible, and cannot be related to a source, or fount or origin: 'The truth is that there is no source of value. It does not arise from labour, any more than it does from crime or delusion' (*Science of Money*, p. 16). It is of course with such a thesis, legalistic and functionalist in the extreme, that Pound will have most difficulty. But his dialogue with Del Mar will never be complete, perhaps because he uses Del Mar essentially for the series of concrete details he provides in his bulky *History of Monetary Systems* and not for the entire thesis he represents. Yet at one point he voices his disagreement:

> And then Amsterdam (1609) busted the Wisselbank
> and said who shd/ deal in exchange,
> But Mr Del Mar does not, at this point,
>   connect issue with backing,
> though he is all for a proper total proportion
>   between total issue and buyables,
> Ike, '55, had got that far.   (xcvii, p. 672)

The question of backing is by definition absent from Del Mar's problematic or from his descriptions, because he situates his analysis in the sole circuit of distribution: 'so that the actual unit or measure of value is the whole legal or tale sum of circulating money, of whatever material or material it may be composed' (*Science of Money*, p. 17). Hence, prices, for instance, are only defined as the 'relation between money and exchange *in time*' (ibid., p. 23), as a factor of the velocity of exchanges and the conditions of the market. Money is measured, but it remains a relation, the rapport of two figures. Value is left to oscillate between a supply and a demand which cannot be calculated: 'Hence we have for value a complex numerical ratio of exchange, but precisely measurable by money; and for money, a measure susceptible of precise limitation, but, as the case now stands, actually left to vary between illimitable demand and the more or less uncertain supply' (ibid., p. 17). Thus money is defined by the almost mystical right of the community at large to fix value by stamping any kind of symbol it wishes and by letting it circulate. Whoever attempts to exploit the sovereignty, identical with the 'right to issue' commits a sin. As Del Mar underlines, *valeo* means 'to have power', and this power is an intangible essence:

> Rome   versus Babylon
> no sense of quiddity in the sovreignty
>   i.e. the power to issue
> The slaves were red herring,
>   land not secure against issuers
>   (ciii, p. 732)

In the case of Rome, the mystical sense of 'issue' was lost, the relation was not kept by law and justice, and devaluation despoiled peasants of their lands. So, if Pound follows Del Mar's inquiry into the causes of downfall or perversion at the level of entire systems of exchange, he keeps in mind the necessity of referring the 'issue' to some natural order.

Del Mar, on the other hand, writes in the context of the American crisis at the end of the nineteenth century, the controversy over the demonetisation of silver, the issue of greenbacks, the national debt after the Civil War – and thus his main objective is to restore a sense of sovereignty in the American Congress, and to forbid the 'monetary crimes' of 1868, 1870 and 1873.[80] The origin of the crimes is always the same: a group of private interests plays on the public's inevitable fetish for gold or silver, and exploits it to its own advantage. Del Mar traces the loss of distinction between value and precious metals back to the Middle Ages, when the Greek wisdom still manifested by the Byzantine Empire was obliterated in a 'disintegration' of value (and subsequently of values). Money and words undertook the same course: 'Words followed a similar process of decomposition' (*Science of Money*, p. 111). At times, indeed, Del Mar touches on themes with a definitely Poundian ring: 'There is a parallelism in the decay and subsequent revival of the conception of money and the arts of music and poetry. During the Dark Ages the ancient art of music was lost, and poetry, which in the classical ages went by numbers, now went by accent' (p. 112, n. 2). In spite of possible disagreements with the chronology, Pound would no doubt have agreed on the whole, and indeed, when he takes copious, if cryptic, notes from Del Mar's *History* in Canto xcvii, he notes a parallel between what Del Mar calls the 'grammar of money' and the evolution in prosody by a rhyming pun on Byzantine taxes:

>   ... wheat 12 pence a quarter
>   that 6 $\frac{4}{5}$ ths pund of bread be a farden
>   Act 51, Henry Three. If a penny of land be a perch
>   that is grammar
>   nummulary moving toward prosody
>   πρόσοδος φόρων η ἐπέτειος..
>   μεταθεμένων after Dandolo got into Byzance
>   & worsened AND...   (p. 671)

Del Mar explains how the division of the pound into twenty parts, each subdivided into twelve, was extended by Henry III to the division of the pound weight used for bread. The complicated account of these measures interests Pound because the precision of numbers is coupled with the idea that numismatics creates not only a grammar but a prosody of its own, which might supply a new quantitative meter. The Greek sentence means the 'yearly procession of taxes', and *prosodos* is echoed by 'prosody', while the science of the 'change of meters' is coupled with the tag from Aristotle criticising those who change the unit of money to gain a profit. Dandolo is of course the Doge who helped to bring about the fall of Constantinople, putting an end to the domination of Byzantine coining in the Mediterranean world. Del Mar had noted that, from Augustus to the thirteenth century, approximately thirteen centuries had been spent with one source of mint, that of the King.[81] For the right to coin was and still is the first sign of sovereignty.

This is why Pound glosses the fight between Abd-el-Melik and Justinian II caused by the Caliph's decision to pay tribute in his own coin – a gesture which, Del Mar says, constituted 'an insult, a defiance, and a sacrilege' because the Caliph appeared in effigy on the coin, having a drawn sword in hand, along with Mohammedan religious formulae. This provides Pound with a rhetorical flourish with which to open the Canto:

> Melik & Edward struck coins-with-a-sword,
> 'Emir el Moumenin' (Systems p. 134)
>> six and ½ to one, or the sword of the Prophet,
> SILVER being in the hands of the people   (xcvii, p. 668)

For Pound, who follows Del Mar rather literally, this Caliph, eventually defeated, represents the first rebel of money, because he refused to let his rule be jeopardised by the centralisation of 'issue'. The Micah tag 'each in the name of his god' should apply to the right of issue, both being connected. The reference to 'six and a half' and to 'silver' concerns the ratio between gold and silver, different in the Roman Empire (1 : 12) from in the Arab countries, India and elsewhere (1 :6½). Enormous profits could be made by transferring precious metals from one part of the world to the other, but there was a political rationale behind the discrepancy: gold was possessed by the nobles, and silver was the people's currency – already – and the Arab rulers wished to conciliate the peoples of the countries they conquered by a revaluation of silver currency. While Pound learns a lot in this long inquiry, and also teaches a little, he seems to hesitate to let the 'system' function without the assured foundation of a 'backing'. Is it to be found in land? Del Mar proves that this is not the case. It cannot be the precious metal, nor work. Thus the only real backing left to Pound remains the calculation of demand in the cycle of supply and demand.

Of course, Pound cannot attempt to revise the fundamental notions of classical economy, and he always proceeds in the disjointed, paratactic fashion with which he approached Del Mar. Del Mar's vision of coherent, closed systems, whose interaction explains the political and social history of the periods considered, would not easily fit in with the pattern of vital interest already sketched by Pound before the war. While Del Mar remains an Aristotelian, always on the look-out for those who 'change the currency' (*metathemenon* . . .) he appears to foreclose the claims to an Other, something outside the system. Money for him, must be 'the Same', and he quotes with approval a note issued as an official resolution by the English Privy Council in 1604 which says that 'Money should not be falsified, by making the same generally more or less' (*Science of Money*, p. xi). If 'an appeal to reason is about a 13% / appeal to reality' (Canto xcvi, p. 655), Pound may avail himself of this appeal and attempt a last time to find a foundation in human nature.

This implies a rereading of Aristotle, on whom so many of Pound's other sources were similarly founded. And indeed, through the inconsistencies of terminology and the constantly shifting ground, there remains in Pound's obdurate quest for the root or the source of money a wish to absorb all new knowledge so as to be in position to test it against some kind of *arche*. Thus the symptomatic terminological hesitations take a sharper outline if one relates them to the early summary of the *Guide to Kulchur*. Pound had embarked on an ambitious reading of the *Nicomachean Ethics* – to which I shall return in order to give a complete account of Pound's textual manoeuvres – and had come to the point where Aristotle defines money as a measure, which meets Pound's entire approval. And suddenly Pound thinks he has spotted a blunder in the translation. I quote the entire passage:

He [Aristotle] has, and let no one fail to credit him with it, come at money from the right side, as a measure. A means of ascertaining the proportionate worth of a house and a pair of shoes.

In the hierarchy of its constituents he has got hold of the chief reason for money's existence.

Yet again it makes an infinite difference whether you translate χρεία as *demand* or USE. Here the black curse of university obfuscation descends on Rackham. The man has met somewhere a university professor of economics or some work exuded from such licery. He falls into class-room jargon and translates χρεία as demand.

The value of a thing depends on USUS, its price may be distorted by its OPUS. (*GK*, pp. 323–4)

And Pound heaps more abuse on poor Professor Rackham, accusing Aristotle himself of not having 'made his paragraph fool-proof'. Indeed, the passage is fundamental, since Aristotle is about to define the essence of money as being constituted by custom: it deserves the term *nomina* by derivation from *nomos*, as we have seen. The general measure which assures that all commodities have found a common standard is determined by something else: 'And this standard is in reality demand [*chreia*], which is what holds everything together [*panta sunekei*], since if men cease to have wants or if their wants alter, exchange will go on no longer . . . .'[82] Rackham has thus translated the sentence, choosing among the several senses of *chreia*, which range from 'use' and 'function' to 'question', 'subject', 'relationship', 'profit', 'advantage', and finally 'need', 'necessity', 'want'. Pound adds a footnote to explain that the word is tricky and presents one of the text's 'wangles': 'To want, to be in want OF, to need, are not identical conditions' (*GK*, p. 324). In 1938, therefore, Pound doggedly sticks to his belief that an appeal to *usus* can be the only answer to *usura*, which leads him to choose the opposite pole of the verbal spectrum of *chreia* from that selected by the translation.

Imagine, then, the reader's surprise when he goes on reading through the *Guide to Kulchur* and comes to the series of 'Addenda' dated 1952! For this time Pound himself makes the blunder for which he blamed Rackham and placed him in the 'pimp's paradise of indefinite verbiage' (*GK*, p. 324); while carefully cautioning us against mistranslation ('ONE WORD WILL RUIN IT ALL'), he gives as his first example 'The mistranslation, or rather the insertion of the word "value", where Aristotle said χρεία, demand. Money is not a measure of value. The price is caused by demand' (p. 357). Now, there is nowhere in Rackham's text an interpolation of the word 'value', though it does occur in a long footnote by Rackham which discusses 'values' in the arithmetical example given by Aristotle,[83] and in the passage which defines money as 'a measure of all things, and so of their superior or inferior value'. Pound reiterates his statement in the

'Chronology for school-use' he adds at the end of the volume, a chronology which starts with Aristotle, who 'saw that money is not a measure of value, but of demand. Price indicating the demand. XREIA' (*GK*, p. 359). The difference between 1938 and 1952 turns out to be simply that Pound has read Del Mar in between, and acknowledges his influence: 'Work does not create wealth, it *contributes to the formation of it.* Nature's productivity is the root (ref/ also Del Mar: interest is due teleologically to the increase of domestic animals and plants)' (p. 357). The opposition between *use* and *demand* has given way to an opposition between *value* and *demand.* This time the motive of complete circulation freed from any 'clog' in the sphere of demand is taken as the basis of economics. The problem of the 'producers' who 'use' the earth and should 'own' it has been replaced by that of deciding who issues the money and for what purpose. Money is both an instrument of policy and a mark of authority. The just leader is he who satisfies all the needs of his people. Distribution according to needs prevails over the just claims of producers.

Yet, when one again tries to locate the exact points of disjuncture between all these notions in the *Cantos*, another surprise lies in wait, for the terms used in 'Rock-Drill' and then in 'Thrones' are subtly divergent; when Pound examines the problem of 'issue' in Canto LXXXVII, he sees it as the 'source' (p. 569) and comments on its necessary enforcement by law:

> 'But', said Antoninus,
> > 'Law rules the sea'.
> 'And that the state shd/have benefit
> > from private misfortune,
> > > not in my time, not under me.'
> Until Salmasius, wanting precision:
> > > > > Want, χρεία,
> 'Common practice!' sd/Ari re business . . . .   (p. 570)

This time the punning echolalia seems to replace monetary questions by a pure play on signifiers, with the rhymes on 'wanting', 'want' and 'Ari'/'re'; we cannot tell whether *chreia* is the object of discussion implied by Antoninus (and let us not forget that among other meanings, *chreia* signifies a 'subject' of conversation) or refers humorously to a failing in Salmasius's thinking.

Two other snippets from 'Thrones' merely add to our perplexity: 'in Xreia, to dissociate demand from the need' (Canto CIV, p. 739); and

> river gold is from Ko Lu;
>
> price from XREIA;
>
> Yao and Shun ruled by jade
>
> (CVI, p. 753)

In this last repeat of the theme, 'XREIA' cannot be translated, it remains as an enigmatic ideogram inserted in the Chinese mythical past. 'XREIA' functions as a shifter, linking Artemis and Circe with the emperors Yao and Shun.

What Pound constantly emphasises is the dissociation to be achieved, a subtraction almost, taking need out of demand, and demand out of need. Demand, in this widening context, tends to mean the circuit of exchange at large, seen from the point of view of those who are ready to part with their liquidities for goods, or the reverse. Needs are the objectives to be satisfied in terms of services or products, and are ultimately grounded in the physiological nature of man. The subtraction of *usus* from *usura* entails a complex interaction of gaps within a totality that refuses to allow for closure; no sooner has Pound quoted Bracton's words 'Uncivil to judge a part in ignorance of the totality' (Canto CIX, p. 771), than he must add 'nemo omnia novit' (nobody knows everything), which dismisses the appeal to a knowledge of the totality. Totality would be acquired by a general view of the whole circuit of exchange *and* an insight into the total nature of man, including physiological desires and metaphysical concerns. This desire to know is revealed to be impossible, as Lacan formulates it in his dialectic of 'desire', 'need' and 'demand':

> Desire is that which is manifested in the interval that demand hollows within itself, inasmuch as the subject, in articulating the signifying chain, brings to light the want-to-be, together with the appeal to receive the complement from the Other, if the Other, the locus of speech, is also the locus of this want, or lack.
>
> That which is thus given to the Other to fill, and which is strictly that which it does not have, since it, too, lacks being, is what is called love, but it is also hate and ignorance.
>
> It is also what is evoked by any demand beyond the need that is articulated in it, and it is certainly that of which the subject remains all the more deprived to the extent that the need articulated in the demand is satisfied. (*Ecrits/S*,[84] p. 263)

Desire manifests itself when the need is satisfied and when demand is not reductible to this satisfaction; their inadequation appears as a gap which might be the equivalent of Pound's version of the *A + B* theorem in Douglas. Pound provides the most general formulation in Canto xcvii (the Del Mar Canto):

> Assyria, Babylon, Macedonia,
> 　　　　always more somewhere than somewhere,
> but the (*abbreviare*) the great gap declining.　　　　(p. 674)

The remainder that he cannot but '*abbreviare*' tells the reader that the total system can never be presented at once, and therefore that a residue remains, a lack covered and revealed at the same time by the parenthesis which attracts to his own utterance and writing-process. Douglas is then added to Del Mar's *History* ('Steed asked Douglas about the rupee'), and a second signal of 'abbreviation' confirms this reading.

> And if, say, we had a pope, like Pisani?
> 　　　　abbreviare
> faster than it distributes the power to buy,
> 　　　　but the interval, 15, 16, (vide Benton)
> as from 12 to 6 and one half,
> 　　　　but by that time they found some other wangle,
> by '78, T. C. P. said 'non-interest-bearing'
> 　　　　　　　　　　　　　　　　　(xcvii, p. 677)

The montage of fragmented quotations has acquired maximum velocity there, and all the elements are explained by other parts of the poem. What should be pointed out is the importance of the circulation of a lack (Gesell's money-as-loss) to make up for the unjust gap between the production of value and the power to buy. The distinctions are all important, for in that context they can be anarchically multiplied 'with ever-shifting change' (ibid.).

> 'All true,' said Griffith
> 　　　　　　　'but I can't move'em with it'.
> Ownership? Use? there is a difference.　　　　(p. 678)

Lacan's analysis can help us go beyond certain perplexities, since it shows how the subject is trapped by the enigma of desire as 'causing' him:

For the unconditional element of demand, desire substitutes the 'absolute' condition: this condition unties the knot of that element in the proof of love that is resistant to the satisfaction of a need. Thus desire is neither the appetite for satisfaction, nor the demand for love, but the difference that results from the substraction of the first from the second, the phenomenon of their splitting (*Spaltung*).   (*Ecrits/S*, p. 287)

Such a 'gap' cannot be filled by merely putting triumphant phallic sexuality in its place, as Pound repeatedly tried to do, until the attempt failed to locate the cause of his desire (a desire already split by the division or multiplication of objects, be they women or concepts). The only solution lies in the possibility of finding a signifier of the lack, and this pertains to the function of the phallus:

In any case, man cannot aim at being whole (the 'total personality' is another of the deviant premises of modern psychotherapy), while ever the play of displacement and condensation to which he is doomed in the exercise of his functions marks his relation as a subject to the signifier.

The phallus is the privileged signifier of that mark in which the role of the logos is joined with the advent of desire.

It can be said that this signifier is chosen because it is the most tangible element in the real of sexual copulation, and also the most symbolic in the literal (typographical) sense of the term, since it is equivalent there to the (logical) copula. It might also be said that, by virtue of its turgidity, it is the image of the vital flow as it is transmitted in generation.   (Ibid.)

These remarks then help us understand how Pound can attempt to bridge the gap in his economics only by resorting to the expedient of leaving signifiers to stand for themselves, while they all point toward his absent and underlying signature, the pound of flesh he has had to pay for his desire. Lacan speaks of desire as branding the subject's shoulder, by the action of a signifier which cuts through his body: 'This moment of cut is haunted by the form of a bloody crap – the pound of flesh that life pays in order to turn it into the signifier of the signifiers, which it is impossible to restore, as such, to the imaginary body; it is the lost phallus of the embalmed Osiris' (p. 265). The phallus introduces the question of the symbol in another key, since it can now be related to a debt from which the subject is never free, rather than to the tension against chaos. Money becomes the symptom of an effort to assert desire without having to pay off the symbolic debt.

The only factor which, for Pound, can unify natural production and the accumulated inheritance from the past lies within the 'power to issue', in which sovereignty consists and on which it insists, but which can also be turned awry, perverted against the source. The 'production' is irremediably split between an unapproachable origin and a continuous movement of creation. Money is therefore both symptom and symbol; as symptom, it tells of the endless mutilation at work through *Leihkapital*, and, as Del Mar points out, 'the forgery of books, the defacement of monuments, the perversion of evidence'[85] reveal the amount of interpretative effort required to reach the key to the system, a key which in optimistic moments Pound sees as lying out there, within reach ('and with one day's reading a man may have the key in his hands' – Canto LXXIV, p. 427), but which recedes into the distance as soon as the inquiry faces the indefinite field of an entire symptomatology: 'the history of money lies scattered and hidden in the chronicles of law, religion, slavery, wars, natural philosophy, mining, metallurgy and archeology'.[86] But, as 'symbol', money gives the true basis which mere signs lack, even if it is constantly attacked: 'We find two forces in history: one that divides, shatters, and kills and one that contemplates the unity of the mystery. // 'The arrow hath not two points.' // There is the force that falsifies, the force that destroys every clearly delineated symbol. . . . But the images of the gods, or Byzantine mosaics, move the soul to contemplation and preserve the tradition of undivided light' (*SP*, pp. 276–7). To bridge the gap between symptom and symbol, between desire and debt, Pound's answer lies in his writing, in the signature it attempts to leave as a trace, a signature which has to be erected again and again, but in a sacred space: as a temple.

Templum

If Pound's name has played the role of a fate for him, it is not simply by the obsessive recurrence of puns linking his signature with economic theories; it is rather in the means of which he availed himself to transform this fate into the fate of a nation, and, perhaps, of language in general.

Pound signed his first economic pamphlets with the £ symbol (*Money-Pamphlets by £*[87]), and at one point used this character to cross out words and sentences in his drafts and letters,[88] until this sign was transformed into the ideogram *cheng*[4], 正 , which concludes the fifth decad of the *Cantos*, and is the first character to appear in the older Faber edition. By a play on the Confucian sense of the ideogram, Pound reminds the reader of the connection between a just doctrine and his own name, inscribed in a chain of echoes, displacement and subject-rhymes. Pound goes as far as punning his name into the three ideograms he put on the cover of the first edition of 'Thrones', *pao*[3] *en*[1] *te*[2], meaning 'keeper', 'goodness' and 'virtue'.[89] *Cheng*[4] means to regulate, and Pound uses it in relation with *ming*[2], in the phrase 'to regulate the name': the rectification of names becomes the erection of the name into a symbol or a hieroglyph.

In the 'Pisan Cantos', Pound finds a way of simplifying the *cheng* ideogram by linking the *chih*[3] ideogram with his own 'position':

what's the name of that bastard? D'Arezzo, Gui d'Arezzo
notation

      3 on 3

    chiacchierona   the yellow bird

  to rest   3 months in bottle

                (auctor)
by the two breasts of Tellus

                        (LXXIX, p. 487)

Pound is looking at the birds on electric wires, and they irresistibly call up the image of a score, which reminds him of the inventor of musical notation, Gui d'Arezzo. The reference to the *Book of Poems* in the *Ta Hsio* transforms a lyrical description ('The twittering yellow bird . . . comes to rest in the hollow corner of the hill') into a philosophical argument: 'Kung said: comes to its rest, alights, knows what rest is, what ease is. Is man, for all his wit, less wise than this bird of the yellow plumage that he should not know his resting place or fix the point of his aim?' (*Con*., p. 39). The 'resting place' derives a negative connotation from the juxtaposition of 'bottle', which refers to the prison of the Camp, but the most important link established is the direct transition from 'auctor' to 止 (*chih*[3]), which will then dot the later Cantos in a regular fashion; it will be superimposed on the sense of a 'gnomon', the stick used by the Chinese to measure the time from the observation of shadows, and then used for its main sense of 'arrest':

Ver novum
        are protected of course,
        hic est medium

                        chih in the 3rd/ tone
                        and a radical

                        (LXXXVII, pp. 570–1)

The character becomes the real root of Confucian doctrine, because in the *Analects* Confucius says about Yen Yuan, 'Alas, I see him advance, I never see him stop (take a position)', and Pound adds the following comment: 'There is no more important technical term in the Confucian philosophy than this *chih*³ the hitching post, position, place one is in, and works from' (*Con.*, p. 232). It is a way of stopping the reader, as with the ploces of 'Rock-Drill' and 'Thrones', but this time the name has turned into a signature:

                Quos ego Persephonae

      chih³

        not with jet planes,
The holiness of their courage forgotten
        and the Brescian lions effaced,
Until the mind jumps without building

      chih³

and there is no *chih* and no root.

                        (CX, p. 780–1)

The insistent repetition of the 'point of rest' is a way of taking 'position' (and in that case it means 'resisting' the 'black-out', saving fragments out of ruins) without intruding a shrill personal voice, for indeed the 'ego' has disappeared within the symbol. This silent mode of presentation corresponds to the higher level of the analysis of usury and money, the move upward towards the light, out of 'the hell of money' into 'the undiscussable Paradiso' (*GK*, p. 292). The monetary sign £, the Chinese rectification of names and the cryptic assertion of a mute signature all signal the possibility of a vision, and, the less said, the better it sounds: ideograms make money appear as symbol rather than as symptoms. The dream of a voice encrypted by the signature underlies the desire to arrest the name in the space of writing constituted by a *templum*: then can the birds sing on the wires, and bring a portent on the lines. Pound's finest example of such a mute utterance which discloses the ultimate meaning of life is that of an old duchess who never spoke: 'She nodded. She had the dignity of a temple image, and various nods and bobs eliminated all need of verbal expression' (*GK*, p. 83). Like Peeperkorn, who in Thomas Mann's *Magic Mountain* imposes silence on all verbose discourses by a simple gesture of the hand, Pound still dreams of a pure *deixis* which would nevertheless point to the presence of the mystery.

This is why the moment of arrest symbolised by *chih*[3] finds a direct economic and religious equivalent in the temple, which is symbolised by a little drawing: it appears in the Del Mar Canto as a counterpoint to the chronicle of the changes in monetary systems:

> The temple ⎏⎐ is holy
> because it is not for sale. (XCVII, p. 676)

Like the Greek temples, Pound's temple is 'not for sale' but keeps value; it can serve as a bank, with the offerings to the gods and the deposits of the community, and, because it remains outside time, in a direct bond with the eternal, it is the ideal bank, because it never attempts to make time pay. The gods guarantee any deposit, and, furthermore, transform the name – the 'auctor's name' – into solid stone:

> 'Got no stone' said Knittl ⎏⎐
> (p. 681)

Furthermore, as Aristotle notes at the end of the *Nicomachean Ethics*, the gods can be called truly 'immortal' because, among other things, they do not require any money: 'Besides, it would be absurd to suppose that [the gods] actually have a coinage or currency [*nomisma*] of some sort' (x.viii.7). In the realm of the transcendent, debt is abolished, and the Law becomes synonymous with the city and civilisation, as Pound recalls when he uses a palindrome to collapse the *walls* back into *laws*: 'must fight for law as for walls' (Canto XCVIII, p. 685). But the tragic consequence is that a total arrest, a total identification with the gods, brings about the subject's disappearance, and Pound adds immediately, 'Heracleitos' parenthesis', which alludes to the last scene of *Women of Trachis*, in which Heracleitos is trying to give courage to his son, who refuses to kill him in order to stop his agonising pain: 'And put some cement in your face, / reinforced concrete, make a cheerful finish / even if you don't want to' (*WT*, p. 70). The exact allusion in the Greek text is to the iron staples used to clamp together and seal the stones of city walls. The ultimate 'sealing' of the Temple entails therefore the same sealing of the mouth, and the price the community pays for its coherence is the death of the hero. His death yields the ultimate 'symbol' or *sumploke* (total interweaving of essences[90]), because he understands that 'all has come to pass' because of the Law written by the Father, Zeus.

And, exactly as the 'Temple' and *chih*[3] motifs dot the later Cantos, the *Leitmotiv* of the *sumbainei* recurs in the interwoven quotations to stress that the perception of a full light means the death of the subject. Lifting from the concluding soliloquy of the tortured Herakles the sentence *taut 'oun epeide lampra sumbainei* ('these things thus happen clearly, brilliantly'), Pound forces the translation, giving it a stronger emphasis because, as he writes in a note, 'this is the key phrase, for which the play exists':

> SPLENDOUR,
>   IT ALL COHERES (*WT*, pp. 66–7)

The *sumbainei* stresses the etymological sense of *sumbolon* (*synballein*, to throw together), already implied by the 'halves of a seal' in Canto LXXVII, since it originally meant to stand with feet together, to put both feet together, only later to acquire the meaning of to happen, to come to pass, to tally with, to correspond with. *Chih*[3] on the other hand derives from the imprint of a foot, thus meaning to stop, which creates a submerged link with *sumbainei* and also with Oedipus – etymologically the 'man with the swollen foot' – since the assertion of the Law must nevertheless always walk in the traces of transgression, a transgression which is redoubled when the hero wants to know the truth at all costs, thereby bringing about his own ruin.

Indeed, Marcel Granet has shown that Confucius used the term *cheng ming* for the first time when confronting the scandalous situation of incestuous relationships within the family of the Duke of Ling, whose wife slept with the Duke's son, a little like Parisina and Ugo d'Este in Canto XX:

In Wei, the wife did not behave as a wife, the husband did not behave as a husband, neither the father as a father, nor the son as a son. This is expressed by saying that either no one was in his proper place (*kiu*) or that the father and the son had swapped their designations (*yi ming*): the situation being interverted, it was as if the designations themselves had been interverted.[91]

The *cheng* requires that the wife should be a wife, the son a son, the father a father 'indeed', in the normal economy of house and family; only then can the economy of the Empire be regulated on a sound basis, and the good order of language be founded on the order of society and the *cosmos*.

The tragedy of a divided subject who can be reconciled with the law of desire just at the moment of his sacrifice – in a complicated imbrication of roles to which I shall come back – is thus identical with the desire to establish a just system of economy. The name functions as the keystone of the system, but because of its sym-bolic value (threatened, as it were, by the splitting movement of the evil other, the diabolic *dia-bolon*), it can only be written in stone letters, hieroglyphs, incisions, steles. Its function is arresting; it stops the reading, underlines, repeats, but also permits the circulation of another type of symbols.

Pound's name links him with his paternal heritage, which not only gave him descent from Homer (his father's name, which sounded so well to him that he called himself 'homerovitch'), but also related him to his grandfather's struggle when he invented a money of his own, which could be exchanged for timber:

> Trying (T. C. P.) 50 years later to keep some of the
> non-interest bearing etc.
>> in circulation
>> as currency
>> (CIII, p. 733)

Before the Second World War, Pound had made several reproductions of his grandfather's 50-cent scrip, issued by the Union Lumbering Company of Chippewa Falls, Wisconsin, and he used these as postcards, writing on the other side a description and a commentary. For instance, he sent one to Roosevelt with the following text: 'Lest you forget the nature of money / i.e. that it is a ticket. For the govt. . . . You can see that the bill here photod. has SERVED (I mean by the worn state of the note.) Certificates of work done.'[92] Pound's dream was that, by sending the reproduction and the commentary to Mussolini and to Roosevelt, he would suddenly illuminate them, make them see what money *is*. Both sides were signed, T. C. Pound's paraph clearly visible on the scrip,[93] underwritten by his grandson's signature. The double signature, allegorically condensing all of Pound's beliefs on economics, afforded the opportunity for a supplementary profit: money could become writing, and the sign could become money. The act of sending this complex symbol, currency and index, icon and signature, worn-out note and monument salvaged from the dust of archives, enabled him, moreover, to show all the credit which could be attached to his name, since he not only meant what he said, showed what he mentioned, disclosed a truth so simple that it was blinding, but also appeared as the respectful, reverent inheritor of a long legacy, of an important political and ethical responsibility. Between an almost mythical grandfather and a mystical new symbolic father, between the inventor and experimenter out there in the wilderness of America and the enlightened ruler, a double letter could serve as the token of a circulation of symbols: a debt which abolishes itself as it circulates, because its very circulation is a discharge from debt.

It is important to understand that Pound needed both moments or movements: the erection of an unmovable and cryptic signature as Temple, and the circulation of signs as currency; but the gap he could never bridge between the two logics of signification enacted the movement of splitting and difference he feared. Whenever Pound insists on the direct legibility of the symbol, whenever he thinks he can dispense with discourse, the name breaks down, collapses unable to underwrite the major issues of history. When he wants to make people open their eyes, money becomes the real thing: he cannot then help disavowing the symbolic structure of language, which entails that division should be experienced through absence, death, castration. At the time of this illusion, contemporary with the ideological investment of his work, he thought anyone could read the same truth as he saw in any coin, any note – as is shown by an anecdote narrated by his daughter, describing their life in Venice before the war:

Sometimes Izzo brought some shy young man interested in poetry. Babbo would immediately challenge the newcomer by pulling out a ten-lira note and telling him to look at it carefully, to read the fine print. What did it mean, what did it say, what did he know about the nature of money? Nothing. Unless he understood the nature of money he could not understand or write good poetry. Then followed a list of assignments. The young men seldom came a second time.[94]

The note is to be read like an ideogram in Confucius's story about the dog: one sees that it is the perfect drawing of a dog. However, what one 'sees' in a banknote is the endless ramification of a symbolic structure condensed by a metonymy. Pound attempts to close the symbol chain whilst turning money into a challenge for our hermeneutic skills. The conceptual tools are not situated in an abstract theory which would disclose the truth of money through a rational discourse; they too are caught up by the hallucinatory demand of an immediate gaze. That this constitutes a kind of hermeneutic circle is Pound's important victory, but the price he has to pay is the splintering of the symbol; being intermittent in its disclosure, it becomes, like the name which bears it, *spezzato* – it shines forth at intervals leaving only agony as a more persistent state of mind.

On the other hand, it is probably because of Pound's failure to give a satisfactory account of the production of value and signs that he can inscribe his name in a text which becomes identical with the fate of contemporary writing. The reality of language and the reality of history negotiate an interaction of vortices which Pound calls money. Money becomes his privileged vantage-point for a reading of symptoms and symbols. The last note written by Pound, five months before his death, sums up his ambivalence and perplexities:

> re Usury:
> I was out of focus, taking a symptom for a cause.
> The cause is AVARICE.
> > Venice, 4th July, 1972.
> > > (*SP*, p. 6)

The date is not fortuitous: just as the decision to write on a postcard representing his grandfather's efforts may appear as a wish to write directly on the map of America, the calendar situates any attempt at disclosing the truth in a familial and collective history. And, as long as money continues to oscillate in status between cause and symptom, it may represent the main 'issue' deserving all our 'interest', while Pound's imaginary world continues to build a temple and a city in our minds.

6 From Ethics to Hermeneutics

I did not cheat
nor fake inspiration,
what I wrote was right then,

auguries, hermetic definition;
yet, I would have left initiates, many times
for a red rose and a beggar . . .

(HD, *Hermetic Definition*[1])

Taught and the not taught. Kung and Eleusis
to catechumen alone.

(Canto LIII, p. 272)

The discussion of certain monetary concepts has taught us that, if a certain circularity is perceptible in most arguments advanced by Pound, this does not lead to a complete reversibility of all analyses, and that the interactions are positive – for instance in the case of words and money – as soon as some type of circulation is established. I would now slightly displace the ground of such circulation, and approach the tactics by which Pound circulates between texts and also uses his text to hold a dialogue with his reader. The circulation of knowledge about a few economic facts is a prerequisite for a just circulation of goods among the people, just as any statement, any work of art, bears the imprint of a state of exchanges in a given society, and reveals the presence or absence of usury. The circle is therefore a circle of communication, which can find a very simple psychological explanation, as quoted by Pound from Frobenius: 'It is not what a man says, but the part of it which his auditor considers important, that measures the quantity of his communication' (*GK*, p. 59). But, on the other hand, Pound wants the critic to commit himself, to start from personal measurements, 'pick out for himself' (*ABCR*, p. 30). This is how his many guides and ABCs display a series of unconnected statements, all starting from some experience in dissociation of values and ideas, which then must be 'picked up' by the reader. The strategy imposed by the *sumploke* constituted in the ideogram cannot directly attack bad language: first, because it would be pedagogically unsound; and secondly because it would not stay true to the selection of 'peaks' or 'high points'.

> It would be particularly against the grain of the whole ideogrammic method for me to make a series of general statements concerning Elizabethan katachrestical language.
> The way to study Shakespeare's language is to study it side by side with something different and of equal extent.   (*ABCR*, p. 59)

Pound's refusal to engage in any kind of confrontation with what is not the best leads him to present the results, the findings, the pearls, and not the general process by which he comes across the passages from given authors, or whole authors. Despite his titles, his guides are guides to a reading which has been done, not to the reading-process. This is first experimented with in the *Guide to Kulchur*, with the reading of Aristotle, and is therefore interesting as much for what it reveals of the process as for the conclusions. In 'Rock-Drill', such an experimental attitude to texts is developed, and explains the great contrast between the later Cantos and the early ones. Pound then appears ready to quote even catachrestic examples of language or documents in order to re-create the total interpretative circle, and to include the reader in it.

This entails a re-evaluation of the term 'interpretative', which had been used in a rather arrogant way by the Pound of *The Spirit of Romance*: 'An art is vital only so long as it is interpretative, so long, that is, as it manifests something which the artist perceives at greater intensity, and more intimately, than his public' (p. 87). Interpretation only touches on the artist's sense of integrity, his keenness of perception, his ability to 'distinguish between the shades and the degrees of the ineffable' (ibid.). Without ever relinquishing the idea of the 'ineffable', Pound knows that his poetry misses its aim if he is the only one to 'enter arcanum' (Notes for Canto CXVII, p. 802). Not that he would wish to drag in a crowd! But the naming of people and things can bring back some illumination, shared at least for an instant ('by naming over all the most beautiful things we know we may draw back upon the mind some vestige of the heavenly splendor' – *SR*, p. 96). I shall hence follow the reading- and naming-process which leads to a finer perception of values, showing the transformation it undergoes after the 1950s.

A guided tour of Aristotle

The process of reading is never a straightforward act harmonising a chosen, well-defined perspective with a printed object. Reading cannot be reduced to the various visual manoeuvres required for some ideal clarification, for, when I read a text, this text reads me, as it were, and the only way of examining the complex forces invested and displaced at the same time is to join the criticism *of* the text in a dynamic spiral to the criticism *in* the text. The awareness of such dialectical interaction is revealed by Pound in his letters just after he sent off the typescript of his *Guide to Kulchur*. To Rouse he writes, 'I hope my lambasting of Arrystotle will arouse a little *real* interest as distinct from the bureaucratic exploitation' (*L*, p. 295); and to Eliot, 'An I hope you won't find I overdid Aristotle, cause I got to do somfin so't of thorough, fer to kork up deh *end* (de TELOS or termination). Can't just go butterflying all deh time' (*L*, p. 294). The object of the *Guide*, which Pound preferred to call 'The New Learning' in his first drafts, was to show 'what Ez don't know' – 'How much does Ez git fer eggsposin hiz iggurunce?' (*L*, p. 288) – and also to offer a kind of compendium of philosophy, literature, beliefs, economics and history as he has read, digested and experienced them. It is in a way the equivalent of a general treatise of 'ideology', if one understands the word in its historical sense: a story of man's vital representations and of their relation to actual life and society.

Pound thus embraces the whole of Western epistemology, and, drawing a lot from Francesco Fiorentino's *Storia della Filosofia*, he selects Greek philosophy as a decisive starting-point: 'It cd. be argued that the "main ideas" were all present in Greek philosophy . . .' (*GK*, p. 25). The conditional comes from his recourse to another model of wisdom, Chinese thought as defined by Confucius; but, whenever Greek and Christian concepts are opposed, Pound prefers to return to the root in the early philosophers. His confrontation with Aristotle is therefore a fundamental step in his assessment of values, for, up to this point, he had regarded him as the originator of the 'syllogistic method', which stood in direct opposition to the 'ideogrammic method'.

Besides, his early readings had all tended towards Platonism, and he had only met Aristotle when grappling with the main terms of literary criticism ('The triumph of literary criticism is that certain of its terms – chiefly those defined by Aristotle – still retain some shreds of meaning' –*SR*, p. 13) or the question of money (in which case, Pound derived his main quotations from secondhand sources such as Montgomery Butchart's *Money*[2]). Aristotle had repeatedly been praised for his conception of metaphor as 'swift perception of relations',[3] but before Pound engages in a detailed confrontation, in 1937, the picture one gets of him remains blurred. The insertion of the tag *metatheme-non* . . . in the dynastic Cantos is therefore posterior to this major reading. Even on page 278 of the *Guide*, Pound states his doubts: 'Aristotle did not implant a clear concept of money in the general western mind. He saw that money was a measure. The pregnant phrase is that wherein he says it is called NOMISMA because it exists not by nature but by custom *and can therefore be altered or rendered useless at will*.'

The starting-point for Pound's complete examination of the *Ethics* is a sense of closure – since Aristotle laid the foundations of Western thought – allied with the awareness of some original inadequacy. If Aristotle 'anchored human thought for 2000 years' (*GK*, p. 39), if 'what he didn't define clearly remained a muddle for the rest of the race' (ibid.), how is it possible that no just system could be erected on his definitions? Again, Pound is looking for the source of the error, and thinks he can trace it back to some document, read as a monument bearing the traces of subsequent obliteration and defacement. The sense of the closure of Western metaphysics is all the more important as Pound is not entirely sure whether he is going to situate himself 'in' or 'out' of it, and even in 'Thrones' he relates the attempt to erect a temple with an 'interest in equity' which will not be confused with logical splitting, while alluding to Aristotle's famous classification of his treatises, which put 'metaphysics' simply after 'physics' in a logical order of reasons:

> an interest in equity
> > not in mere terminology
> μετά τὰ φυσικά
> > metah, not so extraneous, possibly not so extraneous
> most *'metas'* seem to be in with.
> 'Had not *thought* about government', Adams;
> > 'or civilization' said Monsieur Bonaparte,

> at least I think it was Bonaparte.
>   The artigianato bumbles into technology,
> 'Buckie' has gone in for structure (quite rightly)
>   but consumption is still done by animals.
>
> (XCVII, p. 680)

The suggestion that 'metaphysics' must be included in physics is coupled with denunciation of a technological perversion (quite similar to what Heidegger calls the *Gestell*, or age of technological domination of nature), while the ineradicable components of human nature are here sarcastically replaced by 'animals'; Pound is parodying Mussolini's tag, 'Production is done by machines but consumption is still performed by human beings' (*SP*, p. 232). All this belongs to the concept of a closure which nevertheless leaves a sense of government and social responsibility as the only escape-route: ethics and politics can be founded on the ruins of metaphysics.

Thus, in the *Guide to Kulchur*, Pound's objective is to test Aristotle's 'interest in equity', and this is why he prefers the *Nicomachean Ethics* to any other text. But verbal precision is indispensable, and the mediaeval doctors are praised for their integrity: 'There flourished during the best age of "scholastic thought" a very great and high verbal culture. Having almost nothing but words to deal with, the ecclesiastical doctors cared for (that is took care of) their terminology' (*GK*, p. 26). Pound wishes to retain this verbal clarity, while developing a sense of social values necessary to create a *paideuma*. This is achieved by means of the 'ideogrammic method', which functions here in a new way: Pound does not merely want to replace syllogisms by parataxis, and he even agrees that the Stoics 'got their teeth into something' when they used the syllogism as pure 'grammatical form' 'for hypothesis and dissociation' (p. 123) – an insight which can be related to the role of Anselm in the later Cantos ('but had a clear line on the Trinity, and/ By sheer grammar' – Canto cv, p. 750). Fenollosa's attacks on 'mediaeval logic' for transforming thought into a kind of 'brickyard', submitting reality to the imperialism of the copula 'is',[4] had to be related to a more comprehensive definition of an 'epoch' than his *Epochs of Chinese and Japanese Art*[5] provides, and be based on the vital organic development of cultures as suggested by Frobenius. This is why Pound had put himself on the stage, to show how a true verbal picture of the word – such as exemplified by the Chinese character – can lead to a new direction of human interests, will, dreams, desires. The disposition of the speaking subject, caught up by the closure of the system of values, and trying to connect unconscious urges with an almost mythical perception of 'light', becomes the focus of an experiment in reading and writing.

The subject as such will have to rely on his memory and his fundamental 'position' in the world (*chih*³) to introduce some order into the statements he has produced and which do not represent him. This is the way to a new learning:

It may or may not matter that the first knowledge is direct, it remains effortlessly as residuum, as part of my total disposition, it affects every perception of form–colour phenomena subsequent to its acquisition.

Coming even closer to things committed verbally to our memory. There are passages of the poets which approximate the form–colour acquisition. (*GK*, p. 28)

The 'verbal sign' thus participates in both the oral and the written, since the 'culture of ideas' which de Gourmont grafted onto the 'instinct' of man, and the 'unconscious' *paideuma* observed by Frobenius condense into a common paradigm: the writing of experience as a series of traces in a subject's memory. This is also why Fenollosa can so wholeheartedly bypass the oral aspect of the sign, insisting on a reading of visual clues which have 'no basis in sound':[6]

But Chinese notation is something much more than arbitrary symbols. It is based upon a vivid shorthand picture of the operations of nature. In the algebraic figure and in the spoken word there is no natural connection between thing and sign: all depends upon sheer convention. But the Chinese method follows the natural suggestion.[7]

Pound is starting out with the same effort in his *Guide*, with the difference that he attempts this time to engage the whole of our present culture. Whereas Fenollosa decided to see in Chinese poetry a verbal representation of 'actions or processes' as they are observed in nature, Pound wants to reread the whole array of seminal influences which have slowly built up mental habits, in order to dissociate positive trends from negative influences. While Fenollosa believed that a mere glance at radicals might bring us closer to a direct intuition of the reality of the universe ('In *reading* Chinese we do not seem to be juggling mental counters, but to be watching things work out their own fate"[8]), Pound integrates this immediate reading of characters into a collective memory. Just as Confucius recommended the *Odes* to form one's character, Fenollosa recommends a reading of characters to see the world as it is. Pound fuses the two senses of 'character' when he goes back to *ethos*, meaning character, disposition, custom and customs, and finally ethics.

> quand vos venetz al som de l'escalina
>
> $\mathring{\eta}\theta o\varsigma$ gradations
>
> These are distinctions in clarity
>
> ming[2] 明   these are distinctions
>
> (LXXXIV, p. 539)

What interests Pound is, then, the 'whole tone, disposition, Anschauung of Confucius recommending the Odes' (*GK*, p. 28), or, in other words, the roots of that 'great sensibility' which echoes throughout 'Rock-Drill'. But he will have to express this interest by presenting his own reading of a text, Aristotle's *Ethics*, in such a way that it will remain entirely personal and completely symptomatic of a whole culture. If 'man reading shd. be man intensely alive' (*GK*, p. 55), it is also because 'man intensely alive' is man reading the superposition of his *ethos* onto the *ethics* of his city and civilisation; reading, in a word, his fate in signs, documents, objects, and his own memory.

This is why the *Guide to Kulchur* cannot engage in a complete 'reading' of Confucius, although he is tempted ('I can't at this day Ap. 16, '37 have any sense of proprietorship in the Nichomachean Ethics. Ease might tempt me to use a Chinese philosopher recently edited' – *GK*, p. 304). Pound is referring to his article on Mencius, to which I shall return later. What stands out is that Chinese thought serves as a constant point of reference, which offers an impressive series of quotations, and this fixed reference is an 'axis' by contrast to which all the rest is measured, 'tested'. Confucius and Mencius allow for the reading of other texts, providing measures by which to evaluate them and eventually subvert them. 'You may, by contrast, contend that Christian thought has never offered a balanced system' (*GK*, p. 29). Pound's reading of classical texts will consequently be critical, deconstructive, polemical. Staunchly buttressed by the core of wisdom he has found in Confucius and a few mediaeval philosophers, having transformed this into 'his own ideogram of culture', he can launch a new reading. Francis Bacon will appear as an ally in the subversive reading, but his *Novum Organum* does not figure in Pound's ideogram of culture. Therefore two moments can be sketched: the first one, to which he referred as 'butterflying', describes the movement by which Pound's memory has turned into a text, a vital text full of illuminating insights; the second is the confrontation with a 'new text', which is used as a 'tabula rasa' (*GK*, p. 305). In a way, the *Guide* was finished, the entire ideogram was given, respecting the pledge not to open new books: 'In the main, I am to write this new Vade Mecum without opening other volumes, I am to put down so far as possible only what has resisted the erosion of time, and forgetfulness' (p. 33). The bold gesture of self-exposure is the only way to start a new process of learning which entices the reader to examine himself or herself in turn. In short, this initiates the hermeneutic circle. But, once the fragments have been scattered on the page or in the reader's memory, they need some *telos*: an 'end', an achievement, an issue, a whole text which yields both a foundation and a way out of the system of dead concepts.

For Pound, the closure of the system and the dissociation of sensibility are one. After Plato and Aristotle, all the 'ideas' had been given; what remained were different ways of putting them into action. 'In a sense the philosophic orbit of the occident is already defined, European thought was to continue in a species of cycle of crisis. . . . Originality of speculative research (guess work) was exhausted with Arry Stotl' (*GK*, p. 120). This is phrased by Fiorentino as 'ethics and politics are no longer one' (ibid.). Aristotle is, then, a good example of symptomatic production, since he wrote in a period which saw the end of the system of the *polis*, the little independent city, and would not transform Alexander into an enlightened ruler (save when Alexander paid for the debts of his campaigning soldiers, but no one attributed this to Aristotle.[9])

Pound thus swears he is going to be impartial ('I take the oath of impartiality' – *GK*, p. 305), and to prove this he leaves his notes as they were written, for instance refusing to modify a positive statement that one could 'dig a lot of acute sense out of Aristotle' (p. 45) and merely leaving a note to say that, if he disagrees after having gone through the *Ethics*, he leaves it to the reader to 'measure the difference, if any, between this "residuum" left in my memory or whatever, and the justification or unjustification given in detail later'. Once he has started reading, he repeats this warning and incitation to 'gauge' the difference between the 'residuum' and the examination proper. We are thus meant to see Pound's notes as a series of immediate reactions, a kind of recorded monologue taking place in front of our eyes. And, very soon, the old misgivings surface again: 'I have not got through 4 pages before my gorge rises. Here indeed we have a swine and a forger. . . . He is not a man with the truth in him' (*GK*, p. 306). Here, it is mainly style which serves as the measure to decide whether Aristotle is worth reading, his 'hedging, backing and filling' not being equal to Schopenhauer's essay on style.

What is quite remarkable is that Pound not only does not explain why these first pages fill him with such disgust that he now concurs with the prohibition of his doctrine by the Sorbonne in 1313, but also touches on themes which will recur with great frequency in his *Cantos*: it is as if the total rejection had functioned as a denegation of what can only be accepted later. For in these pages Aristotle situates the Supreme Good as the end of any activity, decides that his investigation of ethics is inseparable for a clear conception of politics, and finally opposes the arts and activities which find an end in themselves to those which have this end outside themselves, thereby defining the terms which will regulate the notions of *praxis* and *poiesis*. What is more, it is in the middle of the fourth page that Aristotle declares that 'the young are not fit to be students of Political Science' (*Ethics*, I.iii.5, p. 9[10]), a quotation which Pound uses again and again in the 'Pisan Cantos' and after:

> each in the name of its god
> or longevity because as says Aristotle
> philosophy is not for young men
> their *Katholou* can not be sufficiently derived from
>   their *hekasta*
> their generalities cannot be born from a sufficient
>   phalanx of particulars
>
> (LXXIV, p. 441)

Pound's memory in Pisa works by sudden jumps and condensation, and he conflates the passage on 'young men' quoted with a passage from *Ethics*, VI.xi.4, on which he comments cryptically in the *Guide*, 'a platitude never sufficiently grasped./ ἐκ τῶν καθ ἔκαστα γὰρ τὰ καθόλου / rules are based on particular cases'(*GK*, p. 329). In fact, Aristotle is examining prudence, or *phronesis*, as a stable concept on which to found maxims of practical morality. Pound has in mind another passage, which he does not quote in *Guide*, but which provides the link between the first remark on young men and prudence: 'we do not consider that a young man can have Prudence. The reason is that Prudence includes a knowledge of particular facts [*hekasta*] and this is derived from experience, which a young man does not possess . . .' (*Ethics*, vi.viii.5, pp. 349–51). In this passage, which goes beyond the 'platitude' it could be reduced to ('for experience is the fruit of years'), the intent of Aristotle's demonstration is to prove that a general rule of the particular can be stated by philosophy. Prudence apprehends the 'ultimate particular things', an apprehension which derives from perception only. Aristotle manages to relate a direct perception of things with a virtue which has severed all ties with a world of Platonic essences; Pound does not quote the end of the sentence in *Ethics*, vi.xi.4, but it will echo through the later Cantos: 'hence we must have perception of particulars, and this immediate perception is Intelligence [*nous*]' (p. 363).

Whatever the ultimate causes of Pound's disagreement with the first few pages of the *Ethics*, he himself is so surprised by his reaction that he expresses it: 'This is not by any means an opinion I had this morning expected to write down this evening (16 Ap. 1937)' (*GK*, p. 306). For a short but very irrational moment, Aristotle is to blame for every instance of terminological weakness, even down to Mussolini! 'I wd. even go further and state in parenthesis with the date Ap. 16 anno XV, that the things still needing to be remedied in the Italian State are due to an Aristotelic residuum left in Mussolini's own mind' (p. 309). He then decides to give a kind of 'sottisier', listing 'imbecilities' 'yatter' and phrases of value; what he offers is then totally indecipherable for someone who is not willing to go back to the Greek text with a pencil in his hand, for the two columns merely quote words or groups of words in Greek with the reference, 'IF the reader wants to do his own thinking' (p. 311).

Two main tenets of Aristotelian thought were nevertheless likely to appeal to Pound, for they correspond to his fundamental beliefs. The first is the idea that one acts against the Good only from ignorance, an idea which goes back to Socrates (and Pound mentions the filiation which could bypass Plato – p. 307). But Aristotle restricts the kind of intellectual idealism revealed by Socrates, and adds that 'it is not surprising that a man should do what he knows to be wrong if he is not conscious of the knowledge at the time' (*Ethics*, vii.iii.5, p. 389). This develops into the famous 'practical syllogism' which attempts to differentiate between good and bad justifications. With this style of 'hair-splitting' analysis, we know how much Pound disagrees. The second point also leads to a 'perversion' of a sound principle in Pound's eyes; since there cannot be *a priori* principles in the world of private actions, as the theorems of prudence have shown, it follows that there must somehow be a law of particulars. The 'equitable' is 'a rectification of law where law is defective because of its generality' (v.x.6, p. 317). A certain indefinition of the principle is unavoidable, and this is expressed by the image of the 'leaden rule used by Lesbian builders'. Since law involves a risk of error, it is better to have a rule which adapts to corners and angles as in building a temple with polygonal stones, and this is not reducible to ignorance or error. This time, there is an ontological impossibility: if indetermination is ontological, it is because it obeys an undetermined rule.[11] Pound was not ready for such an opening of law to indeterminacy at the time of his *Guide to Kulchur*, and he prefers to concentrate on the gallery of portraits, such as those of the 'Generous' or 'Magnanimous', instead of developing the theme of a correction brought to law and justice by equity. Nevertheless these reflections already point in the direction his later texts take.

And, even when Aristotle defines virtue by a sense of proportion, which becomes the 'just mean', or *meson* (middle), Pound refuses to equate him with Confucius: 'My imaginary opponent may say: well, Aristotle preaches the doctrine of the mean' (*GK*, p. 314). On the contrary, Aristotle's 'mean' is a symptom of decadence: 'the Greeks had already collapsed. Conscious or unconscious subversivism?' (p. 315). No reason is given for this rejection of a concept which is indeed remarkably similar to Confucius, since in both cases there must be a relationship between the elements and the whole *cosmos*. For Aristotle, the same proportionality is observable in a work of art, from which nothing could be taken or added (*Ethics*, II.vi.9, p. 93), and in the definition of money as a just measure. Anyhow, a few days after having started his 'reading', Pound was ready to 'chuck the job, as a waste of my time, and my comment likely to be a waste of the reader's' (*GK*, p. 319). And, even if he finds some points of interest in the discussion of money, and the discussion of the faculties or different types of knowledge, the main impression is negative. What stands out as Aristotle's highest achievement is provided by a last footnote in which Rackham explains that Aristotle had 'compiled or caused to compile descriptions of the constitutions of 158 Greek states' (*Ethics*, p. 642). This turns him into a 'serious character' with 'concrete particulars assembled for examination' (*GK*, p. 342). This is the only positive picture which seems to fit Aristotle: the empiricist who works from precise documents or elements (in the case of natural sciences). The limitations of Pound's reading derive from this general framework; it is as if Pound had started his analysis with Bacon's criticism in mind, and had finally found Aristotle less abstract, less syllogistic – in a word, more 'ideogrammic'. This eventually forbids an acknowledgement of the deeper hints contained in the *Ethics* – such as the conclusion on man's desire for immortality. This is simply not mentioned by Pound.

The critical importance of Pound's reading is nevertheless enormous, especially since this attempt at a synthesis of beliefs becomes impossible after the war: in 'Rock-Drill' and 'Thrones', the Cantos provide the only locus which can take an actual reading in this sense, which of course makes them more difficult and fragmentary. What stands out is the dogged attempt at reading an author against himself, to subvert him or to understand how his insights have been subverted: 'I am not attacking the conscious part of Aristotle, but the unconscious, the "everyone says", or "everyone admits" . . .' (*GK*, p. 331). This special attention to the 'unconscious' element of a text implies an oversensitive reaction to the author's style (even if he knows these are merely notes taken during lectures) and a searching-out of the weak spots, the gaps in the argumentation, the unsatisfactory hinges. And, finally, Pound's reading has to uncover such a gap. The first gap disclosed is a historical gap: 'The greeks [*sic*], being *maqueros* (happy men) with no moral fervour, left a *hole* or a *sense of lack*, and into that *hole* there poured a lot of crass zeal' (p. 330, emphasis added). He means that it was easy to fill in the *Ethics* with a Judaeo-Christian theology completely foreign to its whole concept, and there is an element of truth in the remark.

The other gap is unfortunately found too late for the discussion in the *Guide*. I have underlined Pound's quarrel with the translation of *chreia*, but soon after he had finished his manuscript he realised that the editors of the *Magna Moralia* had deleted the first mental faculty, or *techne*, from the list he quotes (*GK*, p. 351). In his discussion of the Greek text, Pound does not emphasise *techne*, merely remarks that it 'can exist without the others' (p. 328); but, after he has discovered the disappearance of this word, it becomes charged with an enormous weight, all the more so as his publisher, Faber, refused to modify the sheets of the book still in the press. The hand of finance was clearly visible, and the same process of historical degradation repeated itself: Morley, the editor at Faber's with whom Pound corresponded for *Guide to Kulchur*, had 'cut my *main* point' (*L*, p. 321), and the *Guide* would now have to be completed by the paper on Mencius, which attempted to make up for the omission: 'The curse of European thought appeared between the Nichomachean notes and the Magna Moralia. Aristotle . . . began his list of mental processes with TéXne, τέχνη, and the damned college parrots omitted it. This was done almost before the poor bloke was cold in his coffin' (*SP*, p. 100). The difference between two texts becomes a major symptom of historical destruction of the evidence: 'the damn Greek lecturers had just slid over Aristotle's teXne in the list of components of kinds of intelligence. This was the beginning of the end' (*L*, p. 298). This is again invoked in a letter to Eliot mentioning the 'growth of historiographic *teXne*' (p. 336).

The importance of *techne* is not limited to the historical omission of the word from the *Magna Moralia*, but it is fully ascertained by Pound in poetic texts only, once the *Cantos* had taken over responsibility for all the 'readings'. Pound implicitly agrees with Aristotle's formula according to which 'Art, being concerned with making, is not concerned with doing' (*Ethics*, VI.iii.5, p. 335), but does not discuss these concepts in the *Guide*. They nevertheless provide the later Cantos with their main conceptual framework. Art as *techne* is linked with *poiesis* and not with *praxis*, which defines rational action or conduct. Art brings something into existence (*genesis*) which would not have existed otherwise, and is therefore on the side of chance (*tuche*) and not necessity. Aristotle quotes a line by Agathon which twice links *techne* with *tuche* ('Chance is beloved of Art, and Art of Chance' – *GK*, p. 335). Chance introduces a world ruled by Fate, a Fate which will recur in the last Cantos as *Fortuna*. As Aubenque writes, 'Chance only happens in a world in which accidents – that is, that which befalls things, *sumbainei* – cannot be reduced to essence, a world where everything is not deducible, and where the infinity of possible accidents renders it impossible to calculate the resulting combinations.'[12] Production as *poiesis* and action as *praxis* have been primordially separated; but through the term 'prudence', which defines an aptitude to deal with unforeseen events taking the form of chance, in a world from which the gods – and their oracles – have vanished, they find an asymptotic meeting-point: it can be described as the tragic interrogation on the lack of validity of laws, and the tragic assertion of man's creativity through art, in order to give a shape to the chaos of his life. Between reverential prudence, defined by a respect for the rites, and poetic *poiesis* the *Cantos* attempt a complicated and almost doomed periplus: the reconciliation of the world of Fate and the world of shapes has to be achieved through the polarisation of a symbol untying and uniting at the same time the divergent senses of *sumbainei*.

Thus Pound exploits minimal hints provided by the Chinese Chronicle to come back to a central concept of *techne*:

> study with the mind of a grandson
> and watch the time like a hawk
> taó tsi
> 1/2 research   and 1/2 Τέχνη
> 1/2 observation,   1/2 Τέχνη
> 1/2 training,   1/2 Τέχνη
> Tch'eng T'ang for guide
> (LXXXV, p. 550)

The cue is a little sentence in which the sage Prime Minister Iue advises the Emperor to follow the path of his grandfather Tch'eng T'ang and to observe virtue by studying: 'La science s'acquiert (moitié par l'étude), molitié par l'enseignement'[13] – 'Science comes half from study, half from teaching'. It is not difficult to see that *techne* has now taken for Pound the sense of the technical skill gained by the practice of art, thereby exploiting the double sense of the word, which is used for 'craft' as well as for 'art'. Heidegger remarks for instance that, if the craftsman and the artist are called by the same name of *technites*, it is because *techne* is knowledge, not a mere technique.

> The word *techne* denotes rather a mode of knowing. To know means to have seen, in the widest sense of seeing, which means to apprehend what is present, as such. For Greek thought the nature of knowing consists in *aletheia*, that is in the uncovering of beings. It supports and guides all comportment toward beings. *Techne*, as knowledge experienced in the Greek manner, is a bringing forth of beings in that it *brings forth* present beings as such beings *out of* concealedness and specifically *into* the unconcealedness of their appearance; *techne* never signifies the action of making.[14]

Thus, this 'production' which 'uncovers' is more concerned with contemplation than with the *praxis* of politics, for instance. Heidegger's commentary merely develops the intuition contained in the *Ethics*, and explains why Pound engages in combinations which would not seem warranted from a restrictive reading of Aristotle:

Perspicax qui se excolit ipsum,
Their writings wither because they have no curiosity,
This 'leader', gouged pumpkin
        that they hoist on a pole,
But if you will follow this process

not a lot of signs, but the one sign
      etcetera
   plus always Τέχνη
and from Τέχνη back to σεαυτόν

                   (LXXXV, pp. 545–6)

I In's words, quoted from the Latin version in Couvreur's *Chou King* (p. 123), mean 'an intelligent prince cultivates himself', and this leads Pound to intone the same hymn to curiosity and study: Aristotle and Confucius, Dante, Richard of St Victor and Erigena are finally reconciled against all those who have declared 'total war on CON-TEMPLATIO'. Their *techne* leads back to 'self-knowledge' and finally knowledge in general (*seauton*).

By 1941, Aristotle has definitely been integrated into Pound's pantheon, having been exculpated[15] of the terminological hesitation with which he, chiefly, was charged. He is now placed among the founders of political science, is seen as the basis of Canon Law on the 'just price', and can be superimposed on Confucius: 'Thought hinges on the definition of words. Aristotle and Confucius bear witness' (*SP*, p. 320). And Pound recommends the *Nicomachean Ethics* and the *Politics* (from which he quotes with increasing frequency to stress the philosopher's awareness of the manipulation of silver money, 'a common practice of commerce'[16]), along with the four Confucian books.

In his exemplary and symptomatic reading of the *Nicomachean Ethics*, Pound manages to fuse all his previous definitions of reading, uniting the philological precision of a de Gourmont with the almost Nietzschean concept of 'reading for power' (*GK*, p. 55). This privileged textbook manages to mobilise his energies long enough to give a sense of focus to the usually discontinuous ideograms of culture, so that he not only reaches a sense of process but also finds precise measures: values are gauged in their historical context, to the point where a whole crisis appears in a nutshell, as the difference between two texts and the elimination of one word; as he wrote to Santayana, 'The decline of the West occurred between the Nicomachean Ethics and the Magna (or fat) Moralia' (*L*, p. 333). But he still needed to find a locus for the articulation between ethics and politics, between *praxis* and *poiesis*, which became identical with the question of pure *contemplatio*.

'Neo-Platonicks' against 'Plato Inc.'

The *Guide to Kulchur* repeatedly expresses favourable comments on the neo-Platonists, whilst both Plato and Aristotle seem to be the butts of pervasive attacks which oscillate between mild deprecation and harsh abuse. Pound always feels more at home with the unorthodox schools of thinkers than with the great names of classical philosophy. In the *Spirit of Romance*, he nevertheless ascribes to Plato's *Phaedrus* the origin of certain perceptions leading to Dante's Paradiso (*SR*, p. 140): the attempts in the *Guide* to situate Plato's mystical inspiration retain some respect for the visionary power of this text, although he quotes, in an almost parodic vein, snatches of enthusiast rhetoric. These descriptions of ecstasies remain 'prose rhapsody' and smack of adolescence (*GK*, p. 222). Pound meets Eliot in a global rejection of such rhetoric: 'it is this sort of writing which causes Mr Eliot to break out against Plato Inc. (or rather not incorporated in any but the "société anonyme" sense)' (ibid.). Plato is thus banded with hellish anonymous societies of the soul and, of course, the worst side of oriental religions, the Hindu and 'non-Confucian China'. However, Pound soon qualifies this criticism, distinguishing between a sound appeal to contemplation and negative fanaticism. The basic truth remains for him the personal experience of an ecstasy which need not be antisocial: 'the ecstatic-beneficient-and-benevolent, contemplation of the divine love, the divine splendour with goodwill toward others' (*GK*, p. 223). This is the complex ideogram which 'Rock-Drill' attempts to write down.

At this point, Pound definitely chooses a class of thinkers who all allude to Plato, but who are more 'neo' than 'Platonic', and the first name he quotes in the *Guide* is Gemisthus Plethon, because of his association with Malatesta and his political ideal of restoring unity and independence to a Greece occupied by the Turks. The difference between Plethon and Plato is that, whereas Plato is intent on singing of the 'heaven above the heavens', Plethon relates his *cosmos* to the names of classical gods, deriving his *'concret Allgemeine'* from the sea and Neptune.[17] At any rate, he had 'a nailed boot for Aristotle' (*GK*, p. 224) and can be allied with Ficino, Porphyry, Psellos, Iamblichus, and Hermes Trismegistus, all of whom stress contemplation and fusion with the divine *nous* or intelligence.

Thus it may come as a surprise that what is allowed to these neo-Platonic philosophers should be expressly forbidden to Aristotle. Throughout his long examination of the *Nicomachean Ethics*, Pound explains that he keeps a sentence from Rackham's introduction in reserve; it will come as the final conclusion, and he finally quotes, 'Man's welfare thus is ultimately found to consist not in the employment of all his faculties in due proportion, but only in the activity of the highest faculty, the "theoretic intellect" ' (*GK*, p. 342). In this sentence, he assumes that he detects the 'rift' between Aristotle's praiseworthy political efforts, the examination of the 158 constitutions, and pure mind: 'Therein is the scizophrenia [*sic*] in its almost invisible embryo' (p. 343). Aristotle becomes the prototype of the split nature of modern man; but the movement Pound describes is nevertheless the same as that of his *Guide*'s! He himself hurriedly juxtaposes Aristotle's list of categories with the three modes of intellectual activity he derives from Richard of St Victor, and these culminate in 'contemplation, the identification of the consciousness with the object', and finally *atasal*, or union with the divine (*GK*, p. 328).

The discrepancy might appear as a linguistic quibble or equivocation, Pound admitting without difficulty the *sophia* and *nous* in the list, which starts *techne*, but balking at 'theoretic intellect'; but Pound knows enough Greek to relate contemplation with *theoria*, and he quotes the word in a context which proves he is aware of its real sense: 'In x.vii.2 Aristotle comes out with the unsympathetic word theoretike, but the pp. 2/3/4 give the key to his place in mediaeval esteem. He plugs for contemplation as the noblest form of activity' (*GK*, p. 338). The comment might suggest a favourable impression, since this leads to Dante, but Pound resolutely opts for a negative judgement: Aristotle has not found an adequate terminology – 'Arry has . . . a good deal of trouble in finding a verbal manifestation that won't fit tennis playing as well as contemplation', and 'Arry's argument wd. apply to onanism quite nicely' (pp. 338–9). The whole drift of Book x of the *Ethics* is questioned and rejected; Aristotle argues that intellectual contemplation is the highest form of action (*praxis*) which can be achieved in concordance with virtue. Practical prudence and the laws of particulars are finally dominated and even replaced by *sophia*, or contemplative wisdom. The argument is simple: whilst production as *poiesis* finds an end outside itself, in the genesis of some form or object *praxis* or action can find its end in itself, acting can be the end of action. This type of action is superior to production because it is 'self-sufficient'; man can only find his autonomy or 'autarky' (*autarkeia* – *Ethics*, i.vii.6) in a just action which finds a first aim in social and political life: 'The term self-sufficient, however, we employ with reference not to oneself alone, living a life of isolation, but also to one's parents and children and wife, and one's friends and fellow-citizens in general, since man is by nature a social being' (i.vii.7, p. 129). The 'social' being in man is in fact his 'political' being (the term used is *politikon*). Autarkic activity resides in the agent, and this has to be achieved by integration of the agent into the city or political system. And the end or conclusion of the *Ethics* is precisely the *Politics*.

Thus Pound is right to consider it a distortion to equate the Supreme Good residing in contemplation with an integrated activity; Aristotle reflects that political activity is always more interested, less autonomous than intellectual contemplation, which brings man close to the gods. He concludes that 'we ought so far as possible to achieve immortality, and do all that man may to live in accordance with the highest thing in him' (*Ethics*, x.vii.8, p. 617). Pound is thus right when he says that Aristotle has lost the 'Homeric vigour', 'with its sympathetic rascality, its irascible goguenard pantheon' (*GK*, p. 331). Pound favours contemplation when it is turned toward the gods, who, as we have said, can be *named*. Their names recall their close links with a city, a region; they evoke a complete myth. The type of immortality Aristotle advocates may appear cut off from the integration of ethics, politics and the pantheon of gods, since it replaces the glory of a name – a hero's or a god's name – by seemingly introspective and private activity: 'Aristotle was interested in mind, not in morals' (*GK*, p. 331).

The displacement observed in Aristotle's ethics therefore leaves a gap which only an ineffable god can fill; it will not be submitted to man's or the city's naming-power: 'Aristotle leaves a yawning chasm into which a mediaeval or neoPlatonic or even Mesopotamian god has to be shoved' (*GK*, p. 339).

Pound rightly situates the origin of the split in the distinction between *production* and *action*, and his criticism of Aristotle paralleled by his commendation of neoPlatonism is not as inconsequential as it might seem. A passage from 'Thrones' proves this:

> KALON KAGATHON, and Marengo,
>   This aura will have, with red flash,
>   the form of a diamond, or of crimson,
>   Apollonius, Porphery, Anselm,
>   Plotinus EN THEORIA 'ON NOUS EXEI
>   had one vision only, and if the stars be but unicorns...
>
> (CI, p. 726)

Pound presents the roll-call of major neo-Platonists, and quotes Plotinus ('In contemplation, the mind possesses the One', which comes from different lines of the *Enneads*, III.8: 'On Contemplation') before alluding to the 'one vision' Porphyry had. Porphyry explains in his *Life of Plotinus*[18] that, whilst Plotinus had 'contemplated the god without form nor essence' four times, he himself has known such ecstasy only once, when he was sixty-eight. The series of visions merges into a view of the earthly paradise of the Na-Khi, to which I shall come back, and blends with Napoleon's victories.

> Mint grows at the foot of the Snow Range
>   the first moon is the tiger's,
>   Pheasant calls out of bracken
>   Rossoni: 'così lo stato...' etcetera
>   Delcroix: 'che magnifica!'
>   (prescrittibile)
>
> (CI, p. 726)

Rock's description of Na-khi funeral-ceremonies is juxtaposed with approval of projects for monetary reform encountered among Mussolini's ministers and friends:[18] the redeeming vision of mint in Pisa (LXXIV, p. 438, and LXXXIII, p. 533) is here again incorporated into the tripartite universe, in which gods, men and nature are at one. The last line, taken from a Na-khi prayer, concludes on a note of harmony: 'His body and soul are at peace' (p. 727).

Now, what allows for such incorporation is the neo-Platonic wisdom which Pound discovers in the *Enneads* for instance. When discussing *theoria*, contemplation, Plotinus starts with a sort of joke which then is taken seriously: and if not only men, but also animals and plants were 'contemplating'? The beginning of *Enneads*, III.8 uses a direct quotation from Aristotle's *Nicomachean Ethics* (x.i.2, p. 579), according to which 'all creatures move in the direction of their supreme good'. Pound's concept of *semina motuum*, the 'seeds of movements' which describe 'the inner impulse of the tree' (*Con.*, p. 59) and the 'intelligence' that makes a tree grow,[19] owe a lot to this idea that the generation of plants, animals and beings (not even excluding stones and mountains) comes from a contemplation of nature. This contemplation is a *poiema*, a production, a generation at the same time. Thus, since 'it is shown that production is a contemplation' (*Enneads*, iii.8.3[20]), Pound's reference to Plotinus manages to bridge the 'gap' opened by Aristotle's distinction between activity and production.

This should not, however, lead one to conclude that Pound simply takes Plotinus as the answer to all metaphysical or ontological problems arising from the unstable coexistence of so many different elements. The youthful fervour felt in the poem 'Plotinus' was already founded on a distinction between 'accurate record of sensation' and 'mere theorizing'.[21] Plotinus's concept of 'emanations' was translated in psychological terms, and led to the necessary creation of masks. In the later Cantos, the portrait of Plotinus is relatively ambivalent, and he is even accused of 'perversion' (a word never used for Aristotle):

> And Plotinus, his bellyache,
> A great perversion
>   from Plotinus his bellyache,
> Though he still thought: God of all men.
>   The body is inside.
>
>   (xcix, p. 700)

Compared with Chinese wisdom, which takes care of people's bodies ('People have bodies / ergo they sow and reap, / Soldiers also have bodies, / take care of the body as implement' – pp. 705–6), the teachings of Plotinus appear unsound, bordering on the ascetic. Pound is here commenting on *The Edict of K'ang Hsi*, and the grafting in of neo-Platonic mysticism proves less satisfactory than when it is mixed with more ethereal visions of paradise. The main weakness of Plotinus comes from his alleged 'shame' over his own body; Porphyry is the initiator of this tradition, since he explains in his *Life of Plotinus* (2.1) that his aging master suffered from frequent colics, and stubbornly refused to take any enema or cluster.[22] The first sentence of his biography is, indeed, 'Plotinus seemed to be ashamed of having a body'. Pound pinpoints this refusal of the body by the term 'bellyache', which violently undermines the vision. By contrast, Plotinus's idea that the soul lives around the body, and not the reverse, stresses the divine nature of all men who participate in the One or *nous*.

The unhealthy feature associated with Plotinus again appears when Anselm is introduced:

> Anselm versus damn Rufus
> 'Ugly? a bore,
>   Pretty, a whore!'
>   brother Anselm is pessimistic,
>   digestion weak,
>   had a clear line on the Trinity, and
> By sheer grammar: Essentia
>   femine
>   Immaculata   (cv, p. 750)

The weak digestion of the saint is connected with his surprising antifeminism, presented in ironically rhyming idiom. In fact, Pound is merely gently teasing Anselm, whom he has shown as a nature-loving man who was not above indulging a little delicacy when ill ('And he said '. . . eh . . ./ I might eat a partridge' – p. 748[23]), and ready to equate intellectual knowledge with 'Sapor, the flavour':

> Sapor, the flavour,
>   pulchritudo
>   ne divisibilis intellectu
>   not to be split by syllogization
>
>   (v, p. 748)

Anselm thus joins Plotinus, their fight against Aristotelian 'logic-splitting' is a kind of premonition of what Eliot calls the 'objective correlative'. Pound had discovered Anselm when reading Charles de Rémusat's *Saint Anselme de Cantorbéry*,[24] and then took to reading his works in Migne's *Patrologia*. The conclusion to *Saint Anselme* attempts to situate his famous 'ontological argument' in a tradition going back to Plato: 'Let us be content with the great and deep truth which we have learnt from Anselm and Descartes, but which Plato knew before them.'[25] And Rémusat was also able to show how Anselm's committed spiritualism, finding its origin in Erigena and Denis the Aeropagite, had political bearing as well. Since God is the being who is devoid of principle, a pure *anarchos* as Erigena said,

Anselm, helped by such transcendent 'anarchism' of the soul, could defend the rights of men and fight against the tyranny of kings, such as 'damn Rufus' in England. Not only do the *ratio cognoscendi* and the *ratio essendi* merge in the idea of the most perfect being, a being who must henceforth necessarily be, but they point toward a principle of active resistance to dictatorship. Pound's approval of this struggle, which he was soon to relate to the fight for the Magna Carta, indicates how far he had come from the totalitarian theses developed in the *Guide to Kulchur*.

The neo-Platonists are thus the complementary aspect of Aristotle's insistence on the accumulation of concrete particulars yielding precise political knowledge and anthropology:

> And is here among serious characters
> and not reasoning from a belly-ache.
> Or that Ari. might have heard about the fishes,
> thank Alex. (CXIV, p. 791)

This time the pendulum seems to have swung back to Aristotle, who is superposed on Agassiz's strict empiricism because he collected zoological data and information about curious fish met in the course of Alexander's conquests. The 'belly-ache' has come to represent all that Pound feels he has to sublimate. It denotes not only a repression of the body, but also the source of perverted thinking. The same image occurs in *Jefferson and/or Mussolini*, in a passage which attempts to refute Freud and the Bloomsbury aesthetes who had fallen for his theories (unlike Cocteau, who wrote an *Oedipe* without 'falling into the Freudian mess' – *SP*, p. 404). Under the heading 'Freud or . . .', Pound writes, 'That which makes a man forget his bellyache (physical or psychic) is probably as healthy as concentration of his attention on the analysis of the products or educts of his stomach-pump' (*J/M*, p. 101). The confidence expressed in these lines is then shattered during the experience at Pisa, and, even if Freud is still violently rejected afterwards (he is part of the 'sewage' and 'dung' denounced in Canto XCI, p. 614), what takes place in the 'Pisan Cantos' can be described as a reappraisal and an internalisation of the 'bellyache'.

In Pisa, Pound gradually discovers that anality cannot merely represent a Hell 'for other people', as T. S. Eliot had objected in *After Strange Gods*. His stay 'amid what was termed the a. h. of the army' or 'in the a.h. of the army' (Canto LXXIV, pp. 437, 443) enables him to fuse the 'great night of the soul' with a suitably hellish environment:

> nox animae magna from the tent under Taishan
> amid what was termed the a. h. of the army   (p. 437)

The reference to St John of the Cross is then expanded as he spirals
down towards despair and death:

> . . . Νύξ animae?
>   is there a blacker or was it merely San Juan with a belly ache
>   writing ad posteros
>   in short shall we look for a deeper or is this the bottom?
>   Ugolino, the tower there on the tree line
> Berlin   dysentery   phosphorus   (p. 438)

In a fantastic juxtaposition, Pound brings together the circumstances
in which Saint John composed his *Cantico*, imprisoned in a foul
dungeon full of his excrement, and Ugolino's tragic fate as described in
Inferno, XXXIII (although the tower Pound could see was not the prison
in which Ugolino, starving, devoured the corpses of his children). Thus
the subsequent links between anality and tragic climax allow for
reversals and interpenetrations which would have been impossible ten
years before:

> [I heard it in the s. h.   a suitable place
>   to hear that the war was over]   (LXXVII, p. 467)

The discovery of 'Whitman or Lovelace / found on the jo-hous seat at
that / in a cheap edition' (LXXX, p. 513) is one more instance of these
happy twists of fate which enabled him to survive. The anal element
has then to be introduced into the scale of gradations, or a sense of
ethos.

This fits in with Plotinus's vision of the world, in which evil is
reduced to a lower degree of being, a lack in being. As the lover, when
he desires a beautiful object, strives to be united with a pure essence, so
the artisan who creates ugliness has only not respected the full form or
eidos. We now understand why Plotinus has replaced Virgil to help the
poet emerge from the excremental Hell of Cantos XIV and XV. Plotinus
is not just pictured as a new poetic 'guide' out of the Inferno of Geryon;
he also plays the part of Theseus, who petrifies Medusa with his shield
held as a mirror, and of Hermes, who leads the hero out of perils:

and again Plotinus:
>   To the door,
> Keep your eyes on the mirror.
> Prayed we to the Medusa,
>   petrifying the soil by the shield,
> Holding it downward
>   he hardened the track
> Inch before us, by inch,
>   the matter resisting,
> The heads rose from the shield,
>   hissing, held downwards.   (xv, p. 66)

Medusa's head, which according to Freud represents castration by the image of raised snakes,[26] intervenes here to petrify the ground ('The serpents' tongues / grazing the swill top, / Hammering the souse into hardness'), because division must stop the anal proliferation: castration is the condition of phallic ascent towards the sun. But a mirror acts as mediator to what would once more bring blinding and killing light to the poet's eyes ('Keep your eyes on the mirror' – exactly as the Medusa was to petrify herself by looking at her image). It is then quite logical that this Canto should conclude with the word 'unconscious':

> 'Ηέλιον τ' 'Ηέλιον
>   blind with the sunlight,
> Swollen-eyed, rested,
>   lids sinking, darkness unconscious.   (p. 67)

As with Wondjina, castration and blindness turn out to be positive; at least, one escapes from the endless 'scission' of 'skin-flakes, repetitions, erosions, / endless rain from the arse-hairs' (p. 65). The catharsis is an ascension at the same time, and we witness it in a similar pattern just at the end of the 'Pisan Cantos', in a passage already quoted, linking 'quand vos venetz al som de l'escalina' (Arnaut Daniel, speaking in his own language, describes the purgatorial ascent to Dante: 'When you shall come to the top of the stairs' – *Purgatorio*, 26, 146) with *ethos* understood as 'gradations' and 'distinctions in clarity' (Canto LXXXIV, p. 539).

Plotinus uses a mirror to convert the threat of castration into a weapon and a contrivance against anal matter. The image of the mirror is one of the most consistently recurrent in the *Enneads*, and it is no surprise to see it reappear in the presentation of Anselm:

'non genitus' Caput 57, 'discendendo'
      Guido C. had read 'Monologion'
vera imago
      and via mind is the nearest you'll get to it,
'rationalem'
      said Anselm.
              Guido: 'intenzione'.
Ratio,
    luna,
             speculum non est imago,
                mirrour, not image
                    (cv, pp. 747–8)

Pound starts from a meditation on love in the *Monologion* (ch. 56, col. 203) which conveys the idea that it is not simply produced by the Father and the Son (united in ch. 57) but is an integral part of their being.[27] 'Discendendo' should be 'discedendo' (separating itself from), for Pound mistakenly decides to read it as the Italian word for 'descending', a misreading which is symptomatic of the whole drift of his argument, as we shall see.

In chapter 67 of the *Monologion*, Anselm writes that the 'mind itself is a mirror of [the Highest Nature] *and* its image';[28] Pound decides to contradict Anselm on this point, adding a 'not' and repeating the idea with 'mirrour, not image'. The distinction is therefore important for him, and it takes its full significance when envisaged in the neo-Platonic context of Guido Cavalcanti's 'Canzone d'Amore', which is here alluded to ('Guido C. had read "Monologion" '). Pound's theory is that Cavalcanti can only be understood when relocated in a tradition which goes back to Averroes, and finally Plotinus. But, while in the *Literary Essays* (pp. 173–6) Pound hesitates to be so precise about Cavalcanti's source, the last Cantos manage to sum up all aspects of divine and human love in one single concept. Part of this terminological harmonisation is the discovery of a principle, the divine emanation of *nous*, which has to solve Pound's main philosophical problem: the compatibility of unity with division.

In the passage quoted above, Anselm has a vision of love flowing directly from a united Godhead, and leaving a trace in the mirror of memory: mind is a mirror but not an image, because the image in the mirror is love as trace left or indeed written by God. Such an organic unity can be apprehended not by a logical division ('ne divisibilis intellectu') but by a natural division – the division of the trace, as it were, leaving imprints or shapes. Love is the key to the synthesis of pure and undivided vision and of separated forms: each form is an image which leads back to the mirror reflecting the One. This is borne out by an earlier passage which already attempts to find a source for Cavalcanti's 'Donna mi Pregha'.

$$\textit{come in subjecto}$$

lisses
    amoureuses
        a tenir
EX OUSIAS...HYPOSTASIN
III, 5, 3   PERI EROTAS

          ⊔⊔⊔   hieron

nous to ariston autou
        as light into water compenetrans
that is pathema
        ouk aphistatai'
           thus Plotinus
               per plura diafana
neither weighed out nor hindered;
           aloof. 1 Jan '58
              (c, pp. 721–2)

Pound's montage is rather elaborate, starting with 'chome in subgetto' (lifted from 'Donna mi Pregha'), which the first translation renders by 'as in a subject ready' (*LE*, p. 156). The whole passage from the poem is crucial:

        VIEN da veduta forma ches s'intende
        Che'l prende
               nel possibile intelletto
        Chome in subgetto
               locho e dimoranza
        E in quella parte mai non a possanza
                   (*LE*, p. 164)

This is translated by:

> Love is created, hath a sensate name,
> His modus takes from the soul, from heart his will;
> From form seen doth he start, that, understood,
> Taketh in latent intellect –
> As in a subject ready –
>   place and abode,
> Yet in that place it ever is unstill   (p. 156)

The differences from the new version in Canto XXXVI are striking:

> Cometh from a seen form which being understood
> Taketh locus and remaining in the intellect possible
> Wherein hath he neither weight nor still-standing,
> Descendeth not by quality but shineth out
>   (XXXVI, p. 177)

The 'descendeth' of the last line is the equivalent of 'non disciende', which had brought about the misreading in Anselm's *Monologion*. Pound adds a repeat of Villon's hymn to sensuality and profane love in his 'Belle Heaulmière' ('lisses amoureuses . . .'[29]), only to move toward the real source of the Italian poem, the description of love as 'hypostasis' in the *Enneads*. For Plotinus, love is 'an essence proceeding from essence' (*Enneads*, III.5.3; the treatise 'On Love' should have been transliterated as 'Peri Erotos') and comes from vision: 'From this soul which directs its glance toward the object of its vision and from what emanates therefrom, the eye is hence filled with the object it contemplates, a vision which is never imageless, Eros, whose name can be derived from the fact that it owes its existence to vision [*orasis*].'[30] The Egyptian temple provides a perfect sacred locus for this god of love and vision, while the absence of weight and the mystical transparency of Cavalcanti's diaphane meet and blend in a spiritual elation or elevation.

Pound continues quoting from Plotinus, leafing through the *Enneads*, and finds *pathema* and *ouk aphistatai* in the following book, which deals with the essence of the soul. Intelligence or mind, *nous* is the 'most noble part' (*to ariston autou*) of the Being (*ousia*) found by contemplation. Plotinus depicts the world of the intelligible as a realm of pure essences, without division. But souls exist in bodies and at the same time participate in the totality of *nous*: love is the experience by which the soul turns back to its origin, desiring an image of beauty and eternity. The soul is 'wholly given to the whole body, where it stays undivided; but since it is in all bodies, it is divided' (IV.1.21).[31] This is the central paradox which the second part of the treatise tackles; it can be enounced as a paradox: 'the souls are both separated and not separated' (IV.3.5)[32]. The infinite power of the mind embodies a total division, so to speak. The simplicity of the soul requires that it be not detached, *ouk aphistatai*. The essence 'comes into bodies, and by accident, divides itself in bodies', while at the same time 'giving itself entirely to bodies' (ibid.). Or, 'thus when it comes into a body, were it the largest and extended to everything, it gives itself entirely to this body, without ceasing to be one'. The division comes from bodies, 'because bodies, owing to the division proper to them, cannot receive it without division; this division is therefore an affection [*pathema*] of the body and not of the soul itself' (IV.2.1).[33] It is with the idea of a similar division that Cavalcanti concludes his poem:

> Being divided, set out from colour,
> Disjunct in mid darkness
> Grazeth the light, one moving by other,
> Being divided, divided from all falsity
> Worthy of trust
> From him alone mercy proceedeth.   (XXXVI, p. 179)

This division has been the object of a complicated negotiation of places between vision and fusion, action and passion, colour and 'the white light that is allness'. Love moves everything, even the stars of Dantean or Plotinian visions, and it remains still; moving all other beings, it brings them closer to the division which the object of desire causes in them, and heals it at the same time, 'drawing all to his stillness'. When gold rhymes with god's love, it gathers and divides the light radiating about and against the gloom.

Such a movement of division within a totality slowly leads the subject to the ecstasy of time, time which 'gives' itself as identical with the loving *logos* which disseminates the *semina motuum* and the characters on the page.

Hermetic circulation

The reunion of *praxis and poeisis*, the creative move toward *contem-*

platio, and the recurrent hymn to a love from which everything flows are at the same time the objects of the poem, its imaginary counters, the themes it plays with time and again, and the texture of the poem itself: in describing love as a source, the *Cantos* describe themselves as well, situating their rhapsodical or jagged epiphanies in a circle – or a spiral – which takes in the reader's perception of the text. Readers must be 'moved': they are alter-egos whose ignorance is fought away by a progressive tactical circling of motifs. Pedagogical manoeuvres thus dominate. But one must be 'touched' and 'delighted' as well: marvel and wonder! The eye undergoes a silent revolution, perceives the light and love flowing from a dilating 'pupil'; one is caught up by the whirl of voices, the snatches from other texts, the abrupt sparseness of hieratic ideograms.

These two interlocking movements are parallel to what as specialist in pagan mysticism and hermeticism has to say about the fundamental attitudes implied by neo-Platonism. Festugière sees Plotinus as having initiated the two main directions subsequently taken by Hellenistic philosophies of the *arcanum*, and developed by the 'Platonic academy' of the Renaissance Pound describes so well ('You had, ultimately, a 'Platonic' academy, messing up Christian and pagan mysticism, allegory, occultism, demonology, Trismegistus, Psellus, Porphyry, into a most eloquent and exciting hotch-potch . . .' – *GB*, p. 112). The two fundamental attitudes have both been explored by Pound.

The first consists in a feeling that somehow Being is deficient, that there is a lack of being in sensible existence, by comparison with a supreme principle which transcends language and intelligibility. This opens the way to the ineffable, the mystic speechless illumination in a progression from being to Being which escapes perception. Thus an ontological difference is both the obstacle to and the motive for the intellectual quest.[34]

The second attitude starts from a belief that the lack is a lack in order, not in being. Disorder is restricted to the lower spheres of the sublunary world, and contemplation of the universal *logos* or *nous* brings back the mind toward order. This may turn into a desire to save the world at all costs, since a mystical atonement can result from a radical cleansing of the grossest elements. Pound's starting-point lies in the second attitude; for him, the major perversity lies in the wrong direction taken by man's will alone, from the early declarations that 'will and consciousness are our vortex' (*GB*, p. 110) to the later assertion that Dante's *directio voluntatis* and the Confucian 'phallic heart' are the keys to Paradise. But, if man's will is perverted, it also comes from a more Manichaean state of affairs, which Pound ascribes to the dark forces of evil embodied by Usura. There, the 'serpent' is already at work in the garden of Eden, gnawing the fruit and the light from within, splitting up totalities, ruining symbols, obliterating documents, falsifying records, multiplying lies in an endless production of frauds, forgeries and felonies.

Thus the critical gesture which prepares for the reawakening of a sense of life in its pristine identity and intensity does not only hammer around the dotted line in a circle of truths: it leads the reader in twisting ascent toward the ineffable, the transcendent. The verbal rock-drill working with ploceic repetitions and polyphonic rhymes does more than destroy deadened and anaesthetised mind or matter: it mimes the ascent to values of another order. In other words, meaning in its search for coherence and eventually closure is dependent on judgement, in its ethical, political and religious senses. But since, for strictly historical reasons, the validation-procedures have all proved wrong or false, the movement in which the play of mirrors constituted by the paratactic juxtaposition of signifiers attempts to break from its circle is not a movement which leads to the world of action, in an overtly ideological mode, but one which leads to a spiral linking readers as coenunciators, as they perceive the faint but persistent glimmer of a sacred light. The 'vision' suggests a world in which ethics and economics, politics and true communication would be synonymous; but their identity cannot be conveyed without some tricks, or some ruse: Apollo's sun needs the help of crafty Hermes to illuminate intelligence.

Such a dialectical or dialogical process might map out Pound's hermeneutical progression, which grows increasingly complex with the passing of time and the accumulation of heterogeneous evidence. Part of the complexity stems from the fact that he has himself to be integrated into the process of interpretation; but, if we know quite well the extent to which he wrote 'about' his own life and the multifarious meetings and crossings of traces it came to represent, the writing itself has been so much devoured by the curious economy of reference and devious initiation that the situation of transparent communication is no sooner mimed than it is lost. Although we know the man, the writer and his books, to read him introduces another scene, a scene in which our interest is kept awake by a thousand puzzles and quizzes, a scene in which our ear is lured astray by the music of sense, and in which we finally find ourselves writing the text we were only supposed to read.

This new textual interweaving can best be described as a tension between hermeneutics, or the science of interpretation, and grammatology, or the science of written signs.[35] The wish to create a hermeneutic circle of comprehension works through anarchic textual displacements, disseminating, disruptive drives, and among the proliferation of almost illegible fragments torn from intractable texts or from the *obiter dicta* of a subjective memory. The reader who follows in his tracks learns how to join in the hermeneutic process, and cannot help feeling divided, threatened by dismemberment in the constant rewriting of the gods' names, obliged to confront his own historical sense with a montage of at-times entirely biased documents. So that Pound's text finally leaves us with a tangled trace, the graphic reminder of a superhuman effort towards totality and transcendence, as intricate as the footprints left by the cattle stolen from Apollo by his brother Hermes, who had them walk backwards while he himself covered his tracks by fantastic wickerwork patterns.[36]

Pound's hermeneutics must then be referred to Hermes as well as to a safer and more solar god of the lyre – a lyre he exchanges with Hermes in order to make peace. Indeed, Hermes is one of the most congenial gods of the *Cantos*, since he embodies the principles which make Odysseus a *polumetis* at the level of the divinities. And this is also why the god of messengers and thieves is called the god of poets, as Heidegger points out:

The expression 'hermeneutic' derives from the Greek verb ἑρμηνεύειν. It refers to the noun ἑρμηνεύς, which can be approximated with the name of the god Hermes ('Ερμῆς) in a play of thought more compelling than scientific rigour. Hermes is the messenger of the gods. He announces fate; ἑρμηνεύειν is an exposition which brings news, in so far as it can hear a message. Such an exposition then becomes an exegesis of what has been said by poets who, according to the word used by Socrates in Plato's dialogue Ion (534e), are themselves ἑρμηνῆς εἰσιν τῶν θεῶν, messengers of the gods.[37]

Pound indeed believes in his role of 'messenger' when he transmits his *arcanum*:

> This I had from Kalupso
> who had it from Hermes
> (CII, p. 728)

Hermes is thus indispensable in bringing a little Homeric humour, and deflating the pose of the would-be secret-monger. Pound is fond of alluding to the declaration by which Hermes frees Odysseus from the bondage of Calypso: 'I am so Xtian that a lying god tickles my funny bone / *You a goddess ask of me whom am a god, / Nevertheless I will tell you the truth.*' (*L*, p. 275). Hermes is the best example of the 'goguenard pantheon' which had vanished when Aristotle was writing. The 'touch of irony' (*GK*, p. 329) in his formulation is a symptom of verbal agility allied with an awareness that no truth is assured in statements, but has to be referred to a sense of utterance. Hermes provides the key to Pound's polytheism: the refusal of monotheism is not so much a critique of reverence and rites as the rejection of monologic discourse. Gods can lie, thereby provoking interpretation. But, whenever they lie, they do not cease to manifest the numinous in their speech.

This is why Pound decides to conclude Canto xxiv by an ideogram splicing in Hermes' answer to Apollo, and the degradation of sacred places symbolised by the transformation of the Schifanoia palace into a tannery; Hermes is a reminder of the ambivalent energy of people like Paris, who brought ruin to Troy, Ugo d'Este, who was beheaded, and Niccolo, with his insatiable sexual urges. But he opposes the mere profanation of 'temples' for economic reasons:

'Is it likely Divine Apollo,
That I should have stolen your cattle?
A child of my age, a mere infant,
     And besides, I have been here all night in my crib.'

(xxiv, p. 114)

In the same way as Pound does not tell us who is speaking or whether the words quoted are true or untrue, he uses modern versions of Hermes to catch our *interest*, an interest which is less and less dissociable from interpretation. Thus, Baldy Bacon is one of the rare positive figures of business-men:

Pollon d'anthropon iden,
Knew which shipping companies were most careless;
    where a man was most likely
To lose a leg in bad hoisting machinery;
Also fire, as when passing a whore-house,
Arrived, miraculous Hermes, by accident,
Two minutes after the proprietor's *angelos*
Had been sent for him.

(xii, p. 54)

His faculty for and speed in adapting render him the equal of the god, and even when he looks obsessed by money he is redeemed by his curiosity: 'Baldy's interest/ Was in money business./ 'No interest in any other kind uv bisnis' (p. 53). He is one of the active characters who do not reappear in the chronicle but intervene to flesh out what would otherwise drift too easily toward the realm of gods and heroes. Hermes is well represented in the roll-call of gods who, for instance, preside over the foundation of Venice in Canto xvii. There Hermes is placed side by side with Circe, through an allusion to Aeëtes, because, as Circe incites Odysseus to go down to Hell, so Hermes leads Aeneas in the *Aeneid* and provides him with the sacred golden bough:

> 'For this hour, brother of Circe.'
> Arm laid over my shoulder,
> Saw the sun for three days, the sun fulvid,
> As a lion lift over sand-plain;
>   and that day,
> And for three days, and none after,
> Splendour, as the splendour of Hermes
>
>   (xvii, p. 79)

This repeats and inverts the theme of the 'golden bough of Argicida' concluding the first Canto; Hermes, the slayer of Argus, leads both into and out of Hell, thereby granting some of his splendour to Plotinus (who comes into play in Canto xvii, inserted between these two moments).

Hermes as the 'god of thieves' reappears symbolised by the caduceus of the US Army doctors in the 'Pisan Cantos', but he also more seriously emerges as a comforter who gives eternal value to his comrades' help:

> magna NUX animae   with Barabbas and 2 thieves beside me,
>   the wards like a slave ship,
>   Mr Edwards, Hudson, Henry   *comes miseriae*
>   Comites Kernes, Green and Tom Wilson
>   God's messenger Whiteside   (lxxiv, p. 436)

> Zarathustra, now desuete
> to Jupiter and to Hermes where now is the castellaro
>   no vestige save in the air   (p. 438)

The recognition of human help and compassion harmonises with a more transcendent design which situates the tradition 'in the air' – in the mind of the poet, and in the evanescent link between subjectivities: a tradition of this type only exists in what Pound later calls 'Sagetrieb', a term to which I shall return. After the experience of Pisa, Pound knows he writes for those whose curiosity reaches into greater detail (the *'right . . . to write for a few people with special interests and whose curiosity reaches into greater detail'* is stated p. 659 in the middle of a laborious exercise in comparative philology involving constant parallels between Greek and Chinese words – XCVI, p. 659), and this curiosity is above all a reader's curiosity, but a curiosity about a reading which does not limit itself to written documents:

> They who are skilled in fire
>
> shall read   旦   tan, the dawn
>
> Waiving no jot of the arcanum
>   (having his own mind to stand him)   (XCI, p. 615)

A neo-Platonic light suffuses the Chinese radical, in which the skilled reader has recognised the sun on the horizon. Such a reading which insists on its claims to precision and wholeness makes one the emulator of the gods, for one must possess a mind like Odysseus's to perceive the entire *arcanum*. Man reading becomes an ideogram of vision, thus of pure love:

>   Renew
> jih
> hsin
> renew
> Plus the luminous eye
>   chien[4]   (XCIII, p. 629)

The 'eye' and the 'legs' combine to form the character *chien*[4], meaning see, observe, consider. When the character is used in conjunction with a negative, 'not + see', it means search.[38] Thus the reading Pound engages is situated between those two forms, between a 'seeing' the signs which discloses vision, hence wisdom, and a 'not seeing' which perpetuates the quest for clues.

But the quest for signs and luminosity is part of a collective *techne*, since we have seen that any reading is a writing, and that the subject appears as plural in this process. Thus, when Pound wants to collate the cumulative wisdom he has derived from Chinese chronicles and sacred texts with the anthropology of culture evolved with the help of Frobenius and certain economists, he has to coin a word which cannot be Greek or Chinese, nor totally English, since he has exploited all the English word's associations with 'Culture' or 'Kultur' or 'Kulchur';[39] so he creates 'Sagetrieb'.

naught above just contribution

invicem docentes siu   M.2835

that is Sagetrieb

hsü, in the first tone
kiaó. chiao,[1-4]

(LXXXV, p. 557)

Pound comments on a passage from the *Chou King* in which the sage minister Tcheou koung explains to the future Emperor that there had been a mythical time when 'state ministers would instruct each other' (which is glossed by 'invicem docentes' in the Latin text[40]). The two characters, *siü* and *kiao* in Couvreur's transliteration, *hsü* and *chiao*[1-4] in Mathews's *Dictionary*, mean mutually, and teach, instruct, education. 'Sagetrieb' is first an equivalent of 'education', but it keeps the sense of its two German roots, *Sage* (meaning legend, saga), and *Trieb* (compulsion, drive, instinct). In the German coining, the two words are polarised and retain something of their derivation: *Sage* comes from *sagen*, (say), and *Trieb* from *treiben*, (push), and the word could be rendered as 'the urge to say', 'the compulsion to utter'. It also suggests a collective process of myth-making, and resembles closely the concept of *Sprachkraft*, which von Humboldt and the Humboldtians have used.[41]

This is a step in the direction of a new conceptual vocabulary, since Pound does not quote a word, but builds a synthetic compound. What is stranger is that, for the same reasons – namely, to avoid the trap of overdetermined words, and in order to bypass metaphysical concepts – Heidegger has elaborated a similar coining, *Sage*, to replace *Sprache* (language) in his post-fifties' texts. Furthermore, the necessity for such a coining appears when Heidegger (H) is in the middle of a dialogue with a Japanese professor (J) who attempts to define 'hermeneutics'. The Japanese has just answered a question asking him to define 'language' in Japanese; he calls it *koto ba*, and explains that *koto* would correspond to 'the ecstasy of a beckoning stillness'.

H. What then does the term *koto ba* mean as a name for language?

J. Hearing the word rightly, it says: petals of flowers coming out of *koto*.

H. A truly astonishing and marvellous word, thereby inexhaustible. It names something entirely different from the expressions which remain in the realm of metaphysics: γλῶσσα, *lingua, langue* and *Sprache*. For a long time, I have only reluctantly used the term *Sprache* [language] when trying to think of its essence.

J. But have you found something more fitting?

H. I believe I have found it, but I would be wary of using it as a general-purpose word, or of falsifying it as the definition of a concept.

J. Which word do you use?

H. The word *Sage* [fable, legend, the 'say' of 'saying']. It means the saying and what the saying says, as well as what it is to say something.

J. What does 'say' [*sagen*] mean?

H. This word probably means the same as 'show' [*zeigen*], in the sense of letting appear and letting shine [*erscheinen- und scheinen-lassen*], although still in the guise of a wink.

J. *Sage* is consequently not the word for the speech of men . . .

H. . . . but rather for its essence, to which your Japanese term *koto ba* alludes: *das Sagenhafte* [the legendary, fabulous; the 'imbued with saying'] . . .

J. . . . . And I now feel more at home in the winks of this word thanks to our conversation, so that I see more clearly that Count Kuki was well inspired to attempt a meditation on hermeneutics under your guidance.[42]

No correspondence can be found between Pound's *Sagetrieb* and Heidegger's *Sage* beside the historical coincidence, and the appeal to the plastic conceptual possibilities of German. What matters more is the idea which dominates in both texts: the difficulty of naming language with a word distilling all the richness of the experience of speaking and all the epochal determinations. The result is a tactic of estrangement, the violence of the new term obliging the inventor and the reader, or, in the case of Heidegger, the philosopher and the Japanese professor, to engage in a dialogue. Any attempt at a redefinition of language is forced to end in a dialogue which hinges around language while talking about language.

Objective and subjective categories are interverted: the simplest utterance is at the same time a deep personal urge, an unconscious drive, and a collective myth; in the same way, a dynasty can be founded on 'sensibility':

LING²

Our dynasty came in because of a great sensibility.

All there by the time of I Yin.

All roots by the time of I Yin.

Galileo index'd 1616,

Wellington's peace after Vaterloo

                chih³

                a gnomon,

Our science is from the watching of shadows;

That Queen Bess translated Ovid,

         Cleopatra wrote of the currency,

Versus who scatter old records

        ignoring the hsien² form

        and jump to the winning side

                      (turbae)

II.9. have scopes and beginnings   tchŏung

                      (LXXXV, pp. 543–4)

Pound had already noted in the *Guide to Kulchur* the importance of sensibility in approaching Confucius: 'Our general notion of Confucius

(Kung) has perhaps failed to include a great sensibility. The Conversations are the record of a great sensibility' (*GK*, p. 232). This would tend to confirm the relationship between 'Sagetrieb', *Sage*, 'great sensibility' and the idea of a dialogue, a living speech between different men, with the added nuance that it becomes part of a tradition; the term 'record' is important in this context, since it recurs in the Canto: those who 'scatter records' cannot understand the word for 'virtuous, honest' (*hsien²*).

Advancing in his meticulous deciphering of the *Chou King*, Pound meets a sentence which seems to call up the same 'sensibility': 'Les empereurs de notre maison de Tcheou (Wenn Wang et Ou Wang), *à cause de leur grande bonté* (*ling²*) furent chargés d'exécuter l'oeuvre du roi du ciel.'[43] The ideogram *ling* is then transformed into a majestic porch, signalling that henceforth the ideograms will be more than underlinings: they tend to occupy more and more space, and are glossed in successive layers of interpretation (thus we still find echoes of *ling* in Canto CIV, pp. 738 and 740, where the circularity is stressed with 'Ling by ling only', and a new reading added to the sense of 'goodness': 'under the cloud / the three voices'[44]). In 'sensibility', the worlds of men and gods are one: 'the heaven speaks'. Indeed, the 'sensibility' also derives from a perfect adequation of the world of politics with the decrees of fate, since the 'mandate of heaven' can be lost by a dynasty, so justifying a popular rising and the victory of a new pretender to the throne, who will, in his turn, found another dynasty.[45] An acute perception of signs is indispensable, since, when unhappy peasants are crushed by taxes or a certain degree of corruption exists at court, Nature declares a ruler illegitimate. Thus a certain type of welfare state is founded on a mystique of light.

Pound then moves back six centuries to the time of I In T'ang's sage minister, who educated the young Emperor T'ai Kia (1753–1720 BC). His speech defines good government and recalls the principle of conformity with the laws of Nature and the four virtues, 'humanity, justice, urbanity and prudence' (*Chou King*, p. 109). From the vantage-point of an ordered society with a sound prince, Pound examines the present degradation of Europe, marked by two names, Galileo's condemnation (called up by the memory of the Jesuits[46]) and Napoleon's defeat at Waterloo. The delayed knowledge of the earth's revolution, and the conspiracy against the last condottiere before Mussolini relate the light of the sun and the Father's name in another European ideogram. 'Vaterloo' takes on these further significations, since the transcription not only mimics the Belgian pronounciation but also indirectly alludes to the absence of the Father by echoing the

German word *vaterlos* (fatherless) and the new imperial capital of *Lo* which the Emperor is planning at the precise passage in the *Chou King* alluded to.[47]

The *gnomon* becomes a name and a measure. Granet explains how the Chinese calculated the exact centre of the world, on which precise spot Lo should be founded, by using a gnomon, or rough sun-dial made with a stick. The Chinese omphalos is where the sun leaves no shadow at midday in the middle of the summer. Of course, Pound relates this to his 'hitching post' or *chih*[3], since it points to the exact site for a dwelling. Granet also explains that the fusion of all contraries at that precise spot indicates the 'way' or *tao*, which used to refer to a pole or gnomon around which light and darkness proceeded.[48] This turns into a 'hierogamy'[49] uniting masculine and feminine principles, which explains why two feminine names correspond to two masculine names. Women can unite love and ordered administration as well as men.

The unity of this Chinese universe is based on the four virtues, which also correspond to the four cardinal points, or the four books of Confucius, and the four seasons: 'and the whole creation concerned with "FOUR" ' (Canto XCI, p. 616), as Heydon had already said.[50] Pound finds a confirmation of this when he glosses the *Edict* in Canto XCIX: 'But the four TUAN/ are from nature' (p. 711). Frobenius stresses the importance of the number four for the Chinese *paideuma*: 'Four is the number of totality for Chinese wisdom', since 'The four is the boundary of space.'[51] And Frobenius uses this ancient concept to demonstrate that a culture is time multiplied by space; for the Chinese, '$4x$ equal all x'. Similar considerations have probably influenced Heidegger's concept of the 'Fourfold' (*das Geviert*), which unites men and gods, earth and sky: 'By a primal oneness the four – earth and sky, divinities and mortals – belong together in one.'[52]

Pound and Heidegger thus approach in a similar way the sacred space ready for a foundation, and which the poem memorialises. The simple roll-call of emperors, even when they are just alluded to by their characters, yields the impression of the continuity of a legend which one must keep alive, while the stress on pure enunciation is repeated, as in:

'O nombreux officiers

Imperator ait.

Iterum dico   (LXXXV, p. 556)

This points to the source of 'Sagetrieb': the iteration of correct statements. Assuredly, the repetition is already there in Couvreur, since the Emperor emphasises that, if the 'many officers' of the defeated army want to live in Lo under his rule, they shall be forgiven.[53] However, the fact that Pound quotes declarative verbs without quoting what is said leaves a teasing gap in the text, which has to be filled by an absent enunciator (the Emperor, Pound, ourselves) or by an ideogram: almost devoid of meaning, it survives the successive degradations of values to bear witness to a natural order of space and signs. Thus the *legenda* become *agenda*, ideas to be put into action by being reread, gathered anew, enunciated.

Thus hermeneutics lead to apophantics, the simple 'showing'-forth of light in the world, which points to a continuity of Being. Being can be read because it discloses a sacred space, a *templum*, and this reading needs no real verbal or written sign:

> Being, as itself, spans its own province, which is marked off (*temnein, tempus*) by Being's being present in the word. Language is the precinct (*templum*), that is, the house of Being. The nature of language does not exhaust itself in signifying, nor is it merely something that has the character of sign or cypher. It is because language is the house of Being, that we reach what is by constantly going through this house. When we go to the well, when we go through the woods, we are always already going through the word 'well', through the word 'woods', even if we do not speak the words and do not think of anything relating to language.[54]

This is also the key to Pound's insight into a nature constituted of 'monuments' and 'signatures' which disclose a 'proportion' men can keep as a rule for building temples or the room in Poitiers in which one can stand at midday without throwing any shadow on the ground.[55] Between this human artefact and the natural sign given by the gnomon indicating the omphalos, there exists an unbroken link, although no sacred book contains the key to it ('The mysteries are *not* revealed, and no guide-book to them has been or will be written' – *L*, p. 327). This accounts for the ideogram of Canto LXXXVII:

> The tower wherein, at one point, is no shadow,
> and Jacques de Molay, is where?
> and the 'Section', the proportions,
> lending, perhaps, not at interest, but resisting.

The false fronts, barocco.
      'We have', said Mencius, 'but phenomena.'
monumenta. In nature are signatures
      needing no verbal tradition,
oak leaf never plane leaf. John Heydon.
      Σελλοί sleep there on the ground
And old Jarge held there was a tradition,
      that was not mere epistemology.   (p. 573)

Jacques de Molay, the great Master of the Templars, destroyed for
financial reasons; the English mystic John Heydon, known as the
'secretary of nature' because he could read the secrets of nature; old
Santayana, musing on philosophy in Rome; and the sacred Selloi, who
kept the oracle for Heracles – all these knew about the golden rule, 'la
section d'or' (*LE*, p. 154), a principle inherent in nature. The
conclusion of this montage is the assertion of a meaning in the world:
'In short, the cosmos continues' (LXXXVII, p. 573).

    When the time of palinodes and doubts comes, Pound does not
renege on this belief; the mistakes all come from a 'chaos' which is both
within him and in the world, according to the tension I have outlined:
'Error of chaos. Justification is from kindness of heart' (Canto CXIII,
p. 788). Pound does not write 'Error *from* chaos', which might suggest
a demonic principle as origin of the disorder in his thoughts or in the
world. 'Ignorance' is still reserved for 'them': 'Nothing new but their
ignorance' (ibid.). What then increases is the divorce between the
hidden, secret coherence of the *cosmos*, and the attempts to 'make
Cosmos':

Came Neptunus
            his mind leaping
                  like dolphins,
These concepts the human mind has attained.
To make Cosmos –
To achieve the possible –
Muss., wrecked for an error,
But the record
      the palimpsest –
a little light
            in great darkness –   (CXVI, p. 795)

We have seen how any moment of despair could be retrieved by a dialectical twist of concepts and moods; there is no recantation of faith here, but the reasons for fragmentation and failure go deeper than a simple alternation of psychic movements upward and downward. The same familiar 'but' still points to renascent possibilities:

> But to affirm the gold thread in the pattern
> > (Torcello)
> al vicolo d'oro
> > (Tigullio).
> To confess wrong without losing rightness:
> Charity I have had sometimes,
> > I cannot make it flow thru.
> A little light, like a rush light
> > to lead back to splendour.   (p. 797)

Indeed, there is no rupture of the hermeneutical circle, since there remains a hope that someone will 'copy this palimpsest', that someone will see the light in spite of subjective incoherence, aphasia and ataraxia. However, the hermeneutic circle (or spiral) now begins to rotate around the rift: the division of ontological difference between Being as light and beings as struggling in darkness. Ontological difference has started cleaving the signs of the text, everything now hinging around an 'it' which coheres and a 'they' always liable to err, in the sense of Heidegger's phrase already quoted, 'He who thinks greatly must err greatly.' The 'ego' appears split, divided, torn apart in this disclosure, which nevertheless brings it closer to its truth.

If the 'mysteries' have always been there, in a tradition which hovers in the air or in signatures which constellate on the ground, this implies that in a way everything has always already been said; the hermeneutic progression starts, however, from the realisation that the saying is more important than what is said, that they never can be reduced to one another, that an 'Iterum dico' will duly register a man's efforts against chaos and embody his signature. Pound's daughter explains that at one point, her father thought that 'Dante ha[d] said everything there is to be said',[56] which led him to start with Malatesta. In the fight for 'Eleusis', the sacrament, the true tradition, and against any 'Ersatz religion' (*L*, p. 303), the repetition (*iterum*) opens the way (*iter*) by rearranging the letters in their correct order; in the periplus of the subject these same letters compose his name and hint at the subject's becoming text and the text's opening to other subjects.

Another, easier way to the *arcanum* would have been to seal off completely the hermeneutic circle, to indulge in an autarkic vision of private splendour. There are several indications which point this way, such as the creation of idiosyncratic divinities which tend to fuse masculine and feminine characters.[57] It is true that the perfect sexual fusion of the sun and the moon yielding total light (日 月) can be interiorised in a moment of ecstasy, while the libidinal circulation I have attempted to describe in economic terms would thus be held back 'in the mind, indestructible'. But Pound's grandeur lies in his refusal to comply with the Jungian temptation of hermetic bisexuality, even if he plays with its images. He cannot evade the intense pain caused by desire and an ontological rift which divides the subject. Besides, he is too close to Dante not to have refused, like his mentor, the model of 'hermaphroditic' poetry which Guido Guinicelli represents. Guido, a famous poet writing before Dante, is in Purgatory, for his sin lies in his choice of a fusion between dialectics (Hermes) and rhetorics (Aphrodite).

> For us, hermaphrodite was our offence....
> I am Guido Guinicelli and purge me in flame
> Because, ere the end, my sins repented were.
>
> (*Purgatorio*, XXVI.82, 92–3[58])

The exchange between the two poets may well be of durable 'traces':

> And he to me: 'Such trace, by what men say,
> Thou leavest printed in me, and one so clear,
> That Lethe cannot drown or make it grey.'   (ll. 106–8)

Guido Guinicelli nevertheless acknowledges the entire superiority of the best craftsman, 'miglior fabbro', Arnaut Daniel, who then speaks in his own language:

> 'Ara vos prec, per aquella valor
> que vos guida al som de l'escalina,
> sovenha vos a temps de ma dolor!'   (ll. 144–7)

This might well be what Louis Zukofsky has in mind when he refutes the fear that 'all language might be one' if the Chinese were to adopt the Latin alphabet; for, like Arnaut and Dante, and thus Pound, he wishes to retain the exact shape of a living speech which leads to the 'legend' ('For it is what each says exactly to each / That matters to us most') and then quotes from the legend, listing the four corners of the horizon and the seasons in Chinese:

> *Yü* – North's black winter water
> *Chiao* – East's blue spring wood
> *Kung* – Compass' center yellow prevails
>   over all four seasons' earth
> *Shang* – West's white autumn metal
> *Chi* – South's red summer fire.
> So what if we don't know Chinese
> Don't we become legend
> Come back to read from one book
> I do see your face –   ('A–13')[59]

Reading and writing the 'legend', Pound has indeed become one: the 'last surviving monolith' (*L*, p. 343) of a tradition which still leads us to vision and wisdom.

Hermes may well be the god of circulation, messages and translations: he keeps his staff of *psychopompos* and leads the way along the endless tracks which form a trace – footprints, characters, sites, temples, signatures. The hermeneutic moment of dialogical comprehension is then framed, contained, within a more monumental history in which a whole culture attempts to read its fate.

This entails that the binary divisions between speech and writing, physics and metaphysics, man and woman are repeated and displaced, finding a new basis in the huge tetrad: the *templum*, founded on the Fourfold, men, gods, earth, sky; this seals a writing which still exhibits its ruptures, fissures and di-visions – opening history to endless exegesis:

> ELIZABETH
>   Angliae amor,
>   ad valorem reducta.
> To take wood to melt ore
>   non extat memoria
>   ...ardendam, fundendam
> & souls of the dead defrauded
>   35 Edward

send or cause to be sent out of the
                    Kingdom
and that the seal be in custody of four men dignioribus
                                        (cviii, pp. 768–69)

Such a 'seal' becomes a 'character': a fate and a face, both familiar and
forbidding, if not forbidden.

Conclusion: the Legendary Rite – Writing and Tragedy

Pound always desired to arouse strong feelings, to awake passions and interests, which at times find a better expression in vocal criticism than in the cautious selection of the more palatable poetic translucencies which many prefer to make in order to avoid being swept along by too chaotic a flux of images, quotations, diatribes.

His work can still be quite correctly described in harsher terms as the conjunction of an early aestheticisation of politics and economics, in a movement strikingly parallel to the evolution of totalitarian ideologies, with a later moralisation of economics and history. Aestheticisation of politics, moralisation of economics, the freezing of a history reduced to sectarian praise of a few well-chosen heroes – all this rings a familiar bell, and describes the locus of most reactionary ideologies in a phallocentric system from which no one, today, can be sure to have escaped.

Yet these terms sound strangely inadequate, and hardly do justice to Pound's lifelong effort recorded in his *Cantos*. If he is aware of his deep commitment to an ideology, amidst ideological wars of planetary importance, what remains as an irreducible crux is the reason for a transformation of this ideology into an idiom, an idiolect almost. It is through this movement that Pound is still modern, and continues to pose vital questions, the most poignant of which is perhaps the division of the ideological subject.

Pound's theses could be reduced to a few propositions if it were not that precisely the division of the subject forbids any such summary. Life has been 'impoverished' by economic 'sabotage and obstruction'; the active values retained by a series of 'classics' and certain practical proposals can bring back the integrity of life.[1] Literature and sound economics need only unite, and the earthly paradise is at hand.

However, we have seen the ambivalence in the thematic network as subsidiary to an economic ambivalence, in a system which oscillates between *arche* and *telos*, production and distribution, speed and slowness – to name but a few examples. Moreover, Pound's main

287

failure from a scientific point of view lies in his inability to account for the logic of capitalistic production. But, by a curious movement of reversal, it appears that his main strength resides in this failure: it is because he cannot understand the genesis of surplus value that he is able so effortlessly to reach the foundational point of view. His progressive equation of production with nature, of production with contemplation, provides him with the lyrical language in which he can not only think but also enact the 'step back' out of metaphysics.

The foundation Pound is looking for through the question of language is to be found in an awareness of time as free gift *and* discontinuity, in a consciousness of the ontological rift which cleaves the *cosmos* as well as the speaking subject. Writing takes its origin from the perception of the absence of stable origin: it spans the distance between a root and the negation of the root, in endless rhymes:

> But the lot of 'em, Yeats, Possum and Wyndham
>   had no ground beneath 'em.
>
> Orage had.
> Per ragione vale
> Black shawls for Demeter.   (xcviii, p. 685)

and some Cantos later:

 But the lot of 'em, Yeats, Possum, Old Wyndham

>   had no ground to stand on
>   Black shawls still worn for Demeter
>   in Venice,
>   in my time,
>   my young time
>   (cii, p. 728)

The ideogram *pu* here reproduced means 'no, not' and is the most common form of negation. But Pound has remarked that the character *pen*, 本 , which means 'root, fundament, origin' is almost the same, with the difference that the ground is marked by a stroke.[2] The absence of ground is demonstrated by a visual play which is redoubled in the meaning of 'not'; surely a 'no one' or 'no man' is not far removed. The root is best approached through its lack, just as a vanishing bird, lost in the sky, tells of ephemeral things.

If Orage possessed this ground it was because he had *rectitudo*: 'On that rock was his edifice' (*SP*, p. 416). The notion of justice and integrity finds a real site in rites, which becomes even clearer in the last fragments:

> Here from the beginning, we have been here
> from the beginning
> From her breath were the goddesses
> ²La ²mun̲ ³mi
> If we did not perform ²N̄daw ¹bpö
> nothing is solid
> without ²Mùan̲ ¹bpö
> no reality   (CXII, p. 784)

In the Na-khi kingdom, Pound thought he had at last discovered an earthly paradise. The overwhelming sense of rituals which pervades all activities in this Tibetan region affords a glimpse of total harmony of natural and divine realms, if not precisely of personal happiness. But, essentially, Pound has found Chinese – or oriental – gods, who were absent from his Confucian world-picture. Wyndham Lewis, Yeats and Eliot may have had their beliefs; they did not lead the reader to their foundation. Orage's mysticism did, because it was allied to a sense of social justice. The Greek cosmos and Chinese wisdom must be reunited in a new perception of rites and divinities.

The key word for the Chinese sense of balance and gradations is *li*, the rites. As we have seen, the entire social order derives its stability and coherence from an integration of the will of rulers, the will of the people and the decree of Heaven. Pound's prime motive when 'writing through' Chinese documents and historiography is to capture the root of this feeling and to apply it to his own world, including America. Rites are closer to music and dance in Confucian philosophy, and they are preferable to the compulsory enforcement of prohibitions: order has to come organically, and Radcliffe-Brown explains that rites and sacrifices belong to the world of myth which religious orthodoxies try generally to subdue. They cannot accept their plastic freedom and creativity, associated with a sense of the right gesture defined by tradition. Rites neverthless fulfil a more essential role than religions, because they effect the connection, the *re-ligere*, the harmonisation of the human world with the divine world. Radcliffe-Brown proposes to make his own the sentence from the *Book of Rites*, or *Li Ki*, which says, 'Ceremonies are the bond that holds the multitudes together, and if this bond be removed, those multitudes fall into confusion.'[3]

The rite's function is only outwardly that of bringing a direct result; the belief is a belief in the social efficacy of rites, not in their magical power: 'The rites gave regulated expression to certain human feelings and sentiments and so kept these sentiments alive and active. In turn it was these sentiments which, by their control of or influence on the conduct of individuals made possible the existence and continuance of an orderly social life.'[4] This is the recurrent image of China which Pound attempts to create in his *Cantos*, and which he sums up by the term 'great sensibility'. From this assured intuition of a harmonised whole, he can then redefine politics in our Western sense. Confucius completes the hints given by Aristotle or Dante, as his scope is enlarged by reference to the United States or Byzantium:

> And there were guilds in Byzantium.
>   'Not political', said Dante, a
>   'compagnevole animale'
> Even if some do coagulate into cities
>   πόλις, πολιτική
> reproducteur,
>   contribuable. Paradis peint
> but πολεύω meaning to plough
>   πολύγλωσσος
>   There were many sounds in that oak-wood.
>   (xcv, pp. 643–4)

Jules Nicole's edition of the Eparch's book confirms the soundness of a system of corporations regulated by strict laws (and he himself warns the reader of the political danger of such an organisation, in which he perceives a dangerous totalitarian spirit[5]). And, in his discussion of Aristotle, Dante merely translates 'political' by *compagnevole* without stressing the difference. Pound notices it, and chooses to read it as very significant.[6] Dante then distinguishes three levels of political organisation, which could also correspond to economic strata: the village or neighbourhood (*vicinanza*), the city, and finally the state. The political drift is clear, since he appeals to the Emperor to save the Italian cities. Pound conflates this in a pastoral dream of the origins, linking the etymology of *polis* (city) to *poleuo* (plough, and, by extension, to inhabit a city, as in *Odyssey*, XXII. 223). The city is thus related to the rites of foundation which give birth to it and delimit the sacred space with a ritual ploughing; from Greek or Roman rites, we can then move toward basic Chinese virtues:

> The State is corporate
> as with pulse in its body
> & with Chou rite at the root of it,
> The root is thru all of it,
> a tone in all public teaching:
> This is not a work of fiction
> nor yet of one man:
> . . .
> From of old the sovereign likes plowing
> & the Empress tends the trees with reverence;
> Nor shrink from the heat of labour
> 茈 an omen
> The plan is in nature
> rooted
>
> (XCIX, pp. 707–9)

The *Edict* keeps the fertility rites alive; the Emperor ploughs in the spring to ensure abundance: 'There is worship in plowing / and equity in the wedding hoe' (p. 711). The other motifs fused in this primarily agrarian utopia add more ominous counterpointing: de Gourmont's cynicism, which replaces Aristotle's definition of the political nature of man with 'animal reproducteur, animal electoral, animal contribuable';[7] a tag from Villon's 'Ballade pour prier Notre Dame';[8] and finally, by a strange acceleration, after a possible allusion to Electra's grief,[9] a reference to the oracle which announced that Heracles would be killed by a dead man (the Selloi had written their prophecy under the dictation of the 'thousand-voiced oak', *poluglossou druos*, – *Women of Trachis*, l. 1168: a line which Pound had omitted from his own translation, replacing it by a mention of Zeus, the Father[10]).

Thus from the pastoral rites of ancient China and the corporate state of Byzantium, we have come closer to the meaning of sacrificial violence, always preserved and kept at bay by ritual. Paternity implies a dangerous legacy of duties and funeral rites, which finds their real mode of expression in Greek tragedies. This is the other side of the idealised order of Chinese dynasties: another pastoralism is inhabited by jealous gods and vengeful demigods, by tragic heroes who must die in order that they may see the light. If the rites only domesticate the dionysiac components of tragedy, the ultimate quest for a foundation must go deeper; and this is why *The Women of Trachis* is such an important key to the understanding of the later Cantos. Indeed, one might even say that the move into the rural splendour of the Na-khi kingdom had been forced by the need to reconcile a tragic vision of life with a real epic which would end on the promised *Paradiso*.

To pose the question of genres in this necessarily rapid discussion seems a little idle, since Pound himself, who repeatedly alluded to his *Cantos* as an 'epic poem',[11] nevertheless discredited the relevance of such traditional and Aristotelian categories. Since no 'Aquinas map' is valid, it would be rash to superimpose an Aristotelian map. During the composition of the middle Cantos, Pound is very close to the epic pattern, sincerely believing that he is writing a historical chronicle containing economics. But, if the first sequence or decad appears much closer in spirit to Dante's model, while the later part of the *Cantos*, devoured by philological annotation, haunted by the apocalyptic disclosure of an *arcanum*, fuses personal memories and a definition of political justice, one might wonder what 'epic' then means.

Pound himself warned against an adequation of Dante's 'comedy' with an epic: 'The Divina Commedia must not be considered as an epic; to compare it with an epic poem is usually unprofitable. It is in a sense lyric, the tremendous lyric of the subjective Dante' (*SR*, p. 153). What happens to Pound's lyric voice, split and broken after Pisa, might be better approximated by a hesitation between comedy (defined by a positive ending) and tragedy (defined by a negative ending). But the distinction cannot lie in the *dénouement* (or *lusis* in the *Poetics*); it is found in the new sense of 'plot', or *ploke*, or interweaving of several fates, which the voice itself creates, precisely by an insistent repetition of similar names. The voice thus enacts the tragedy of history while it lends weight, credit, authority to the quotations it animates. The 'Pisan Cantos' can therefore be described as the moment when the epic structure finds a resolution and an opening in tragedy (for Aristotle, indeed, tragedy is more complex than the epic, since it possesses elements lacking in epic poems[12]). Besides, the more and more complex intrication of generic models explains why Pound's poem can no longer 'include economics' (since this was his definition of an epic poem): the poem itself becomes an economy of a new type, the economy of a foundational movement which has to be expressed in 'many voices'.

In its quest for forgotten 'Sagetrieb', the foundational poem examines several ethical and political systems, analyses monetary history, and in the complex *sumploke* its repetitive polyphonic rhymes create, goes beyond history to the point where, indeed, the historical becomes the original, as Adorno says about Hölderlin.[13] The poem thus loses in historical precision, and even in historical appreciation, but, instead of situating a few economic verities in the stream of a basically American chronicle, it creates a new literary space for a social and individual *ethos*.

And the more disquieting verbal tactics of the later Cantos find a justification when examined in the context of the tragedy. In ancient Greece, tragedy flourished for only a short while before falling victim to the dislocation of the Greek city. Philosophy, Aristotle in particular (although we have seen that the concept of prudence owed a lot to the tragic vision), came to replace the world of dynamic tensions between the gods and men with an appeal to conceptual definition and clarification. As such, tragedy appears, by contrast, to be poised between the world of a mythical past and the present of political life.

Tragedy is an expression of the city; it needs the point of view of the 'political animal'. But, as Vernant and Vidal-Naquet have noted, if the roles of the heroes were played by professional actors, the chorus was composed of citizens, who were in a way sent by the city to represent it. And, by a curious chiasmus, while the heroes speak a language which is relatively close to everyday speech, in a metre which breaks down in moments of agitated passion to something like free verse, the chorus always speaks in heightened diction, to sing mostly of gods and ancient myths.[14] The inverse relation of roles and idioms assures the interweaving of voices and gives the main condition for the ritual function of tragedy: the purgation of passions by the instauration of a circle of transference and interpretation. Pound's translation of *The Women of Trachis* observes the original's discrimination in idiom, the notoriously slangy passages belonging to the heroes and the hieratic language to the chorus. Thus we find the same range of tones and accents as in the *Cantos*, from the crude impersonations of frontier dialect to the sacramental invocations of the gods.

The plot of *The Women of Trachis* requires further comment: in this play, it is the father himself who orders his son to commit parricide and symbolic incest, when he understands that his death is willed by his own divine Father. He arranges the marriage of Hyllos, his son, with the slave he has brought back as his lover, thereby causing his ruin: 'No other man but you shall have her' (*WT*, p. 69). Hyllos at one point asks, 'Good lord, you want me to be a murderer / and a parricide?' (p. 68). The poison is likewise the source of considerable dramatic irony. Brought in a packet sealed by Daysair's signet, carried by a messenger who keeps comparing himself to Hermes, the poisoned tunic which creates such intolerable pains for Heracles has been in fact smeared by the dying Centaur's sperm.[15] Thus a passage in which Heracles laments his fate acquires weird overtones:

> It sticks to my sides and
>   has gnawed through to my furtherest in'nards.
> . . . . / . . . Nor Greeks,
> nor foreigner whose countries I had cleaned up,
> but a piddling female did it,
>   not even a man with balls.
> Alone and without a sword.

> Boy, you start showing whose son you are. I.e. mine,
> and as for the highly revered title to motherhood,
> you get that producer out of her house
> and hand her over to me . . .   (*WT*, p. 62)

The play seems to dramatise the way the poison of Usura destroys domestic economy: a malevolent force, whose origin the hero mistakes, attacks him from within. But, as soon as the real cause is disclosed by the oracle given at the Selloi's oak, the sequence of priorities is re-established in a flash of pure vision:

> Time lives, and it's going on now.
> I am released from trouble.
> I thought it meant life in comfort.
> It doesn't. It means that I die.
> For amid the dead there is no work in service.
> Come at it that way, my boy, what

> SPLENDOUR,
>   IT ALL COHERES.   (p. 66)

One is not sure whether Heracles is ravished at discovering the subtle ambiguities in the phrasing of the oracle, or at feeling united with his Father's law. However, Pound's translation of *sumbainei*, which I have already mentioned, shows how it can be taken for 'the key phrase, for which the play exists' (*WT*, p. 66n.): seeing 'clearly' fate and death means seeing in its fullness the white light of truth. This light abolishes all hates, jealousies, incestuous motives and involuntary treacheries.

When Pound laments the fact that he is not 'a demigod' and 'cannot

make it cohere' (Canto CXVI, p. 796), he essentially deplores the
impossibility of a reconciliation with the laws of the universe. It is not
so much that the task of writing a 'painted paradise' is now doomed and
unachievable, but rather that the adequation of Hell and the ephemeral, Purgatory and the recurrent, Paradise and the eternal can no
longer be valid. On the contrary, the eternal only appears in flashes
now, opening to a discontinuous Paradise, whilst Hell seems to move in
recurring cycles and moods of persistent depression. Indeed, the
dominant attitude, the *Grundstimmung*, is purgatorial, in the sense
that it leads toward a catharsis that is never totally fulfilled.

Pound's daughter recalls how Pound abruptly quoted his favourite
line from *Electra*, 'Need we add cowardice to all the rest of these ills?',
as he unexpectedly decided to leave a house in which jealousies were
gnawing at his peace of mind.[16]

> When one's friends hate each other
> how can there be peace in the world?
>
> (CXV, p. 794)

and

> For the blue flash and the moments
> benedetta
> the young for the old
> that is tragedy
> And for one beautiful day there was peace.
>
> (Notes for CXVII *et seq.*, p. 801[17])

From a perception of discontinuity in time, a new and intense lyricism
is born, in which dissociation, division, in de Gourmont's sense, is
counterbalanced by repetition, which manages to create the equivalent
of the eternal. A repetitive voice weaves in and out the ploces of the
Father's Law – from Kung to Mussolini, via Adams – a law which can
unite the Four. In that case, the poet himself as go-between men and
gods, the family and society, myth and politics, is often 'one too much':
the excluded one.

In this way the essence of poetry is joined on to the laws of the signs
of the gods and of the voice of the people, laws which tend towards
and away from each other. The poet himself stands between the
former – the gods, and the latter – the people. He is one who has

been cast out – out into that *Between*, between gods and men. . . . It is to Hölderlin himself that we must apply what he said of Oedipus in the late poem 'In the lovely azure there flowers . . .':

> King Oedipus has one
> Eye too many perhaps.[18]

I am not suggesting that the key to the *Cantos* lies in some hidden Oedipus complex, nor that Pound's insistent disavowal of psychoanalysis reveals private motives. But I might point out that at times denegation shows up more than do texts whose explicit objective is the unmasking of the unconscious. The tangle of motifs collated here belongs to what the genre of tragedy has already structured for everyone through the symbolic structure of language, and I have shown that Pound's eminence comes from what he teaches us about the speaking subject and his written signs.

In the main, the strangely elegiac tone of the last fragments draws one away from the robust thrones on which gods and good rulers can sit:

> ubi amor, ibi oculus.
> But these had thrones,
>   and in my mind were still, uncontending –
> not to possession, in hypostasis
>   Some hall of mirrors.   (CXIV, p. 793)

The reference to the lasting impression left by the eyes seen under the tent at Pisa contrasts with a present in which passions have devoured a mythical serenity ('Fear, father of cruelty, / are we to write a genealogy of the demons?' – ibid.). Thus it is quite understandable that one of the key words of the beginning of *Electra, threnos* (lamentation, funeral song),[19] which also supplies the title of one of the earliest poems written by Pound and kept from *A Lume Spento*,[20] should recur in the last fragments as an inversion of 'Thrones':

> Θρῆνος
> And who no longer make gods out of beauty
> Θρῆνος   this is a dying.
>   . . .
> But for the sun and serenitas
>   (19th May '59)

H. D. once said 'serenitas'
>>>>>>>>>>>>>>Atthis, etc.)
>>>>at Dieudonné's
>>>>>>>>>>>>>>in pre-history.
No dog, no horse, and no goat,
The long flank, the firm breast
>>>>>>>>>>and to know beauty and death and despair
and to think that what has been shall be,
>>>>>>>>>>>>flowing, ever unstill.

Then a partridge-shaped cloud over dust storm.
The hells move in cycles,
>>>>>>No man can see his own end.
The Gods have not returned. 'They have never left us.'
>>>>>>They have not returned.
Cloud's processional and the air moves with their living.
Pride, jealousy and possessiveness
>>>>>>3 pains of hell >>>>>>>>>>>>>>(cxiii, pp. 786–7)

I give this long quotation to stress the parataxis of Heaven and Hell, of
the gods and the demons; no synthesis can be achieved, the juxtaposition of mood continues with new alternations, the subject is torn
between shifting poles. The memories of HD's poem 'Atthis'[21] fuse
with a more objective memory: 'And over Li Chiang, the snow range is
turquoise / Rock's world that he saved us for memory / a thin trace in
high air' (Canto cxiii, p. 786). The choice of the Na-khi is highly
strategic: Pound found a community which lives in harmony with its
gods and ceremonies in an ideal landscapes of mountain, lakes and
juniper trees.

>>>>>>>>heaven >>>>>>>>earth

>>>>>>in the center

>>>>>>>>>>is

>>>>>>juniper >>>>>>>>>>>>(cx, p. 778)

But tragedy also finds place in this paradise, and Pound quotes the
ceremony of '²Har-²la-¹llü-³k'ö', which is the ceremony propitiating
the spirits of suicides. Joseph Rock explains that after the Chinese
gained control of the Na-khi's territory in 1723, they imposed
Confucian laws and the custom of forced marriages. The Na-khi,
whose religion was a mixture of animism, shamanism and lamaism, and

who had formerly practised free love, could not accept the new laws without despair:

> The forced marriages between couples who have perhaps never seen each other till the day of their marriage, and the betrothal during early childhood has caused great misery and unhappiness, and many are the couples who, in order to avoid marrying people whom they have perhaps never seen or perhaps dislike, go up to the mountain and commit suicide. There exists a ceremony for the propitiation of the spirit of people who have died a violent death, who it is believed become headless demons or wind demons; this ceremony is called ²Har-²la-¹llü-³k'ö, nowadays one of the most frequently performed ceremonies.[22]

Thus Pound sees that love is not only the form of philosophy and illumination, but also a concrete force which, when thwarted, may lead to suicide; the rites are all the more necessary since in this case there is no possibility of bumping off 'some nuisance'.[23] The striking union of an earthly paradise,[24] of a pervasive religiosity and of the recurrent temptation to disappear, either by suicide or by silence, corresponds to Pound's last imaginary periplus. The voyage to the country of the Na-khi follows a 'thin trace in the air', and finds a new balance between natural contemplation and social rites which leaves the voice mute but heals all the wounds. The Law of the Master, Confucius, has finally been subverted, since it appears in a context in which it signifies oppression and tyranny. Thus the disciple may choose to imitate his Master in his more contemplative moods:

1. He said: I'd like to do without words.
2. Tze-kung said: But, boss, if you don't say it, how can we little guys pass it on?
3. He said: Sky, how does that talk? The four seasons go on, everything gets born. Sky, what words does the sky use? (*Con.*, p. 277)

Notes

INTRODUCTION

1. The most developed and consistent reference is to be found in Anthony Woodward, *Ezra Pound and the Pisan Cantos* (London, Routledge and Kegan Paul, 1980) pp. 87–8.

2. See Heidegger's Preface to William J. Richardson, *Through Phenomenology to Thought* (The Hague: Martinus Nijhoff, 1963) p. x. The distinction between *Sein* and *Seiendes*, which is basic in Heidegger's philosophy, has to be translated by '*B*eing' and '*b*eing' respectively in English, which is a very Poundian instance of the importance of typography for philosophical discourse.

3. Richardson, *Through Phenomenology*, pp. 229–54. On p. 243 he speaks of the 'problem of the two Heideggers'. Heidegger himself does not disown this rupture but qualifies it in his letter. The cleavage can be dated in the thirties.

4. Martin Heidegger, *On Time and Being*, trs. Joan Stambaugh (New York: Harper, 1972). It is this side of Heidegger's thought which is relevant to an understanding of Pound rather than the thinker of 'being-towards-death'.

5. Heidegger was Rector from April 1933 to January 1934, a period during which he publishes the most committed of his papers, *Die Selbstbehauptung der deutschen Universität* ('The Self-assertion of German Universities'), in which he calls for the Nazi 'Service of Work' (*Arbeitsdienst*). He resigned in February 1934, and left the Party. Pound had an interview with Mussolini on 30 January 1933, a treat which, despite all his efforts, was never repeated. See Noel Stock, *The Life of Ezra Pound* (Harmondsworth: Penguin, 1974) pp. 389–90.

6. Theodor W. Adorno, *Jargon des Eigentlichkeit. Zur deutschen Ideologie*, (Frankfurt: Suhrkamp, 1964).

7. Martin Heidegger, 'The Thinker as Poet', in *Poetry, Language, Thought*, essays trs. by Albert Hofstadter (New York: Harper, 1971) p. 9.

8. Stock, *The Life of Ezra Pound*, p. 431.

9. Ibid., pp. 430–431.

10. The lecture-notes have been published in the monumental *Gesamtausgabe* of Heidegger's complete works: *II. Abteilung, Vorlesungen, 1923–1944*, vol. 39: *Hölderlins Hymnen 'Germanien' und 'Der Rhein'* (Frankfurt: Vittorio Klostermann, 1980). The published essays on Hölderlin are collected in Martin Heidegger, *Erläuterungen zu Hölderlins Dichtung* (Frankfurt, Vittorio Klostermann, 1971). Two of these essays have been translated into English: 'Remembrance of the Poet' and 'Hölderlin and the Essence of Poetry', in

Martin Heidegger, *Existence and Being*, ed. Werner Brock, trs. Douglas Scott (London: Vision Press, 1949).

11. Heidegger, *Gesamtausgabe*, vol. 39, p. 26, where Spengler and Rosenberg are criticised. Heidegger was fighting against the exploitation of Hölderlin as a purely nationalist poet by Nazi propaganda.

12. Ibid., p. 254. References to this volume are henceforward given in the text.

13. See Heidegger, *Existence and Being*, p. 301. I prefer 'dialogue' to 'conversation' (as used by Scott) to translate *Gespräch*.

14. Quoted by Heidegger in *Gesamtausgabe*, vol. 39, p. 54.

15. For a good introduction to the question of 'gods' in Pound's early poetry, see Hugh Witemeyer, *The Poetry of Ezra Pound. Forms and Renewals 1908–1920* (Berkeley, Calif.: University of California Press, 1969) pp. 23–43.

16. I could just sketch a few striking parallel axes, which should not, obviously, be understood as individual or psychological determinations, but as epochal markers: a similar strategy of 'translation', which emphasises literal rendering – George Steiner's book *After Babel* (London: Oxford University Press, 1975) esp. pp. 322–33, helps situate the parallel tendencies; exile and wanderings, final silence and 'contemplation'; a sense of tragedy in the absence and presence of the gods, linked with a 'national' (in a broad sense) responsibility of poetry, and the question of the elaboration of a new idiom 'to think in' (*LE*, p. 194).

17. Heidegger, *Poetry, Language, Thought*, p. 11.

18. Ibid., pp. 61–2.

19. Theodor W. Adorno, 'Parataxis', *Noten zur Literatur III* (Frankfurt, Suhrkamp, 1965) p. 164.

20. Hugh Kenner, *The Poetry of Ezra Pound* (New York, New Directions, 1951), and *The Pound Era* (London: Faber, 1972) p. 81–93.

21. Adorno, *Noten zur Literatur III*, p. 193. References to this work are henceforward given in the text.

22. This has been extremely well elaborated and documented by Eva Hesse, first in her postscript to her edition and translation of Pound's last drafts and fragments, *Ezra Pound, Letzte Texte* (Zürich: Arche, 1975) pp. 55–78, and in her monumental Ezra Pound, *Von Sinn und Wahnsinn* (Munich: Kindler, 1978), which is a shortened version of an unpublished book with the same title.

23. Jacques Lacan, 'Traduction de "Logos" de Heidegger', *La Psychanalyse*, 1956, no. 1, pp. 59–79. For a philosophical approach to Lacan's interpretation of Heidegger, see the very critical remarks of Philippe Lacoue-Labarthe and Jean-Luc Nancy, *Le Titre de la Lettre* (Paris: Galilée, 1972).

24. Jacques Lacan, 'Hommage fait à Marguerite Duras du Ravissement de Lol V. Stein', *Cahiers Renaud-Barrault* (Paris: Gallimard, 1965) p. 9.

25. Roland Barthes, *Leçon* (Paris: Gallimard, 1978) p. 20.

26. Roland Barthes, *S/Z*, trs. Richard Miller (London: Jonathan Cape, 1975) p. 21.

27. The best survey of this tradition is to be found in Catherine Fuchs, 'Les problématiques énonciatives: esquisse d'une présentation historique et critique' *DRLAV-Revue de linguistique* (Paris) vol. VIII, no. 25 (1981) pp. 35–60.

28. Georges Mounin and Nicolas Ruwet have been among the more vocal defenders of Saussurean orthodoxy, but a more relevant criticism will be found in Jean-François Lyotard, *Discours, Figure* (Paris: Klincksieck, 1971).

29. Jean-Luc Nancy, *Ego Sum*, Paris, Aubier-Flammarion, 1979, p. 18.

30. For the terminological problems in English, see Oswald Ducrot and Tzvetan Todorov, *Encyclopedic Dictionary of the Sciences of Language*, trs. Catherine Porter (Oxford: Blackwell, 1981) p. 323–8.

31. In a paper which cannot have failed to attract Lacan's attention, since it was published in the *Journal de la Psychiatrie* in 1958. 'De la subjectivité dans le langage' has now been collected in *Problèmes de Linguistique Générale*, vol. I (Paris: Gallimard, 1966) pp. 258–66. See also 'Remarques sur la fonction du langage dans la découverte freudienne', ibid., pp. 75–87.

32. Jacques Lacan, 'Subversion of the Subject and the Dialectic of Desire in the Freudian Unconscious', in *Ecrits. A Selection*, trs. Alan Sheridan (London: Tavistock, 1977) pp. 292–325. I shall refer to this translation as *Ecrits/S*, to distinguish it from the complete French text: *Ecrits* (Paris: Seuil, 1966) pp. 793–837. See also Jacques Lacan, *The Four Fundamental Concepts of Psycho-analysis*, trs. Alan Sheridan (Harmondsworth: Penguin, 1979).

33. *Ecrits/S*, p. 90. References to this collection are henceforward given in the text.

34. Jacques Lacan, *Le Séminaire*, vol. II: *Le Moi dans la Théorie de Freud et dans la Technique de la Psychanalyse* (Paris: Seuil, 1978) p. 59.

35. *Ecrits*, p. 439 (my translation).

36. See Antoine Compagnon's remarks in *La Seconde Main ou le Travail de la Citation* (Paris: Seuil, 1979) pp. 57–92.

37. Lacan, *Four Fundamental Concepts*, p. 141.

38. Sigmund Freud, *Jokes and their Relation to the Unconscious*, trs. James Strachey (London: Routledge and Kegan Paul, 1960) p. 100.

39. Ibid., p. 144.

40. See Luce Irigaray, 'Communications linguistique et spéculaire', *Cahiers pour l'Analyse* (Paris), no. 3 (May 1966) pp. 39–55.

41. 'If I thought that my reply would be to someone who would ever return to earth, this flame would remain without further movement; but, as no one has ever returned alive from this gulf, if what I hear is true, I can answer you with no fear of infamy' (Dante, *Inferno*, XXVII.61–6). Guido da Montefel is thus as deceived by 'what he hears true' in Hell as by the Pope's false promise when he was living: the Pope had promised that he would be absolved of his sins in advance, as it were, but the devils do take him all the same. For Eliot, this symbolises in a nutshell the impossibility of 'telling all' the truth without having recourse to the Other.

42. Lacan, *Four Fundamental Concepts*, p. vii.

43. See Carroll F. Terrell's indispensable *Companion to the Cantos of Ezra Pound* (Berkeley, Calif.: University of California Press, 1980) pp. 32–4.

44. This is the conclusion of Canto XC, p. 609 ('Love is where the eyes is', taken from Richard of St Victor). See Chapter 6.

45. 'In Pound I am confronted by the tragic Double of our day. He is the demonstration of our duality. In language and form he is as forward, as much the revolutionist as Lenin. But in social, economic and political action he is as retrogressive as the Czar' – Charles Olson, 'Canto 3, Jan. 24. 1946', in *Charles*

302 *Notes*

Olson and Ezra Pound. An Encounter at St Elizabeths, ed. Catherine Seelye (New York: Viking, 1975) p. 53.

CHAPTER ONE: SYMPTOMS AND VOICES

1. Rémy de Gourmont, *La Culture des Idées* (Paris: Mercure de France, 1964) p. 17. (Originally published 1900).
2. See Roland McHugh, *Annotations to Finnegans Wake* (Baltimore: Johns Hopkins University Press, 1980) p. v.
3. See Christine Brooke-Rose, *A ZBC of Ezra Pound* (London, Faber, 1971). The phrase comes at a point when Pound plays with the delayed anticipations created in his reader: 'Without ²muan ¹bpo . . . but I anticipate./ There is no substitute for a lifetime' (Canto xcviii, p. 691).
4. This has been pointed out by Massimo Bacigalupo in *The Forméd Trace. The Later Poetry of Ezra Pound* (New york: Columbia University Press, 1980) p. 400.
5. James Joyce, *Ulysses* (Harmondsworth, Penguin, 1968) p. 190. (Originally published 1922.)
6. James Joyce, *Selected Letters*, ed. Richard Ellmann (London, Faber, 1975) p. 319.
7. Charles E. Yriarte, to whom Pound directly alludes in Canto x, p. 44, was the first to use Malatesta's mailbag for direct information; see *Un Condottiere au XVᵉ Siècle* (Paris, 1882).
8. The Leopoldine Cantos, xlii to xliv, are based on the nine volumes of *Il Monte dei Paschi di Siena e le Aziende in Esso Riunite*, ed. N. Mengozzi (Siena, 1891–1925), and many unpublished manuscripts Pound studies in Siena and elsewhere. See also Carroll F. Terrell's indispensable *Companion to 'The Cantos' of Ezra Pound* (Berkeley, Calif.: University of California Press, 1980) pp. 170–9.
9. See esp. J. P. Sullivan, *Ezra Pound and Sextus Propertius. A Study in Creative Translation* (London: Faber, 1964).
10. In *How to Read*, Pound distinguished between 'Melopoeia', a poetry in which the words are 'charged with some musical property' 'over and above their plain meaning'; 'Phanopoeia', 'a casting of images upon the visual imagination'; and 'Logopoeia', 'the dance of the intellect among words' (*LE*, p. 25).
11. Boris de Rachewiltz, who gave Pound the Egyptian documents on which certain late Cantos, such as xc, xciii and xcix, are based, explains Pound's syncretic technique of condensation in 'Pagan and Magic Elements in Ezra Pound's Works', in *New Approaches to Ezra Pound*, ed. Eva Hesse (London: Faber, 1969) pp. 179–83.
12. See Jacques Aubert, *Introduction à l'Esthétique de James Joyce* (Paris: Didier, 1973), and ch. 6 for a discussion of Pound's reading of Aristotle.
13. Such is Max Nänny's thesis in *Ezra Pound: Poetics for an Electric Age* (Bern: Francke, 1973), and esp. 'Oral Dimensions in Ezra Pound', *Paideuma*, vol. vi, no. 1 (Spring 1977) pp. 13–26.
14. See Barbara Eastman, *Ezra Pound's Cantos: The Story of the Text*. One

trivial example: 'Ile des Pinguins' (Faber, 1964, p. 618) becomes 'Ile des Pinquoins' (Faber, 1975, p. 582), instead of 'Ile des Pingouins'.

15. William Carlos Williams, 'Excerpts from a Critical Sketch: A Draft of xxx 'Cantos by Ezra Pound', *Selected Essays* (New York: New Directions, 1954) p. 105.

16. Williams, 'Pound's Eleven New "Cantos" ', *Selected Essays*, p. 169.

17. Walter Sutton, 'A Visit with William Carlos Williams', in *Interviews with William Carlos Williams*, ed. Linda Wagner (New York: New Directions, 1976) p. 44.

18. Williams, *Selected Essays*, p. 109.

19. Charles Olson, *Call me Ishmael* (New York, 1947).

20. Charles Olson, 'Mayan Letters', *Selected Writings*, ed. Robert Creeley (New York: New Directions, 1966) pp. 81–2.

21. Olson, 'Projective Verse', *Selected Writings*, p. 17.

22. Wyndham Lewis, *Time and Western Man* (London, 1927).

23. Pound quotes this sentence often (for example, *SP*, p. 382), but admits in the *Guide* that he cannot find the exact source for it in the original when rereading his *Poetics* (*GK*, pp. 315–6).

24. 'A Visiting Card', written in Italian (*SP*, p. 288).

25. Pound, 'Totalitarian Scholarship and the New Paideuma', *Germany and You* (Berlin, 25 April 1937), quoted in Forrest Read, *'76, One World and the Cantos of Ezra Pound* (Chapel Hill: University of North Carolina Press, 1981) p. 287.

26. Donald Davie, *Pound* (London: Fontana, 1975) p. 90.

27. For a gloss on the exact origin of the cartouche, see de Rachewiltz, *New Approaches to Pound*.

28. "Sort of ignorance", said the old priest to Yeats in a railway train, / "is spreading every day from the schools!" ' (Canto CI, p. 725).

29. *CSP*, pp. 86–7, and 248.

30. Leo Frobenius, *Erlebte Erdteile: Ergebnisse eines deutschen Forscherlebens* (Frankfurt: Veroffentlichung des Forschungsinstitutes für Kulturmorphologie, 1925–9).

31. Ibid., vol. IV: *Vom Völkerstudium zur Philosophie: Der neue Blick* (which is a new version of *Das Paideuma*) p. 18.

32. Ibid., vol. VI: *Monumenta Africana: Der Geist eines Erdteiles*, p. 453.

33. Ibid., pp. 412 and 453. The concept of 'symptom' is found on almost every page from p. 412 to p. 525.

34. Dante's line should read: 'si che'l Giudeo di voi tra voi non rida'. Beatrice explains to Dante the necessity for relinquishing envy, and the fact that Christians have the Old Testament as a guide should suffice for their salvation.

35. Cf. *GB*, pp. 20–4.

36. 'Significato di Leo Frobenius' (1938), repr. in *Il Luto di Gassire, Legenda africana di Leo Frobenius, con due scritti di Ezra Pound* (Milan: Vanni Scheiwiller, 1976) p. 9.

37. 'Continuity', in *'Ezra Pound Speaking'. Radio Speeches of World War II*, ed. Leonard W. Doob (Westport, Conn.: Greenwood Press, 1978) p. 192.

38. 'Poetry = Emotional synthesis, quite as real, quite as realist as any prose (or intellectual) analysis' – *LE*, p. 324n. See also Ch. 5.

39. He starts calling it 'ittisâl' ('Sufi doctrine of union') in his Cavalcanti essay, which relates Cavalcanti to Averroes and Avicenna (*LE*, p. 186). See *GK*, p. 328, for 'atasal', simply glossed as 'union with the divine'.

40. *CSP*, p. 75.

41. 'Je m'habituai à l'hallucination simple. . . . Puis j'expliquai mes sophismes magiques avec l'hallucination des mots!' – 'Alchimie du verbe', from Artur Rimbaud, *Une Saison en Enfer, Oeuvres Complètes* (Paris: Gallimard, 1972) p. 108.

42. An excellent summary of Lacan's definitions of the Real has been given by Stephen Heath in 'Anata mo', *Screen*, vol. 17, no. 4 (Winter 1976–7) pp. 50–5.

43. *The Poetical Works of Longfellow* (New York: Oxford University Press, 1965) pp. 316–17.

44. See particularly Ronald Bush, *The Genesis of Ezra Pound's Cantos* (Princeton, NJ: Princeton University Press, 1976) pp. 75–86; and Leon Surette, *A Light from Eleusis* (Oxford: Clarendon Press, 1979) pp. 9–14.

45. The text of Pound's *Three Cantos* is most easily available in Ronald Bush, *Genesis*, pp. 53–73 (here, p. 53).

46. *LE*, p. 97, and *SR*, p. 58.

47. *ABCR*, pp. 188–91; and *Three Cantos*, in Bush, *Genesis*, p. 54.

48. 'So much for Eglamor. My own month came . . .' (*Sordello*, II.296), which refers to Browning's birthday in May. I use the Centenary edn of *The Works of Robert Browning* (London: Ernest Benn, 1912) vol. I, pp. 179–359.

49. *Three Cantos*, in Bush, *Genesis*, p. 57.

50. Daniel Stempel, 'Browning's *Sordello*: The Art of the Makers-See', *Publications of the Modern Language Association*, vol. 80, p. 561.

51. ' "Et omniformis", Psellos, "omnis/"Intellectus est" ' (Canto XXIII, p. 107). Psellus is a neo-Platonic philosopher who is then linked with Gemistus Plethon. Pound means that the mind can take 'any form' or 'all forms'. See Eva Hesse, *Ezra Pound*, pp. 62–7.

52. *Three Cantos*, in Bush, *Genesis*, p. 57.

53. William Butler Yeats, 'A Packet for Ezra Pound', *A Vision* (London: Macmillan, 1981) pp. 4–5. (Originally published 1931.)

54. William Butler Yeats, Introduction to the *Oxford Book of Modern Verse*, (Oxford: Clarendon Press, 1936) p. xxiv.

55. The only rule Pound gives to a musician is the following: 'A sound of any pitch, or any combination of such sounds, may be followed by a sound of any other pitch, or any combination of such sounds, providing the time-interval between them is properly gauged; and this is true for any series of sounds, chords or arpeggios' ('The Treatise on Harmony', *SP*, p. 77).

56. The leader of the chorus says, 'Silence ! . . .', and Agamemnon answers, 'Again, I have been struck a second time.' Pound has just quoted the two lines as one, and repeats here the 'Silence!' already heard.

57. '*Caina attende*' ('Caina is waiting') comes from *Inferno*, v.107, and means the punishment of traitors.

58. The subject of Euripides' *Bacchae* is the blindness of King Pentheus, who refuses to acknowledge Dionysus and is then torn apart by the Maenads, his mother taking the lead.

59. 'Argicida' refers to Hermes, killer of Argus. See Kenner, *The Pound Era*, p. 361.

60. Malatesta alludes to homosexuality among the Papal legates and officers; cf. Terrell's *Companion*, p. 55.

61. See Chapter 5 for a fuller treatment of 'positive interest'.

62. His suggestion of a 'weekend at the Metropole' is a direct homosexual proposal, owing to the reputation of that hotel in Brighton ('The Fire Sermon', l. 214).

CHAPTER TWO: IDEOGRAM AND IDEOLOGY

1. Letter quoted in Gilbert Chinard, *Jefferson et les Idéologues, d'après sa Correspondance Inédite* (Baltimore: Johns Hopkins University Press, 1925) p. 257. Jefferson answered about a month later and defined 'ideology': 'Tracy comprehends under the word "Ideology" all the subjects which the French term *Morale*, as the correlative to *Physique*. His work on Logic, Government, Political Economy and Morality, he considers as making up the circle of ideological subjects . . .' (11 Jan. 1817, ibid., p. 259).

2. *The New English Weekly*, vol. III, no. 4 (11 May 1933) p. 96.

3. Bush, *Genesis*, pp. 3–20.

4. See Richard Sieburth's excellent synthesis in *Instigations. Ezra Pound and Remy de Gourmont* (Cambridge Mass.: Harvard University Press, 1978).

5. *ABCR*, pp. 36 and 97.

6. See, for instance, Brooke-Rose, *ZBC*, pp. 109–10.

7. Marcel Granet, *La Pensée Chinoise* (Paris: Albin Michel, 1968) p. 48. (Originally published 1934.)

8. Ibid., p. 49.

9. Ibid., pp. 49–50.

10. *'Ezra Pound Speaking'*, p. 382 (script dated early 1941).

11. Ibid., p. 89.

12. For a complete appraisal of the Idéologues' influence on Stendhal, see Emmet Kennedy, *A Philosophe in the Age of Revolution. Destutt de Tracy and the Origins of 'Ideology'* (Philadelphia: American Philosophical Society, 1978). De Tracy is mentioned twice in the Cantos (pp. 420 and 572).

13. Kennedy, *A Philosophe in the Age of Revolution*, p. 46.

14. Ibid., p. 47. See also Georges Gusdorf, 'La conscience révolutionnaire. Les Idéologues', in *Les Sciences Humaines et la Pensée Occidentale*, vol. VIII, (Paris, Payot, 1978); and Michel Foucault's brief but illuminating analysis in *Les Mots et les Choses* (Paris: Gallimard, 1966) p. 95–136.

15. Chinard, *Jefferson et les Idéologues*, p. 196.

16. In Canto LV, Napoleon is superposed on Chi-Tsong through a humorous allusion to the tag attributed to Napoleon's mother ('Pourvu que ça dure' – 'If only it could last!', spoken with a Corsican accent): 'Red the robe of his dynasty/pourvou que ça doure, said his mother/He said: let brothers inherit . . .' (p. 294). For a recent analysis of Pound's shifting relationship to Napoleon, see Andrew J. Kappel, 'Napoleon and Talleyrand in the Cantos', *Paideuma*, vol. XI, no. 1 (Spring and Summer 1982) pp. 55–78.

17. Jefferson sent the translation of de Tracy's *Economie Politique* to John

Adams in November 1818 with the comment that he had hopes 'of advancing our countrymen somewhat in that science; the most profound ignorance of which threatened irreparable disaster during the late war, and by the parasite institution of banks is now consuming the public industry' (Chinard, *Jefferson et les Idéologues*, p. 182). Adams approved, and Jefferson replied in March 1819, 'I am delighted with your high approbation of Tracy's book. The evils of this deluge of paper money are not to be removed, until our citizens are generally and radically instructed in their cause and consequences, and silence by their authority the interested clamors and sophistry of speculating, shaving and banking institutions' (ibid., p. 272).

18. Ibid., p. 182.

19. Cf. *GK*, pp. 35–7, and Chapter 5 for a discussion of Pound's economics.

20. The *Guide* was written in 1937, published in 1938. The dynastic Cantos were published in 1940 by Faber, along with the Adams Cantos.

21. I have not attempted to be consistent in my transliterations from the Chinese, following Pound's example in that matter; when Pound quotes French sources, up to the Pisan Cantos, he uses the old French transliteration of de Mailla's *Histoire*; he then shifts to Mathews's newer system in the later Cantos. I am here using Jacques Gernet's handy synthesis in *Le Monde Chinois*, (Paris: Armand Colin, 1972) pp. 301–2, which follows the modernised Chinese spelling.

22. See Carroll F. Terrell, 'The Chinese Dynastic Cantos', *Paideuma*, vol. v, no. 1 (1976) pp. 95–9. The best presentation of what is called the 'Quarrel of rites' is to be found in Jacques Gernet, *Chine et Christianisme. Action et Réaction* (Paris: Gallimard, 1982).

23. H. G. Creel, *Confucius, the Man and the Myth* (New York: John Day, 1949) pp. 273–8.

24. Joseph Anne-Marie de Moyriac de Mailla, *Histoire Générale de la Chine*, 13 vols, ed. M. le Roux des Hautesrayes (Paris, 1777–85).

25. Arthur Griffith appears in the Cantos on p. 85 with this phrase, which recurs in the later Cantos. Cf. *GK*, p. 105.

26. Cf. *CSP*, p. 205; and the remarks made by Peter Brooker in *A Student's Guide to the Selected Poems of Ezra Pound* (London: Faber, 1979) p. 192.

27. Paul Fort, 'Ballades Françaises' (1917) in *On Loge à Pied et à Cheval, Oeuvres Complètes*, vol. x, with a foreword by Remy de Gourmont (Paris: Flammarion, 1947) p. 109.

28. *Confino* is the Fascist term for exile, *ammassi* means the system of grain-stores invented by the Italian regime, and *fondego* refers back to the Leopoldine reforms of Siena.

29. Séraphin Couvreur, *Chou King, Les Annales de la Chine* (Paris: Cathasia, 1950) p. 189.

30. See Thomas Grieve's useful edition and annotation of the passages from the *Chou King* quoted by Pound in 'Rock-Drill', *Paideuma*, vol. iv, no. 2–3 (Fall and Winter 1975) pp. 362–508, esp. p. 429 n. 1.

31. See, for instance, Sarah Kofman, *Camera Obscura. De l'Idéologie* (Paris, Galilée, 1973); Terry Eagleton, *Criticism and Ideology* (London: New Left Books, 1976); and Olivier Reboul, *Langage et Idéologie* (Paris: Presses Universitaires de France, 1980).

32. Gernet, *Le Monde Chinois*, pp. 93–4.

33. This has disappeared from the 1975 Faber edn, but is still retained in the 1968 edn.

34. This is the aim of Etiemble's book *Confucius (Maître K'ong)* (Paris: Gallimard, 1966).

35. I refer to the transformation of the note on p. 446 in which the 1968 edn of the *Cantos*: 'Rays ideogram from Fenollosa collection', which becomes in the 1975 edn, 'Rays idiogram from Fenollosa collection' (p. 255). See also pp. 167–8 of the present book.

CHAPTER THREE: EZRA POUND AND PECUCHET

1. James Joyce, *Letters*, ed. Stuart Gilbert (London: Faber, 1957) p. 297.

2. See the long, inspired essay 'James Joyce and Pécuchet' (1922), in Forrest Read's edn of the correspondence between Joyce and Pound, *Pound/Joyce. Letters and Essays* (London, Faber, 1968) pp. 200–10.

3. Frederick K. Sanders, *John Adams Speaking. Pound's Sources for the Adams Cantos* (Orono: University of Maine Press, n. d. [1975]). I follow his practice, and shall refer to *The Works of John Adams*, 10 vols, ed. with a biography and notes by Charles Francis Adams (Boston, Mass.: Little, Brown, 1850–6) as *WJA*, with volume and page number.

4. Surette, *A Light from Eleusis*, p. 166.

5. Quoted in Stock, *Life of Pound*, p. 480.

6. Stéphane Mallarmé, 'Crise de vers', *Oeuvres Complètes*, ed. H. Mondor and G. Jean-Aubry (Paris: Gallimard, 1945) p. 366.

7. T. S. Eliot, *After Strange Gods. A Primer of Modern Heresy* (London: Faber, 1934) p. 41.

8. Ibid., p. 29.

9. ' "If he wd/ *only* get rid of Ciano' groaned the admiral" ' note the 'Pisan Cantos' (p. 470), and the several remarks in this sequence about the 'dishonesty' of Italian officials aim above all at Ciano's nepotism.

10. Stock, *Life of Pound*, p. 480.

11. See the suggestions proposed in Terrell's *Companion*, p. 273.

12. Walter Benjamin, 'Karl Kraus', *Über Literatur* (Frankfurt: Suhrkamp, 1969) pp. 133–5.

13. See, for instance, G. C. F. Mohnike, *Kleanthes der Stoiker* (Greifwald: Ernst Mauritius, 1814) pp. 24–5, and text p. 114.

14. Walter Benjamin, 'Theses on the Philosophy of History', *Illuminations*, trs. by Harry Zohn (London: Fontana, 1973) p. 256.

15. See the end of Voltaire's *Le Siècle de Louis Quatorze* (Paris: Garnier Flammarion, 1967) vol. II, pp. 150ff. I owe this point to Joel Shapiro's unpublished thesis on Pound and Segalen.

16. For a full treatment of Coke's role in the Cantos, see David M. Gordon, 'The Azalea is Grown', *Paideuma*, vol. IV, no. 2–3 (Fall and Winter 1975) pp. 223–99.

CHAPTER FOUR: THE 'PISAN CANTOS'

1. David Jones, *Anathemata* (London: Faber, 1952) pp. 28–9.

2. See Thomas Szasz, *The Myth of Mental Illness* (New York, 1961), and *The Manufacture of Madness* (New York, 1970); Eva Hesse, *Ezra Pound*, pp. 339–419; Michel Foucault, *Histoire de la Folie à l'Age classique*, nouvelle édition (Paris: Gallimard, 1972).

3. *Charles Olson and Ezra Pound*, pp. 55 and 75.

4. Ibid., p. 46.

5. Sigmund Freud, 'Über den Gegensinn der Urworte' (1910), in *Studienausgabe*, vol. IV: *Psychologische Schriften* (Frankfurt: Fischer, 1978) pp. 229–34.

6. Ibid., p. 233. Upward is important in that context because he offered a very early model of mythical ambivalence, pointing out the reversal of the priest/victim in all models of sacrificial divinities. See the very stimulating paper by A. D. Moody (A. D. Moody, 'Pound's Allen Upward', *Paideuma*, IV, no. 1 (Spring 1975) pp. 55–70.

7. Nicolas Abraham and Maria Torok, *Cryptonymie: Le Verbier de l'homme aux loup* (Paris: Aubier-Flammarion, 1976).

8. Jacques Derrida, 'Fors', Foreword to *Cryptonymie*, p. 70.

9. *Ezra Pound Speaking*, p. 119.

10. I follow the text of the 1968 Faber edition, the 1975 being incorrect.

11. Victor Bérard, *Les Phéniciens et l'Odyssée* (Paris, Armand Colin, 1902–3) vol. II, pp. 563–4.

12. Ibid., p. 561.

13. See Guy Davenport, 'Pound and Frobenius', in *Motive and Method in the Cantos*, ed. Lewis Leary (New York: Columbia University Press, 1954) p. 52. About the legends of the Wandjina, see I. M. Crawford, *The Art of the Wandjina (Aboriginal Cave Paintings in Kimberley, Western Australia)* (Oxford University Press, 1968), and Hans Nevermann, Ernest A. Worms and Helmut Petri, *Die Religionen der Südsee und Australiens* (Stuttgart: Kohlhammer, 1968). This last book describes the Wandjinas discovered by the Frobenius expedition of 1938–9, thus Pound's direct source for this fertility cult (pp. 219–21). The cave paintings are painted afresh by each travelling aborigine, thus the colours never seem to get old, and fertility is ensured.

14. See Serge Boulgakov, *Le Paraclet*, translated from the Russian by C. Andronikov (Paris: Aubier, 1946).

15. See Pound's 'divagation' on sperm as a metaphor for intelligence, currency and creation in his *Postscript* to Remy de Gourmont's *Natural Philosophy of love*, and Chapter 5 in the present study.

16. Europa is described by Ovid, *Metamorphoses*, II, 832–75, and the legend has subsequently been integrated into Christian allegories, such as the *Ovide moralisé*, which took Augustine and Raban Maur as authorities.

17. *Ezra Pound speaking*, p. 227.

18. Which Pound had written *digenes* in the first versions of these *Cantos*. See Moody's 'Pound's Allen Upward'.

19. Eva Hesse, 'A Redefinition of the Problem of mo 畧 (M 4557) in *Canto* 74 in the Light of its Source', *Paideuma*, vol. VIII, no. 3 (Winter 1979) pp. 407–8.

20. 'In the Pentateuch, the verb *gala* is often used to refer to the gesture of uncovering a man's or a woman's genitals. . . . YHWH can also be the agent of such an exposure' (André Chouraqui, 'Liminaire pour l'Apocalypse', in *Un*

Pacte Neuf: Lettres, Contemplation de Yohanân, trs. A. Chouraqui (Paris: Desclée de Brouwer, 1977) p. 157.

21. See Davenport's paper in *Motive and Method*, n. 13.

22. Quoted in Stock, *Life of Pound*, p. 530.

23. See Walter Baumann, 'Carleton, Paquin and Salzburg', *Paideuma*, vol. XI, no. 3 (Winter 1982) pp. 442–5.

24. *CSP*, p. 269. The poem has a caption which reads, 'Beauty is the marking-time, the stationary vibration, the feigned ecstasy of an arrested impulse, unable to reach its natural end.' And, when Pound pictures himself as 'Old Ez' ('Old Ez folded his blankets / Neither Eos nor Hesperus has suffered wrong at my hands' – Canto LXXIX, p. 488), he subtly alludes to Hulme's poem 'The Embankment', which describes the 'fantasia of a fallen gentleman' and concludes, 'Oh God, make small / The old star-eaten blanket of the sky, / That I may fold it round me and in comfort lie' (*CSP*, p. 270).

25. See Bernard Renaud, *La Formation du Livre de Michée. Thèse de la Faculté de Théologie de Strasbourg* (Lille, 1976) p. 201.

26. The structuring-function of Morris Speare's *The Pocket Book of Verse* in the 'Pisan Cantos' has not yet been fully explored.

27. Clark Emery has shown in *Ideas into Action. A Study of Pound's Cantos* (Coral Gables: University of Miami Press, 1958) pp. 9ff., the influence of Thaddeus Zielinski's *La Sibylle* (Paris, 1925).

28. Quoted in Stock, *Life of Pound*, p. 530.

29. See the motif of Jewish Law in Pound's economics, as developed in Chapter 5.

30. *Charles Olson and Ezra Pound*, p. 77.

31. See John R. Searle, 'Proper Names', in *Philosophy and Ordinary Language*, ed. C. E. Caton (Urbana: University of Illinois Press, 1963) pp. 154–61; and Leonard Linsky, *Referring* (London: Routledge and Kegan Paul, 1967).

32. Published in *Paideuma*, vol. VIII, no. 3 (Winter 1979) p. 456.

33. Quoted by Mary de Rachewiltz in 'Fragments of an Atmosphere', *Agenda*, vol. 17, nos 3–4 vol. 18, no. 1 (Autumn, Winter and Spring 1979/80) p. 164.

34. *'Ezra Pound Speaking'*, p. 178.

35. *'Ezra Pound Speaking'*, p. 262.

36. Quoted by de Rachewiltz, in *Agenda*, vol. 17, nos 3–4 vol. 18, no. 1, p. 165.

37. Basil Bunting, *Collected Poems* (London: Faber, 1978) notes on p. 148.

38. Kenner, *The Pound Era*, p. 430.

39. Michael Reck, *Ezra Pound: A Close-up* (New York: McGraw-Hill, 1967) p. 152.

40. Hugh Kenner, 'The Possum in the Cave', in *Allegory and Representation*, ed. Stephen J. Greenblatt (Baltimore: Johns Hopkins University Press, 1981) p. 140.

41. See the recent interpretation of that song written in the 1910s by P. Marinier and L. Lelièvre, 'La Biaiseuse', in Marie Paule Belle, *Mon Premier Album* (Paris: Carrère, 1982).

42. For relevant information, see *Fabulous Fashion, 1907–1967*,

Catalogue of the Costume Institute, Metropolitan Museum of Art, New York (n.d.). See also Baumann, in *Paideuma*, vol. XI, no. 3.

43. *Ezra Pound and Music. The Complete Criticism*, ed. R. Murray Schafer (London: Faber, 1978) p. 219.

44. '. . . en casque de crystal rose les baladines' is repeated p. 480 and rhymes with the old French song 'o-hon dit que'ke fois au vi'age/qu'une casque ne sert pour rien/'hien de tout . . .'. Pound quotes Stuart Merrill's sonnet he praised in a paper repr. in *Make it New* (1935). See Bacigalupo's *The Formèd Trace*, pp. 355–56.

45. Pound spells it 'ittisâl' in *LE*, p. 186.

46. The Homeric 'Hymn to Aphrodite' is translated by Hugh G. Evelyn-White in *Hesiod. The Homeric Hymns and Homerica* (Cambridge, Mass.: Loeb Library, Harvard University Press, 1977) p. 417. (Originally published 1914.)

47. Ibid., p. 427. This second hymn to Aphrodite is the one from which Andreas Divus translates, thus finding its place in the first Canto.

48. Cf. 'Mauberley 1920': 'Drifted . . . drifted precipitate,/ Asking time to be rid of . . ./ Of his bewilderment; to designate/ His new-found orchid. . . . He had passed, inconscient, full gaze,/ The wide-banded irides/ And Botticellian sprays implied/ In their diastasis' (CSP, pp. 217–18).

49. William Carlos Williams, *Paterson* (New York: New Directions, 1963) pp. 77–8.

50. Williams explains that his poem proposes a riddle, 'the riddle of a man/ and a woman' (*Paterson*, p. 107), 'a riddle (in the Joyceian mode –/ or otherwise,/ it is indifferent which)' (p. 105). Part of the riddle is explained by the analysis of 'credit', which follows the lines of Pound (cf. Ch. 5), p. 193); part is explained by history: Williams has chosen the town of Paterson because it is situated on the Falls of the Passaic, thus taking up the theme of his earliest long poem, *The Wanderer*, and also because it was a site elected by Hamilton for its industrial potential – by a kind of submerged pun, Hamilton and Paterson, the founder of the Bank of England, are united on an American ground. But, of course, the core of the riddle lies in the coincidence of the opposites, man and woman, father and son.

51. *Paterson*, p. 78.

52. See the excellent analysis Michael Bernstein devotes to the link between the *Cantos* and *Paterson* in *The Tale of the Tribe. Ezra Pound and the Modern Verse Epic* (Princeton, NJ: Princeton University Press, 1980) pp. 201–16. I am not reproaching Williams for having omitted real names; indeed, such creations as Sam Patch and Mrs Cumming, even if they appear just once, are unforgettable, and more emblematic than either Paquin or Blunt in the *Cantos*. But Williams's relative failure comes perhaps from his inability or refusal to fuse the two modes, the prose passages and the poetic or lyrical moments, in a general surface made up of particulars. Indeed, at one point Williams considered transcribing the newspaper-cuttings into a sort of verse. See Mike Weaver, *William Carlos Williams. The American Background* (Cambridge: Cambridge University Press, 1971).

53. The whole of the *Guide to Kulchur* could be read as a 'nomenclature' in a new mode, and the ultimate example of the genre.

54. Giambattista Vico, *The New Science*, trs. T. Bergin and Max Fisch (Ithaca, NY: Cornell University Press, 1970) Book II, ch. 4, section 433.

55. Ibid., p. 141.

56. Especially in 'Spring and All', a sequence of poems showing Williams at his best, in *Imaginations* (New York, New Directions, 1970) pp. 88–151.

57. James J. Wilhelm, *The Later Cantos of Ezra Pound* (New York: Walker, 1977) p. 99.

58. *The Sacred Edict of K'ang Hsi*, trs. F. W. Baller (Orono: University of Maine, 1979) Foreword, p. iv. (Originally published 1921.)

59. Cf. *GK*, pp. 133 and 266; and *SP*, p. 283.

CHAPTER FIVE: POUNDWISE

1. John Ruskin, *Unto This Last* (London: Dent, 1907) Essay IV, pp. 170–1.

2. 'The more I read your poetry, the more I am convinced it is the best of its time. And your economics are *right*. We see it more and more in Vietnam. You showed us who's making a profit out of war' – Allen Ginsberg, 'A Conversation between Ezra Pound and Allen Ginsberg' (1968), quoted in Reck, *Pound: A Close-up*, p. 154. It is thus interesting to follow Ginsberg's allegiance, from his early administration of Williams, as he still lived in Paterson, to his approval of Pound's theories, although he felt very much a Jew and a Buddhist.

3. Kurt Heinzelman, *The Economics of the Imagination* (Amherst: University of Massachussetts Press, 1980) p. 269.

4. Brooks Adams, *The Law of Civilization and Decay* (London: Swan, Sonnenschein, 1895) p. 294.

5. Kenner, *The Pound Era*, p. 324. See also Hugh Witemeyer, 'Ruskin and the Signed Capital in Canto 45', *Paideuma*, vol. IV, no. 1 (Spring 1975) pp. 85–88.

6. See Philippe Jaudel, *La Pensée Sociale de John Ruskin, Thèse Paris IV*, (Lille, 1972), for a detailed analysis of Ruskin's economics.

7. John Ruskin, *The Political Economy of Art* (New York: John Wiley, 1870). References are given in the text.

8. See above all Marc Shell, *The Economy of Literature* (Baltimore: Johns Hopkins University Press, 1978) and Eva Hesse, *Ezra Pound, Von Sinn und Wahnsinn*, for a discussion of these terms in relation to Pound. I have also used Arnaud Berthoud, *Aristote et l'argent* (Paris: Maspéro, 1981).

9. Quoted as a footnote by Pound, added by Cookson (*SP*, p. 270).

10. See entry 'Usury' in the *Encyclopaedia Judaica* (Jerusalem, 1971) vol. 16, pp. 27–32.

11. Cf. Daniel Pearlman's fascinating and provocative paper 'Ezra Pound: America's Wandering Jew', *Paideuma*, vol. IX, no. 3 (Winter 1980) pp. 461–80.

12. André Pézard, *Dante sous la Pluie de Feu* (Paris: Vrin, 1950).

13. Christopher Hollis, *The Two Nations. A Financial Study of English History* (London, Routledge, 1935) pp. 251–2.

14. See Jacques Derrida, 'La pharmacie de Platon', *La Dissémination* (Paris: Seuil, 1972).

15. See Ch. 4, n. 52. In *The Two Nations* Hollis quotes Paterson (p. 30), and refers to Ruskin and Disraeli as his main authorities.

16. Karl Marx, *Das Kapital. Kritik der politischen Ökonomie*, in Karl Marx and Friedrich Engels, *Werke* (Berlin: Dietz, 1970) vol. 23, p. 513.

17. Ibid., p. 517.

18. Karl Marx, *Capital: A Critical Analysis of Capitalist Production*, trs. from the 3rd German edn by S. Moore and E. Aveling (London: Allen and Unwin, 1938) p. 780. (Edition originally published 1889.)

19. *'Ezra Pound Speaking'*, p. 392.

20. The question Mussolini asked to Pound is quoted in *J/M* and *GK* (for instance, p. 105) several times, but strangely enough only appears in the *Cantos after* the tragedy of Pisa and Mussolini's death: see Canto LXXXVII, p. 569.

21. Jürgen Habermas, *Technik und Wissenschaft als 'Ideologie'* (Frankfurt: Suhrkamp, 1968) p. 163.

22. Silvio Gesell, *The Natural Economic Order*, trs. Philip Pye (London: Peter Owen, 1958) p. 372. (Gesell's sentence is: 'Marx finds nothing to criticise in money', which concludes an analysis of 'interest' deriving from the 'form of money'.)

23. *'Ezra Pound Speaking'*, p. 353.

24. Ibid., p. 12.

25. Ibid., p. 18.

26. This is the passage on 'interest-bearing capital' which Pound later alludes to by the tag 'Das Leihkapital'; I translate rather literally a long sentence in Marx, *Das Kapital* Bk III, pt 5, ch. 21 (*Marx–Engels Werke*, vol. 25, p. 357).

27. Ibid., p. 359.

28. See *Charles Olson and Ezra Pound*, p. 65.

29. On this point, see Eva Hesse, *Ezra Pound, von Sinn und Wahnsinn*, pp. 198–222; and, for a more detailed presentation of the Proudhon–Marx controversy, Eva Hesse, *Die Wurzeln der Revolution, Theorien der individuellen und der kollektiven Freiheit* (Munich: Hanser, 1974) pp. 336–73.

30. Marx, *Das Kapital, Marx–Engels Werke*, vol. 25, p. 617.

31. On this point see Eva Hesse, *Ezra Pound*, pp. 214–19. Proudhon had rediscovered John Law's insight, merely transforming the creation of paper-money by state-controlled institutions into a free credit controlled by workers' organisations. Pound finally found out in Venice that Law had been rehabilitated by Napoleon, or, less directly, by Alexander Law Lauriston, Governor of the Venetian Province, in 1808. Canto C, which praises Napoleon's 'Code out of Corsica' (p. 714), quotes Law's marble funeral plaque in the pavement of San Moise in Venice: "29, John Law obit / as you may read in San Moisé, in the pavement, / SUMBAINAI' (p. 714). The plaque actually reads: 'Honori et Memoriai / Joannis Law Edinburgensis / Regii Galliarum aerarii / Praefecti Clarissimi / A. MDCCXIX Aet. LVIII Defuncti / Gentilis sui cineres / Ex aede D. Geminiani Diruta / Huc transferri curavit / Alexander Law Lauriston / Napoleoni Maximo / Adiutor in Castris / Praefectus Legionis / Gubernator Venetiarum / A MDCCCVIII.' It will by now have become obvious that one should relate John Law and John Adams, at least by the evocative magic of their 'reassembled' (*sumbainai*) names.

32. I quote from Karl Marx, *Capital* vol. III (Moscow: Foreign Language Publishing House, 1962) p. 583. References to this edition are henceforward given in the text.

33. Marx, *Das Kapital, Marx–Engels Werke*, vol. 25, p. 405.

34. Aquinas, *Summa Theologica*, ii.2, q. lxxviii, art. i: 'He commits usury who seeks to get a retribution *twice*, once as the equivalent of the object exchanged, once as the use of its value.' See John T. Noonan's useful synthesis, *The Scholastic Analysis of Usury* (Cambridge, Mass.: University of Massachussetts Press, 1957) pp. 53–4 and *passim*.

35. Ibid., pp. 106–17.

36. Ibid.

37. Ibid.

38. See Sieburth, *Instigations*, p. 17 and *passim*.

39. *'Ezra Pound Speaking'*, p. 150.

40. Gianni Toniolo, *L'Economia dell' Italia Fascista* (Rome: Laterza, 1980) pp. 183–6.

41. Ibid., p. 290.

42. Mary de Rachewiltz, *Discretions. Ezra Pound, Father and Teacher* (New York: New Directions, 1975) p. 70.

43. R. H. Tawney, *Religion and the Rise of Capitalism* (Harmondsworth: Penguin, 1966) p. 55. (Originally published 1926.)

44. Noonan, *Scholastic Analysis of Usury*, p. 44.

45. A.R. Orage, 'Social Credit', *The Social Credit Pamphleteer* (London: Stanley Nott, 1935) pp. 12–13.

46. Ibid.

47. Gesell, *The Natural Economic Order*, p. 281.

48. Ibid.

49. John Maynard Keynes, *The General Theory of Employment, Interest and Money* (London: Macmillan, 1964) pp. 353–8. Further references are given in the text. (Originally published 1936.)

50. In Canto xxii, pp. 101–2. See also Earle Davis, *Vision Fugitive. Ezra Pound and Economics* (Lawrence: University Press of Kansas, 1968) pp. 60–7.

51. A. R. Orage, *An Alphabet of Economics* (London, Fisher Unwin, 1917) p. 90.

52. 'Money', ibid., p. 87. See also Hilaire Belloc, *Economics for Helen* (London: Arrowsmith, 1924).

53. Remy de Gourmont, 'La dissociation des idées' (1899), in *La Culture des Idées*, pp. 65–7. As he makes plain on p. 64, the entire field covered by these two terms would be that of *catachresis* ('De telles associations sont nécessairement des plus fugitives, à moins que la langue ne les adopte et n'en fasse un de ces tropes dont elle aime a s'enrichir; il ne faudrait pas être surpris que ce pli d'un câble s'appelât le "genou" du cable'). Dissociation aims at discovering the original tropological movement of language.

54. Ibid., p. 68.

55. De Gourmont gives a small number of examples, starting with the dissociation of 'decadence' and 'Byzantium', and curiously concluding the dissociation of 'love' from 'generation' by a convoluted allusion to the practice of incest among the lower classes. (pp. 72–3)

56. *The Social Crediter*, 28 July 1945, quoted by Dennis Klinck in 'Pound, Social Credit, and the Critics', *Paideuma*, vol. iv, nos. 2–3 (Fall and Winter 1975) p. 234.

57. Alexander del Mar, *A History of Monetary Systems* (New York: Kelley, 1969). (Originally published 1895.)

58. *'Ezra Pound Speaking'*, p. 202.

59. Bacigalupo, *The Forméd Trace*, p. 349.

60. For a survey of psychoanalytical theories of money since Freud, see Ernest Borneman, *Psychoanalyse des Geldes* (Frankfurt: Suhrkamp, 1973), to be contrasted with the classic by Norman O. Brown, *Life against Death* (London: Sphere, 1968).

61. Stock, *Life of Pound*, p. 296.

62. Pound, Postscript to Remy de Gourmont, *The Natural Philosophy of Love*, trs. Pound (New York: Rarity Press, 1931) p. 170. (References are henceforward given in the text.) The same mistake about 'male' is reproduced in *PD*, p. 204.

63. For a modern development of the same idea from a psychoanalytical point of view, see Tobie Nathan, *La Psychanalyse et son Double. La Copulation des insectes est l'Actualisation de nos Fantasmes Sexuels* (Claix: La Pensée Sauvage, 1979).

64. Alain de Lille, *Summa de Arte Praedicatoria*, XXVI; quoted in Pézard, *Dante sous la Pluie de Feu*, p. 303, no. 5. (Verboseness comes from semen which did not fructify.)

65. Dante, *Convivio*, IV.21 (pp. 267ff.).

66. Joseph Needham, *Science and Civilization in China*, vol. 2: *History of Scientific Thought* (Cambridge: Cambridge University Press, 1962) p. 150, n. *a*.

67. Cf. Ian F. A. Bell, *Critic as Scientist. The Modernist Poetics of Ezra Pound* (London: Methuen, 1981) pp. 211–16.

68. *Pound/Joyce*, p. 144.

69. Among which I would select the excellent chapter 'Identity and the Other Face', in Alan Durant, *Ezra Pound. Identity in Crisis* (Hassocks: Harvester, 1981) pp. 129–66.

70. Joyce, *Ulysses*, pp. 205–206.

71. See the connection between 'Mitteleuropa' and 'Madame *'ΰλη'* in Canto XXXV, pp. 172–5.

72. It is Giulio del Pelo Pardi who discovered these ancient canals and attempted to put the system into practice. See Eva Hesse's note in *Ezra Pound. Letzte Texte*, p. 85.

73. Stock, *Life of Pound*, pp. 350–1.

74. Marx, *Das Kapital, Marx–Engels Werke*, vol. 25, pp. 357 and 516.

75. *The Sacred Edict of K'ang Hsi*, p. 53.

76. The text says 'not take more than 36 per cent. interest', but Baller's note explains that it means 3 per cent (*The Sacred Edict of K'ang Hsi*, p. 32).

77. See Bernhard Karlgren, *Analytic Dictionary of Chinese and Sino-Japanese* (New York: Dover, 1974) p. 240. (Originally published 1923.)

78. Del Mar, *History of Monetary Systems*, p. vii.

79. Ibid., p. viii. Del Mar refers here to his *Science of Money*, (1885; repr. Hawthorne: Omni Publications, 1967): the quotation is the title of ch. 8. References to *The Science of Money* (1967 edn) are henceforward given in the text.

80. See Alexander del Mar, *A History of Monetary Crimes* (1899; repr. Hawthorne: Omni Publications, 1967).

81. Del Mar, *History of Monetary Systems*, pp. vi and 115–16.
82. Aristotle, *The Nicomachean Ethics*, trs. H. Rackman, Cambridge, Mass.: Loeb Library, Harvard University Press, 1975) p. 285. (1st edn 1926; rev. 1934.)
83. Rackham, in his edn of Aristotle's *Ethics*, p. 283.
84. See Introduction, n. 32, for full details.
85. Del Mar, *History of Monetary Systems*, p. 178.
86. *Science of Money*, 1st edn (London: George Bell, 1885) p. 13.
87. *Money Pamphlets by £* (London: Peter Russell, 1952).
88. See *Pound/Joyce*, pp. 13–14 and 16, n. 1. This sign looked more and more like a swatiska during the 1940s, the cross on the 'L' trailing down to the left.
89. Eva Hesse, 'Answer to Question 14', *Paideuma*, vol. II, no. 1 (Spring 1973) p. 144.
90. The term is used by Plato in the *Sophistes*, 259e, in the sense of an 'interweaving' of generic natures, and 240c, in the sense of an 'interweaving' of being and non-being. See Derrida's 'La pharmacie de Platon', in *La Dissemination*, and Jean-Luc Nancy, 'Le ventriloque', in *Mimesis Desarticulations* (Paris, Aubier-Flammarion, 1975) pp. 308–334.
91. Marcel Granet, *La Pensée Chinoise*, p. 364.
92. Charles Norman, *The Case of Ezra Pound* (New York: Funk and Wagnall, 1968) p. 29.
93. As reproduced in Eva Hesse, *Ezra Pound*, p. 442.
94. Mary de Rachewiltz, *Discretions*, p. 100.

CHAPTER SIX: FROM ETHICS TO HERMENEUTICS

1. HD, *Hermetic Definition* (Oxford, Carcanet Press, 1972) II p. 26.
2. Montgomery Butchart, *Money* (London: Stanley Nott, 1935) quotes del Mar.
3. *SP*, p. 422 and *passim*.
4. Ernest Fenollosa, *The Chinese Written Character as a Medium for Poetry* (San Francisco: City Light, 1969) pp. 25–7. (Originally published 1936.)
5. 'From the building of a great temple to the outline of a bowl which the potter turns upon his wheel, all effort is transfused with a single style. Thus classification should be epochal, and in attempting thus to treat it for the first time it becomes possible partially to trace style back to its social and spiritual roots' – Ernest Fenollosa, *Epochs of Chinese and Japanese Art* (New York: Dover, 1963) vol. I, Preface, p. xxvii. (The 1963 edn is a reprint of the 2nd, 1913, edn.)
6. Fenollosa, *The Chinese Written Character*, p. 8.
7. Ibid.
8. Ibid., p. 9 (emphasis added.)
9. From Canto LXXXVI, p. 564 ('Alexander paid the debts of his soldiery') onward, the *Leitmotiv* of Alexander links economic justice and positive – 'Napoleonic' – imperialism.
10. I quote Rackham's edn of *The Nicomachean Ethics* throughout this chapter.

11. See Pierre Aubenque, *La Prudence chez Aristote* (Paris: Presses Universitaires de France, 1963) pp. 43–4.

12. Ibid., p. 77.

13. Couvreur, *Chou King*, p. 159.

14. Heidegger, *Poetry, Language, Thought*, p. 59. The word *techne* derives from *tikto* (bring forth or produce).

15. See '*Ezra Pound Speaking*', p. 391, to find Aristotle placed alongside Adams and Karl Marx.

16. *SP*, p. 151, and Canto LXXXVII, pp. 570 and 572.

17. Pound uses the strangely Hegelian-sounding expression in Canto VIII, p. 31. He borrows it from Fritz Schultze's examination of Gemisthus Plethon, *Georgios Gemistos Plethon und seine reformatorischen Bestrebungen* (Jena, 1874); see Terrell's *Companion*, pp. 35–40.

18. Cf. Bacigalupo's presentation in *The Forméd Trace*, pp. 402–403.

19. This concept owes a lot to the 'spermatic *logoi*' of the Stoics, which Pound knew of through Fiorentino's *History of Philosophy* (*GK*, p. 128), and can easily be integrated into a neo-Platonic world-view.

20. Pound probably used Stephen MacKenna's translation of the *Enneads* (5 vols., 1930), rev. B. S. Page (London, Faber, 1962). I also use Emile Bréhier's edn and translation in six volumes: *Ennéades*, 2nd edn (Paris: Les Belles Lettres, Collection Budé, 1954).

21. Note in *CEP*, p. 296.

22. Plotinus, *Ennéades*, pp. 1–2.

23. James J. Wilhelm, *The Later Cantos of Ezra Pound* (New York: Walker, 1977) p. 161, explains how a servant found a 'martin' with a partridge in its mouth just after the saint had expressed such a wish.

24. Charles de Rémusat, *Saint Anselme de Cantorbéry, Tableau de la vie monastique et de la lutte du pouvoir spirituel avec le pouvoir temporel au onzième siècle*, 2nd edn (Paris: Didier, 1868).

25. Ibid., p. 458.

26. Sigmund Freud, 'Das Medusenhaupt' (1922), in *Gesammelte Werke* (Frankfurt, Fischer, 1966) pp. 47–48.

27. See Wilhelm, *The Later Cantos*, p. 158.

28. Migne's *Patrologia Latina*, vol. 158, ch. 67, col. 213 (part of *Patrologiae Cursus Completus, series (Latina) Prima*, ed. Jacques Paul Migne, 221 vols, Paris, 1844–64). See Wilhelm, *The Later Cantos*, p. 159, which nevertheless does not notice the difference or even contradiction between the original and Pound's version.

29. Pound inverts the order of the words: 'Petits tetins, hanches charnues,/ Elevees, propres, faitisses/ A tenir amoureuses lices . . .' – François Villon, *Oeuvres Poétiques*, ed. André Mary (Paris: Garnier-Flammarion, 1965) p. 66. Cf. *GK*, p. 364, for the score of this passage of his 'Opera'.

30. Plotinus, 'Peri Erotos', *Ennéades*, vol. 3, p. 78.

31. *Ennéades*, vol. 4, pp. 4–5.

32. '. . . *meristhai kai ou meristhai*' – ibid., p. 70.

33. Ibid., p. 9.

34. A. J. Festugière, *Hermétisme et Mystique Païenne* (Paris: Aubier-Montaigne, 1967) pp. 14–16.

35. I am much indebted to Jean Greisch, *Herméneutique et Grammatologie*

(Paris: Editions du Centre National de la Recherche Scientifique, 1977), for a general comparison of Derrida and Gadamer. See also Jean-Luc Nancy, *Le Partage des Voix* (Paris: Galilée, 1982).

36. 'Hymn to Hermes', in *Hesiod. The Homeric Hymns and Homerica*, p. 369.

37. Martin Heidegger, 'Aus einem Gespräch von der Sprache Zwischen einem Japaner und einem Fragenden', *Unterwegs zur Sprache* (Pfullingen: Neske, 1979) pp. 121–2. (Originally published 1959.)

38. Karlgren, *Analytic Dictionary*, p. 130.

39. 'I suggest *The New Learning* as a be'r title than *Guide to Kultur*. The public mightn't take the Guide idear seereeyus. However, if your public is rough you kin call it the *Guide to Kulchur*, so long as you don't call it the Gide' (*SL*, p. 289).

40. 'Tcheou koung dit: "Oh! j'ai entendu raconter que dans l'antiquité les ministres d'Etat eux-mêmes s'instruisaient et s'avertissaient entre eux, se défendaient et s'aidaient mutuellement, se formaient les uns les autres aux bonnes habitudes . . ." ' (Couvreur, *Chou King*, p. 295).

41. Cf. Canto LXXXIX, p. 598: 'Out of von Humboldt: Agassiz, Del Mar and Frobenius.' It is not clear whether Pound alludes to Alexander or to Wilhelm von Humboldt, although the link between Wilhelm von Humboldt's linguistic theories and Frobenius is indubitable. See Wilhelm von Humboldt, *'Über die Verschiedenheit des menschlichen Sprachbaues und ihren Einfluss auf die geistige Entwickelung des Menschengeschlechtes* (Bonn, Dümmler, 1968) section 9, p. lxx. (Originally published 1836.) Von Humboldt is for Heidegger the modern exponent of a linguistic philosophy, just as Aristotle stands for classical and 'metaphysical' theories of language.

42. Heidegger, *Unterwegs zur Sprache*, pp. 144–5.

43. Couvreur, *Chou King*, p. 285.

44. Couvreur glosses this ideogram – the most elaborate of the radicals, with twenty-four strokes – as 'intelligent, good, soul of a dead man' (ibid., p. 461).

45. 'L'indignation du peuple était un signe manifeste de la colère du ciel' (Couvreur's note, ibid., p. 283).

46. 'So the Jesuits brought in astronomy / (Galileo's, an heretic's) . . .' (Canto LX, p. 328).

47. Tcheou koung explains Tch'en wang's decrees to the officers of the Chang or In dynasties, then defeated, who are obliged to move to the new city of Lo (Couvreur, *Chou King*, pp. 281 and 288).

48. Granet, *La Pensée Chinoise*, pp. 266–7.

49. Ibid., p. 268.

50. See Walter Baumann, 'Secretary of Nature, J. Heydon', in *New Approaches to Ezra Pound*, ed. Eva Hesse (London: Faber, 1969) pp. 303–18. The theme of the quadripartition of space is developed with haunting effects in Cantos XCII ('The four altars at the four coigns of that place' – p. 619) and XCIX, but it goes back to Hanno's Carthaginian periplus: 'Out of which things seeking an exit / To the high air, to the stratosphere, to the imperial / calm, to the empyrean, to the baily of the four towers / the NOUS, the ineffable crytal: / Karxèdonion Basileos / hung this with his map in their temple' (XL, p. 201).

51. Leo Frobenius, *Dokumente zur Kulturphysiognomik. Vom Kulturreich des Festlandes* (Berlin, 1923) p. 104.

52. Heidegger, *Poetry, Language, Thought*, pp. 149–50. See also pp. 153, and 178–9.

53. Couvreur, *Chou King*, pp. 288–9. The ideogram reproduced by Pound signifies 'town', 'region'.

54. Heidegger, *Poetry, Language, Thought*, p. 132.

55. The room of the Tour Maubergeon, Palais de Justice, Poitiers, is shown in Kenner's *Pound Era*, p. 331.

56. Mary de Rachewiltz, *Discretions*, p. 159.

57. See Boris de Rachewiltz, 'Pagan and Magic Elements in Pound's Works', in *New Approaches to Ezra Pound*, pp. 177–81, which refers to the 'Isis Kuanon' of Canto xc and Princess 'Ra-Set' of Canto xci.

58. *The Portable Dante*, ed. Paolo Milano (Harmondsworth: Penguin, 1977) pp. 324–5. (Edn originally published 1947.)

59. Louis Zukofsky, *A* (Berkeley, Calif.: University of California Press, 1978) p. 300.

CONCLUSION: THE LEGENDARY RITE

1. I am here glossing a typical letter (*SL*, p. 263).

2. In the *Cantos*, the *root*, *pen* (xciv, p. 640) echoes the *wood* of p. 553 already commented on and the *wood* of cxiv, p. 792. See Karlgren's *Analytic Dictionary*, p. 218 for *pen* (the stroke can be taken as the root or as the ground) and p. 46 for *pu*. Useful glosses of the radicals can be found in Kyril Ryjik, *L'Idiot Chinois* (Paris: Payot, 1980) p. 404 for *pen*, and p. 314 for *pu*: Ryjik explains that *pu* can be interpreted either as representing a flower, hence something which does not last, or as a bird vanishing from sight in the sky, hence its meaning of a limited negation, something which is not there now.

3. A. R. Radcliffe-Brown, *Structure and Function in Primitive Society* (London: Cohen and West, 1952) p. 159.

4. Ibid., p. 160.

5. 'Nowadays, a whole political school demands in fact the re-establishment of corporations and the State's interference in the domains of production and exchange. . . . Tyranny, a tyranny thousand times more heavy and sterilizing than one man's . . .' – Jules Nicole, Preface to *Le Livre du Préfet ou l'Edit de l'Empereur Léon le Sage sur les Corporations de Constantinople*, (Geneva and Basle: Georg, 1894) pp. 7–8.

6. 'E pero dice lo Filosofo (= Aristotle) che l'uomo naturalmente è compagnevole animale' (Dante, *Convivio*, iv.4); see also iv.27.3.

7. Sieburth, *Instigations*, pp. 80–1, comments on this passage.

8. Villon, *Oeuvres Poétiques*, p. 84: 'Femme je suis pauvrette et ancienne,/ Qui ne rien sais; oncque lettre ne lus./ Au moutier vois, dont suis paroissienne,/ Paradis peint ou sont harpes et luths,/ Et un enfer ou damnés sont boullus.'

9. Electra expresses her grief with 'many voices' (ll. 641 and 798).

10. ' . . . under my father's tree' (*WT*, p. 66).

11. See Bernstein, *The Tale of the Tribe*, for a very comprehensive definition of what Pound means by an 'epic'.

12. And the reverse is not true: all the elements of the epic are found in tragedies, according to Aristotle, *Poetics*, v. 49b.

13. 'In Hölderlin, one can understand that the historical is original and more ancient [*das Geschichtliche sei urgeschichtlich*], all the more so as it is more historical' Adorno, in *Noten zur Literatur*, III, p. 174.

14. J.-P. Vernant and P. Vidal-Naquet, *Mythe et Tragédie en Grèce Ancienne* (Paris: Maspéro, 1977) p. 27 and *passim*.

15. Although this legend is not directly mentioned in Sophocles' play.

16. Quoted as the key phrase of the play by Pound (*WT*, p. 67). See Mary de Rachewiltz, *Discretions*, p. 306. She adds, 'But by now we had all had enough of Greek tragedy.'

17. As Pound writes in Canto XXIX, 'There is no greater incomprehension / Than between the young and the young. / The young seek comprehension; / The middleaged to fulfill their desire' (p. 144).

18. Heidegger, 'Hölderlin and the Essence of Poetry', *Existence and Being*, pp. 312–13.

19. Electra is constantly mourning her father and her brother in a 'funeral song' (ll. 88, 104, 231, etc.).

20. With the burden 'Lo the fair dead!' ('Threnos', *CEP*, p. 30, and *CSP*. p. 17).

21. See Kenner, *The Pound Era*, pp. 55–62.

22. Joseph F. Rock, *The Na-khi Nāga Cult and Related Ceremonies*, Serie Orientale Roma IV, no. 1 (Rome, 1952) p. 5.

23. See Canto XCIII: 'The suicide is not serious from conviction / One should first bump off some nuisance. / From sheer physical depression, c'est autre chose' (p. 625). Plotinus wrote a short treatise against suicide, and prevented Porphyry from committing suicide.

24. Peter Goullart, who also lived among the Na-khi, describes their country as a kind of earthly paradise haunted by despair: 'And it is no substitute for paradise to be eternally preoccupied with sickness, misery, filth and rags. Paradise is perhaps the transformation of both through wisdom and love and the knowledge that the work has been well done' – *Forgotten Kingdom* (London: John Murray, 1955) p. 211.

Bibliography

I   WORKS ON POUND

Ackroyd, Peter, *Ezra Pound and his World* (London: Thames and Hudson, 1980).
Alexander, Michael, *The Poetic Achievements of Ezra Pound* (London: Faber, 1979).
Bacigalupo, Massimo, *The Forméd Trace. The Later Poetry of Ezra Pound* (New York: Columbia University Press, 1980).
——, *L'Ultimo Pound*, rev. Italian edn of *The Forméd Trace* (Rome: Edizioni di Storia e Letteratura, 1981).
Baumann, Walter, *The Rose in the Steel Dust. An Examination of the Cantos of Ezra Pound* (Bern, 1967).
Bell, Ian F. A., *Critic as Scientist. The Modernist Poetics of Ezra Pound* (London: Methuen, 1981).
—— (ed.), *Ezra Pound. Tactics for Reading* (London: Vision, 1982).
Bernstein, Michael André, *The Tale of the Tribe. Ezra Pound and the Modern Verse Epic* (Princeton, NJ: Princeton University Press, 1980).
Brooker, Peter, *A Student's Guide to Ezra Pound* (London: Faber, 1979).
Brooke-Rose, Christine, *A ZBC of Ezra Pound* (London: Faber, 1971).
——, *The Structural Analysis of Ezra Pound's Usura Cantos* (The Hague: Mouton, 1976).
Bush, Ronald, *The Genesis of Ezra Pound's Cantos* (Princeton, NJ: Princeton University Press, 1976).
Chace, William M., *The Political Identities of Ezra Pound and T. S. Eliot* (Stanford, Calif.: Stanford University Press, 1973).
Contino, Vittorugo, *Ezra Pound in Italy. From the Pisan Cantos* (Venice: Gianfranco Ivancich, 1970).
Cornell, Julien, *The Trial of Ezra Pound. A Documented Account of the Treason Case by the Defendant's Lawyer* (New York: John Day, 1966).
Davenport, Guy, 'Pound and Frobenius', in *Motive and Method in the Cantos of Ezra Pound*, ed. Lewis Leary (New York: Columbia Uiversity Press, 1954).
Davie, Donald, *Ezra Pound: Poet as Sculptor* (London: Routledge and Kegan Paul, 1964).
——, *Pound* (London: Fontana, 1975).
Davis, Earle, *Vision Fugitive. Ezra Pound and Economics* (Lawrence: University Press of Kansas, 1968).
Dekker, George, *Sailing after Knowledge. The Cantos of Ezra Pound* (London: Routledge and Kegan Paul, 1963).
Durant, Alan, *Ezra Pound. Identity in Crisis* (Hassocks: Harvester, 1981).

Edwards, John Hamilton, and Vasse, William V., *Annotated Index to the Cantos of Ezra Pound* (Berkeley, Calif., and Los Angeles: University of California Press, 1957).

Ellmann, Maud, 'Floating the Pound: The Circulation of the Subject of *The Cantos*', *Oxford Literary Review*, vol. 3, no. 3 (Spring 1979) pp. 16–27.

Emery, Clark, *Ideas into Action. A Study of Pound's Cantos* (Coral Gables: University of Miami Press, 1958).

Espey, John J., *Ezra Pound's Mauberley: A Study in Composition* (Berkeley, Calif.: University of California Press, 1955).

Fang, Achilles, 'Materials for the Study of Pound's Cantos' (unpublished PhD thesis, Harvard, 1958).

Gallup, Donald, *A Bibliography of Ezra Pound*, 2nd edn (London: Rupert Hart-Davis, 1969).

——, *On Contemporary Bibliography, with Particular Reference to Ezra Pound*, University of Texas Bibliographical Monograph no. 4 (Austin, 1970).

Gordon, David, 'The Sacred Edict', *Paideuma*, vol. III, no. 2 (Fall 1974) pp. 169–90.

——, 'More on the Sacred Edict', *Paideuma*, vol. IV, no. 1 (Spring 1975) pp. 121–70.

——, 'The Azalea is Grown', *Paideuma*, vol. IV, no. 2–3 (Fall and Winter 1975) pp. 223–99.

Grieve, Thomas, 'Chinese Material in *Rock-Drill*', *Paideuma*, vol. IV, no. 2–3 (Fall and Winter 1975) pp. 362–508.

Hansen, Miriam, *Ezra Pounds frühe Poetik und Kulturkritik zwischen Aufklärung und Avantgarde* (Stuttgart: Metzler, 1979).

Harper, Michael F., 'Truth and Calliope: Ezra Pound's Malatesta', *Publications of the Modern Language Association*, vol. 96, no. 1 (Jan. 1981) pp. 86–103.

Hesse, Eva (ed.), *New Approaches to Ezra Pound* (London: Faber, 1969).

——, *Die Wurzeln der Revolution. Theorien der individuellen und der kollektiven Freiheit* (Munich: Karl Hanser, 1974).

——, *Ezra Pound. Letzte Texte* (Zurich: Arche, 1975).

——, *Ezra Pound. Von Sinn und Wahnsinn* (Munich: Kindler, 1978).

Heymann, C. David, *Ezra Pound: The Last Rower. A Political Profile* (New York: Viking, 1976).

Homberger, Eric, *Ezra Pound: The Critical Heritage* (London: Routledge and Kegan Paul, 1972).

Hutchins, Patricia, *Ezra Pound's Kensington. An Exploration 1885–1913* (London: Faber and Faber, 1965).

Jackson, Thomas H., *The Early Poetry of Ezra Pound* (Cambridge, Mass.: Harvard University Press, 1968).

Kenner, Hugh, *The Poetry of Ezra Pound* (New York: New Directions, 1951).

——, *The Pound Era* (London: Faber, 1972).

Leary, Lewis (ed.), *Motive and Method in the Cantos* (New York: Columbia University Press, 1954).

McDougal, S. Y., *Ezra Pound and the Troubadour Tradition* (Princeton, NJ: Princeton University Press, 1973).

Mancuso, Girolano, *Pound e la Cina* (Milan: Feltrinelli, 1974).

Mondolfo, V. I., and Hurley, M. (eds), *Ezra Pound: Letters to Ibbotson; 1935–1952* (Orono: University of Maine Press, 1979).

Moody, A. D., 'Pound's Allen Upward', *Paideuma*, vol. IV, no. 1 (Spring 1975) pp. 55–70.

De Nagy, N. Christoph, *The Poetry of Ezra Pound. The Pre-Imagist Stage* (Bern: Francke Verlag, 1960).

Nänny, Max, *Ezra Pound. Poetics for an Electric Age* (Bern: Francke, 1973).

——, 'Oral Dimensions in Ezra Pound', *Paideuma*, vol. VI, no. 1 (Spring 1977) pp. 13–26.

——, 'Ezra Pound and the Menippean Tradition', *Paideuma*, vol. XI, no. 3 (Winter 1982) pp. 395–405.

Nassar, Eugene Paul, *The Cantos of Ezra Pound. The Lyric Mode* (Baltimore: Johns Hopkins University Press, 1975).

Neault, James, 'Apollonius of Tyana', *Paideuma*, vol. IV, no. 1 (Spring 1975) pp. 3–36.

Norman, Charles, *The Case of Ezra Pound* (New York: Funk and Wagnall, 1968).

Olsson, Theodore Charles Alexander, 'Usura: Economics and Ethics in the Cantos of Ezra Pound' (Unpublished PhD thesis: University of California, 1974).

Pearlman, Daniel D., *The Barb of Time. On the Unity of Ezra Pound's Cantos* (New York, 1969).

——, 'Ezra Pound: America's Wandering Jew', *Paideuma*, vol. IX, no. 3 (Winter 1980) pp. 461–80.

Pleynet, Marcelin, 'La compromission poétique', *Tel Quel*, no. 70 (Summer 1977) pp. 11–26.

Rabaté, Jean-Michel, 'Sounds Pound: History and Ideology in the China Cantos', in *Myth and Ideology in American Culture*, ed. R. Durand (Lille: CERNAC, 1976).

——, 'Pound anathème', in *Language et Ex-communication*, *Degrés* (Bruxelles) no. 26–7 (Spring–Autumn 1981) pp. i-1–i-16.

——, 'Lectures Critiques de Hermann Broch, James Joyce et Ezra Pound (après *Ulysses: Finnegans Wake, Der Tod des Vergil, The Cantos)*', Thèse d'Etat, 1980, Université de Paris VIII (Service des Thèses de Lille–III, 1984).

De Rachewiltz, Boris, *L'Elemento Magico in Ezra Pound* (Milan: Del Pesce d'Oro, 1965).

——, 'Pagan and Magic Elements in Ezra Pound's Works', in *New Approaches to Ezra Pound*, ed. Eva Hesse, pp. 174–97.

De Rachewiltz, Mary, *Discretions. Ezra Pound, Father and Teacher* (New York, New Directions, 1975). (Originally published 1971.)

——, *A Catalogue of the Poetry Notebooks of Ezra Pound* (New Haven, Yale University Library, 1980).

——, 'Pound and Frobenius', *Komparatistische Hefte* (Beyreuth) no. 2 (1980) pp. 92–101.

Read, Forrest (ed.), *Pound/Joyce. The Letters of Ezra Pound to James Joyce, with Pound's Essays on Joyce* (London: Faber, 1968).

——, *'76. One World and The Cantos of Ezra Pound* (Chapel Hill: University of North Carolina Press, 1981).

Reck, Michael, *Ezra Pound. A Close-up* (New York: McGraw-Hill, 1967).

Riddell, Joseph N., 'Pound and the Decentered Image', *Georgia Review*, vol. XXXIX, no. 3 (Fall 1975) pp. 565–91.

De Roux, Dominique (ed.), *Cahiers de l'Herne. Ezra Pound*, nos 6 and 7 (Paris, 1965).

Ruthven, K. K., *A Guide to Ezra Pound's Personae* (Berkeley, Calif.: University of California Press, 1969).

Sanders, Frederick K., *John Adams Speaking. Pound's Sources for the Adams Cantos* (Orono: University of Maine Press, 1975).

Schafer, R. Murray (ed.), *Ezra Pound and Music. The Complete Criticism* (London: Faber, 1978).

Schneidau, Herbert N., *Ezra Pound. The Image and the Real* (Baton Rouge: Louisiana State University Press, 1969).

——, 'Wisdom Past Metaphor: Another View of Pound, Fenollosa, and Objective Verse', *Paideuma*, vol. V, no. 1 (Spring and Summer 1976) pp. 15–29.

Seelye, Catherine (ed.), *Charles Olson and Ezra Pound* (New York: Viking, 1975).

Stallart Flory, Wendy, *Ezra Pound and the Cantos. A Record of Struggle* (New Haven, Conn.: Yale University Press, 1980).

Sieburth, Richard, *Instigations. Ezra Pound and Remy de Gourmont* (Cambridge, Mass.: Harvard University Press, 1978).

Stock, Noel (ed.), *Ezra Pound. Perspectives* (Westport, Conn.: Greenwood, 1977). (Originally published 1965.)

——, *Reading the Cantos. A Study of Meaning in Ezra Pound.* (London: Routledge and Kegan Paul, 1967).

——, *The Life of Ezra Pound* (London: Routledge and Kegan Paul, 1970).

Sullivan, J. P., *Ezra Pound and Propertius. A Study in Creative Translation* (Austin: University of Texas Press, 1964).

—— (ed.), *Ezra Pound* (Harmondsworth: Penguin, 1970).

Surette, Leon, 'A Light from Eleusis. Some Thoughts on Pound's Nekuia', *Paideuma*, vol. III, no. 2 (Fall 1974) pp. 191–216.

——, *A Light from Eleusis. A Study of Pound's Cantos* (Oxford: Clarendon Press, 1979).

Sutton, Walter (ed.), *Ezra Pound. A Collection of Critical Essays* (Englewood Cliffs, NJ: Prentice-Hall, 1963).

Terrell, Carroll F., 'The Sacred Edict of K'ang-Hsi', *Paideuma*, vol. II, no. 1 (Spring 1973) pp. 69–112.

——, 'The Eparch's Book of Leo the Wise', *Paideuma*, vol. II, no. 2 (Fall 1973) pp. 223–42.

——, 'John Adams Speaking: Some Reflections on Technique', *Paideuma*, vol. IV, no. 2–3 (Fall and Winter 1975) pp. 533–8.

——, *A Companion to the Cantos of Ezra Pound*, vol. I (Berkeley, Calif.: University of California Press, 1980).

Wilhelm, James J., *Dante and Pound. The Epic of Judgment* (Orono: University of Maine Press, 1974).

——, *The Later Cantos of Ezra Pound* (New York: Walker, 1977).

Witemeyer, Hugh, *The Poetry of Ezra Pound. Forms and Renewals 1908–1920* (Berkeley, Calif.: University of California Press, 1969).

——, 'Ruskin and the Signed Capital in Canto 45', *Paideuma*, vol. IV, no. 1 (Spring 1975) pp. 85–91.

Woodward, Anthony, *Ezra Pound and the Pisan Cantos* (London: Routledge and Kegan Paul, 1980).

Zapponi, Niccolo, *L'Italia di Ezra Pound* (Rome: Bulzoni, 1976).

For the latest critical and biographical contributions, one should consult *Paideuma: A Journal Devoted to Ezra Pound Scholarship*, ed. Caroll F. Terrell (Orono: University of Maine), which also publishes bibliographical checklists. Invaluable contributions can be found in *Agenda*, ed. William Cookson (London), which, besides two issues entirely devoted to Ezra Pound – vol. 8, no. 3–4 (Autumn and Winter 1970) and vol. 17, no. 3–4 / vol. 18, no. 1 (Autumn, Winter and Spring 1979–80) – regularly publishes articles on Pound. Since 1982, *Sagetrieb: A Journal Devoted to Poets in the Pound-Williams Tradition*, ed. Basil Bunting, George Oppen and Carroll F. Terrell (Orono, University of Maine), provides detailed studies of the new poetic tradition and situates Pound in a contemporary context.

II GENERAL WORKS

Abraham, Nicolas, and Torok, Maria, *Cryptonymie. Le Verbier de l'Homme aux Loups,* preceded by Jacques Derrida, *Fors* (Paris, Aubier-Flammarion, 1976).

Adorno, Theodor W., *Jargon der Eigentlichkeit. Zur deutschen Ideologie* (Frankfurt: Suhrkamp, 1964).

——, *Noten zur Literatur*, 3 vols (Frankfurt: Suhrkamp, 1960, 1961, 1965).

——, *Ästhetische Theorie* (Frankfurt: Suhrkamp, 1970).

Alleman, Beda, *Hölderlin und Heidegger*, 2nd rev. edn (Zürich and Freiburg: Atlantis, 1954).

Aubenque, Pierre, *Le Problème de l'Etre chez Aristote* (Paris: Presses Universitaires de France, 1962).

——, *La Prudence chez Aristote* (Paris: Presses Universitaires de France, 1963).

Barthes, Roland, *S/V* (Paris: Seuil, 1970).

——, *Roland Barthes* (Paris: Seuil, 1975).

Baudrillard, Jean, *Pour une Critique de l'Economie Politique du Signe* (Paris: Gallimard, 1972).

Benjamin, Walter, *Das Kunstwerk im Zeitalter seiner technischen Reproduzierbarkeit*, (Frankfurt: Suhrkamp, 1963).

——, *Über Literatur* (Frankfurt: Suhrkamp, 1969).

——, *Illuminations*, trs. Harry Zohn (London: Fontana, 1973).

——, *Ursprung des deutschen Trauerspiels* (Frankfurt: Suhrkamp, 1978). (Originally published 1928.)

Benveniste, Emile, *Problèmes de Linguistique Générale*, 2 vols (Paris: Gallimard, 1966 and 1974).

Bérard, Victor, *Les Phéniciens et l'Odyssée* (Paris, Armaud Colin, 1902–3).

Blanchot, Maurice, *L'Entretien Infini* (Paris: Gallimard, 1969).

——, *L'Ecriture du Désastre* (Paris: Gallimard, 1980).

Bloom, Harold (with Paul de Man, Jacques Derrida, Geoffrey Hartman, J. Hillis Miller), *Deconstruction and Criticism* (London: Routledge and Kegan Paul, 1979).

Borneman, Ernest, *Psychoanalyse des Geldes* (Frankfurt: Suhrkamp, 1973).

Brown, Norman O., *Life against Death* (London: Sphere, 1968). (Originally published 1959).

Charles, Michel, *Rhétorique de la Lecture* (Paris: Seuil, 1977).

Chinard, Gilbert, *Jefferson et les Idéologues* (Baltimore: Johns Hopkins Press, 1925).

Compagnon, Antoine, *La Seconde Main ou le Travail de la Citation* (Paris: Seuil, 1979).

Davis, Robert Con (ed.), *The Fictional Father. Lacanian Readings of the Text* (Amherst: University of Massachussetts Press, 1981).

De Felice, Renzo, *Mussolini il Fascista. La Conquista del Potere, 1921–1925* (Turin: Einaudi, 1966).

——, *Mussolini il Duce*, vol. I: *Gli Anni del Consenso, 1929–1936* (Turin: Einaudi, 1974); vol. II, *Lo Stato Totalitario, 1936–1940* (Turin: Einaudi, 1981).

Derrida, Jacques, *La Dissémination* (Paris: Seuil, 1972).

——, *Glas* (Paris: Galilée, 1974).

——, 'Limited Inc', trs. S. Weber, *Glyph*, no. 2 (1977).

Descombes, Vincent, *L'Inconscient malgré lui* (Paris: Minuit, 1977).

Détienne, Marcel. *Les Maîtres de Vérité dans la Grêce Archaïque* (Paris: Maspéro, 1967).

—— and Vernant, Jean-Pierre, *Les Ruses de l'Intelligence. La Mètis des Grecs* (Paris: Flammarion, 1974).

——, *Dionysos mis à mort* (Paris: Gallimard, 1977).

Ducrot, Oswald, and Todorov, Tzvetan, *Encyclopedic Dictionary of the Sciences of Language*, trs. Catherine Porter (Oxford: Blackwell, 1981).

Eagleton, Terry, *Criticism and Ideology* (London: New Left Books, 1976).

——, *Walter Benjamin, or Towards a Revolutionary Criticism* (London: New Left Books, 1981).

Felman, Shoshana (ed.), *Literature and Psychoanalysis. The Question of Reading: Otherwise* (Baltimore: Johns Hopkins University Press, 1982). (Originally published 1977.)

Festugière, A. J., *Hermétisme et Mystique Païenne* (Paris: Aubier-Montaigne, 1967).

Foucault, Michel, *Les Mots et les Choses* (Paris: Gallimard, 1966).

——, *Histoire de la Folie à l'Age Classique*, new extended edn (Paris: Gallimard, 1972).

——, *Surveiller et Punir. Naissance de la Prison* (Paris: Gallimard, 1975).

Frank, Manfred, *Die unendliche Fahrt* (Frankfurt: Suhrkamp, 1979).

——, *Das Sagbare und das Unsagbare. Studien zur neuesten französischen Hermeneutik und Texttheorie* (Frankfurt: Suhrkamp, 1980).,

Freud, Sigmund, *Werke. Studienausgabe*, 11 vols. (Frankfurt: Fischer, Conditio Humana, 1969–79).

Frobenius, Leo, *Erlebte Erdteile*, 7 vols (Frankfurt: Forschungsinstitut für Kulturmorphologie, 1925–9).

Gadamer, Hans-Georg, *Wahrheit und Methode. Grundzüge einer philosophischen Hermeneutik* (Tübingen: Mohr, 1967).
——, *Kleine Schriften*, 3 vols (Tübingen: Mohr, 1967–72).
Gernet, Jacques, *Le Monde Chinois* (Paris: Armand Colin, 1972).
——, *Chine et Christianisme. Action et Réaction* (Paris: Gallimard, 1982).
Goux, Jean-Joseph, *Marx, Freud, Economie et Symbolique* (Paris: Seuil, 1973).
Granet, Marcel, *La Pensée Chinoise* (Paris: Albin Michel, 1968). (Originally published 1934.)
Greisch, Jean, *Herméneutique et Grammatologie* (Paris: CNRS, 1977).
Habermas, Jürgen, *Erkenntnis und Interesse* (Frankfurt: Suhrkamp, 1968).
——, *Technik und Wissenschaft als 'Ideologie'* (Frankfurt: Suhrkamp, 1970).
—— (ed.), *Hermeneutik und Ideologiekritik* (Frankfurt: Suhrkamp, 1971).
Hartman, Geoffrey H. (ed.), *Psychoanalysis and the Question of the Text* (Baltimore: Johns Hopkins University Press, 1978).
Heath, Stephen, *Vertige du Déplacement. Lecture de Barthes* (Paris: Fayard, 1974).
——, 'Anata mo', *Screen*, vol. 17, no. 4 (1976) pp. 49–66.
——, 'Notes on Suture', *Screen*, vol. 18, no. 4 (1977–8) pp. 48–76.
Heidegger, Martin, *Existence and Being*, four essays trs. Douglas Scott and R. F. C. Hull and Alan Crick, with an Introduction by Werner Brock (London: Vision, 1949).
——, *Identität und Differenz* (Pfullingen: Neske, 1957).
——, *Unterwegs zur Sprache* (Pfullingen: Neske, 1959).
——, *Erläuterungen zu Hölderlins Dichtung* (Frankfurt: Vittorio Klostermann, 1971).
——, *Poetry, Language, Thought*, essays trs. Albert Hofstadter: 'The Thinker as Poet', 'The Origin of the Work of Art', 'What are Poets for?' 'Building, Dwelling, Thinking', 'The Thing', 'Language', '. . . Poetically Man Dwells' (New York: Harper, 1971).
——, *On Time and Being*, trs. Joan Stambaugh (New York: Harper, 1972).
——, *Sein und Zeit*, rev. and annotated edn (Tübingen: Max Niemeyer, 1979). (Originally published 1927.)
——, *Gesamtausgabe II. Abteilung. Vorlesungen 1923–1944*, vol. 39: *Hölderlins Hymnen 'Germanien' und 'Der Rhein'* (Frankfurt: Vittorio Klostermann, 1980).
Irwin, John T., *American Hieroglyphics* (New Haven, Conn.: Yale University Press, 1980).
Iser, Wolfgang, *The Implied Reader* (Baltimore: Johns Hopkins University Press, 1974).
——, *Der Akt des Lesens* (Munich: Fink, 1976).
Jameson, Fredric, *Fables of Aggression. Wyndham Lewis, the Modernist as Fascist* (Berkeley, Calif.: University of California Press, 1979).
Kofman, Sarah, *Camera Obscura. De l'Idéologie* (Paris: Galilée, 1973).
Kristeva, Julia, *La Révolution du Langage Poétique* (Paris: Seuil, 1974).
Lacan, Jacques, *Ecrits* (Paris: Seuil, 1966). Partly trs. as *Ecrits. A Selection*, trs. Alan Sheridan (London: Tavistock, 1977).
——, 'L'étourdit', *Scilicet* (Paris) no. 4 (1973) pp. 5–52.
——, *Le Séminaire. Livre XI. Les Quatre Concepts Fondamentaux de la*

Psychanalyse (Paris: Seuil, 1973). Trs. Alan Sheridan as *The Four Fundamental Concepts of Psycho-analysis* (London: Tavistock, 1977; Harmondsworth: Penguin, 1979).

——, *Le Séminaire. Livre II. Le Moi dans la Théorie de Freud et dans la Technique de la Psychanalyse* (Paris: Seuil, 1978).

Lacoue-Labarthe, Philippe, and Nancy, Jean-Luc, *Le Titre de la Lettre* (Paris: Galilée, 1972).

——, 'Typographie', in *Mimesis Desarticulations* (Paris, Flammarion, 1975).

—— and Nancy, Jean-Luc, 'Le peuple juif ne rêve pas', in *La Psychanalyse est-elle une Histoire Juive?* (Paris: Seuil, 1981).

Lyotard, Jean-Francois, *Discours et Figure* (Paris: Klincksieck, 1971).

Marx, Karl, *Das Kapital*, in Karl Marx and Friedrich Engels, *Werke*, vols 23–5 (Berlin: Dietz, 1970).

MacCabe, Colin, *James Joyce and the Revolution of the Word* (London: Macmillan, 1978).

—— (ed.), *The Talking Cure* (London: Macmillan, 1981).

De Man, Paul, *Blindness and Insight* (New York: Oxford University Press, 1971).

Metz, Christian, *Le Signifiant Imaginaire* (Paris: 10/18, 1977).

Milner, Jean-Claude, *L'Amour de la Langue* (Paris: Seuil, 1978).

Nancy, Jean-Luc, 'Le Ventriloque', in *Mimesis Desarticulations* (Paris: Galilée, 1975).

——, *Ego Sum* (Paris: Flammarion, 1979).

——, *Le Partage des Voix* (Paris: Galilée, 1982).

Nathan, Tobie, *La Psychanalyse et son Double* (Claix: La Pensée Sauvage, 1979).

Needham, Joseph, *et al.*, *Science and Civilization in China* (Cambridge: Cambridge University Press, 1954).

Noonan, John T., *The Scholastic Analysis of Usury* (Cambridge, Mass.: Harvard University Press, 1957).

——, *Contraception. A History of its Treatment by the Catholic Theologians and Canonists* (Cambridge, Mass.: Harvard University Press, 1966).

Perloff, Marjorie, *The Poetics of Indeterminacy* (Princeton, NJ: Princeton University Press, 1981).

Pézard, André, *Dante sous la Pluie de Feu* (Paris: Vrin, 1950).

Reboul, Olivier, *Langage et Idéologie* (Paris: Presses Universitaires de France, 1980).

Richardson, William J., *Heidegger. Through Phenomenology to Thought* (The Hague: Martinus Nijhoff, 1963).

Ricoeur, Paul, *La Métaphore Vive* (Paris: Seuil, 1975).

Rosolato, Guy, *Essais sur le Symbolique* (Paris: Gallimard, 1969).

Safouan, Moustapha, *Etudes sur l'Oedipe* (Paris: Seuil, 1974).

——, *L'Inconscient et son Scribe* (Paris: Seuil, 1982).

Schürman, Reiner, *Le Principe d'Anarchie. Heidegger et la Question de l'Agir* (Paris: Seuil, 1982).

Shell, Marc, *The Economy of Literature* (Baltimore: Johns Hopkins University Press, 1978).

Steiner, George, *After Babel* (London: Oxford University Press, 1975).

——, *Martin Heidegger* (New York: Viking, 1978).

Suleiman, Susan R., and Crosman, Inge (eds), *The Reader in the Text* (Princeton, NJ: Princeton University Press, 1980).

Toniolo, Gianni, *L'Economia dell'Italia Fascista* (Bari: Laterza, 1980).

Wittkower, Rudolf, *Architectural Principles in the Age of Humanism* (London: Academy Editions, 1973). (Originally published 1949.)

Young, Robert (ed.), *Untying the Text. A Post-Structuralist Reader* (London: Routledge and Kegan Paul, 1981).

Indexes

Conceptual Index

329

Index of Names

Index of Cantos